Global Text

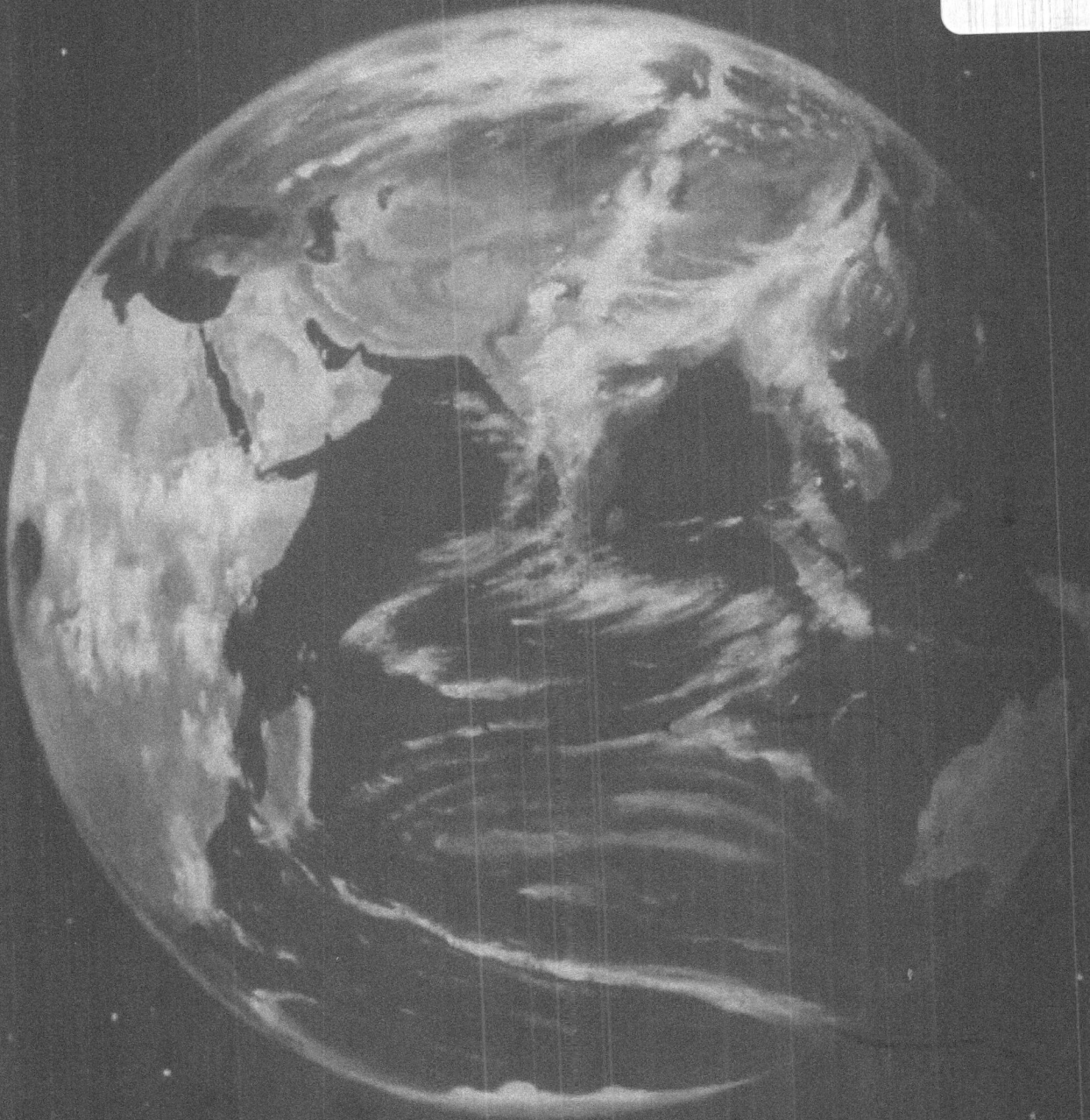

Business Fundamentals

Business Fundamentals

Donald J McCubbrey

Copyright © 2009 Donald J McCubbrey

Editor-In-Chief: Donald McCubbrey

Associate Editor: Marisa Drexel

Editorial Assistant: Jackie Sharman

For any questions about this text, please email: drexel@uga.edu

The Global Text Project is funded by the Jacobs Foundation, Zurich, Switzerland

Table of Contents

Preface

The Global Text Project (http://globaltext.org/) was initiated in early 2006 to develop a series of free, open content, electronic textbooks. A description of the Global Text Project is available on the project's website.

The first book in the series is on information systems, because the founders of the Global Text Project are both Information Systems professors who knew many other IS academics who wanted to help start the book. IS professors have a long history of cooperating with each other on a global scale. Creation of an open content textbook on information systems required the cooperation of the worldwide community of faculty and their students, as well as practitioners.

The IS community, of all academic communities, should be the one that is an early adopter of technology that holds the promise of being able to create a state-of-the-art open electronic textbook. The Information Systems textbook created by the community aims to evolve over time to be best-in-class, up-to-date, and, perhaps most importantly, make available at no cost to students anywhere in the world, but particularly to students in the developing world.

The impetus for developing the business fundamentals text as the second of the proof of concept texts was based on the realization that it is a mistake to teach information systems in a vacuum, i.e. without giving students an appreciation of the organizational settings in which they operate. Accordingly, a table of contents was prepared and volunteers were recruited to serve as chapter editors and reviewers for a book on business fundamentals. Most chapter editors are academics who wrote their own chapters while, in other cases, teams of graduate students wrote segments of a chapter as a part of a course assignment. All contributions are gratefully acknowledged and the contributors names are noted at the beginning of each chapter.

We learned some things from developing the two proof of concept texts:

- Faculty members are busy people *and,* in most instances, a contributed book chapter is not as highly regarded for promotion and tenure as a peer-reviewed article in a highly-rated academic journal. As a result, delivery times of chapters varied widely. For example, one faculty member wrote his chapter over spring break in 2008, and two other chapters were finally written by new authors after it became clear that the original authors were not going to deliver.

- In the meantime, publicity received by Global Text attracted the attention of authors who either had manuscripts ready to be published or had texts that were out of print (most often as a result of consolidations in the publishing industry) that could be scanned, and published quickly by Global Text. Consequently, we are continuously searching for high quality titles in every higher education discipline. The plan is to create communities to get updated and to extend contributed texts.

- The idea of having students write a book as a part of a course assignment proved to be bear fruit as a books on IT Management and Change Management were created by graduate classes at the University of Denver and the University of Washington, respectively, during the spring of 2009. As discussed on the GTP website, the XML book that was created by students at the University of Georgia in 2004, and updated by successive classes since then, was a major inspiration behind the idea of the Global Text Project.

And now a bit about the focus of this text:

1. The business eco-system: Your path to finding the pot of gold at the end of the rainbow!

The Business Fundamentals text is designed to introduce students, particularly those in developing economies, to the essential concepts of business and other organizations. It does this by focusing on small, entrepreneurial start-ups, and expanding the discussion in each chapter to include issues that are faced in larger organizations when it is appropriate to do so. Traditional business models are discussed as well as eBusiness models, with appropriate links to the IS Global Text and other relevant websites. All major functional areas of modern organizations are covered.

A common thread in most, if not all, chapters will be applicable principles of sustainable development and corporate social responsibility, although these topics are covered in depth in Chapter 12. In keeping with the community-based content development principles of the Global Text Project, active participation of members of the global community of academics, students, and practitioners in its creation and continuing maintenance is strongly encouraged.

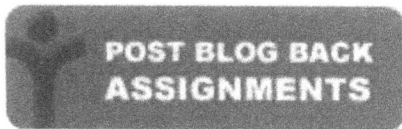

POST BLOG BACK ASSIGNMENTS

Chapter 1 and 2 feature a unique interactive option for readers.

Visit http://www.mentorography.com to post the Blog Back assignments to share your insights and comments on others' postings.

1. The business eco-system: Your path to finding the pot of gold at the end of the rainbow!

Editor: Molly Lavik (Vatel International Business School Los Angeles, USA)

Reviewer: Debbi D Brock (Berea College, USA)

Exhibit 1: Striking gold

Image created by: Taissia Belozerova,
Graphic Designer, Artist, MBA Candidate
at Pepperdine University Class of 2009

Dedication: In Memory of Nancy Wachs who believed in everyone's Startup time!

The business eco-system: Your path to finding the pot of gold at the end of the rainbow!

There are many ways to live your life. One of the most exciting yet challenging ways to live your life is to start your own business or work for someone who has their own startup. People who start their own businesses are known as entrepreneurs. Entrepreneurs throughout the world are extremely enthusiastic individuals who devise visionary methods to accomplish their new venture ideas while simultaneously convincing others to help.

Merriam-Webster Online defines the term "entrepreneur" as follows:"Etymology:

French, from Old French, from entreprendre to undertake — more at ENTERPRISE

Date: 1852 : one who organizes, manages, and assumes the risks of a business or enterprise"[1]

Are entrepreneurs born or made?

There is a long-standing discussion throughout the world that delves into whether you are born predisposed to become an entrepreneur or is it necessary for you to work and study hard to make yourself into one. There are many examples of individuals who were told they would never amount to anything and yet they went on to become very successful entrepreneurs. So, if you think that you are unlikely to be an entrepreneur, please realize it is possible for you to become an entrepreneur and to, potentially, even become a very successful one. With that said, there are characteristics and an overall mindset you can adopt that will help "predispose" you to having a greater opportunity of becoming a successful entrepreneur. Some of the most common characteristics of an entrepreneur include the following attributes:

"The Mindset of an Entrepreneur"

Vision: Able to create and communicate an easily understandable mission for what the new venture does in order to successfully launch a new business. This is accomplished while inspiring others to join you in your new enterprise.

Creativity: Ability to inject imagination and uniqueness into a new business venture. It takes skill and ingenuity to create a new venture equipped with strategies to outsmart the competition.

Focus: Able to maintain the vision of the company with unwavering diligence. It's very easy to get sidetracked especially if you find it necessary to evolve the original vision. Ironically, we have encountered many successful entrepreneurs who get bored easily...

Passion: Desiring to succeed under your own steam [initiative] on a business venture...

Drive: Possessing intrinsic energy to accomplish the business goal even in the face of adversity.

Perseverance: Able to keep going even when faced with seemingly insurmountable obstacles.

Opportunistic Nature: Sees the possibilities even before they exist. Can take advantage of an upcoming trend or unite unrelated processes to create a unique business venture...

Problem Solving Ability: Thrives on coming up with solutions to complex challenges...

Self-discipline: Able to be organized and regimented in pursuit of a successful business venture.

Frugality: Knows how to stretch every cent so that expenditures are as low as possible.

---

1   Merriam-Webster's Online Dictionary, "Merriam-Webster Online," http://www.merriam-webster.com/dictionary/entrepreneur (Assessed, August 30, 2008).

Empathy: Able to put yourself in another's shoes and therefore able to show sensitivity and understanding of what others are communicating in the startup environment...

Social Responsibility: Ethics, caring and humanitarianism are characteristics that are commonly found in today's entrepreneurs...

Spirituality: We have found that successful entrepreneurs have often devoted time to spirituality development. Meditation and positive affirmations are two common examples of spirituality.

Good Timing: Able to identify a market opportunity and know when it's the optimum time to launch a new venture or expansion of an existing enterprise.

Luck: Can a person be predisposed to be lucky: Is luck a human behavior or a karmic universal predisposition?"[2]

Read on: Chapter 2 is dedicated to this topic and delves deeply into "The mind of an entrepreneur".

Blog Back 1: Mindset

Blog Back: Is an entrepreneur born or made?

What characteristics are necessary for an entrepreneur to be successful and why? What additional entrepreneurial mindset characteristics could be added to the list and why?

Go to: http://www.Mentorography.com and make your case.

The business eco-system

Whether you possess the characteristics of an entrepreneurial mindset, or work for someone who does, you can still be instrumental in starting a new venture by understanding the business eco-system. What is a business eco-system? A business eco-system is a set of business components that form the foundation of a new venture's creation. Figuratively, the business eco-system is like a wheel that rolls your new venture forward which is why we represent the business eco-system in a wheel-shaped model.

---

2 "The Mindset of an Entrepreneur" is reprinted and adapted with permission from Mentorography, Inc. © 2008. All Rights Reserved. Entrepreneurial Marketing; Real Stories and Survival Strategies by Molly Lavik and Bruce Buskirk, introduction pages xxviii-xxx.

1. The business eco-system: Your path to finding the pot of gold at the end of the rainbow!

BUSINESS ECO-SYSTEM WHEEL

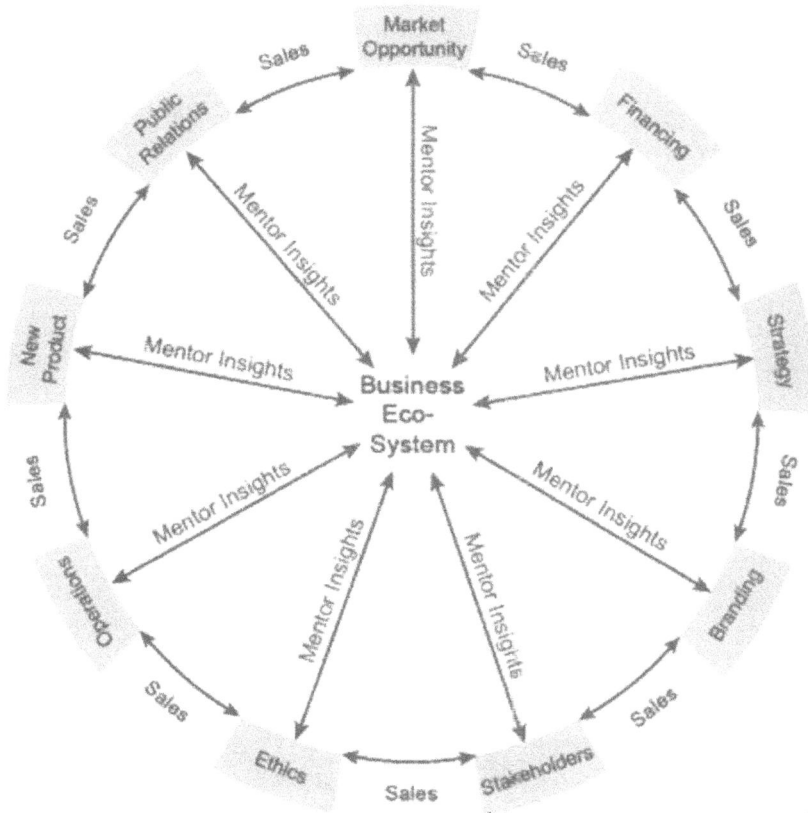

Exhibit 2: Business eco-system wheel

The Business Eco-system Wheel is reprinted and adapted from the Entrepreneurial Marketing Wheel with permission from Mentorography, Inc. © 2008. All Rights Reserved. Entrepreneurial Marketing; Real Stories and Survival Strategies by Molly Lavik and Bruce Buskirk, Preface, page xxii.

Exhibit 3: Caption: Rising sun

Image created by: Taissia Belozerova,
Graphic Designer, Artist, MBA Candidate
at Pepperdine University Class of 2009

The sun rise of your new business
Accessing market opportunity: the initial rim of the wheel

Market Opportunity is positioned at the top of the Business Eco-system Wheel for a reason. Every new venture starts with a single seed or kernel of an idea to do something in business that will result in money being exchanged. Since there is always some risk associated with starting a new business, you will have to take special care to plant the idea seeds of your new venture in a way that allows these seeds to some day bloom into a successful venture.

When to plant your market opportunity seeds

Without a doubt it's challenging to know when to move forward and plant your new venture ideas in the "business garden" where you want to grow your career.

Entrepreneurs who are considering moving forward with a new venture idea can utilize the following questions and the "Stop and Go Signs for Accessing Market Opportunity Matrix."

"Stop and Go Signs for Accessing Market Opportunity Matrix"

"Is there a customer for this product or service? Is there someone who will buy the product or service you're considering selling? You can't effectively answer this question until you have personally spoken to the potential customer and ascertained that this person will buy your product. You need to know as much about this customer as the customer knows about himself: What are the demographics of this customer? What influences his buying behavior? What factors could lead to this customer changing his mind about buying the product or services? What will be the impact of a crisis during an emerging trend?

What will it cost to make a sale to this customer? If there is a common pitfall for entrepreneur, it's greatly underestimating the cost to acquire and repeatedly sell to a customer. The entrepreneurial marketer must account for every last expense it will take to make the sale. Commonly missed expenses include: staff time, travel and related expenses, overhead for office, payroll taxes, social security employer matching expenses (which occurs in the United States so your countries' equivalent,) unemployment payroll related expenses, marketing expenses, and the overall amount of time it takes to make a sale.

Is my timing right for this market opportunity? You will have a brief window of opportunity to launch your new venture or expansion of an existing enterprise. Misjudging your timing is often the difference between success and failure with assessing market opportunity. If you are too early, you have the right product or service but your market is not ready for it yet. If you are too late, giant competitors may have acquired a loyal following, blocking new entries to the market.

Can I sell this product or service for a profit? Even if you have an existing customer, and have accurately estimated what it will cost you to acquire that customer; you might not have a sustainable business model until revenues outweigh the expenses...You need to find the incremental steps you can take to get to profitability. This is not easy. Again, there is no road map, but remember that patience is needed to reach profitability." (One solution that is becoming a common practice throughout many parts of the world is micro-financing. Micro-financing is where a small loan is made available to an entrepreneur in a developing country. While micro-financing is arguably one form of financing micro-financing has been documented to be a more sustainable form of financing because the amount of the loan is made in such a small (micro) amount that the recipient of the loan does not have to leverage the startup's best interests and assets in order to pay the loan back. The small amount of money loaned to the entrepreneur can usually be paid back from the revenues that the new venture is generating. Check out this micro financing website: http://www.acion.org.)

"Be open and flexible and recognize that along the way to profitability you might stumble on to a product or service that is in higher demand than the original concept.

When do I give up on my product or service? When should I pull up the roots of my new venture?

In the characteristics of an entrepreneur...perseverance was listed. There is a point, however, where you need to "pull the plug" and refocus your energies. You know you have reached this point when:

You have run out of resources and can't further leverage any of the methods suggested in this book.

The customers who said they would buy your product during your research phase are no longer interested.

You can't effectively market to your customer.

It costs you more than you make to sell your product or service.

During market opportunity assessment, there are times when the entrepreneur needs to "hit the brakes" and stop. Not stopping fast enough can lead to a failed business and/or bankruptcy. There are also times when an entrepreneur should "step on the accelerator" and drive on to new market opportunity territories. Knowing when to stop and go in your new venture market opportunity assessment isn't easy.

To help you decide when to move forward with and when to forego an opportunity, please see the "Stop and Go Signs for Assessing Market Opportunity Matrix." It's common for an entrepreneurial marketer to get caught up in what seems like a great idea or business concept. This matrix is a concise, easy to reference and somewhat simplistic way to make decisions on judging market opportunity. This matrix suggests four major causes for a new venture to not find a profitable market opportunity.

Recognizing when you are on the verge of going through a Stop Sign without braking is critical. You can refer back to these stop signs in this matrix as constant reminders of when to turn your market opportunity strategy in another direction."

Stop and Go Signs for Assessing Market Opportunity Matrix

No Customers for the Product	Customers' Purchase Motivations Unknown	Unprofitable Sales of the Product	Resources Running Out
STOP	STOP	STOP	STOP
Trends Indicate Emerging Market Opportunity	Timing Right to Attract Customers for the Product	Total Costs for Selling the Product Known	Sales to Customers Yield Sustainable Profitable Results
GO	GO	GO	GO

Exhibit 4: Stop and Go Signs for Assessing Market Opportunity Matrix "When to Access Market Opportunity" text and "Stop and Go Signs for Assessing Market Opportunity Matrix" adapted and reprinted with permission from Mentorography, Inc. © 2008. All Rights Reserved. Entrepreneurial Marketing; Real Stories and Survival Strategies by Molly Lavik and Bruce Buskirk, Mini Module on Assessing Market Opportunity, pages xxxix-xli.

1. The business eco-system: Your path to finding the pot of gold at the end of the rainbow!

> If you encounter any of the four Go Signs when you are assessing market opportunity, don't take time out to pat yourself on the back. This is because if you look over your shoulder you may see someone else realizing what you have discovered. Keep "driving on" if you are encountering all Go Signs."[3]

Read on: Chapters 3 and 6 discuss market opportunity in greater detail.

Blog Back 2: Go Signs

Blog Back: Analyze your new venture's market opportunity; do you have all "Go" signs? If you have all or some "Stop" signs what can you do to remove the roadblocks that are causing your "Stop" signs? Enter your strategy for obtaining all "Go" signs at http://www.Mentorography.com.

Sales: the essential rim of the wheel

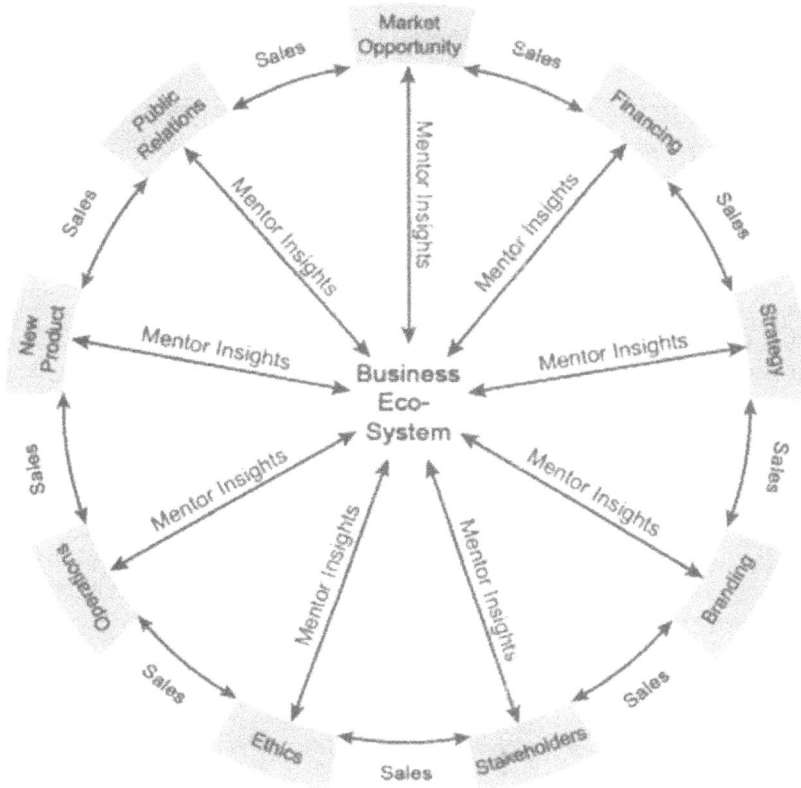

BUSINESS ECO-SYSTEM WHEEL

Exhibit 5: The Business Eco-System Wheel and sales

---

3 "When to Access Market Opportunity" text and "Stop and Go Signs for Assessing Market Opportunity Matrix" adapted and reprinted with permission from Mentorography, Inc. © 2008. All Rights Reserved. *Entrepreneurial Marketing; Real Stories and Survival Strategies* by Molly Lavik and Bruce Buskirk, Mini Module on Assessing Market Opportunity, pages *xxxix-xli.*

Sales are depicted as the inter-connecting factor of each business component on the Eco-system Wheel because without sales you won't have the revenue necessary to keep your business going. Sales help provide the overall shape of the wheel and are a major component of an entrepreneurs' work. When starting a new venture you need to convince others of your vision and eventually bring on strategic partners and vendors to accomplish your vision. You will need to sell your product and/or service to others. Selling is a skill that absolutely can be learned and improved upon. Also, the more people you contact to make a sale, the greater the odds you will actually sell something.

What will I sell?

You can sell a product or service. A product is a physical item while a service is something you would implement or execute on behalf of someone else.

Product ideas to consider selling

- Hand-crafted art and artifacts for exporting

- Fruit for selling at a fruit stand or using in the production of cosmetics

- Honey that you produce as a bee keeper

- Mustard condiments produced from mustard seeds

- Handcrafted furniture

- Paintings by emerging artists

- Recycled goods made into products such as purses made from recycled juice and soda containers

- A restaurant that offers food menus that others enjoy eating

- Yogurt served in containers that are edible

Ideas for services to consider offering

- Providing education to children as well as adults in a school

- Purifying water at the site of wells that may be tainted with arsenic

- Providing guide services to travelers

- Developing marketing campaigns for local businesses

- Running food stands for others

- Providing tailoring services

- Manufacturing furniture for businesses and residences

- Offering cooking services to families

- Selling wireless phones for phone corporations

- Providing people to build buildings, houses, roads and or bridges

1. The business eco-system: Your path to finding the pot of gold at the end of the rainbow!

- Offering out-sourced from other countries call center services

- Providing computer consulting services

Places for inspiration

"**Kiva** (www.kiva.org) is the world's first person-to-person micro-lending website, empowering individuals to lend directly to unique entrepreneurs in the developing world."[4] Kiva provides a list of entrepreneurs who seek loans and a description of these entrepreneurs' business concepts. Visit the Kiva website to read the inspirational stories of these entrepreneurs. http://www.kiva.org/app.php?page=businesses.[5]

"**Aid to Artisans** (ATA), (http://www.aidtoartisans.org) an international nonprofit organization, is a recognized leader of economic development for the craft industry. By linking artisans to new markets and buyers to culturally meaningful and innovative products, ATA provides needed economic opportunities to artisans while preserving the beauty of global handmade crafts."[6]

Financing: the fundamental rim on the wheel

One of the greatest talents that most successful entrepreneurs possess is the ability to persuade others to invest funds and resources in a startup during the idea creation phase of a new venture. You are not alone if you have major concerns about attracting the finances you need to get your startup idea "off the ground". If you are reading this and thinking you do not know anyone who would consider investing in your startup we suggest transforming your thinking into a more constructive thought process in which you believe in yourself and your own ability to achieve financing.

Financing opportunities

- **Micro-financiers** (Do a Google search at www.google.com using the key word "micro-finance" to find potential micro-financiers that you may want to research as one method of financing your startup costs.)

- **Family** traditionally is the first place to look for funds to pay for some of the startup costs associated with a new venture. Even if your family has no resources to offer you can still talk to family members about introducing you to people they know who might be able to help. More money then you can imagine has been raised in this manner.

- **Friends**, even casual acquaintances, can at times provide financing and resources for a startup. Even if a friend is not able to directly help, you should ask each friend or person you contact for help to also provide you with 3 names of others they know who may be able to help.

- **Governmental support** is also a possibility. If applicable, you can also let the local non-governmental agency associated with what you are doing know your needs in case there is some support available.

- **Barter** or trade is a method by which you could provide a needed service such as consulting/management advice in return for the resources needed for your startup.

---

4   Kiva, "About: What is Kiva?," http://www.kiva.org/about (Accessed January 11, 2009).

5   Kiva, "Lend," http://www.kiva.org/app.php?page=businesses (Accessed January 11, 2009).

6   Aid to Artisans, "About Us," http://www.aidtoartisans.org (Accessed January 12, 2009).

- **Savings** take a long time and effort to accumulate in the amount most people need to start a new venture. There are many risks involved and you may not ever be able to replenish the amount of money you took from your savings to invest in a startup. On the positive side though, if you use your own savings you do not have a loan to pay back.

- **Bank loans** are not usually available to early-stage entrepreneurs unless you have a track record of a previous success and/or the assets to put up such as a home you own in return for securing the bank loan.

- **Networking** refers to attending events, conferences, seminars, and any activity where by you can meet others who might be able to help your further your startup's development.

- **Online networks** are online websites where you can connect with people you know to ultimately gain connections to people they know. One well-known online network is LinkedIn at <u>www.linkedin.com</u>. According to the About LinkedIn website, "LinkedIn is an online network of more then 30 million experienced professionals from around the world, representing 150 industries."[7] LinkedIn is available in English, French and Spanish. You can use the search field at the top of every LinkedIn web page to search for people and companies that might be willing to finance your startup. You can sign onto LinkedIn and connect with others that would in turn potentially be willing to connect you to the people you are trying to meet.

- **Memberships** in community organizations may be a place where you can meet like-minded individuals interested in your startup idea. Use the opportunity to share some information about your startup with the people you meet. You may find others who want to help you make your startup a success.

Read on: Chapter 10 contains more material on financing your business.

Strategy: the tactical rim on the wheel

Strategy is the method you utilize to go about achieving the underlying goal of your startup. It's recommended that prior to spending any money on your new venture that you first come up with the strategy or strategies you plan to utilize to make your startup successful. Devising the right strategy often requires a great deal of market research on the history of your competition, potential customer needs and wishes as well a taking into consideration the economic climate and cultural factors that could impact your startup.

Examples of startup strategies:

- **Low cost leader** by charging less than the competition

- **Luxury cost leader** by charging more than the competition

- **First to market** by having your product or service in the market place prior to anyone else. This strategy is often referred to as the "first mover advantage."

- **Creating sustainable growth** for a startup means that the new venture will eventually make more money then it takes to operate the company and that the profitability of this venture is possible over an extended period of time.

---

7 LinkedIn, "About LinkedIn, <u>http://www.linkedin.com/static?key=company_info&trk=hb_ft_abtli</u> (Accessed August 15, 2008).

1. The business eco-system: Your path to finding the pot of gold at the end of the rainbow!

- **Creating societal wealth** means the company you are starting wants to create a product or service that will make the world a better place. The product or service you plan to create will enhance societal value. Educational institutions and schools are good examples. Another example is providing foods in the market place that are nutritional in value can have a major positive impact on a society's health.

- **Paradigm shifting brand** for a startup means creating a product or service that revolutionizes the world! Examples include the first developers of airplanes that not only manufactured the airplane but also found a way to commercialize the product in the market place. An emerging product in this category is space ships. Although it may sound far-fetched today, there are several corporations today developing the design and plans for the day where by we get in our space ship the way we get in our car or on our bicycle. Some wealthy business owners are even today adding space ports to their garages.

Read on: Chapters 3 and 6 both contain more information in setting your strategy.

Blog Back 3: Strategy

Blog Back: Imagine that you are starting a new venture utilizing the strategy of creating a paradigm shifting brand. What product and or service might you develop to implement such a strategy?

Go to: http://www.Mentorography.com and share your idea as well as post a comment on what you think of two other ideas that others shared regarding their paradigm shifting idea.

Exhibit 6: Mid day

Image created by: Taissia
Belozerova, Graphic Designer, Artist,
MBA Candidate at Pepperdine
University Class of 2009

Branding will make your blossoms bloom!
Branding: The memorable rim on the wheel

Branding is the core foundation of your startup that is necessary to make your product or service blossom and grow. "Branding" is a commonly used marketing term that refers to a distinctive image, usually in the form of a logo or company mark that represents a company or product. In recent years a company's brand has become an asset with a financial worth known as "brand equity". The marketing use of the word "brand' is borrowed from the process of burning a rancher's mark into the hide of a calf for identification purposes. When building your brand, the following checklist is helpful for making your startup bloom.

Branding coaching

What is the meaning behind the message your product and/or service represents?

Coaching: Try writing the history of why you are starting this venture and what is the deeper meaning behind why you are doing this and what you hope the legacy of the new venture will be in the market place. Review the history and pull out any information that seems relevant toward the meaning. Then write up some draft messages you hope to communicate when marketing the product or service.

What is the brand essence of your new product or service?

Coaching: The brand essence of your venture is the "heart and soul" behind the product and service you plan to develop; the core DNA of your product or service. The brand essence is the foundation of your brands true identity and the brand essence typically stays the same over time. An example of brand essence is the medical corporation International Patient Assistance Centre headquartered in Singapore. A review of the corporation's website (<u>http://www.ipac.sg/en/About/</u>[8]) leads one to believe the brand essence for the medical company is "dedicated and experienced patient care teams". If you are not able to come up with the brand essence for your venture try reverse engineering the process by asking yourself what would you like the brand essence of your venture to be and then make a list of action items you would have to do to achieve creating a company with this type of brand essence.

What is the brand advantage?

Coaching: What sets our brand apart from that of the competition?

Try answering the following:

"What is distinctive about the brand?

What differentiates this brand from the competitor's?

How do customers perceive the brand?

What emotion does the brand evoke?

Who appreciates the brand? Why?

What do customers get from the brand?

Where do customers go to find the brand?

---

8   IPAC, International Patient Assistance Care, <u>www.ipac.sg/en/About/</u> (Accessed January 2, 2009.)

1. The business eco-system: Your path to finding the pot of gold at the end of the rainbow!

What do customers see in the brand that the founders didn't?"[9]

Source: "Understanding the Essence of Brand Advantages" questions reprinted with permission from Mentorography, Inc. © 2008. All Rights Reserved. Entrepreneurial Marketing; Real Stories and Survival Strategies by Molly Lavik and Bruce Buskirk, Branding that Works, page 79.

What can you do from the start to make sure that others cannot use the mark or brand name?

Coaching: Investigate what the trade-marking regulations are for protecting your brand. What are the governmental processes for securing a trademark for your brand? *"Trade marking"* is the process one goes through to register with a government entity the text and or visual depiction of your business name and, if applicable, the business mark that accompanies the venture. A *"logo"* is the word utilized typically to describe the visual depiction of the business name.

If you plan to trademark your logo or the text version of your business name for protection you can find out the necessary details of this process at the World Intellectual Property Organization at:

http://www.wipo.int/portal/index.html.en[10] by specifically utilizing the Madrid System for International Registration Marks explained further at:http://www.wipo.int/madrid/en/.[11]

As of October 27, 2008, countries' statuses are listed regarding the Madrid Agreement Concerning the International Registration of Marks and the Protocol Relating to the Madrid Agreement Concerning the International Registration of Marks. View this information at:

http://www.wipo.int/export/sites/www/treaties/en/documents/pdf/madrid_marks.pdf.[12]

Looking for inspiration?

You can find many examples of logos in the process of being trademarked in the United States through the United States Trademark and Patent Office website that posts online "The Trademark Gazette". Here is an example of one issue of The Trademark Gazette: http://www.uspto.gov/web/trademarks/tmog/20081230_OG.pdf.[13]

---

9 "Understanding the Essence of Brand Advantages" questions reprinted with permission from Mentorography, Inc. © 2008. All Rights Reserved. Entrepreneurial Marketing; Real Stories and Survival Strategies by Molly Lavik and Bruce Buskirk, Branding that Works, page 79.

10 World Intellectual Property Organization, http://www.wipo.int/portal/index.html.en (Accessed January 11, 2009).

11 World Intellectual Property Organization, "Madrid System for International Registration Marks," http://www.wipo.int/madrid/en/ (Accessed January 11, 2009).

12 World Intellectual Property Organization, "Madrid Agreement Concerning the International Registration of Marks and Protocol Relating to the Madrid Agreement Concerning the International Registration of Marks," http://www.wipo.int/export/sites/www/treaties/en/documents/pdf/madrid_marks.pdf (Accessed January 11, 2009).

13 United States Trademark and Patent Office, "The Trademark Gazette," http://www.uspto.gov/web/trademarks/tmog/20081230_OG.pdf (Accessed December 24, 2008).

Once you have secured the trademark for your business name, you then process a legal standing to protect against other businesses using your company name in the category you are doing business in. Trademarks are considered assets to a business and have a monetary value if and when you want to sell or merge your venture.

The Brand Identity Guide: A blueprint toward success

Once you have developed your business name into a logo and are in the process of trade-marking that name, many entrepreneurs begin widespread use of the logo in marketing materials to raise awareness of their product or service to their targeted customers. Well-known branded businesses assign someone the task of making sure the logo is properly utilized, with the correct color ink, in the correct size, in the correct location of the page layout especially when used in conjunction with other logos. A style guide for the use of the logo is often called a "brand identity guide".

Blog Back 4: Brand Identity

Blog Back: Brainstorm the development of a Brand Identity Guide to illustrate the use of your logo in any materials you or others create to market the product or service you would like to create.

What is your brand essence?

What is your brand advantage?

What font and font size will you utilize for your logo?

What if any visual image/drawing/illustration will accompany the text of your logo?

What colors will you utilize for your logo? Using the pantone color chart, select the exact color(s) you wish to utilize.

Will your logo be depicted differently if it's used in a horizontal vs a vertical page lay out?

What is the smallest size your logo can appear?

What rules govern your logo's use when it appears with logos from other companies such as may be the case with a sponsorship?

In what countries would you like to trademark your logo?

Is there anything else you would like to share about the brand you plan to create?

Go to: <u>http://www.Mentorography.com</u> and share an outline of your Brand Identity Guide.

Stakeholders: the connective rim on the wheel

Your brand cannot bloom unless you ensure that you develop your brand in a way that will please everyone who comes into contact with your business. The people who come in contact with your business's brand are known as your startup's stakeholders. Who will be your startup's stakeholders? "Take aim" carefully as you decide. Consider establishing contacts with some of the following suggested stakeholder categories common to new venture enterprises mentioned in the "Startup Stakeholder Arrow".

Startup Stakeholder Arrow

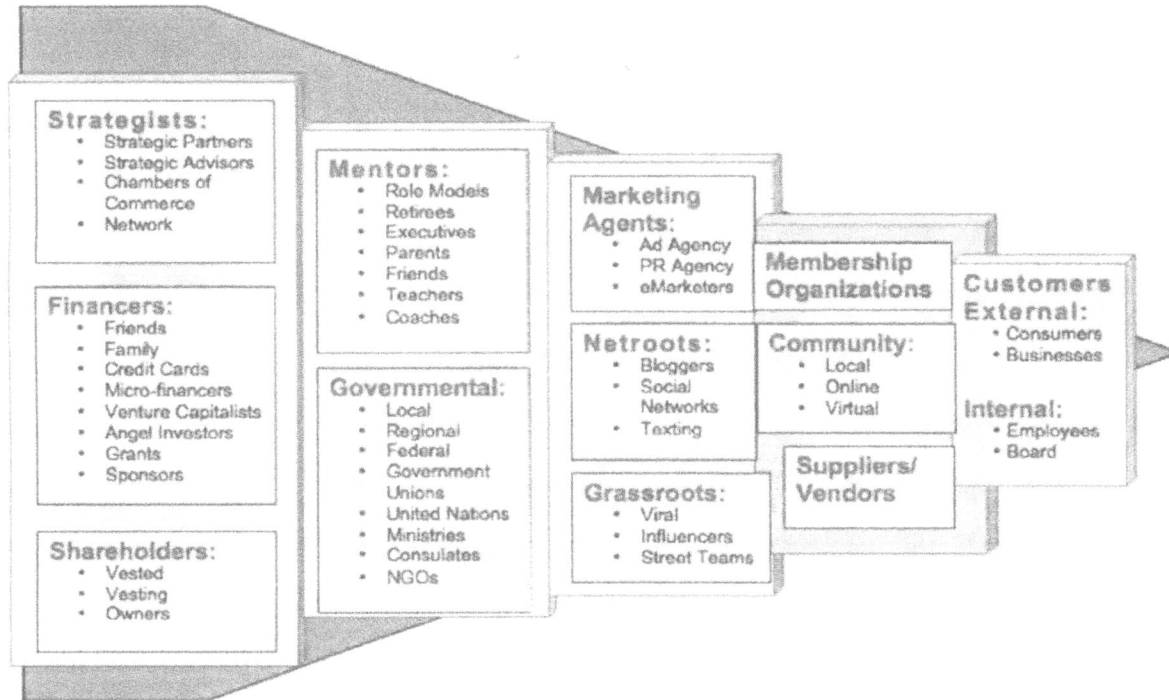

Strategists:
- Strategic Partners
- Strategic Advisors
- Chambers of Commerce
- Network

Financers:
- Friends
- Family
- Credit Cards
- Micro-financers
- Venture Capitalists
- Angel Investors
- Grants
- Sponsors

Shareholders:
- Vested
- Vesting
- Owners

Mentors:
- Role Models
- Retirees
- Executives
- Parents
- Friends
- Teachers
- Coaches

Governmental:
- Local
- Regional
- Federal
- Government Unions
- United Nations
- Ministries
- Consulates
- NGOs

Marketing Agents:
- Ad Agency
- PR Agency
- eMarketers

Netroots:
- Bloggers
- Social Networks
- Texting

Grassroots:
- Viral
- Influencers
- Street Teams

Membership Organizations

Community:
- Local
- Online
- Virtual

Suppliers/ Vendors

Customers External:
- Consumers
- Businesses

Internal:
- Employees
- Board

Exhibit 7: "Startup Stakeholder Arrow" created by Molly Lavik, founder, Mentorography, Inc., January 12, 2009. Reprinted with permission from Mentorography, Inc. © 2009. All Rights Reserved.

The stems of growing startups: definitions of "startup stakeholder arrow" selected terms

Strategists: A strategist is a skilled person who may be adept at taking your overall vision for the business and developing the plan of action for achieving the overarching goals. Strategists are experts at coming up with the winning maneuvers for laying the foundation of having a successful venture. The term strategy was originally utilized to define military maneuver plans.

1. The business eco-system: Your path to finding the pot of gold at the end of the rainbow!

Exhibit 8: Mid day (Adapted)

Image created by: Taissia Belozerova,
Graphic Designer, Artist, MBA Candidate
at Pepperdine University Class of 2009

Strategic advisors: Advisors are people typically with experience in an area that you wish to learn more about. Advisors impart valuable wisdom that you can utilize to learn valuable lessons regarding generating revenue and profits for your planned venture.

Chambers of Commerce: Chambers of Commerce are large memberships of business federations representing hundreds and sometimes thousands of business owners.

Network: Your business contacts that can help you today or in the future accomplish your goals. Entrepreneurs need vast networks of people's assistance to achieve the venture's goals.

Financiers: Financiers are comprised of people or a business entity that provides financial resources for your new business to utilize.

Micro-financiers: These are people who make cash loans in very small amounts to entrepreneurs in emerging countries to people who have very little if any resources. Often the people who receive micro-financed loans have little to no experience in business. A website where people can see micro-financing in action is located at: http://www.accion.org.

Venture capitalists: These are people who have a high net worth of resources or are part of an institution that has a fund of high net worth. Venture capitalists seek out entrepreneurs who are starting new ventures that have an opportunity to make a large and fast return on the financial resources invested. The main category that venture capitalists have previously invested in has been the technology industry. A venture capitalist does not make any money until the new venture sells, merges or makes an initial public offering known as an IPO when for the first time that business offers common stocks to the public. Entrepreneurs have had a "love and hate" relationship with venture capitalists because if the new venture doesn't make the anticipated return on investment predicted the venture capitalists usually has the legal right to take over part or all of the ownership of the new venture leaving the entrepreneurship often out of the venture from that point forward. Venture capitalists also have the ability to provide the cash as well as mentoring resources needed for the new venture to thrive.

Angel investors: These are private individuals that typically have large amounts of resources to invest in your startup. Angel Investors choose to invest in your startup because they share a common interest in what you are doing.

Shareholders: A person who owns or holds stock in a business.

Vesting: Vesting occurs when a person associated with a business venture is granted legally the right to possess stock-options if they work for a specified term. By way of example a person's stock options could vest over a three year period with the person earning stock-options incrementally and fully vesting in all the promised stock-options at the completion of the three year term.

Mentors: These are role models who you can receive instruction, advice and coaching from regarding important lessons to follow to make your new venture a success.

Ministries: These are offices that provide service to the country or state of origin.

Consulates: These are the official offices of a government appointee. These offices can be located in the country of the government that made the appointment and or abroad NGOs: Stands for non-governmental organization and NGOs are run by people who are not part of the government although governments can partially fund an NGO as long as the funding government agency doesn't retain any type of representative or leadership role in the NGO. In the United States a type of NGO is referred to as a non-profit organization. NGOs typically have organization missions and goals that are dedicated to creating greater societal value versus existing to stay solely focused on generating profits.

Ad agency: This is a company that you hire to develop for pay advertisements to ensure that your targeted market is aware and enticed to purchase your product or service.

PR agency: A company that you hire to generate favorable publicity about your new business to people who have been found through market research potentially interested in buying your product or service

eMarketers: A group of people that you hire to implement your digital media strategy for the online and potentially via cell phone marketing of your new business. eMarketers utilize ultimately any form of electronic media to promote and advertise your business.

Netroots: This word is a newly coined termed that combines portions of the words Internet and grassroots to define a type of marketing that targets blogs and digital media in order to cause powerful action for achieving your new venture goals. The term originally described political action and has recently been utilized to describe business action. Bloggers: This term describes someone who keeps an online diary/journal/log of his or her activities or comments on others' activities. One of the most popular blogs in the world is about entrepreneurs and is kept by

1. The business eco-system: Your path to finding the pot of gold at the end of the rainbow!

Guy Kawasaki called, How to Change the World: A practical blog for impractical people. Check it out: http://blog.guykawasaki.com.

Social networks: These are websites dedicated to fostering a community of individuals around a topic. We mentioned LinkedIn earlier; Facebook is another social networking example. According to Facebook's website, "Millions of people use Facebook everyday to keep up with friends, upload an unlimited number of photos, share links and videos, and learn more about the people they meet."[14]

Readers of this chapter are invited to join my Facebook page by registering to become a Facebook member at http://www.facebook.com (it is free and a social networking site) and then enter Molly Lavik into the search field and click on my name. Then select add as a friend.

Texting: This is when you type in a message with photos or in some cases a video via a cell phone

Grassroots: This is a powerful movement of every day people for a cause. Currently there is a grassroots movement to protect the environment throughout the world.

Viral: This happens when a marketing message is transmitted through people excitedly and enthusiastically spreading the message by telling others who tell others who tell others and so forth. When a marketing message is spread via "word-of-mouth" the message is visually depicted as spreading in the same way a cold virus spreads and multiplies through a growing number of people in the wintertime. Marketers spend a great deal of money to attempt to initiate the spread of messages via word-of-mouth. However, it's easier said than done. An example of a marketing campaign that was spread via word-of-mouth was the marketing campaign for the film *Slumdog Millionaire* which is a film about a poor orphan from Mumbai India's slums who is a candidate for winning millions.

Influencers: Persons who are copied for wearing or embracing a particular fashion or trend. Taste makers are often known as trend setters.

Street teams: This term is used to describe a group of often young people between the ages of 15-25 years old, who travel up and down usually city streets actively promoting the product or service they are paid to market.

Membership organizations: Trade and other forms of professional associations, unions, special interest groups and work related clubs that one can join.

Community: The geographic, psychographic as well as online neighborhood in which your venture operates on a regular basis.

Virtual: Pertaining to your image appearing in a perceived manner, live, somewhere other then where you actually are currently located. The image would appear via a digital format such as through a web camera, simulated artificial intelligent agent and or three dimensional image such as a hologram image.

Suppliers: Companies that provide valuable resources to your new business are true suppliers.

Vendors: Typically the valuable resources are purchased from commercial resources known as vendors.

Consumers: These are people who buy your product or service.

---

14 Facebook, "Molly Lavik," http://www.facebook.com (Accessed December 24, 2009).

Employees: These are individuals that work directly for you and are on your pay roll.

Read on: Several subsequent chapters discuss the importance of stakeholders further.

Blog Back 5: Stakeholder

Blog Back: Decide how you want to "take aim" carefully here. Who will be on your Startup Stakeholder Arrow? Brainstorm ideas for who specifically you would aim to have for your Startup Stakeholder Arrow. Be sure to include exact names of businesses and people and titles for this list. Try to utilize all the aspects mentioned in the provided categories of the "Startup Stakeholder Arrow".

Go to: <u>http://www.Mentorography.com/</u> and post a draft of your Startup's Stakeholder Arrow list.

Ethics: the authentic rim on the wheel

Ethics refers to the "heart and soul" of the activities you engage in while starting your business. How authentic and truthful you are during the startup phase will set the stage for the future ethical threshold of your new venture. As the founder and chief visionary behind the concept you are bringing to market, it is your responsibility to create the values and company culture that will be your business. Once a company culture is set, it is virtually impossible to alter the path that you have set for your new venture to follow. One way to try to ensure the ethical standards of your company is to first make sure that you have a good moral compass.

Your "moral compass" is the ethical stance you take on decisions and actions with your startup.

Here are some questions to consider when developing your own moral compass:

- What will the new venture's code of ethics state?
- How will I make decisions for the startup that will limit my revenue potential but will ultimately be the correct action to take legally and ethically?
- What can I do to ensure that the people I hire have good values?
- Who will I go to for advice when I have a moral/ethical dilemma?
- Will I be capable of following the advice that I receive for taking the right ethical action?
- How will I know what is ethical and what is not?
- What processes will I put in place to make sure that my staff and the stakeholders I associate the startup with are acting ethically at all times?
- What will I do if a staff member or key stakeholder I'm associating with violates my new venture's code of ethics?
- In a crisis how will I communicate to my stakeholders the situation in the most ethical manner possible?
- How often will I cross check that I'm following my new venture's code of ethics?
- What seminars, classes and guidance can I find to make sure I'm acting ethically when running the startup?
- What people can I go to in order to gain a role model/mentor for acting ethically with my startup?

1. The business eco-system: Your path to finding the pot of gold at the end of the rainbow!

- If I end up doing something that was unethical what will be my process to correct the situation and to communicate the situation to my stakeholders?

- Will I listen to my gut if I have a strange ethical reaction to someone or something?

- Is there anything else I should ask myself to develop my moral compass?

It turns out in business that self-awareness of one's action is a key component to understanding how to develop an ethical moral compass. Additionally, the translation of an entrepreneur's moral compass into the development of a new venture leads to the establishment of the businesses' company culture. The "company culture" is the values you decide to instill in the new venture.

Making good: elements of a values-based company culture

- Provide a safe work place and clean work environment.

- Pay fair wages to all employees.

- Provide benefits of some kind for employees that may include health insurance, dental insurance, vision insurance, a retirement investment plan, a pension of partial salary to be paid once an employee retires, and reimbursement for continuous learning.

- Host employee appreciation events.

- Be respectful to all employees.

- Treat all stakeholders with respect and fairness.

- Have a suggestion box or method where by employees and stakeholders can make suggestions that you review and consider.

- Be a good corporate citizen by supporting some NGO/non-profit entities either by paying your employees to volunteer for these named causes or making cash donations or sponsorships to financially help support these organizations. This type of activity is known as CSR (Corporate Social Responsibility.) An example of a company that has been a good corporate citizen and routinely practices CSR is Grupo Bimbo which, according to the company's website, was established in 1945 and is considered one of the most important bakeries in the world. In 2007, Grupo Bimbo's net sales amounted to $ 6.7 billion dollars. In keeping with the company's social responsibility, Grupo Bimbo participates in important community projects such as the reforestation of protected natural areas in Mexico as well as in a series of different projects for community welfare. You can read all about Grupo Bimbo's Social Responsibility work in health, commitment to the environment, commitment to associates, and commitment to society at: http://www.grupobimbo.com/display.php?section=6 [15]

- Adopt a triple bottom line philosophy. "Triple bottom line" means your company cares equally not only about making a profit but also about taking care of the people associated with your company and

---

15 Grupo Bimbo, "Social Responsibility," http://www.grupobimbo.com/display.php?section=6 (Accessed December 28, 2009).

conducting business in a way that is good for sustaining a healthy environment for the planet. So to summarize, the triple bottom line philosophy means you care equally about people, planet and profits.

- Develop sustainable business practices. One who cares about the environment of his business goes to the trouble and expense to make sure that he:

  - has a recycling program for not only garbage but also old electronic devices and toxic waste disposal from batteries and printers.

  - utilizes office cleaning supplies that are environmentally safe and don't outgas. "Outgassing" is a term that refers to indoor air quality and describes the slow release of gas from a manufactured material such as furniture or carpets. Often the term is used to describe the potentially unhealthful attributes of a newly manufactured material as this gas is released indoors.

  - carries out office remodeling and construction in a safe for the environment fashion by using low VOC, ("Volatile organic compounds (VOCs) are emitted as gases from certain solids or liquids. VOCs include a variety of chemicals, some of which may have short- and long-term adverse health effects.")[16], paints that do not out gas as well as insulation made from recycled materials.

  - replaces company light bulbs and lighting fixtures with energy efficient light bulbs.

  - produces marketing materials that use soy-based ink and are printed on recycled paper stock. He uses the recycled logo mark on materials to communicate to stakeholders that he is concerned with sustaining the environment.

  - works with vendors, suppliers and all of his stakeholders that support environmental protection tactics.

  - conserves energy and resources whenever possible. Moving to a four day a week, ten hour a day schedule can by way of example conserve energy and ultimately "cut kilowatts to create a slender gas and electric bill".

  - rewards employees for traveling to and from work in sustainable ways such as walking, riding a bicycle, taking public transportation and when appropriate car-pooling.

  - if applicable, purchases company vehicles that are electric or electric hybrids.

  - stays current with environmental literature to keep employee's knowledge base strong on conserving energy.

Going green on a shoe string

You may be wondering what you are going to do take the ethical stance on your company's proactive sustainability plans to protect the environment when you are in the startup phase of your venture. It happens that doing the right thing for the environment is not just good for the environment but it also can be profitable no matter what your socio-economic state is today with your business. The recommended energy-saving tactics listed above will help you save money on your electric bill. By operating a sustainably-focused company you will be

---

16 U.S. Environmental Protection Agency, "Indoor Air Quality: An Introduction to Indoor Air Quality: Organic Cases (Volatile Organic Compounds-VOCs), http://www.epa.gov/iaq/voc.html (Accessed January 16, 2009).

generating a growing amount of good will for your venture. And good will is something you can take to the bank! "Goodwill" is the difference between what your company is worth and what you are actually able to sell your venture for in the market place. The more goodwill you generate the higher value of your company in comparison to your competition. Some of the most environmentally conscious people in the world live in severely economically-challenged neighborhoods. Do not let your socio-economic status challenge the entrepreneurial ethics behind your startup. The goodwill you are generating from taking care of the environment could potentially come back to you in the form of good karma!

Read on: You'll find more discussion of a socially responsible organization in Chapter 14.

Blog Back 6: Moral Compass

Blog back: Write a draft of your new venture's code of ethics and a description of your moral compasses' stances including what sustainable practices your venture will adopt to go green and have a triple bottom line focus.

Go to: http://www.Mentorography.com and post a draft of your code of ethics, description of your moral compasses' stances and green sustainability practices.

Operations: the logistical rim on the wheel

The operations of your business are the tactics and processes you implement to run your business.

Water your plants: operations hydrate your startup

Operations in a startup begin with the composition of a business plan. A new venture without a business plan is like a car without an engine; it exists but cannot get anywhere. In fact, researching and drafting the new venture's business plan is probably the most important and necessary business practice you will ever under take. Business plans are usually written to obtain financing for a new venture. However, the business document and planning process provides a much more important function. This document will be your road map for getting your venture started. The findings of your research contained in your business plan can tell you from the beginning with pretty good certainty if your new business has a real chance of being successful financially and sustainable in the long run.

Traditional sections contained in a business plan:

- **Company Description** gives a background to the history of your startup and explains what your venture will do.

- **Statement of Mission or Mantra** is a short phrase that explains the purpose of your new venture.

- **Products and or Services** describe what you plan to sell.

- **Target Markets** elaborate on whom you plan to sell to.

- **Marketing Strategy** explains what unique maneuvers your venture will under-take to accomplish the businesses goals.

- **Competitive Analysis** documents who your main competitors are in the market place.

- **Management Teams** are the names, titles and backgrounds of the people who will lead your venture to success.

- **Operations for Investors** explains what tactics you will undertake to finance the venture and the exit strategy you plan to utilize for the initial investors to make a profit on their investment.

- **Financials** document the forecasted sales and expenses for the first five years of the new venture. The financials should be accompanied by a detailed assumption log which summarizes where the numbers entered in your financial spreadsheets originally came from. Most investors want to see your financial documents include balance sheets, cash flows, income statements and key ratios such is when you anticipate breaking even.

- **Long-term Goals** explain what you hope to eventually accomplish with the new venture.

- **Executive Summary** which goes at the beginning of your business plan but is often written last should contain a brief summary of each of the above mentioned business plan sections. Executive summaries should be limited to two or less pages. The Executive Summary is often the most read portion of your business plan so it's important to write and re-write this section until it's absolutely perfect. Some entrepreneurs recommend that you draft the executive summary first and use this document as a planning document to cross check what you need in order to complete the business plan.

After you have completed drafting your new venture's business plan it may be time to establish the legal entity of your business. Check with your local government office to get directed to the rules and regulations and processes you need to follow in order to properly establish your business's legal entity

Some of the most universal company establishments are:

- sole proprietor

- private limited company

- state-owned enterprise

- public-limited company

- NGO

- corporations

If you can get the resources from family and friends to pay for an attorney to help you establish your business legal entity you may lessen some of the risks associated with starting a new venture. The type of business entity you form will more than likely impact the way in which you pay taxes on your products and services and file your country's income tax filing. The definitions for the different forms of company establishments vary from country to country. You will want to check with the portion of your government that grants company established entities for clarification

With a draft business plan in hand and your legal company business entity established it's time to fully map out the operations/processes you plan to utilize to implement your business plan. It's highly recommend that you make a Gantt chart to stay organized with the correct sequence and timing of each business activity.

You can use Microsoft® Excel and setup columns that list:

1. The business eco-system: Your path to finding the pot of gold at the end of the rainbow!

- tasks

- person(s) assigned to complete tasks

- dates that tasks must be completed by as well as proper task sequence

- an area to check off when a task has been effectively completed

- a comment section to keep a historic list of reactions to the considered tasks

- and given your unique plans, you may choose to have additional columns.

It is highly recommended that you post your new venture's Operations Gantt Chart on a wall in a visible location so that as many people as possible have access to this information. This will allow others to make updates as well as understand what you are working on when they are considering interrupting you during the day.

Keep an open mind as you implement your operational plans for the startup. Remain flexible to continuous updates. Remember a startup is an evolving operational process that will need fine turning along the way.

Read on: Operations is the subject of Chapter 7

New product: the tangible rim on the wheel

The new product can be a physical product and or a service offering. Developing a new product is an operational task that goes "above and beyond the call of duty" of utilizing the Operations Gantt chart described in the previous Operations section. Instead, we are recommending that you create a Process Mapping Guide in order to effectively develop your new product offerings. The following section describes in detail how to develop a Process Mapping Guide for your new product offerings

A new product bud is blooming: introducing the "New Venture Instructional Manual to Operational Excellence"

"New Venture Instructional Manual to Operational Excellence"

Start by process mapping all of the organization's processes by creating a process log. Utilize a word processing software program which has auto shapes that features a "flowchart." This will give you the software necessary for developing your process map. It does take a long time to process map the functions within an organization, even a newly formulated venture. It's time well spent.

Process mapping guide

There are many books and publications about process mapping and there are multiple ways to process map. We are going to focus here on showing you how to map the processes that make up new product development and marketing. We suggest the following:

Assemble the people who are involved in the development and marketing of a new product at your organization.

Brainstorm a list of the day-to-day steps that are taken to develop and market a new product.

Review the list with your board, strategic alliance partners, mentors, vendors, and family members for items that may have been missed.

Take the final list and divide it into two categories: repetitive processes and rare processes. Repetitive processes are steps that are taken repeatedly when developing and marketing a new product such as manufacturing the product. Rare processes occur infrequently.

Analyze the rare processes list to see if any of the items mentioned can be combined with or woven into the repetitive processes. Rare processes can drain resources and are often not budgeted for. If you can combine a rare process with a repetitive process, you have taken a valuable step toward improving the operational excellence of your business.

Make a flowchart of the processes within your organization from the list that was prepared and fine-tuned. This is where you take what might be explained in several paragraphs of text and drill it down to several flowchart icons. See Exhibit 1.9.

Process Mapping Diagram

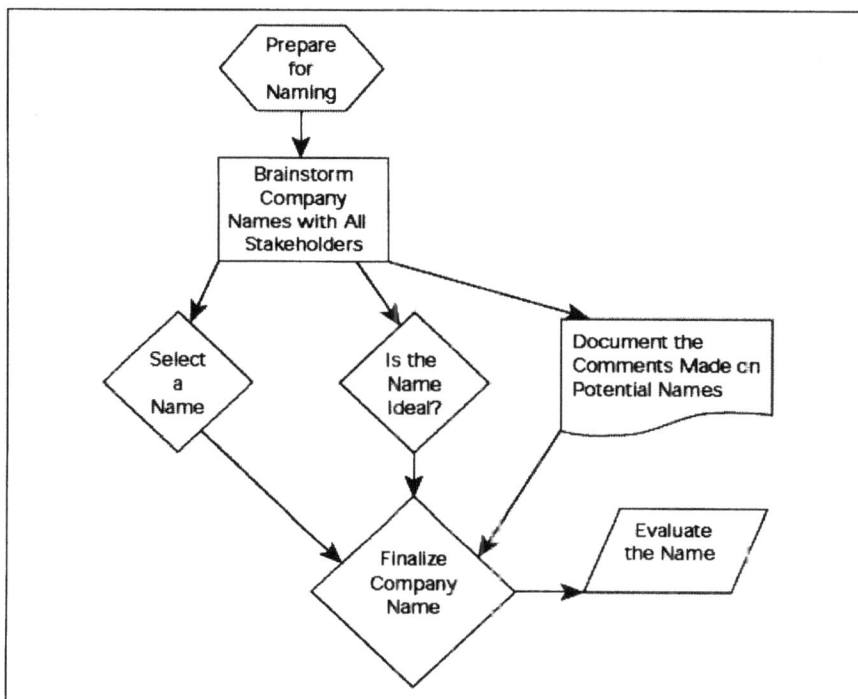

Exhibit 9: The Process Mapping Diagram was developed by Molly Lavik, October 6, 2002

There is a growing trend for corporations to organize their management systems by processes instead of products. Large and mid-size corporations are making this shift to achieve cost savings.

1. The business eco-system: Your path to finding the pot of gold at the end of the rainbow!

Once you have completed your process log you must repeat the analysis phase. Gather your resident experts as well as some new mentors and outside board members to analyze the firm's processes. Look for current processes that could be streamlined.

Because areas to streamline are difficult to see, keep re-examining what has been documented in the process log. Upon exhaustive examination of every possible streamlined scenario, the solution to achieving operational excellence will come into focus. Stay open and flexible to these new ideas.

Log the new process innovations. Embrace the new processes and apply them throughout the organization with the committed support of top management. This can be the most challenging step and requires a change management campaign.

A change management campaign is the internal communication campaign that is targeted at a venture's employees regarding a shift in the way a business is managed. This means you have to take a hands-on role in communicating the changes throughout the organization, making sure that everyone understands the new game plan, and why it is necessary. Inevitably, some won't be willing to go along with the new program and you may need to help them find employment elsewhere. One negative person can delay the whole group's transformation."[17]

Source: "Process Mapping Guide" text and "Process Mapping" Image reprinted with permission from Mentorography, Inc. © 2008. All Rights Reserved. Entrepreneurial Marketing; Real Stories and Survival Strategies by Molly Lavik and Bruce Buskirk, Module on Savvy Strategies for Marketing New Products, pages 188-190.

After your new product bud has bloomed through the implementation of a process mapping guide you are ready to launch your new product offering into the market place. You should consider planning a New Product Launch Event.

Read on: Adding Products or Services is discussed further in Chapter 13.

---

17 "Process Mapping Guide" text and "Process Mapping" Image reprinted with permission from Mentorography, Inc. © 2008. All Rights Reserved. Entrepreneurial Marketing; Real Stories and Survival Strategies by Molly Lavik and Bruce Buskirk, Module on Savvy Strategies for Marketing New Products, pages 188-190.

Exhibit 10: Sunny day

Image created by: Taissia Belozerova,
Graphic Designer, Artist, MBA Candidate
at Pepperdine University Class of 2009

Let the fruits of your labor blossom: the new product/service launch event plan

Your new business may be built around a product or service or both as we earlier discussed. We will discuss, by way of example, a new product launch event but it's worth noting that the same general principles apply whether you are planning a new product or new service launch event.

Events organized around a new product/service launch are typically postponed or cancelled because the new product/service does not turn out as anticipated. Build this scenario into any planned event so that you can recoup some of the costs if the event needs to be cancelled.

"Checklist for a New Product Launch Event

Is the new product going to be fully functional in time for the event? What is your backup plan?

Have you assembled a well-connected board of advisers to help with the production of the event?

Have you determined your budget for the new product launch event? Is there anyone you can bring in to cosponsor the event to help defray the cost?

Have you hired someone to be responsible for the myriad of details that must come together in order for a new product launch event to be called a success?

Have you prepared a detailed spreadsheet, with deadlines, of all the items that need to take place for the event to come together and assigned each item to a responsible person?

> Have you devised the best forum for the new product launch event? Is the event scheduled during an industry tradeshow where every- one will already be assembled and you can easily fold your event into the bigger show, leveraging all the resources available at that event?
>
> Have you outlined how you are going to communicate your new product message at the launch event? (There is nothing worse than producing an expensive new product launch event that everyone may enjoy but attendees leave not having any idea what brand was being promoted.)
>
> Have you invited your targeted press to cover the new product event?
>
> Do you have a contingency plan if few people respond to your invitation to the new product launch event? Do you have takeaway logo items, commonly referred to as premiums, for attendees so they can be reminded of the new product?
>
> Have you decided how you will measure and evaluate your brand building strategy?"[18]
>
> *Source:* "New Product Launch Event Plan" text reprinted with permission from Mentorography, Inc. © 2008. All Rights Reserved. Entrepreneurial Marketing; Real Stories and Survival Strategies by Molly Lavik and Bruce Buskirk, Module on Savvy Strategies for Marketing New Products, pages 191-192.

Read on: Launching your business is the topic of Section 2, Chapters 4, 5, and 6.

Blog Back 7: Launch Plan

Blog back: Develop a plan for your new product launch. Include the name and description of the venue you plan to showcase your new product as well as a detailed budget of the researched expenses and a forecast of the media coverage you hope to gain during the launch event.

Go to: http://www.Mentorography.com and post your new product launch plan.

Public relations: the sensational rim on the wheel

Public relations are the activities one engages in to generate excitement about your new venture so that editorial coverage will occur. Editorial coverage is thought to be much more valuable then advertising in media because people perceive editorial coverage as authentic and of interest. Startups need to generate a great deal of excitement known as "buzz" in order to make the case for media coverage. Because entrepreneurs normally don't have much if any marketing budgets to initially launch his or her new venture, relying on public relations coverage becomes essential for the success of a new venture.

In order to increase your chances for coverage of the new venture you will want to make sure that communications with the media include information about your new venture that is written in what is known as a "tight" manner including, if possible, the following attributes:

---

18 "New Product Launch Event Plan" text reprinted with permission from Mentorography, Inc. © 2008. All Rights Reserved. Entrepreneurial Marketing; Real Stories and Survival Strategies by Molly Lavik and Bruce Buskirk, Module on Savvy Strategies for Marketing New Products, pages 191-192.

- concise/brief summary

- straight-forward

- timely and quite current

- a first of its kind if possible

- attention-grabbing

- authentic and truthful

- tying-in if possible with an emerging trend

- remarkable

- and absolutely accurate

The public relations practitioner's tool kit

Press releases: Newsworthy text regarding the "Who, What, Where, and When" of the story you are pitching to the media.

Video News Releases (VNRs): Usually responsible for coordinating the video production of news announcements known as VNRs which are sent to television/broadcasting stations with the intention of gaining news coverage

Newswire services: The Public Relations practitioner works with a company known as a newswire service to disseminate news announcements to targeted media. One example is CSRwire service found at: http://www.csrwire.com which specializes in disseminating news releases from corporate socially responsible companies often engaged in many CSR pursuits. [19]

News agencies: The public relations practitioner is in direct contact with news services that cover large batches of news happenings in specific regions. MEMERCOPRESS is an example of a news agency. According to this news agency's website, "MERCOPRESS is a news agency concentrating on Mercosur countries which operates from Montevideo, Uruguay and includes in its area of influence the South Atlantic and insular territories."[20] For more information on MERCOPRESS visit: http://www.mercopress.com/about.do.

Media databases: Contain detailed information on how to reach media contacts. The more expansive and current the media database, the more likely you are to achieve optimum press coverage in targeted publications.

Style guides: Provide guidelines on the proper formatting of information to include when quoting from another source and attributing in a citation the quoted source.

Extensive Rolodex: Public relations practitioners are major networkers with vast contacts with the media as well as key stakeholders.

---

19 CSRwire, "Home Page," http://www.csrwire.com (Accessed on August 15, 2008).

20 MERCOPRESS, "About MERCOPRESS, http://www.mercopress.com/about.do (Accessed January 2, 2009).

1. The business eco-system: Your path to finding the pot of gold at the end of the rainbow!

Timelines: Successful public relations practitioners are known for keeping long timelines of checklists to make sure events and campaigns are carried out flawlessly in order to achieve the maximum amount of effective media coverage

Archives: The public relations practitioner usually is the one to maintain the press clipping files documenting media coverage as well as the video and image files. Images are sometimes used by the media so keeping well-organized archive files is essential to any marketing campaign.

Because public relations professionals are dedicated to the tasks surrounding disseminating, documenting and archiving news coverage, these practitioners are usually a great resource to any startup.

Blog Back 8: PR Plan

Blog Back: Write down a list of public relations plans you have for your new venture. Include what you will do to get publicity for your startup. What news sources will you target? Be specific by naming newspapers, magazines, newsletters. Leaflets, signage and other media sources that you plan to target.

Go to: http://www.Mentorography.com and post your Public Relations Plan.

Mentor insights: the "Where the Rubber Meets the Road" spokes on the wheel

Mentor insights are the lessons learned by the protégé/mentee. Mentor insights are depicted as spokes on the wheel because they are the glue that effectively holds together everything else. Understanding your mentor's driving philosophies is essential if you want to gain the wisdom that your mentors possess. There is a tremendous amount you can learn from a mentor's successes as well as their setbacks. Mentors come literally in all "styles, shapes and sizes". When you are away from home be sure to keep a "look out" for people who might have some business wisdom to share with you.

Places you can go to find mentors potentially ideal for coaching you with your startups include:

- faculty at schools
- libraries
- seminars/conferences/workshops
- town meetings
- management from other businesses
- classmates
- family
- friends
- co-workers
- religious institutions
- public markets
- neighbors

- near-by communities

- re-acquainting yourself with people you haven't kept in contact with

- entrepreneurs

- micro-loan recipients

To keep track of the insights that you pick up from mentors try keeping a journal of the lessons you are learning that are applicable to your startup. Mentor insights can come from a business executive or role model who you want to emulate. Mentor insights can also come from observations of others.

I was fortunate to meet a student named Jay Milbrandt while teaching a Social Entrepreneurship course at Pepperdine University's Graziadio School of Business and Management. Jay had recently traveled to Bangladesh and kept journals of his first-hand observations of meeting people who were prospering through micro-finance loans. I found these journal entries extremely inspirational and we hope you will as well. We encourage you to be on the alert for micro-finance opportunities in your country as a proven method for helping those that are less fortunate than yourselves. By reading these journal excerpts you can experience how those less fortunate are finding success no matter what their economic situation. Micro-financed loans are imparting a great deal of opportunity to those that really need it and transforming the economies of developing countries in remarkable ways! The following are excerpts from the journal of Jay Milbrandt.

Jay Milbrandt's Journal Entries from Bangladesh
Not Just Statistics

The shear numbers are impressive. 1.2 billion people throughout the world live in extreme poverty. Accordingly, extreme poverty is defined by the World Bank as living below $1 per day purchasing power parity threshold. The United Nations set the Millennium Challenge goal of eliminating extreme poverty by the year 2025. In Bangladesh, at least, it appears to be well on the way. It's easy to get lost in the numbers. But, when you travel through Bangladesh meeting the microcredit borrowers, you realize that behind every number is a life—real people and real families. Suddenly, the statistics come alive.

I don't know what it's like to live on less than $1 per day. I have, however, met enough people to garner some details about what such a life is like. Simply put, you consume in proportion to what you grow; when you cannot afford more, you beg.

Meet Meera. She used to live on less than $1 per day. Now, she's a twenty-six year old business owner with two daughters, eleven and seven years old. Her husband walked out on her a few years ago, leaving her to fend for herself. In the culture of Bangladesh, she was in a very tough spot. To give birth to only daughters and no sons is unlucky. Likewise, for a husband to walkout on his wife is looked down upon even more. In spite of this, she became one of the most successful women in her village. Through microcredit, she started and built a large poultry farm, raising thousands of chickens and selling them to market. After showing us her farm, she invited us into her home, which was considered a nice home by village standards—four walls, two rooms, a cement floor, and metal roof. Her home was also financed through a Grameen[21] microcredit home loan. And, best of all, she told us how happy she was and how microcredit changed her life.

Although Meera holds the distinction as the first microcredit customer I met, that's the only number associated with her.[22]

Jay Milbrandt's Journal Entries from Bangladesh
Why I Have Hope

"I've got this feeling of hopelessness," I admit to a traveling companion. I'm here to see the hope that microcredit has brought, but our taxi has not even left Dhaka yet and I'm surrounded by the most abject poverty I have ever seen.

I'm on sensory overload. There are so many people that the country seems ready to burst at the seams. More than 140 million people are packed into this country, approximately the size of Iowa. In Dhaka, garbage is everywhere—in the streets, in the ditches. Its obvious that the city does not possess the infrastructure to service its 15 million inhabitants. Judging by the integrity of the city streets, which appear to have been paved once left alone, I'm not the least bit surprised. If the heap of garbage is fresh, a few people would be rummaging through it—looking for a meal, I suspect. If the garbage was old, it served as a bed. Audibly, Dhaka pulses with the sound of non-stop horns— there need be no reason to use it. Dhaka is also a city of smells. Every street has a different smell, many of which I find both unfamiliar and unappealing.

The streets are a labyrinth—if I were lost, I could never find my way back. We round a corner and roll past a lot of wood and metal. A salvage yard maybe? "Those are the slums of Dhaka," our guide explains. Our taxi comes to a stop, waiting for a train to pass. After a few seconds, there's a bang on the window. It's a young boy, maybe seven years old, begging for money. He's yelling in Bengali and motioning to his mouth with his hand. "In Dhaka, people work together in an organized system of begging," my guide explains. He cracks the window and tells the child to leave. We start moving again and the child runs along until he can no longer keep pace.

Little did I know at this point, that over the succeeding two months, I would meet some of the most disadvantaged people in the world: the poorest-of-the-poor, victims of trafficking, prostituted women, refugees, and the illiterate. Despite their perilous circumstances, I'm filled with more hope than ever before. Why? The positive, successful change I would come to witness—and the great potential for continued change.

---

21 Grameen Bank: Banking for the Poor, "Home Page," http://www.grameen-info.org/ (Accessed on December 10, 2007).

22 Jay Milbrandt's Journal Entries from Bangladesh, Pepperdine University JD/MBA alumni, Reprinted with Permission.

My hopelessness, however, would be relieved. What I saw in Dhaka was probably a piece of history for Bangladesh... Due to current laws, Grameen Bank is restricted from operating in urban areas.

I have hope because of Bangladesh. I wish I could have traveled here 20 years ago to experience the change. From the descriptions of the people I met, the change has been Bangladesh—a model for global turn around; the man sitting next to me on the airplane was convinced that, given ten years and right national leadership, the country could shine like Malaysia.[23]

Jay Milbrandt's Journal Entries from Bangladesh
Moving the Mountains of Poverty

How come I have never heard a sermon preached on the elimination of poverty? Christians frequently talk about giving to those in need or feeding the hungry, but I have yet to hear a sermon calling for a solution. Here is one to start with, I would like to call it "Microcredit and the Mustard Seed":

One evening just before dusk, we were riding a rickshaw down a narrow road in the village of Salanga. Suddenly, our guide stopped the driver, had him turn the rickshaw around, and pull up at a small metal building. Inside, the building was dimly lit with an organic smell and the hum of a large engine. We met with the owner, Shameen, who had financed his small business through a Grameen microloan. Before Grameen, he had nothing—barely enough to feed his family—if that year's rice harvest was plentiful. After founding and growing his business through Grameen loans, he started generating income on his own, built a better house, and could afford to send his kids to school. And his business? Processing mustard seeds.

Matthew 17:20 [from The New International Version, NIV, which is the English translation of the Christian Bible] tells us that with the faith the size of a mustard seed, we can tell the mountains to move. I took this verse literally with a good dose of skepticism until this day. Here was a mountain right in front of us: More than 1 billion people clenched in the fist of poverty. In Bangladesh and throughout the world, millions of people are putting a lot of faith in tiny loans—Shameen's faith, ironically, happened to be a mustard seed.

Soon, the entire building was flooded with local people wanting to gaze at the foreigners. Each of these people was a microcredit borrower. None of them in the chains of poverty. This held true for practically everyone in the entire village, followed by millions more throughout Bangladesh. Microcredit was moving the mountain of poverty before my very eyes.

Deuteronomy 15:7-8 says "If there is a poor man among you... do not be ... tightfisted. ...Rather be openhanded and freely lend him whatever he needs." Is it coincidence that the word "lend" is used? I believe microcredit is a sermon that every church should hear. I believe that if Christians were to

23 Ibid.

> join the Muslims and Hindus of Bangladesh in the mustard seed of microcredit, the mountain would move much faster.[24]

Jay Milbrandt's Journal Entries from Bangladesh
What Third World?

The man staring at me has no shoes or shirt. This seems like the perfect opportunity to capture the face of the human condition in rural Bangladesh. As I pull out my camera he mirrors me with none other than a camera phone. I'm photographing him photographing me—something seems wrong here.

Earlier in the day, I spontaneously walked out into a rice field to visit the field workers. They were excited to show a foreigner how fast they cut, then give a brief rice cutting lesson. I just about took a Bengali man's leg off—the sickle blade is sharper than it looks. They cut a few sheaths of rice, then tie the bundle off with one of the stalks. The whole process takes but a few seconds. Rice harvesting has been done this way here for hundreds of year. Occasionally, I would see a billboard for a tractor or modern agricultural convenience, but I never saw any of them in action.

Third world technology transfer is an interesting phenomenon. Is a cell phone really what they need? How about drip irrigation instead? Or maybe a rice harvester?

Grameen created an interesting microenterprise program throughout Bangladesh with village "phone ladies." A woman in each village is allowed to purchase a cell phone through a Grameen loan. The "phone ladies" then sell use of their cell phone to other villagers. The result is that the "phone ladies" have a very profitable business and villages that previously had no phone line at all now have a modern method of communication. As traveling is difficult for the poor of Bangladesh, the villagers no longer have to leave if they need to communicate with a relative in another village or ask a doctor a question. In other villages, the profitability of "phone ladies" has diminished because a majority of villagers now own a personal cell phone.

It's surprising how someone may not have running water, but own a nicer cell phone than I do.[25]

Blog Back 9: Journal

Blog back: Keep a journal of the lessons learned from your own startup time mentor insights.

Go to: http://www.Mentorography.com and post an excerpt of one of your journal entries that is particularly applicable to someone on an entrepreneurial journey.

With the Mentor Insights providing strong spokes; this completes the description and elaboration of the visual model of the Business Eco-system Wheel.

---

24 Ibid.

25 Ibid.

BUSINESS ECO-SYSTEM WHEEL

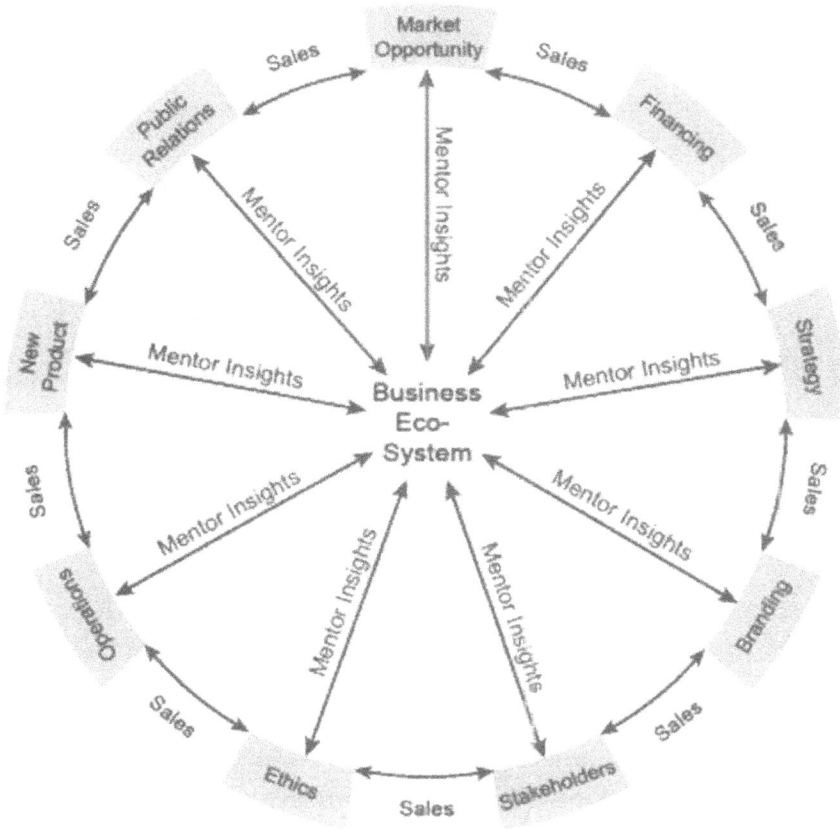

1. The business eco-system: Your path to finding the pot of gold at the end of the rainbow!

Exhibit 11: Striking gold

Image created by: Taissia Belozerova,
Graphic Designer, Artist, MBA Candidate
at Pepperdine University Class of 2009

Early-stage entrepreneurs can rejoice when they invest the time and energy to build well thought out Business Eco-systems. These hard-working, strategic-thinking entrepreneurs increase the chances of creating a startup that has a real opportunity of potentially striking gold at the end of the rainbow!

About this author and acknowledgements:

Editor and Author: Molly Lavik, Founder, Mentorography, Inc. & StartupTime Coach, Molly.Lavik@StartupTime.com, Professor, Vatel International Business School. Very special thanks to the Academic Reviewer: Debbi D Brock, William and Kay Moore Professor of Entrepreneurship and Management, Berea College. Special Thanks to Michael Tanenbaum, Kaushik Shirhatti, and Sumeet Malik my graduate assistants and my former students, Ann Shafer and Luiz Montoya from Pepperdine University's Graziadio School of Business and Management who assisted by providing initial research on preliminary versions of Chapter 1. Special thanks to my former student Jay Milbrandt for providing his journal. Special thanks as well to Taissia Belozerova, Graphic Designer, Artist, MBA Candidate at Pepperdine University Class of 2009. Also, special thanks to Bruce D Buskirk, PhD, Professor of Marketing, Pepperdine University's Graziadio School of Business and Management who co-authored the gratefully acknowledged and appreciated excerpts provided by Mentorography, Inc. from *Entrepreneurial Marketing: Real Stories and Survival Strategies*. Additionally, special thanks to Estelle Holloway.

2. The mind of the entrepreneur: Your entrepreneurial journey begins by embarking on your own hero's journey!

Editor: Molly Lavik (Vatel International Business School Los Angeles, USA)

In chapter 2 we will explore what factors and characteristics are commonly found in an entrepreneurial mindset. These may be characteristics that you can strive to possess and emulate. Perhaps you may need to inherit from your parents a certain combination of entrepreneurial characteristics to become an entrepreneur or perhaps that has absolutely nothing to do with if you are destined to become an entrepreneur. Is an entrepreneur ultimately born or made? That question has no definite answer. We suggest you meet as many entrepreneurs as you can to see if this is how you want to spend your life; then decide if you want to train under these entrepreneurs as an apprentice. You control your own destiny and your life's journey is your own so you decide!

Review:

In chapter 1 we discussed the characteristics of an entrepreneur as possessing the following attributes:

Vision: Able to create and communicate an easily understandable mission for what the new venture does in order to successfully launch a new business. This is accomplished while inspiring others to join you in your new enterprise.

Creativity: Ability to inject imagination and uniqueness into a new business venture. It takes skill and ingenuity to create a new venture equipped with strategies to outsmart the competition.

Focus: Able to maintain the vision of the company with unwavering diligence. It's very easy to get sidetracked especially if you find it necessary to evolve the original vision. Ironically, we have encountered many successful entrepreneurs who get bored easily...

Passion: Desiring to succeed under your own steam [initiative] on a business venture...

Drive: Possessing intrinsic energy to accomplish the business goal even in the face of adversity.

Perseverance: Able to keep going even when faced with seemingly insurmountable obstacles.

Opportunistic Nature: Sees the possibilities even before they exist. Can take advantage of an upcoming trend or unite unrelated processes to create a unique business venture...

Problem Solving Ability: Thrives on coming up with solutions to complex challenges...

Self-discipline: Able to be organized and regimented in pursuit of a successful business venture.

Frugality: Knows how to stretch every cent so that expenditures are as low as possible.

Empathy: Able to put yourself in another's shoes and therefore able to show sensitivity and understanding of what others are communicating in the start up environment...

Social Responsibility: Ethics, caring and humanitarianism are characteristics that are commonly found in today's entrepreneurs...

Spirituality: We have found that successful entrepreneurs have often devoted time to spirituality development. Meditation and positive affirmations are two common examples of spirituality.

Good Timing: Able to identify a market opportunity and know when it is the optimum time to launch a new venture or expansion of an existing enterprise.

Luck: Can a person be predisposed to be lucky: Is luck a human behavior or a karmic universal predisposition?[26]

In Chapter 2 we begin by introducing you to Costa Roussos, a young entrepreneur from the country of Cypress who is creating a global music empire. We will share his story through an interview that Molly Lavik conducted with him and look at his entrepreneurial tendencies and attributes. Then it is your turn to take the Entrepreneur Assessment Survey which can be used as one indication of measuring your own entrepreneurial mindset. However, it should be noted that a true entrepreneur would never rely on a survey to determine how worthy or ready they are to become an entrepreneur. A true entrepreneur would simply begin implementing his or her start up idea.

True story: Costa Roussos was one of my students several years ago and immediately I noticed something quite different from Costa and that was his focus on starting a music company. It seems to take a certain type of person to start a new venture because you do not have the security and structure of a more established company not to mention the challenges of inspiring others to join your unproven venture and to help you meet their deadlines associated with a new business. Do you have the type of mindset that Costa seems to possess to get him through the many setbacks and challenges that faced him or any entrepreneur in the making? If you are not sure do not worry. When the timing seems right you will know if an entrepreneurial journey is your destiny. And you might even become a hero to someone or maybe even an entire group of people such as how you will soon read Costa is becoming a hero to the independent music artist and music listening enthusiast. This is your future we are talking about and it's your decision if you have a hero's journey ahead!

As you read Costa's story pay particular attention to the characteristics described as his entrepreneurial mindset. Do you possess some of the same characteristics? Read Costa's story to find out.

26"The Mindset of an Entrepreneur" is reprinted and adapted with permission from Mentorography, Inc. © 2008. All Rights Reserved. Entrepreneurial Marketing; Real Stories and Survival Strategies by Molly Lavik and Bruce Buskirk, introduction pages xxviii-xxx.

http://www.startuptime.com/costamusicus.html

Do you possess any of the entrepreneurial mindset characteristics that Costa has?

Blog Back 10: Your Mindset

Blog Back: Go to http://www.Mentorography.com and post your own entrepreneurial mindset characteristics.

Still not sure if you are an entrepreneur or if you may some day have your own hero's journey ahead? Try taking the Entrepreneur Assessment Survey but remember, this does not mean if you have the tendency or not, again only you get to decide if you want to go on your own entrepreneurial journey. No one or no survey can tell you that.

Entrepreneur assessment survey

Entrepreneur assessment survey

Directions: Please circle your personal response to each question. Please be sure to go with the answer that is your first choice if and when you are in doubt of how to respond.

1) Do you have an issue that is a major driving force behind your professional goals in life?

Yes   Undecided   No

2) Would you describe yourself as the type of person who gives up easily when faced with adversity?

Yes   Undecided   No

3) Do people who have known you since childhood describe you as the type of person who gives up easily when faced with adversity?

Yes   Undecided   No

4) Have you been successful in the past convincing others to help you to accomplish your goals?

Yes   Undecided   No

5) Do you have a desire to make the world a better place that is a stronger goal for you then your desire to earn money?

Yes   Undecided   No

6) Have you considered becoming an entrepreneur?

Yes   Undecided   No

7) Have you spent a substantial amount of time in your life considering what type of legacy you would like to leave?

Yes   Undecided   No

8) When trying to raise support for an idea, do you ever start by identifying people to form alliances with who may be sympathetic to your goal?

Yes   Undecided   No

2. The mind of the entrepreneur: Your entrepreneurial journey begins by embarking on your own hero's journey!

9) If you were busy with a deadline for work and or school would you miss completing this deadline on time because you gave your own new venture/start up/new product idea a higher priority?

Yes   Undecided   No

10) Will you use your score on this test to ultimately help determine if you should become an entrepreneur?

Yes   Undecided   No

11) How many of the entrepreneurial mindset characteristics do you possess? Give yourself 1 point for each of the characteristics you possess from the list below.

Total Score for characteristics: _____

Some key characteristics of an entrepreneurial mindset

In chapter 1 some characteristics of an entrepreneurial mindset were shared; here are additional characteristics and or similar characteristics to also consider.

Mentor Method 2

Humanitarian **Worth 1 Point** **Add 1 Point_____**	Organizing movements that can take many forms including campaigns, drives, grassroots or net roots movements, lobbying, and/or crusades for the express purpose of providing altruistic or charitable support.
Visionary **Worth 1 Point** **Add 1 Point_____**	Possessing the ability to potentially define the future by making bold unsubstantiated predictions for new enterprises while utilizing a great deal of imagination and foresight in the process.
Values-centered **Worth 1 Point** **Add 1 Point_____**	Demonstrating worthwhile qualities of leadership that are lawful, ethical, considerate, and honest in nature and intent.
Change-oriented **Worth 1 Point**	Adopting a leadership style that attempts to transform the status quo by creating a new method, process or invention for accomplishing tasks.

Add 1 Point_____	
Self-reliant **Worth 1 Point** **Add 1 Point_____**	Depending on yourself to develop solutions for the problem or challenge at hand.
Persuasive **Worth 1 Point** **Add 1 Point_____**	Able to convince others that the new organizations' mission and goals are viable and should be adopted and supported.
Hyper-focused **Worth 1 Point** **Add 1 Point_____**	Maintaining uninterrupted attention and concentration directed at implementing the enterprise's mission.
Passion **Worth 1 Point** **Add 1 Point_____**	Having a tremendous amount of enthusiasm and excitement over the mission and goals of the new organization.
Energetic **Worth 1 Point** **Add 1 Point_____**	Demonstrating an infinite amount of drive and an enterprising nature toward accomplishing an organization's objectives. When starting a new organization especially when starting a social enterprise, it requires a great deal of energy and drive to accomplish all the objectives especially given that social enterprises usually require volunteer staff and unpaid staff for resourcefulness that goes far beyond the standard needs of a traditional, long-established company.
Resilient	Possessing the ability to keep on trying even when

2. The mind of the entrepreneur: Your entrepreneurial journey begins by embarking on your own hero's journey!

	faced with failure, great adversity and seemingly insurmountable obstacles.
Worth 1 Point **Add 1 Point**_____	

12) Ask someone who has known you since you were a child how many of the entrepreneurial mindset characteristics they think you possess? Give yourself 1 point for each of the characteristics they feel you possess.

Total Score for characteristics: _____

Answer key

Answer key for entrepreneur assessment survey

Directions: Please circle your personal response to each question. Please be sure to go with the answer that is your first choice if and when you are in doubt of how to respond.

1) Do you have an issue that is a major driving force behind your professional goals in life?

Yes   Undecided   No

Score: Ten points for Yes, 0 points for Undecided and No.

Reason: One of the first steps toward creating a new company is to have a major reason or issue for your new venture's mission or goal.

2) Would you describe yourself as the type of person who gives up easily when faced with adversity?

Yes   Undecided   No

Score: Ten points for No and 0 points for Yes and Undecided.

Reason: You have to be able to continue through all the setbacks to be successful and ultimately enjoy being a social entrepreneur.

3) Do people who have known you since childhood describe you as the type of person who gives up easily when faced with adversity?

Yes   Undecided   No

Score: Ten points for No and 0 points for Undecided and Yes.

Reason: It typically takes a track record in life of dealing successfully with adversity to build up the confidence and credibility that comes with a No answer for this question.

4) Have you been successful in the past convincing others to help you to accomplish your goals?

Yes   Undecided   No

Score: Ten points for Yes and 0 points for Undecided and No.

Reason: New ventures do not have the funding to afford the staff to get work accomplished. Resourcefulness is the key to succeeding and one must possess the ability to attract and retain volunteers and non-paid experienced help at first to get the tasks completed.

5) Do you have a desire to make the world a better place that is a stronger goal for you then your desire to earn money?

Yes   Undecided   No

Score: Ten points for Yes and 0 points for Undecided and No.

Reason: Entrepreneurs are driven by their need to create societal wealth vs self-wealth. This desire takes precedent and priority over other goals. This does not mean that someday you might not derive a financial bonanza for the work you have been doing associated with the start up. It just means that is not what drives you today.

6) Have you considered becoming an entrepreneur?

Yes   Undecided   No

Score: Ten points for Yes and 0 points for Undecided and No.

Reason: Even if it was a subconscious or passing thought, usually you have to have some propensity or interest toward becoming an entrepreneur for it to be your destiny.

7) Have you spent a substantial amount of time in your life considering what type of legacy you would like to leave?

Yes   Undecided   No

Score: Ten points for Yes and 0 points for Undecided and No.

Reason: Perhaps your legacy is something to be considered in later years. With that said it is never too soon to begin considering what type of footprint you may want to leave. If you have considered trying to leave a legacy of making the world a better place then you may a hero's journey as your entrepreneurial path for future.

8) When trying to raise support for an idea, do you ever start by identifying people to form alliances with whom maybe sympathetic to your goal?

Yes   Undecided   No

Score: Ten points for Yes and 0 points for Undecided and No.

Reason: One of the best ways to increase your chances of being a successful entrepreneur is to enhance your credibility by forging strategic alliances and partnerships with others.

9) If you were busy with a deadline for work and or school would you miss completing this deadline on time because you gave your own new venture/start/new product idea a higher priority?

Yes   Undecided   No

Score: Ten points for No and 0 points for Yes or undecided.

2. The mind of the entrepreneur: Your entrepreneurial journey begins by embarking on your own hero's journey!

Reason: This may appear to be a trick question. A values-centered leader would not sacrifice one important commitment for another even if it was to help a social enterprise. Part of starting a new company is demonstrating ethical and honest business leadership.

10) Will you use your score on this test to ultimately help determine if you should become an entrepreneur

Yes   Undecided   No

Score: Ten points for No and 0 points for Yes and Undecided.

Reason: The truth of the matter is that if you are really meant to be an entrepreneur you do not need a test and or survey to tell you this. In fact; a true entrepreneur does not depend on others to make their decisions. Only you know your destiny; do not let anyone tell you what you can and can't accomplish in life because statistically speaking they would not really know.

11) How many of the entrepreneurial mindset characteristics do you possess?Give yourself 1 point for each of the characteristics you possess.

Total Score for characteristics: The goal is to score a ten for this question. Many entrepreneurs embody these entrepreneurial mindset characteristics.

12) How many of the entrepreneurial mindset characteristics do you possess? Give yourself 1 point for each of the characteristics you possess.

Total Score for characteristics: The goal is once again to score a ten for this question as explained above. If it turns out that you have a very different score for your self-assessment of this question in comparison to what someone who has known you all your life then you need to come to an understanding why others perceive you differently then you perceive your own interests. Perhaps you are repressing or camouflaging your true interests or maybe you have changed. The reason for the difference isn't as important as making sure you are aware of your own interests.

Score:

- A score of 120-110 may mean that you know that you want to become an entrepreneur and you should begin working out a strategic plan to make your goals a reality and to begin your own hero's journey.

- A score of 109-90 may mean that you most likely want to become an entrepreneur and you should begin thinking of this possibility to give yourself a further self-assessment of your interests.

- A score of 89 or lower may mean that you probably are not going to be an entrepreneur but as mentioned before; do not let this assessment be the final or even partial determination; the choice is clearly your own to make.

Blog Back 11: Start-up Story

Blog back: Post a story or interview with an entrepreneur who possesses some of the entrepreneurial mindset characteristics you hope to develop in yourself at: http://www.Mentorography.com. Whether you possess confidence in your own entrepreneurial mindset or hope to enhance or inspire further development there are resources and things you can do today to build your entrepreneurial mindset!

Entrepreneurial mindset enhancing activities

- Set up a Google Alert for the key words: "entrepreneurial mindset" at <u>http://www.google.com/alerts</u>. A Google Alert is a query of key words and allows you to receive in your e-mail inbox a list of all the stories to be posted on the Internet that day associated with your key word. You can set the alert to come to you immediately, daily or weekly.

- Discuss with entrepreneurs what attributes they possess that make these founders particularly adept at starting new ventures. When you talk with these visionary individuals be on the "look out" for unique characteristics that they people possess.

- Take some time and consider today what you want your lasting legacy to be and who you will accomplish those goals. Keep a diary of this journey and try when possible to have journal entries about what type of entrepreneurial characteristics you are developing to help you achieve your legacy goals.

- Do not let others define your entrepreneurial journey! You know who you are and who you want to be. The "naysayers" will always be around to try to prevent you from starting a new venture. Learn to listen to your gut.

- Seek out educational programs and literature that will help you better develop your own entrepreneurial characteristics. Make a list of the attributes you do not yet possess and then develop a plan of action to achieve adding these entrepreneurial characteristics to your own personality traits.

- Schedule time every day for 30 minutes to keep refining your entrepreneurial characteristics and figuring out how to enhance your entrepreneurial personality. Many people think that what you spend time thinking about will become ultimately your own reality.

- While each of you are from different countries and cultures there are some places that often will provide resources for first-time entrepreneurs.

These places include:

- Small business associations

- Banks, financial institutions, and micro-credit agencies

- Educational Facilities

- Business related NGOs

- Libraries

- Community Redevelopment Agencies

- Most family and friends for moral support

- The Internet when using the right search terms associated with developing and or enhancing your entrepreneurial mindset.

2. The mind of the entrepreneur: Your entrepreneurial journey begins by embarking on your own hero's journey!

Now you are ready to go out and potentially create your own hero's journey

Chapter summary

In Chapter 2 titled, "The mind of the entrepreneur", we reviewed the characteristics of an entrepreneurial mindset that were covered in Chapter 1, shared the story and entrepreneurial mindset attributes of Costa Roussos during his start up journey with Music.us followed by sharing with you the Entrepreneur Assessment Survey and answer key ending Chapter 2 with a list of entrepreneurial mindset enhancing activities so that you can begin embarking on your own hero's journey.

Blog Back 12: Hero Post

Blog back: Post entries from your journal regarding your thoughts about your own journey. Then read what others have posted. Do you see anyone who you think is on his or her way toward becoming a hero? Post your thoughts and comments on entrepreneurial mindset characteristics at http://www.Mentorography.com.

3. Business models and marketing:an overview

Editors: Salvador Treviño and Carlos Ruy Martinez (ITESM, Monterrey Campus, Mexico)

Contributors: Carlos Alberto Alanis, Gaspar Rivera, Jorge Echeagaray, Jose de Jesus Montes, Juana Monica Garcia, Ramiro Robles, and Roberto Sanchez

Learning objectives

- how to build and implement a successful business model

- understand the importance of a company to be market vs product oriented in a developing country

- how to identify consumers' wants successfully

- understand Porter's 5 forces of Industry Attractiveness

- how to perform a Market Research study

What is a business model?

Business models can be approached from two perspectives. A general perspective defines a business model as any type of conceptual framework explaining how to organize and evolve a business venture. On the other hand, specific circumstances guide business modeling. For instance, industries such as tourism, banking in the services sector, or automobile or shoe manufacturing demand specific models that take into account critical variables found within the industry's specific environment.

One definition from the general perspective is provide by Alex Osterwalder:

"A business model is a conceptual tool that contains a set of elements and their relationships and allows expressing the business logic of a specific firm. It is a description of the value a company offers to one or several segments of customers and of the architecture of the firm and its network of partners for creating, marketing, and delivering this value and relationship capital, to generate profitable and sustainable revenue streams." (Osterwalder 2005, http://business-model-design.blogspot.com/2005/11/what-is-business-model.html. Accessed November 25, 2007).

Models are simplified representations of things in the real world. You are already familiar with many kinds of models. You have played with a model air plane or boat when you were a child. You may have seen models of buildings, dams, or other construction projects built by architects to show the sponsors of a project how a completed building will look after it is built. In the same way, a business model lets an entrepreneur try out different ways to put together the components of his or her business and evaluate various options before implementing the one that looks the best. This technique is especially important in today's business environment, where technology gives business people so many more options than ever before.

3. Business models and marketing: an overview

Osterwalder goes on to say:

> *"For managers and executives this means that they have a whole new range of ways to design their businesses, which results in innovative and competing business models in the same industries. Before it used to be sufficient to say in what industry you were for somebody to understand what your company was doing because all players had the same business model. Today it is not sufficient to choose a lucrative industry, but you must design a competitive business model. In addition increased competition and rapid copying of successful business models forces all the players to continuously innovate their business model to gain and sustain a competitive edge".*

Based on his search of the literature, Osterwalder lists nine building blocks for managers to use in developing an innovative and effective business model. We list them, along with some comments of our own:

- "The **value proposition** of what is offered to the market"; We have covered this issue earlier in the chapter in general, and with specific reference to how Porter's analytical tools can assist managers in generating a viable value proposition that consumers perceive as one that is superior to what is offered by the competition.

- "The **target customer segments** addressed by the value proposition"; Managers soon learn that they cannot be all things to all people, that what appeals to one segment of the market will not appeal to another. We will discuss this in more detail later in this chapter.

- "The communication and **distribution channels** to reach customers and offer the value proposition"; This issue relates to two of the "four P's" (promotion and place) we discussed briefly when we discussed the marketing mix. For example, do we promote the business by word of mouth, signs on a storefront, ads in a newspaper, ads on TV, ads on the Internet, or some combination of all of these? Place refers to where the product or service is made available to the customer. The three usual choices are in a store, through a mail-order catalog, or from an Internet website.

- "The **relationships** established with customers"; In general, however, the important point is not just to acquire customers, but to serve them in a way that your business retains them as customers. For example, it is usually much more expensive to attract a new customer to your business than it is for you to encourage a previous customer to return.

- "The **core capacities** needed to make the business model possible"; This point refers to the necessity to define the basic capabilities your business must have. For example, if you are opening an art gallery to sell your own work, you had better have some talent as an artist!

- "The **configuration of activities** to implement the business model"; Another way of stating this is to define the business processes that your business must have in order to function properly.

- "The **partners** and their motivations of coming together to make a business model happen"; Partnerships and alliances are increasingly important in today's world.

- "The **revenue streams** generated by the business model constituting the revenue model"; In essence, this is the Price component of the "Four P's". Where does your revenue come from, what are the projections for the future, and what are the plans to sustain the necessary revenue stream as business conditions change?

- "The **cost structure** resulting of the business model". The difference between revenues and costs, of course, is your profit. Without a profit, it will not be possible for you to stay in business very long.

Examples of successful business models

It may be helpful to illustrate the concept of business models with two examples, McDonalds and CEMEX. In the case of McDonalds, it operates franchises all over the world. Franchises are proven and successful business models whose business model "prescription" is successful within the country of origin and even overseas. Dominating the hamburger fast food market, McDonalds' franchise model has also proven to be successful since it quickly adapts and evolves according to the environment. For example, McDonalds USA does not have hot sauces, but in Mexico where Mexicans like a lot of spicy food, they offer hot sauce, as well as spicy meat put into the hamburgers. Another successful example is the Mexican cement maker CEMEX (the world's third largest producer of cement) that has successfully implemented and tested a standard business model called the "CEMEX Way" in all the plants and business units it has within more than 50 countries around the world. Considering it operates in four different continents, except Oceania, with very different cultures and ways of thinking; countries such as the US vs Thailand, or Italy vs Bangladesh; it allows CEMEX to have a very quick response mechanism to adjust to the market demands since it has a standard operational platform. This gives CEMEX a clear competitive advantage against its main rival giants such as Holcim and Lafarge.

Having established what a business model is, it is important to separate it from the design of a model actually implementing it, i.e. testing it and putting it into practice. The design is best defined as the strategy. If a business model design is not well outlined; the implementation and testing will also fail. Taking a very simple framework from Alexander Osterwalder (Business Model Design Blogpost, June, 2006) shown in Exhibit 12, business model design is separated from business model execution, preceded, of course, by business execution implementation and testing. Companies in quadrant "B" with sound business model designs and effective execution are successful companies, and they must focus on staying in that quadrant. Companies in quadrant "C" need to re-examine their business vision and strategy, while companies in quadrant "D" do not have a good design but are effective on its implementation; this latter usually happens with the appearance of **disruptive technologies** that 'shake up" established industries and business models much the way iTunes and the iPod did. It is very common for companies to have a sound business model design but fail to implement and test it properly (quadrant "A").

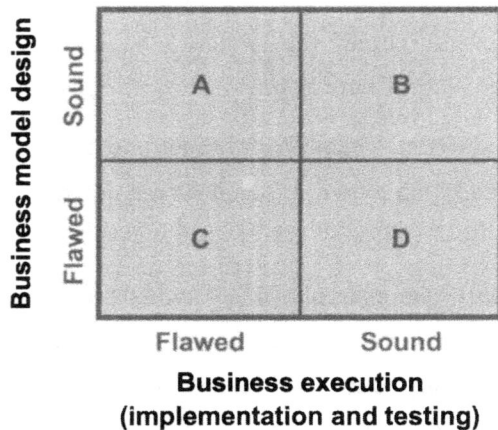

Exhibit 12: Success = Business model design
and implementation

If we seek to have a successful test result from a business model it is mandatory to have a clear vision as well as a sound business model design. The rest is a matter of testing and implementations, or "execution" as it is often called. Still, successful execution is sometimes the most difficult task of all.

The focus of the balance of this section will be to review the main issues companies must consider in order to successfully implement and test a business model.

Model implementation/testing pre-requisites

A model must have the following pre-requisites in order to implement and test it:

1. A company owner/sponsor: Organizational models must manifest themselves as a cascading effect emanating from top to bottom. Therefore, the sponsor must either be the head of the company or other high level executive. Usually sponsors are identified as the head of a company department.

2. Sound budget: Testing a business model will always require funds. The amount provided must be the one demanded by the model to test it, no more and no less.

3. Leader: This is especially important since he/she will be the "authority" or responsible person who will get results.

4. Qualified human resources: The leader gets to choose his/her team. This an important point since the leader must look for the key individuals who are up to the test and have the necessary expertise to successfully implement and test a business model.

5. Effective training: With all the above accomplished, the final part of the pre-requisites is training. A business model automated or manually developed, must be operated by human beings, therefore these persons who will actually test and operate the model must have no doubts and be convinced about the model's processes and the benefits of working accordingly to the business model.

Real expectations outcome: benefits

Usually companies have a tendency to be very optimistic about outcomes when a business model is tested. Companies must be balanced between being aggressive and demanding about the model benefits and be realistic when evaluating outcomes of the test. The main benefits to show when a business model is tested must be outlined around the next three aspects.

Economical: They must reflect tangible economical benefits, such as: cost reductions or sales increases.

Process: They must improve connections between the company's value chain activities such as production, maintenance, procurement, finance, human resources, etc. so they are better coordinated and decision making processes are more effective and timely.

Practice: They must improve the work flow of how things are done in the company. These improvements can be translated into creating better historical data for a company e.g. real time inventory transactions from a plant warehouse, or complete and accurate recording of a maintenance job performed on a specific item of plant equipment. This creates a more accurate data set, later used as important information to make decisions.

Success factors

Once the benefits have been shown, the next step is to preserve them. In order to do so, the following success factors must be kept in mind.

1. Have the appropriate leadership. Person(s) that can make well based and quick decisions to assure the continuity of the model once it has been implemented.

2. Create an internal environment of quick and flexible response. All departments of the company must be flexible and adjust quickly to events

3. Have integrative indicators and measurements. This is a model "thermometer", one that will indicate if everything is going smoothly according to expectations or not. The indicators will show warning signs in order to take corrective action.

4. Have corrective actions or model adjustments. Learn from actual results by quickly adjusting and evolving the business model in an integrative way, being coherent, sound and aligned with the company vision.

Conclusions

After seeing what a business model is and the required issues involved in having a successful business model test and implementation; companies must keep in mind that there is no one time testing of a model and guarantees of success in the business world. In our era, businesses are dynamical propelled by technology that change constantly as we move more and more into a more global world. The keys for companies to succeed are to be always focused and to be flexible enough to adjust its business model quickly and effectively according to the changing demands of customers and markets.

One of the most important functions that companies can have to anticipate competitive threats and to recognize evolving market opportunities is to have a continuing competitive intelligence function within the company. Management failures are frequently associated with the inability to anticipate rapid changes in the markets, respond to new and proliferating competition, or re-orient technologies and the strategic direction of their business toward changing customer needs and new industry standards. Competitive intelligence is an important function in today's rapidly changing business environment.

Consumer marketing models

The formal use of marketing concepts is a fairly recent activity in developing economies. In the past, most companies focused on producing products or offering services without much emphasis on customers and wants. Understanding consumer behavior was not considered to be important. The emphasis was on the product or service per se. Given the emergence of a global economy, however, which brought the opening of markets and increased competition, the traditional approach has changed dramatically. Companies are increasingly focusing on what customers need and/or want. Market-oriented companies are beginning to emerge in every developing economy in the world.

The purpose of this section is to introduce you to the importance of marketing oriented companies in developing economies, as well as identifying business models which follow a **marketing model** rather than a **product model.**

The product model vs the marketing model

According to Philip Kotler, the product model is a management orientation that assumes that if a quality product is produced, and offered to consumers at a price they find to be acceptable, the company will be successful in the market place. Another author who successfully introduced a marketing orientation is Theodore Levitt. His orientation is sometimes referred as a "marketing myopia" approach since companies define their business in terms of products and not in terms of customer needs and wants. For example, a car manufacturer may think they are in the "car business" while they are, in fact, competing in the transportation industry.

Under the product model, management focuses on developing high quality products which can be sold at the right price, but with insufficient attention to what it is that customers really need and want. For example, Apple determined that what customers wanted was the ability to purchase music one song at a time rather than purchase an entire CD with 16 tracks, only three of which were really wanted. They subsequently developed and introduced the iPod and iTunes online store which revolutionized the way consumers buy music. In the meantime, traditional producers of traditional CDs lost market share to Apple, which had a much better understanding of how to satisfy consumers.

The premises implicit in the product model are:

- Consumers buy products more than solutions.

- Consumers are interested basically in product quality.

- Consumers recognize product quality and differences in performance alternative products.

- Consumers choose between different products based on getting the best quality for the money.

- The main task of organization is to keep improving quality and reducing cost as key factors to maintain and attract customers.

The product model used to be applied in developing or closed economies where few, if any choices were available. Advantages of the product model are that the cost of determining consumer preferences and the development of new products and services are minimized or eliminated because consumers are in some way captive. By way of example, compare the automobile industry in developed countries to the automobile industry in the Soviet Bloc countries prior to 1989. Customers had a wide variety of automobile models to choose from while citizens in the Eastern Bloc had few. The latter was operating on a product model rather than a marketing model. Disadvantages of the product model are that as soon as a company could offer a product more oriented to satisfy customers´ needs and desires the companies oriented to products will lose the most if not all of its market share. The traditional CD companies referred to above are a good example of this.

In summary, market orientation is essentially a customer orientation. Understanding customer needs lies at the core of the marketing concept.

The marketing model

The marketing model is a management orientation which maintains that the fundamental task of the organization is to determine needs and wants of customers in the target market and adapt the organization as a whole to satisfy their customers more effectively and efficiently. Satisfying customers more efficiently and effectively than competitive companies increases the chances of the organization's success. The marketing model is an approach whereby companies create value for their customers. This concept can be understood by applying it in the so called **Value Chain Model** introduced by Michael Porter. An application on how this model is applied in marketing is shown Exhibit 13below.

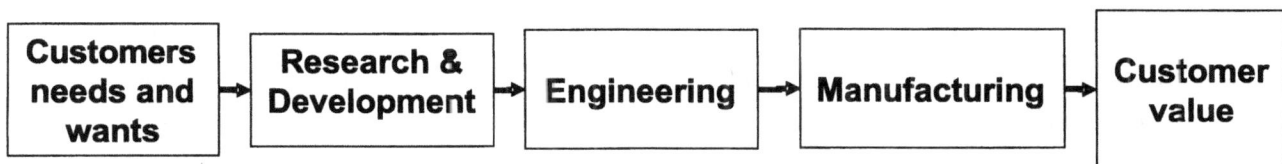

Customers needs and wants	→	Research & Development	→	Engineering	→	Manufacturing	→	Customer value

Exhibit 13: Value chain of marketing

- First, you need to know and understand your customers' needs and wants.

- Based on your understanding of their needs, through research and development you must develop an appropriate product or service that fulfills those needs.

- Based on your engineering capabilities you must define your manufacturing process that delivers the right product in the most efficient and economical way.

- Finally, the product or service must be delivered at the right time and place.

A simple way to understand the creation of value to customers is by examining the following equation:

Value = Benefits / Price

Value is created by increasing benefits to the customers. For this reason, "benefits" is specified in the numerator of this equation (the higher the benefits, the higher the perceived value by the customer); on the other hand, "price" is placed in the denominator since the higher the price the lower the perceived value.

Now you must understand how value is created for your customers. To do so, managers use a technique called the "**Marketing Mix**" (commonly called the four P´s)

- Product: What is the product/satisfactor that best fulfills my customer's needs?

- Price: What should be the appropriate price for this product that reflects not only its cost but also its benefits to compete with other products in the same segment or substitute products?

- Place: In what markets should the company offer the product?

- Promotion: How should the company promote the product or satisfactor?

One of the main advantages of the marketing model approach is that the company tries to be near the customer's needs by understanding them and therefore developing products that fulfill or exceed them in the best possible way. On the other hand, and especially in developing economies, the main disadvantage of this model is the cost in obtaining the information needed to understand the customer.

Identifying market needs

As mentioned previously, the essence of applying the marketing model lies in the finding of needs and filling them wisely. We will assess this issue of "Identifying market needs" by introducing a conceptual framework known as Abraham Maslow's **Hierarchy of Needs**.

This model focuses in the psychological features that explain the basic dimensions of human needs.

Maslow's Hierarchy of Needs

Maslow's Hierarchy of Needs, a staple of sociology and psychology courses, provides a useful framework for understanding how and why local products and brands are being selected and additionally how they can be extended beyond home country borders. Maslow hypothesized that people's desires can be arranged into a hierarchy of five needs. As an individual fulfils needs at each level, he or she progresses to higher levels (see Exhibit 14 Maslow's Hierarchy of Needs). At the most basic level of human existence, physiological and safety needs must be met. People need food, clothing, and shelter, and a product that meets these basic needs has potential for introduction into a specific market. However, the basic human need to consume food and liquids is not the same thing as wanting or preferring a hamburger and a soft drink.

An additional consideration is that preferences are deeply embedded in local cultures. Responding to such differences has required the creation of products and brands for specific regional or country markets.

Mid-level needs in the hierarchy include self-respect, self-esteem, and the esteem of others. These social needs, which can create a powerful internal motivation, driving demand for status-oriented products, cut across the various stages of country development.

Luxury goods marketers are especially skilled at catering to **esteem needs** on a global basis. Some consumers flaunt their wealth by buying expensive products and brands that others will notice. Such behaviour is referred to as **"conspicuous consumption"** or **"luxury badging"**. Any company with a premium product or brand that has proven itself in a local market by fulfilling esteem needs should consider devising a strategy for taking the product global.

self
actual-
isation

esteem

belongingness
&love

safety needs

physiological needs

- calling for self realisation and personal growth
- reputation and prestige, status dominance, recognition or appreciation
- safety, security of home and family, order and stability
- the requirements for survival food, water and shelter

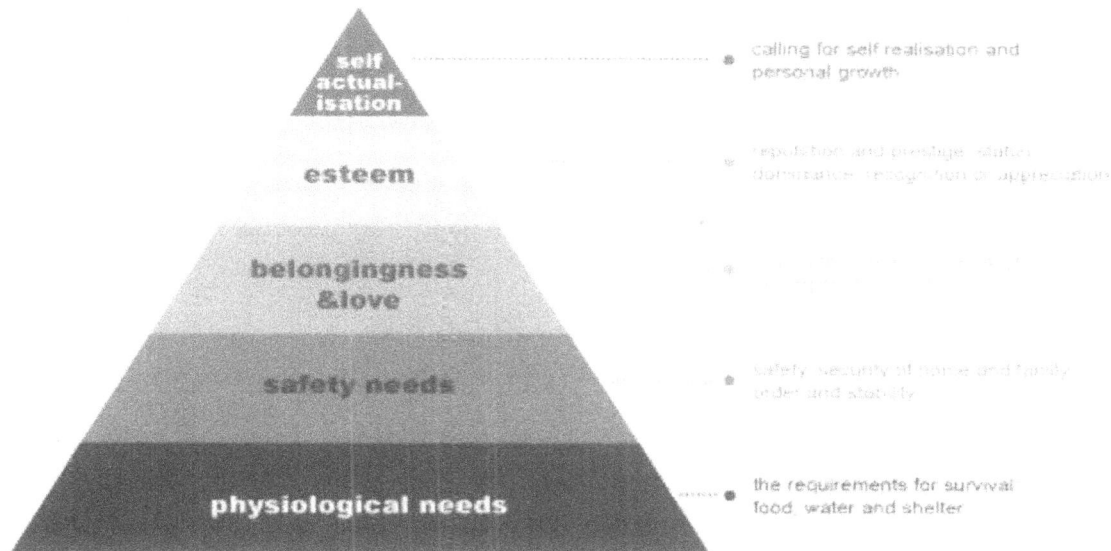

Exhibit 14: Maslow's Hierarchy of Needs

Source: http://www.provenmodels.com/19/image

Identifying customer's wants successfully

A process to determine the actual needs of consumers requires the identification of the market factors that produce them. In this process companies should find real consumption motivators that eventually evolve into product offerings. Furthermore, a correct business definition leads to a natural market orientation; for instance, Charles Revson famous quote "in the factory we make cosmetics; in the drug store we sell hope" (www.thinkexist.com) made possible for the company to develop cosmetic products based on women's hopes rather than product features. Several potential pitfalls should be avoided. First, the natural tendency to impose a personal point of view when launching a new product or entering a new market. Second, simple imitation about competitors' moves. Third, lack of sufficient research and market knowledge to produce market proved ideas. A framework has been proposed to align customer's needs and wants with companies capabilities. This framework was introduced by Sherri Dorfman in her 2005 marketing article entitled "What do Customers Really, Really Want".

In the article aforementioned, Dorfman proposes a three-step process to develop a natural market orientation:

Step 1. **Discovery**: Finding out what customers really need

To learn about customer needs and priorities, to identify opportunities in the company to fulfill these needs, and to create new or enhanced product offerings. These ideas must be incorporated in a market research process involving customers and other clients and suppliers in the Value Chain.

Step 2. **Definition**: Shaping the offerings to meet customer needs

In this step, Dorfman proposes prioritizing features and benefits identified by clients, suppliers, and customers. Different qualitative research techniques such as in-depth interviews, ethnographies, and focus group sessions permit the identification of the core market needs.

Step 3. **Validation**: Insuring your offerings fit into your customer's world.

Further communication with consumers validate the final definition of a market based product or service. This validation takes place as prototypes are assessed by consumers to identify potential problems and to smooth out design issues.

All these models take into account the so-called end consumer perspective, which implies that consumers buying, using, or recommending the products are the driving force behind successful marketing efforts.

However, there are other marketing perspectives that assume that organizations of many sorts, given their importance in the overall size of the global economy are the real forces behind markets' success. This implies that marketing efforts should be aimed at understanding their behaviour as consumption entities, and use this knowledge to develop marketing strategies.

Business to business marketing models
Models of industry attractiveness; the strategic perspective

In order to be successful in business, we must understand what our customer's needs and wants are and deliver them in an efficient and profitable manner. In order to do so, we must also understand the industries in which the companies are immersed and what makes them attractive from the general point of view.

Industry attractiveness was initially described by Michael Porter in his book, *Competitive Strategy* (Porter 1980). Porter's well-known **Five Forces Model** is often used as an analytical tool by companies when they are deciding whether or not to enter a particular industry. According to Porter, what makes an industry attractive or unattractive is determined by 5 forces:

1. Rivalry: This force is measured by how intense the rivalry/competition relationship in an industry is. The factors affecting rivalry are: number of competitors, slow market growth, low levels of product differentiation, how aggressive competing companies are, etc. For example, retailing has always had the reputation of being a highly competitive industry, while the rail road industry is thought to be less competitive.

2. Threat of substitutes: In Porter's model, substitute products refer to products that can be substituted for your own. Substitute products can be found within own or other industries. For example, if you decide to start an inter-city bus company, you have to consider all the other options your customers have to get from one city to another, for instance, city trains, small shuttle service, shared private cars, among others.

3. Buyer power: The power of buyers is the impact that customers have on a producing industry. In general, when buyer power is strong, the buyer has the ability to set the price because usually there are very few buyers and many suppliers. Grain farmers are often used as an example. In most countries, there are many small farmers who grow grain, but few large buyers who have the power to set the price a farmer receives.

4. Barriers to entry: Barriers to entry are unique offerings of companies in an industry that any company wishing to enter that industry must be prepared to overcome. Examples from developed economies are online banking and ATM services for banks and frequent flyer programs for airlines. In many cases, development of these expected products or services is quite expensive for a new entrant, and, thus, it s a barrier to entry.

5. Supplier power: Suppliers are powerful when there are few suppliers for a company to purchase necessary items from. In a situation where there are few suppliers, it is typically difficult for a buyer to get a lower price from another supplier. An example is the oil industry, where they are many buyers, but relatively few suppliers, and most of the suppliers are members of the OPEC cartel which sets common production quotas, thereby controlling the market price for oil.

Michael Porter developed two other tools that are widely used by organizations in their approach to markets: **Three Generic Strategies** and the **Value Chain.**

Porter postulated that a firm should adopt only one of three generic strategies. They are illustrated in :

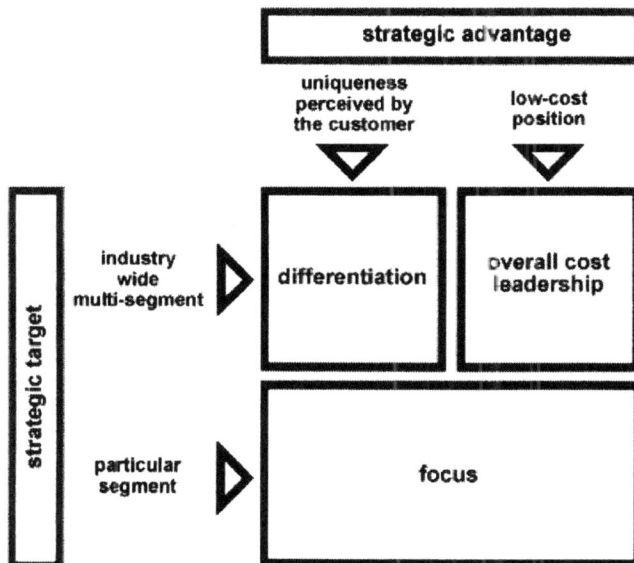

Source: http://www.provenmodels.com/27/image A firm can choose to be the low cost producer for a wide segment of the market; it can offer a differentiated product for a wide segment that customers are willing to pay more for because of its perceived greater value; or it can focus on a market niche as a low cost producer or with a differentiation strategy. For example, the original Volkswagen automobile focused in a broad low-cost market. As a matter of fact, the word in German means "Peoples Car", indicating it was meant to be affordable by everyone. A good example of a differentiated automobile is the BMW. People pay more for a BMW because of the "conspicuous consumption" or "luxury badging aspects" they have managed to create in peoples' minds, not necessarily because the BMW is actually worth 30 per cent more than a comparable automobile from Cadillac or Nissan. An example of a car positioned towards a low cost niche is the Mazda Miata, a two-seat sports car that costs much less than comparable cars. Finally, you can consider the Hummer as a car that appeals to a differentiated market niche.

Porter's other widely-used tool is the Value Chain, which is used to model the firm as a chain of value-creating activities or processes. Porter identified a set of interrelated generic processes common to a wide range of firms. He divided them into primary activities and support activities, as illustrated in Exhibit 15.

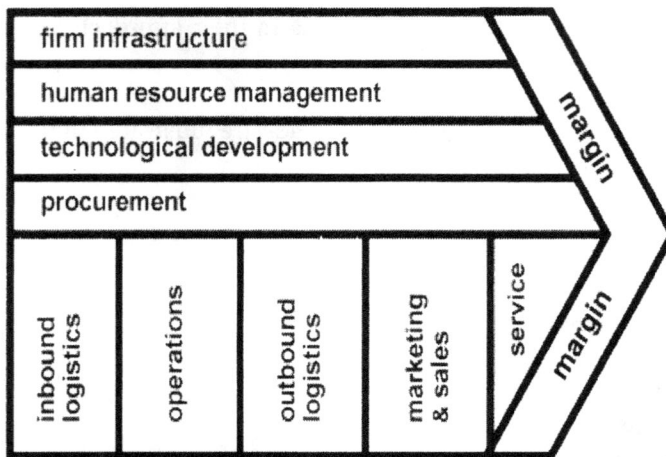

Exhibit 15: Value chain

Source: http://www.provenmodels.com/26/image

The primary activities in the value chain are: inbound logistics, operations, outbound logistics, marketing and sales, and service. The support activities are procurement, technology development and research and development, human resource management, and firm infrastructure (top management). The primary value chain activities are interrelated, to the extent that they can be formed with high quality and low cost, the firm will be able to have value-added that will be returned to the firm as profit. As an example of the way that primary value activities are interrelated, suppose that the inbound logistics process does not do well in identifying raw materials of poor quality. This will cause problems with the next process, operations, and it may cause problems as far down the value chain as service after the sale. The value chain is, thus, a useful tool for analysing a company's business processes and searching for ways to lower costs, improve efficiency or search for process innovations.

Other Strategic Models

There are many other strategic models used by companies to help them formulate their overall business and marketing strategies. Three of best known models are the Boston Consulting Group (BCG) Matrix, the McKinsey Matrix, and Larry Downe three forces. Each of these models is described below.

The BCG matrix

The BCG matrix method is based on the **product life cycle** theory that can be used to determine what priorities should be given in the product portfolio of a Strategic Business Unit (SBU). To ensure long-term value creation, a company should have a portfolio of products that contains both high-growth products in need of cash inputs and low-growth products that generate a lot of cash. This model can be explained in two dimensions: relative market share and market growth. The basic idea behind this model is that the larger the market share a product has relative to its competitors or the faster the product's market grows, the better it is for the company in an economic sense. The key components of the matrix are illustrated in Exhibit 16 and discussed below:

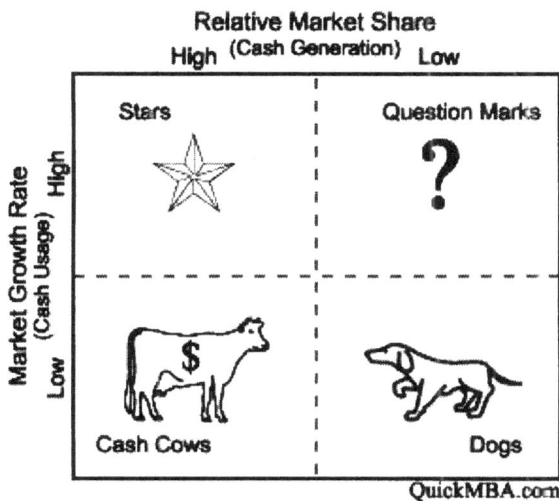

Exhibit 16: BCG Matrix

Source:<u>http://www.quickmba.com/strategy/ma</u>
<u>trix/bcg/</u>

1. Stars (high market growth, high relative market share). These are products that require large amounts of cash and are also leaders in the business and therefore they should also generate large amounts of cash. They are frequently roughly in balance on net cash flow.

2. Cash Cows (low market growth, high relative market share). These are products that generate high amounts of profit and cash, and because of the low growth, investments needed should be low.

3. Given its characteristics, companies should avoid and minimize the number of products in this category. If the product does not deliver cash, it may be discontinued.

4. Question Marks (high market growth, low relative market share). These products have the worst cash characteristics of all, because of high cash demands and low returns due to low market share. If nothing is done to change the market share, question marks will simply absorb great amounts of cash and later, as the growth stops, it

may become a dog. So, managers should either invest heavily in order to improve market share, or sell off/invest nothing and generate whatever cash is possible.

The McKinsey matrix

The McKinsey matrix is a later and more advanced form of the BCG Matrix. It has several differences with BCG's matrix, as discussed below. It is illustrated in Exhibit 17.

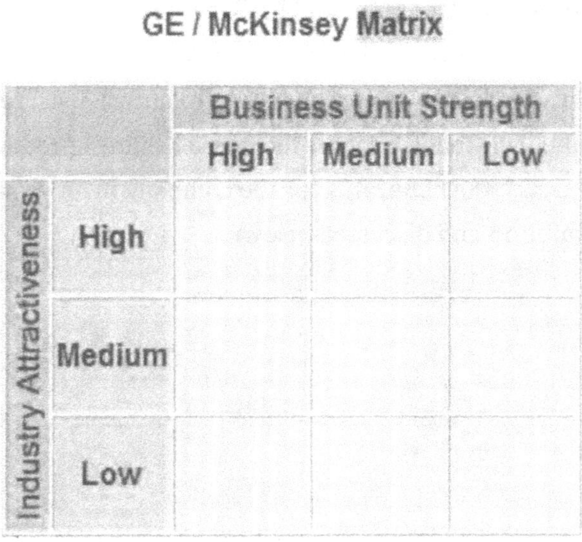

GE / McKinsey Matrix

		Business Unit Strength		
		High	Medium	Low
Industry Attractiveness	High			
	Medium			
	Low			

Exhibit 17: McKinsey matrix

Source:http://www.quickmba.com/strategy/matrix/bcg/

1. Market (Industry) attractiveness replaces market growth as the dimension of industry attractiveness. Market attractiveness includes a broader range of factors other than just the market growth rate that can determine the attractiveness of an industry/market. For example, market attractiveness could be determined using Porter's five forces model.

2. Competitive strength replaces market share as the dimension by which the competitive position of each Strategic Business Unit is assessed. Competitive strength likewise includes a broader range of factors other than just the market share that can determine the competitive strength of a Strategic Business Unit.

3. Finally the McKinsey matrix works with a 3x3 grid, while the BCG Matrix has only 2x2. This also allows for more insight in the analysis of the business.

Downes' three new forces

Larry Downes (1999) identifies three new forces that require a totally different perspective towards a strategic framework and a set of very different analytic and business design tools: digitalization, globalization, and deregulation.

Digitalization: As the power of information technology grows, all players in a market will have access to far more information. Thus, totally new business models will emerge in which even players from outside the industry are able to vastly change the basis of competition in a market. Downes gives the example of the rise of electronic shopping malls, operated for instance by telecom operators or credit card organizations. Those who use the Five Forces Model and who base their thinking on today's industry structure would never see these changes coming in time.

Globalization: Improvements in distribution logistics and communications have allowed nearly all businesses to buy, sell, and cooperate on a global level. Customers, meanwhile, have the chance to shop around and compare prices globally. As a result, even locally oriented mid-sized companies find themselves in a global market, even if they do not export or import themselves. In addition, global and networked markets impose new requirements on organizations' strategies. It is not enough any more to position oneself as a price-leader or quality-leader (as Porter suggests in his Generic Strategies model). Rather, competitive advantages emerge now from the ability to develop lasting relationships to more mobile customers and to manage far-reaching networks of partners for mutual advantage.

Deregulation: The past decade has seen a dramatic shrinking of government influence in many industries like airlines, communications, utilities, and banking in the US and in Europe. Fueled by the new opportunities provided by information technology, organizations in these industries were able and forced to completely restructure their businesses and to be on the lookout for new opportunities and competitive threats. For example, traditional land line telephone companies that did not enter the wireless telephony market found themselves with a shrinking customer base. This is because young people frequently use only cell phones now and do not bother to have a land line phone in their homes.

Chapter summary

While each of these models (and others we have not covered) have their own strengths and weaknesses, what organizations must learn is how to best utilize each of them. Porter still is the best known authority in strategy models and complemented with Downes' digital age model works well for many companies. BCG's Matrix and Mckinsey's Matrix help diagnose the dimensions in a product's life cycle. They are all tools, and just as a workman has many tools in his tool kit, so managers must have many tools in theirs, and know when to use the right tool in a given situation.

Establishing that a market exists

Market research

Understanding the market's needs, competitors' strategies, and to obtain information for decision making, it is imperative to do market research. Next, we will introduce a case that demonstrates the value of market research to any firm willing to spend time and resources using it. After this example is introduced, two sections are developed. One, introducing the market research process, and second, the general guidelines on how to conduct a market research study.

A Candy Store Company with subsidiaries in New York and other large cities in US was interested in opening a store in Monterrey, Mexico.

The New York subsidiary is located in one of the most visited areas of Manhattan. It is housed on three floors, a huge locale focused on selling all type of candies. Every floor has a thematic decoration, characters, and games, depending on the type of candies sold on that floor. Inside they even have a coffee shop. They employ a high price strategy, and most of their visitors are tourists (a differentiated niche in Porter's Three Generic Strategies model).

The plan for the store located in Monterrey was recently completed. It will be a big store, almost the same size as the one in New York, with high prices and focused on high-income consumers. Additional to the thematic areas defined in the New York store, this store will have a space for "old candy brands" to attract older consumers. The store will also have a section for local brands.

A consultant was hired for advising the owners on how to achieve the plan. His first advice was to do some market research to understand the real opportunity. The market research results were astonishing: there was no market in Monterrey. Consumers loved the idea, but they were not willing to pay the high prices or even to visit the store more than once a month and being Monterrey city with a small amount of tourists there would not be enough revenue to maintain the business.

The investment for opening the store in Monterrey was about USD 1 million dollars. The potential entrepreneurs spent around USD 10 thousand in marketing research, which kept them from making a bad investment.

The market research process

There is an inherent risk when trying to expand the market, launching a new product, or starting a new business. Defining that a market exists for your business idea will help in reducing that risk.

You may think that with a bunch of collected data and facts you will be able to decide whether or not to go forward with your idea. But the challenge is not just collecting the data, but how to transform it and how to use it. Market research will support you in collecting, transforming, and getting meaning from the data.

Some of the reasons why market research is so important are:

1. The cost of errors. Launching and selling a new product that is not successful in the marketplace could cause you to lose your entire investment.

2. Conducting market research will help you identify new trends, market segments, and niches.

3. Market research will end up saving you time by developing focused strategies based on a better understanding of your customers.

Market research involves all the activities that allow the company to obtain the required data for decision support. Market research is collecting, interpreting, and communicating the information used for strategic marketing. The most typical approaches are to conduct a tailored, one-time market research study as described below, or to use readily available information such as the periodical information provided by companies like AC Nielsen.

This section will describe how to conduct a market research study. The main steps are:

1. Identify and define the problem: The first step is defining the target or problem to solve for your market research. Most of the time it is more than one problem to solve, but you should prioritize. The right definition of the problem should allow us to obtain the needed data.

2. Define the objectives: The objective should answer the question of what you want to obtain from the market research. In this step you should define the scope and action plan. Developing the objectives should consist of establishing a budget, understanding the environment, developing the approach to analysis, and formulating hypotheses.

3. Developing a research plan: Based upon a well-defined problem and objectives, the framework for the research plan should be apparent. This step requires the greatest amount of thought, time, and expertise. It includes incorporating knowledge from **secondary information**, analysis, qualitative research, methodology selection, question measurement and scale selection, questionnaire design, sample design and size, and determining the data analysis to be performed.

4. Collecting the data: This is the point at which the finalized questionnaire (survey instrument) is used in gathering information among the chosen sample segments. There are a variety of data collection methodologies to consider. For instance: Computer Assisted Telephone Interviewing, Mail Survey, Internet Survey, Mall intercepts, Traditional telephone interviewing, Internet panel, home panel, among others.

5. Performing data analysis: This is the process of analyzing the collected data, and transforming complex to simple information. Less complex analysis on smaller data sets can be handled with any of a number of personal computer office suite tools, like spreadsheets, while more complex analysis and larger data sets require dedicated market research analysis software. Types of analysis that might be performed are simple frequency distributions, crosstab analysis, multiple regression (driver analysis), cluster analysis, factor analysis, perceptual mapping (multidimensional scaling), structural equation modeling and data mining

6. Reporting and presentation: This is one of the most important steps. All business critical information and knowledge that comes from your market research investment are limited by how they are presented to decision makers. There are as many reporting styles as there are research reports, but some are definitely better than others, and there are definitely trends to be aware of.

It is important to mention that market research by itself does not arrive at solutions or marketing decisions. It does not even guarantee your business success. However, when conducting a well-executed market research study you can reduce the uncertainty in the decision-making process, increasing at the same time the probability and magnitude of success.

> To illustrate these concepts in a live situation, we have included a discussion of how a market research study was performed to determine the potential market for a new concept for funeral services in Monterrey, Mexico.

Market research to determine the potential market for funeral services in Monterrey, Mexico

Background: A group of investors thought about developing a new enterprise concept of funeral services in Monterrey, Mexico. The main idea was to offer improved funeral services, satisfying a need not yet covered in the city.

Concept of the project: The company will offer funeral services to people of socioeconomic level A and B+. The new funeral services will include: Sale of coffins or crematory urns, luxury transportation, memorial vigils, chapel, flowers and cafeteria services, religious ceremonies, wide parking with valet parking service, legal requirements, condolences via Internet, publication of brief letters, private room for the family with foods at the request of the client and pre-arranged funeral plans.

The architecture of the place will include many green areas, big spaces and a quiet and peaceful atmosphere.

The added value will be to support the client in his pain, reason why a specific executive will be in charge of all the proceedings and procedures for the memorial vigil and burial of his beloved.

Objectives:

To understand if a potential market exists for a funeral services enterprise in Monterrey City.

Identify current specific needs for the sector.

Evaluate project concept.

Evaluate project location.

Evaluate project name and logo.

Methodology:

Stage I

Qualitative study:

2 sessions group with the following profile:

Session 1: Men between 35 and 50 years of age, from socioeconomic level A and +B who experience in the process of hiring funeral services in the last year.

Session 2: Women between 35 and 50 years of age from socioeconomic level A and +B who had experience with the process of hiring funeral services in the last year.

Stage II

Quantitative study:

The size of sample was of 472 personal interviews to men and women of socioeconomic level A and +B, ages between 35 and 60 years old, who live in Monterrey and its metropolitan area.

Main findings and conclusions:

In this research we found an important opportunity at the funeral logistics services since 76 per cent of the interviewed people consider that it is necessary to have a company of this type in the city, since at the moment the companies that offer these services have many opportunity areas.

"Cedillas del Toro", the most important funeral services enterprise up to date show us some opportunity areas as: lack of parking, mentioned by 15 per cent of the sample; the lack of a comfortable cafeteria, mentioned by 10 per cent of the sample; small chapel, mentioned by 7 per cent of the sample; and the temperature of the very cold climate, mentioned by 7 per cent of the sample, among others.

In the qualitative study, people interviewed mentioned what they dislike about "Cedillas del Toro" is that the memorial vigils have a common area for visits in where you can not identify whom each person is accompanying, turning it very informal.

The challenges that we found at the second more important funeral services company of the city, "Cedillas Carmelo" were: high price (20 per cent of mentions), lack of facilities for handicaps (crowded elevating) (15 per cent of mentions) and poor availability of chapels (only three) (10 per cent of mentions), among others.

The concept of the new funeral services enterprise was very well accepted by most of the people interviewed (70 per cent), mainly the idea of having a person who facilitates all the funeral proceedings, seems to be very helpful and important in those moments of grief.

The proposed location for the new funeral services enterprise had an acceptance of 80 per cent of the people interviewed, mainly because they are near the most important churches of the city with easy accesses.

The options of names people interviewed preferred were "Cedillas Marian" or "Cedillas de Maria" by 45 per cent and 30 per cent respectively.

The people interviewed in the qualitative study suggested some ideas to improve the concept mentioned like: To have a private area with all the comforts (telephone, computer, air condition, bath) for the family who does not wish to receive visits, that have a pleasant decoration (not funeral), and personal attention, among others.

Thanks to this market study, the investors could corroborate the idea that a funeral service enterprise in Monterrey may be a good business opportunity. In addition they could delineate the concept according to the market.

The funeral business has been an economic success so far, thanks to its clear definition of its mission and its market oriented philosophy: always searching for and delivering an excellent service to its customers.

Discussion questions

> ➢ Think of an industry with which you are familiar. Discuss the major elements of a business model and apply it to the industry chosen. What features in the model appear to be a standard compared to other industries?

> ➢ What are the steps in the process of customers' needs and wants identified in the chapter as defined by Dorfman?

> ➢ Or: Refer to the section of this chapter entitled "Identifying customers' wants successfully". In Dorfman's framework three steps lead to the identification of customers' need and wants. This process ends on the validation of needs. What would be a further step geared to identify future needs?

> ➢ Read the case about the Market research to determine the potential market for funeral services in Monterrey, Mexico.

>> ➢ What objectives would you propose for this study?

>> ➢ Methodology suggested?

>> ➢ What policies could be derived from the information obtained by the Marketing Research study?

References

Direccion de Mercadotecnia. Analisis, planeación y control. Philip Kotler, 4ª edicion.

What Do Your Customers Really, Really Want? Sherri Dorfman. June 7, 2005

Osterwalder, Alex. "Success = Business Model Design AND Implementation". June 11, 2006.
    <http://business-model-design.blogspot.com/2006/06/sucess-business-model-design-and.html>.

CEMEX Web site. CEMEX S.A. DE C.V. April 2007. <http://www.CEMEX.com>.

McDonalds Web site. McDonalds Corporation. April 2007. <http://www.mcdonalds.com>.

Wikipedia. Business model definition by Osterwalder, Pigneur and Tucci. 2005.
    <http://en.wikipedia.org/wiki/Business_model>.

4. How to organize and lead an entrepreneurial venture

Editor: John Maynard (The University of Georgia, USA)

Contributors: Suzanne Barnett, Lydia Jones, Carol McDonell, Bernie Meineke, Tammy Segura (Georgia Small Business Development Center, USA)

Reviewer: Dr Gideon Markman (The University of Georgia, USA)

Learning objectives

- differentiate between the growth stages of business organizations

- understand how businesses can organize their tasks and responsibilities

- compare the advantages and disadvantages of tall versus flat organization structures

- distinguish between the various types of business legal entities (see skill head, US legal issues)

Introduction

This chapter discusses organizational issues owners face while operating and attempting to grow their businesses. We examine four stages of organizational growth and the choices business owners face when deciding how to manage tasks and responsibilities. Those management decisions shape an organization's structure, which in turn influences lines of communication and decision-making processes.

The end of the chapter includes a short description of business legal entities. Also, you will find exercises to help you better grasp these concepts and to determine what type of organizational structure and legal entity might best suit your venture.

Moving from a one-person band to an orchestra

Most businesses start like a one-person band. The owner plays all the instruments, some better than others, but all out of necessity.

Like any musical ensemble, a small business includes many roles. In the beginning, the owners are often the best at making or delivering the product or service. Since they have the most at stake, they often assume a wide variety of roles, including sales, accounting, and much more.

Through a combination of skill, planning, talent, and perhaps luck, some businesses manage to grow. This growth leads to new and changing roles in the business for everyone, including the owner. Of all the roles an owner has in the business, perhaps the most important one is to be the *designer* for the business.

In the role of chief designer, business owners have three critical duties:

- **Provide the vision and direction for the company.** Owners set the direction for the values of the company, develop its product and service strategies, and set the tone for its relationships with customers.

- **Develop and refine processes and procedures.** Owners design the "business model", or the big picture formulas and processes of doing business. Then, they must fill in the details by analyzing processes and finding bottlenecks.

- **Create the organization's human resource structure.** Owners identify the positions and types of people the business needs, and then they find the people to fill those roles. In the words of Jim Collins, author of the bestseller *Good to Great*, "Get the right people on the bus, the wrong people off the bus, and get everyone in the right seats."

The payoff for a well-designed business is immense. With clarity of vision, expectations and processes, and with the right people pulling together, there is a strong foundation for growth. Instead of a grim "never take a day off" grind, the business owner can now enjoy the ride—and maybe take a day off from time to time. It is also now possible for the owner to think about a profitable exit, because a business that can run without the owner is worth a lot more than one that falls apart when he or she is not at the controls.

Owners of a growing business eventually have to decide how to organize employees and delegate authority. Doing so can be a frustrating task for many entrepreneurs. Most would rather concentrate on closing sales, producing product, or managing cash. However, they do so at the peril of putting off planning for the future needs of their enterprise.

Organizational issues

Entrepreneurs typically know when their company needs a structural overhaul. The owner can no longer juggle all the critical day-to-day activities. Important decisions are delayed, customer contact suffers, employees feel overwhelmed and confused about their and others' roles in the organization. As the employee count rises, someone other than the owner has to manage and be empowered to make critical decisions. The stress generated by these various dysfunctional symptoms eventually reaches a point where the owner has to decide to either continue growing the business (but in a more managed way) or to restrict its growth to effectively manage the firm single-handedly.

Acme Security Company's (the name has been changed to maintain its anonymity) original organizational structure caused many problems for the company, especially as its customer base began to expand.

The company provides security and fire alarm systems for high rise buildings and large corporate and government customers. It had grown to more than 40 employees in a short time, but was finding it increasingly difficult to provide the service customers expected. The company's organizational structure had evolved to meet the needs of the many family members that worked in the company, but not the needs of the customers.

The company had a product-based structure. The departments included Inspection, Maintenance, and Alarm Installation. Each department had a manager, a sales manager, field crews and administrative support. Even though most customers needed and purchased all of the company's services, no one was responsible for meeting the total needs of the customer. Each department focused on getting its work done. The lack of communication and coordination resulted in scheduling snafus and invoicing problems. A growing number of petty details quickly buried the CEO and prevented her from focusing on the important strategic and financial issues facing the company. She was also a bottleneck that contributed to customer service problems. No wonder she kept a candy dish filled with antacids on her desk!

Acme Security, Inc.

Original Organization Chart

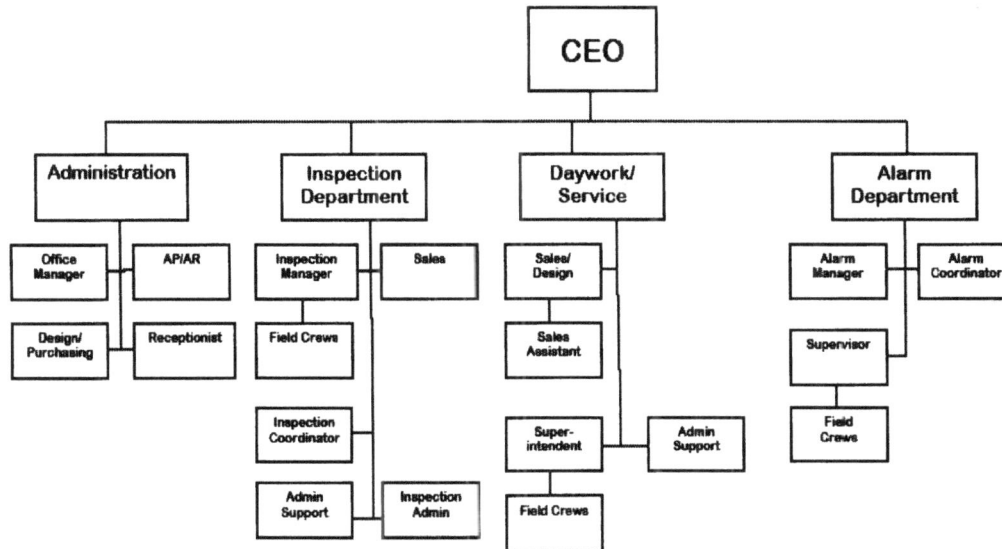

Exhibit 18: A Product-based organization

From the customer's point of view, working with Acme Security was akin to entering a restaurant and having to order the appetizer from the appetizer waiter, entrée from the entrée waiter, and dessert from the dessert waiter. In this scenario, each waiter is only concerned with getting his or her order complete and delivered. The dessert might arrive before the entrée or appetizer. And if the entrée is delivered cold, the other waiters cannot help. Finally, once the meal is over, all the waiters have to get together to figure out the bill. Like Acme Security, the restaurant's structure made it difficult, if not impossible, to deliver quality service.

With the ultimate goal of improving customer service, what should the new and improved Acme Security organizational structure look like? For this company, a function-based rather than a product-based structure was more appropriate. The most important change was to assign one person as the primary contact for each Acme Security customer. This Account Manager would report to the Sales Manager. The new company structure features two other key management positions, an Operations Manager and an Office Manager. These three key managers report to the CEO. The challenge for the CEO was to delegate responsibility and authority to these three managers. Below we will discuss the composition and responsibilities of these three functional departments:

Acme Security, Inc.

New Organization Chart

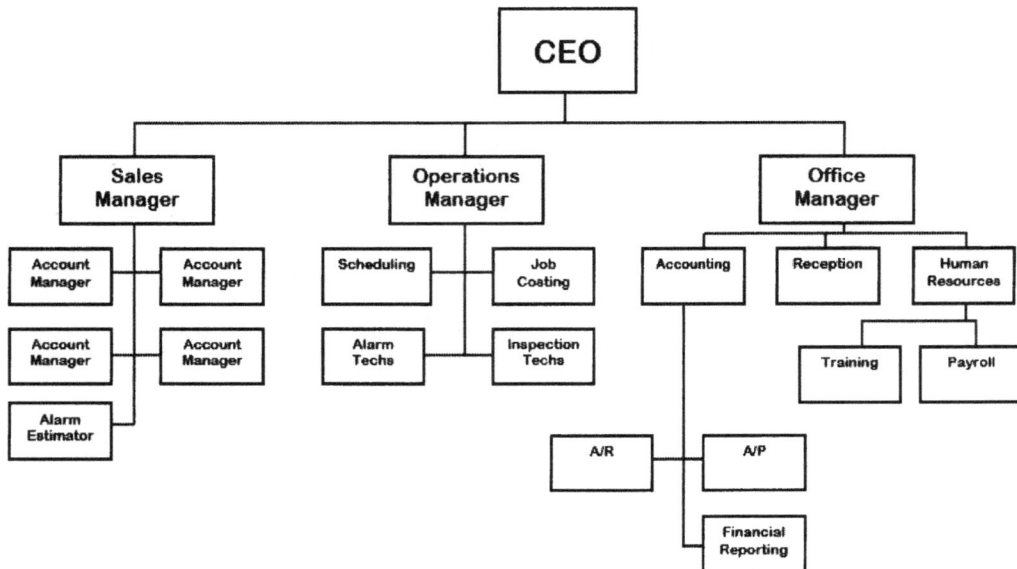

Exhibit 19: A Function-based organization

Sales: *includes the Sales Manager, the account managers and estimators. Account Managers are assigned by building or a major corporate account. This way everyone in the company, and more importantly the customer, knows who is responsible for a question or problem. The Account Manager's primary task is to meet the customer's total needs, and to make sure the invoices for work performed are issued in a timely manner.*

Operations: *includes the operations manager and the field crews. This department includes a position responsible for scheduling all operations work and a position responsible for collecting and entering all job cost information. Operations' primary task is to meet the needs of the Account Manager and the needs of the Office Manager with respect to information required to process invoices and payroll. The department maintains a centralized scheduling system that is accessible to everyone. They notify the Account Manager that a job is complete, provide the necessary job costing and billing information so that the Account Manager can notify accounting that an invoice should be issued.*

Administration *is led by the Office Manager. This department includes the receptionist, Accounting Manager, and Human Resources. This department's primary task is to issue invoices and manage payables, receivables, and to provide management with timely financial reports.*

With improved structure and communication, the CEO of Acme Security can focus on more strategic issues and replace the bowl of antacids with chocolate!

Organizational stages of growth

As an organization grows, it generally progresses through four stages of increasingly formal management structures.[27]

Stage 1: In a one-person operation, the owner does everything: sales, bookkeeping, marketing, production and so on. Many firms remain one-person operations indefinitely due to the owner's family obligations, financial constraints, or contentment with the status quo.

Stage 2: As more people join an organization, the business owner becomes a player-coach. The entrepreneur continues to perform day-to-day tasks, but along with other employees. So the owner assumes additional employee management duties such as hiring, scheduling, supervising, and payroll.

Stage 3: Firms reach a major milestone in organizational development when they add an additional level of supervision. The owner relinquishes some direct control and begins working through an intermediary layer of professional managers.

Stage 4: As a company adds more layers of management and processes, it also adopts written policies, budgets, standardized personnel practices, organizational charts, job descriptions, and control protocols.

Departmentation

New business owners do not ask themselves how they should organize their business. Rather, they organize by objective: what does it take to get a job done, meet a goal or create wealth. How owners organize a company depends on a multitude of factors: for example, are certain tasks performed in-house or out-sourced? Are people (staff and management) with the necessary skills available?

Business scholars have categorized various organizational structures as described below. However, do not assume that a growing business must at one point or another assume one of these structures. Rather, smart entrepreneurs constantly tweak their organizations to remain agile to take advantage of new opportunities or respond to new challenges. Sometimes the changes necessary to move from a small to larger business require gut wrenching decisions: for example, personnel that might have played key roles in establishing a new business might not be the right fit for a larger, more structured organization.

As the business grows, its organizational structure is heavily influenced by function (people grouped with similar responsibilities), process (people involved in similar processes), product (people building a specific product) or projects (members of a project).[28] A firm's structure might be influenced by some or all of these types of departmentation. Large firms usually employ a variety of departmentation styles, selecting the most appropriate form for each subsystem.

---

27 Longenecker, Justin Gooderl, Moore, Carlos W.; Petty, J. William; Palich, Leslie. (1991). Small Business Management: An Entrepreneurial Emphasis. South-Western College Publishing. Mason, OH.

28 "Entrepreneurial Firms: An Examination of Organizational Structure and Management Roles Across Life Cycle Stages," Watson, Kathleen M., Plascha, Gerhard R., paper presented at U.S. Association for Small Business and Entrepreneurship annual conference, Baltimore, Maryland, October 1993)

Departmentation by function

Grouping activities by function is the most widely used form of departmentation. Similar activities are housed in a department or under a single chain of command. For example, sales, advertising, public relations, and promotion might be grouped in a marketing department; employee benefits, employee training and employee regulatory compliance may be housed in the human relations department and so on.

Functional departmentation takes advantage of employees' specialization. Employees with similar training, education, skills, or equipment work together and under a supervisor responsible for that department's activities. Because one supervisor typically oversees a major area of activity, functional departmentation also facilitates coordination. For instance in a larger retail operation, one marketing department supervisor would control and coordinate the work of buyers, merchandisers and the sales force so that information and activities of each function would be more efficient and productive.

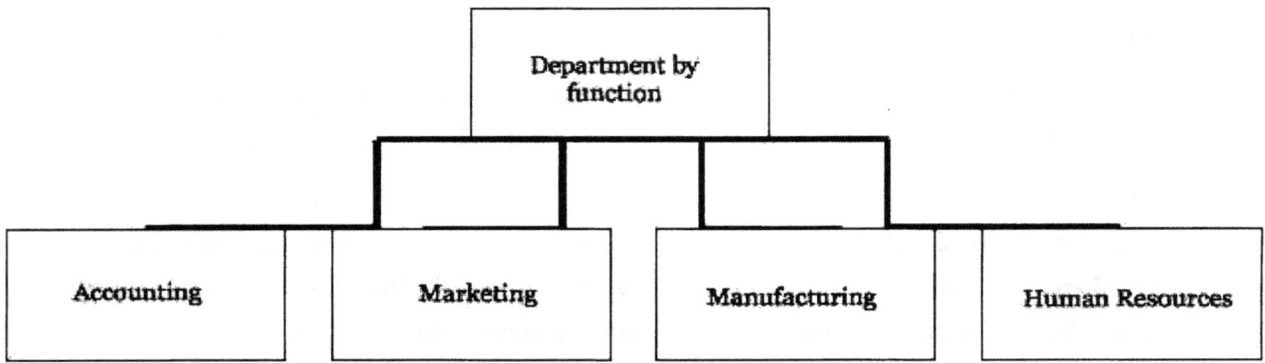

Exhibit 20: Departmentation by function

The process or equipment used in producing a product or service may be the basis for determining departmental units. Since a certain amount of expertise or training is required to handle complicated processes or complex machinery, activities that involve the use of specialized equipment may be grouped into a separate department.

This form of departmentation is similar to functional departmentation. The grouping of all milling machines into one department or the placing of lathes in another department is illustrative of departmentation by equipment or process. As a further example, a large food products firm may be departmentalized by processes such as manufacturing, package design, distribution, and shipping.[77]

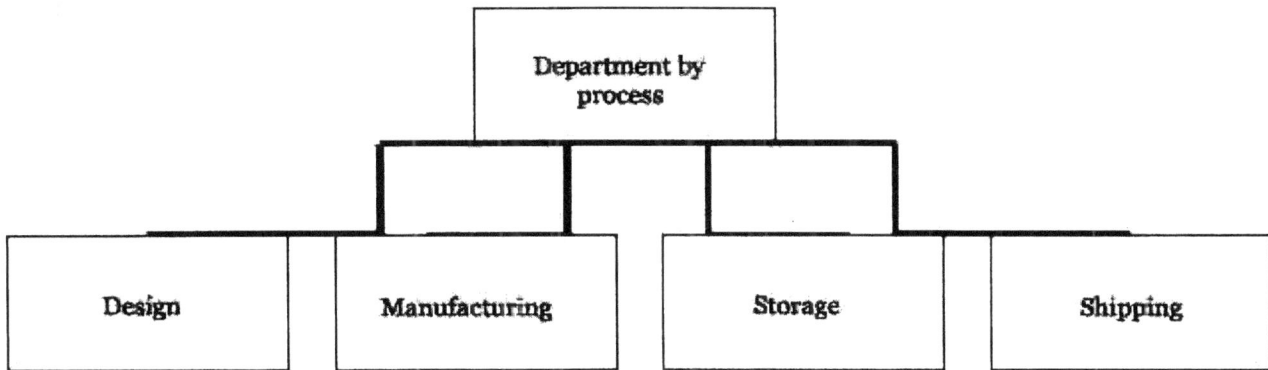

Exhibit 21: Departmentation by process

Departmentation by products

Companies with diversified product lines frequently create departmental units based on the product. To departmentalize on a product basis means to establish each major product in a product line as an independent unit within the overall structure of the company. For instance, retail stores may organize their operations to meet the needs of specific customer groups by forming special departments to cater to house wares, menswear, children's clothing and so forth. Product departmentation can be a useful guide for grouping activities in service businesses as well. Many banks have separate departments for mortgages, checking accounts and commercial loans.

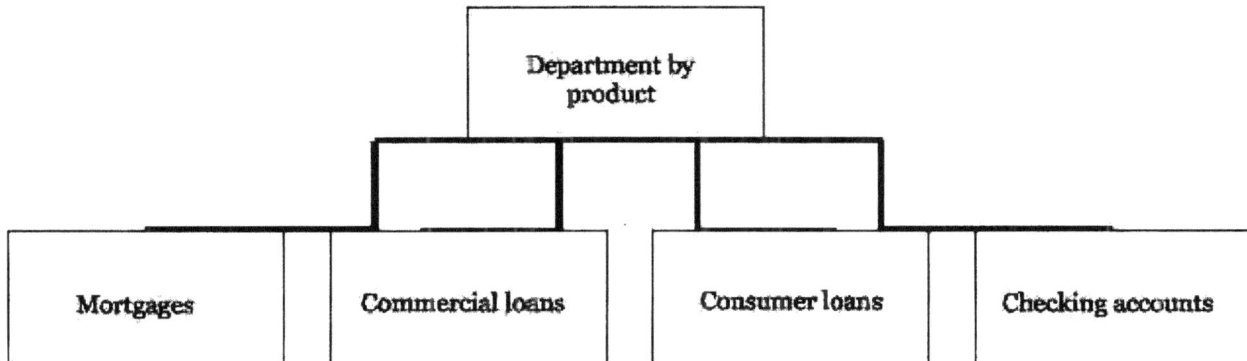

Exhibit 22: Departmentation by product

Departmentation by projects

Project organizations are specifically designed to deal with changing environments. A project in this sense is a series of related activities required to accomplish a work outcome, such as the development of a new product. Projects and task forces or teams are generally unique—designed to work on a nonrecurring project. They are tightly organized units under the direction of a manager with broad powers of authority.

A team is given a project with specific tasks or operational concerns. This team is composed of employees from the firm who have expertise or skills that can be applied directly to the project. The members of the team manage the project without direct supervision and assume responsibility for the results. When work teams function well, the need for a large number of supervisors decreases.

Departmentation by matrix

Some firms are organized by using a mix of departmentation types (matrix organization). It is not unusual to see firms that utilize the function and project organization combination. The same is true for process and project as well as other combinations. For instance, a large hospital could have an accounting department, surgery department, marketing department, and a satellite center project team that make up its organizational structure.

- Once the bases for departmentation are determined, another problem of structure immediately arises concerning how many departments or how many individual workers should be placed under the direction of one manager. This is referred to as a span of management or span of control issue. A number of factors should be considered when deciding upon a span of control:

    - the complexity of the subordinates' jobs and need for interaction with management

    - the complexity of the supervisors' jobs

    - the competence of the supervisors and subordinates

    - the number and nature of the supervisors' other interactions with non-subordinates

    - the extent to which staff assistants provide support.

Flat versus tall organizations

By definition, a small business is typically a flat, centralized organization. The founder/owner is the boss and makes all the critical decisions. However, as the personnel count grows, the firm's structure typically expands either horizontally (flat) or vertically (tall). Again, various factors including the owner's management style, might affect what type of structure a business assumes.

Flat organizations

Flat organizations follow the decentralized approach, or organic system. There are fewer levels of management which creates an environment for faster growth and response between all levels. Organizations that follow this type of structure have wider spans of supervisory control and have more horizontal communication. This type of structure promotes task interdependence with less attention to formal procedures.

More decisions are made at the middle levels of the organization. They are less bureaucratic and less structured. Externally, the organization as a whole becomes more adaptable to its market and can quickly react to changes. Internally, the organization as a whole encourages more participation between all levels of the organization. As a result, all levels have the potential of working more closely together which enhances a closer working environment with better communication and creativity.

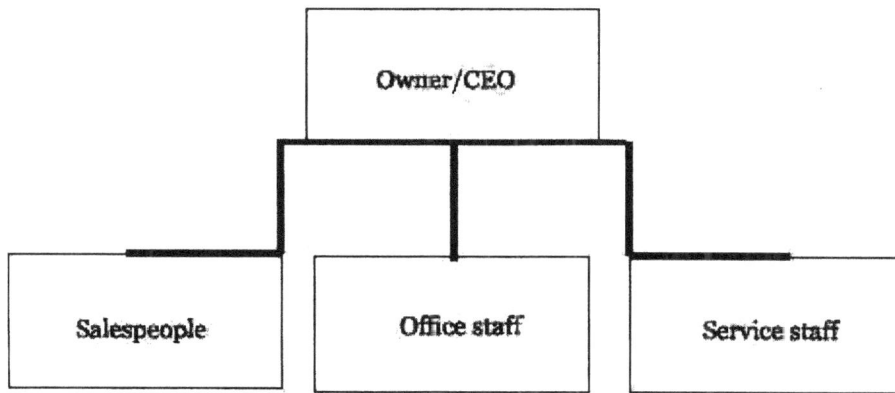

Exhibit 23: Flat organization

Tall organizations

A tall structure is a more formal, bureaucratic organization or mechanistic system. In this environment, multiple levels of management control decision making processes and employees within the organization. When numerous levels become involved in daily operations, decision-making tends to be more impersonal. Since this type of structure has more levels, the division of labor is much more specialized. Departments can become more compartmentalized, which increases the communication within them, but does not lend itself to communication with other departments.

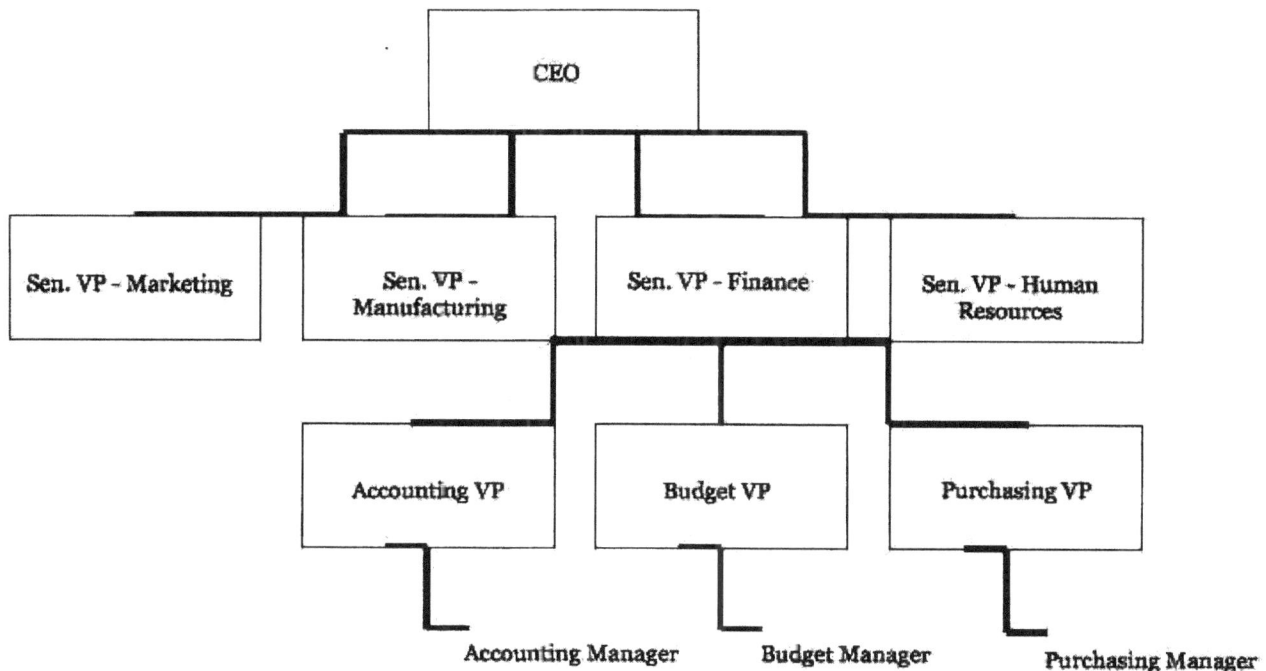

Exhibit 24: Tall organization

Centralized versus decentralized organizations

Communication is essential to disseminate information throughout organizations and can take place at many levels. There are two communication models that are utilized—centralized and decentralized. Again, each style can be effective depending on the environment and each has its advantages and disadvantages, as are outlined below.

Centralized

Centralized organizations require communications flow through a central person or location. Single leaders are prominent and have a great deal of decision-making power. These persons have access to more information and can therefore exercise a great deal of influence over group members by controlling the flow of critical information.

One disadvantage to centralized communication is that as the organization grows, the amount of information can overwhelm the central hub (person or department) that processes this information. One advantage to the centralized approach is that it encourages standardized processes that typically result in cost savings and better quality control.

Decentralized

Decentralized organizations tend to utilize many channels of information flow, allowing for more open communication between group members. This model is more conducive to solving complex problems.

One of the major advantages to decentralized communication is that problems and processes can be solved and changed in a timely manner. Also, the needs of customers and employees are more easily and quickly met because fewer levels of management are involved.

A major disadvantage to a decentralized organization is that departments can easily lose sight of the organization's common mission. To ensure organizations stay on task, upper management should maintain open lines of communication with local management.

Chapter summary

So how does an owner begin to digest and pick between all the choices (function, product, process, project or matrix structure, flat versus tall, centralized versus decentralized) available when it comes to organizing a business?

To design a better business, owners should take these steps:

- Schedule time to work on the business. This applies to start-ups and established businesses. There is an old saying, "If you are chopping wood, you need to take some time to sharpen the axe".

- Write everything down. Document all job descriptions, processes, and procedures, and then refine the processes so the result is reliable and high quality output. In his book *The E-Myth*, Michael Gerber makes the case that entrepreneurs should build and document their business as if it were the first of 5,000 locations, even if they never plan to expand.

- Try to become unimportant to the day-to-day operations. A business that would cease if something happened to the owner has very little value to a potential buyer. If the business is a turn-key operation with documented and reliable processes, it has much greater value to the current owner and future buyers.

- Be prepared to change roles as the business grows. As time goes on, the amount of time an owner spends working in the business should decrease. He or she should embrace the role of a CEO who is working on the business.

In the introduction of this chapter we likened the business owners' role to a musician. In the early stages of the business, the owner had to play every instrument. But if the business is to grow and prosper, the owner must become the conductor of an evolving orchestra. If an orchestra has good musicians, excellent sheet music, and a talented conductor, the result is beautiful music.

US legal issues

Because laws regulating business vary greatly by country and locale, entrepreneurs should pick a legal entity for their business in consultation with a local attorney that specializes in business law. The legal issues discussed below reflect general practices in the United States where laws governing business vary not only by state, but by local jurisdictions within states.

Businesses activities are organized either by individuals, couples or groups of people.

Businesses with one owner (the most common and referred to as sole proprietorships in the United States) can be launched without any legal assistance, and depending on the location, with or without certain permits.

Businesses with multiple owners typically write out explicit guidelines regarding investment and management issues using one of several types of legal agreements designed specifically for business organizations. Thus, one of the first decisions facing new business owners is deciding what legal entity to use for their business. That decision-making process typically weighs the following issues:

(a) how much time or involvement in the business is required

(b) what skills are required

(c) degree of risk associated with the business

(d) amount of capital needed

(e) tax regulations on labor and income earned by the business

In the United States, there are four basic types of business operations:

1. Sole proprietorships

A sole proprietorship is an individual owner of a business (with or without employees). This type of operation is the simplest to form, and the single owner, or sole proprietor, may work as much or as little time as desired. The sole proprietor is generally held accountable for all products and/or services produced by the business, as well as debts and liabilities of the business. Since the owner's personal liability extends well beyond amounts invested in the business or even beyond assets purchased by the business, this type of operation is considered high risk.

The amount of capital required to start a sole proprietorship is generally minimal.

In addition to sole ownership of all assets and liabilities, the proprietor benefits by receiving all profits, which in the United States are taxed as part of the owner's total personal income. The sole proprietor may employ workers or engage independent contractors to increase skills available, but the business ceases to exist upon the owner's death.

A sole proprietor business can be organized at any time into a different legal entity. The owner often decides to reorganize when profits substantially increase the individual's tax liability.

2. Partnerships

When two or more family members or people join together in a business operation, they may choose to establish a partnership which can take the form of a general or limited liability partnership. General partnerships are similar to the combination of a group of sole proprietorships in that the partners share workloads, profits, and liabilities. Limited Liability Partnerships, however, usually include one or more partners who manage daily operations and are generally liable for the debts of the business while other limited partners risk their investment in anticipation of profits.

Initial agreement is essential concerning how the partnership will operate, who will manage daily operations, how profits will be disbursed, and who assumes liabilities and debts. Such an agreement is normally formalized in writing and is known as a "Partnership Agreement".

Partnerships, like sole proprietorships, are generally dissolved upon the death of a partner. Profits are shared in accordance with terms of the Partnership Agreement and reported to taxing authorities on personal tax returns of the partners.

3. Corporations

In the United States, corporations are considered separate legal entities that are chartered and regulated by an authority in each state, such as the Secretary of State. Additionally, a separate agent who acts on behalf of the corporate entity is identified in the initial application process to receive legal notifications. Corporations must also submit identification and governing documents such as Articles of Incorporation and By-Laws. Corporate entities are generally required to be kept in active status through annual updates to a regulatory authority. As a result, this type of entity is deemed slightly more complex to form and manage.

Corporations require investment by one of more owners who are known as "shareholders" or "stockholders", and the amount of investment varies depending on the needs of the business. Since this form of entity provides protection (widely known as the "corporate veil") for the personal assets of owners against certain types of claims, it is generally of lower risk. Corporate entities may vary in numbers of owners from a single shareholder to an unlimited number. States and federal agencies regulate financial activities and reporting requirements that are categorized by the number of shareholders and whether their shares are available to purchase and sell on public stock exchanges. For example, US corporations with publicly traded shares are regulated by the US Securities and Exchange Commission.

The corporation may employ workers and engage independent contractors as needed to increase skills available. Corporations are required, however, to acknowledge formally (in a written document) the individuals who are approved to engage in financial transactions on behalf of the entity.

In the United States, the Internal Revenue Service regulates federal tax codes. There are two taxing options for earnings of corporations: a progressive structure on profits for the traditional corporation and another that allows owners to "flow-through" profits to their personal tax returns.

4. The Limited Liability Company (LLC)

In the United States, the Limited Liability Company (LLC) is the entity of choice for the owner or owners who prefer the limited liability afforded by a corporation and a tax treatment that allows profits to flow from the business to the owner or owners. The LLC must also be registered with a State authority, but requires less documented structure. Ownership is acknowledged by percentage as opposed to number of shares and protection for the owners is similar to that of a corporation.

Discussion questions

- ➤ Describe the characteristics of each of the four stages of growth a business organization might experience?

- ➤ Describe the advantages and disadvantages of a flat versus tall organizational structure.

- ➤ Given your personality and past experience, do you prefer working in a flat or tall organization and why?

- ➤ What are the characteristics of the four types of business legal entities?

References

Collins, Jim. (2001). *Good To Great.* HarperCollins, New York, NY.

Gerber, Michel E. (1995). *E-Myth Revisited: Why Most Small Businesses Don't Work and What to Do About It.* HarperCollins Publishers, Inc. New York, NY.

5. Selecting and managing your team

Editor: Cynthia V Fukami (Daniels College of Business, University of Denver, USA)

Contributors: The students of MGMT 4340, Strategic Human Resource Management, Spring 2007

Learning objectives

- to understand the field of Human Resource Management and its potential for creating and sustaining competitive advantage

- to understand how an organization can effectively recruit, manage, and terminate its employees.

- to know the basic approaches to creating effective reward systems through base pay, benefits, and pay for performance

- to understand the relationship between work design and employee motivation

- to show familiarity with mechanisms to create employee voice and influence

Competitive advantage through human resource management

An introduction, by Cynthia V Fukami

A great deal of recent research has underscored the strategic advantage to be gained from managing employees as if they are assets rather than commodities. Consider the commodities a business employs—pads of paper, ballpoint pens—things that you purchase, use up, and then discard. Investing in a commodity is never considered—refilling a ballpoint pen, for a simple example—because it simply is not worth the expenditure of time and resources. A return on that investment is not expected. On the other hand, consider the assets employed in business—the physical plant, the equipment, and the money—things that are maintained and developed. When the paint peels on the office walls, one does not throw away the building and build a new one; a new coat of paint is sufficient. Making investments in a business's assets makes a great deal of sense, because these investments will bring a return. A growing number of companies, recognizing that their employees are among their most valuable assets, are backing up that recognition with solid investment.

In an important recent book, Professor Jeffrey Pfeffer of Stanford University identified seven management practices that have been associated with producing sustained competitive advantage for the companies that have adopted them. These practices are: employment security, selective hiring, self-managed teams with decentralized authority, high pay contingent on organizational performance, training, reduced status differences, and sharing information. Put together, these practices form the foundation of what is called a "high-commitment" or a "high-performance" management system.

5. Selecting and managing your team

The evidence on the results of implementing a high-commitment management system is striking and strong. Research has been conducted in many industries, from banking to automotive to semiconductors to service. Some research has focused on one industry while others have looked across industries. Some research has included companies from the United States and others have studied companies abroad. Overall, the conclusions of these studies are remarkably similar. High-commitment management systems produce higher organizational performance. Pfeffer summarizes the results into three categories. First, people work harder because they have more control over their work from the high-commitment management practices. Second, people work smarter because they have stronger skills and greater competence from the investments of high-commitment management practices. Third, companies save administrative overhead and the costs by reducing the alienation of their workforce and the adversarial relationship with management.

In a study of firms representing all major industries, Mark Huselid found that a one standard-deviation increased the use of high-commitment practices was associated with a 7.05 per cent decrease in employee turnover, a USD 27,044 per-employee increase in sales, USD 18,641 more in market value per employee, and USD 3,814 more in profits per employee. When he repeated the study several years later, he found that a similar increase in the use of high-commitment management practices was associated with a USD 41,000 increase in shareholder value per employee.

Another noteworthy study examined the management practices of initial public offerings or IPOs to see if there was a relationship between high-commitment management practices and the five-year survival rate of IPOs. This study concluded that the treatment of employees as assets and the use of stock options, profit sharing and gain sharing programs for all employees (versus limiting the programs to key executives) were significantly related to the survival of the IPO to the five-year milestone.

These studies, and many others like them, have put conventional wisdom on its ear. Typically, we have assumed that success was related to factors such as size, or being global, or leading your market, or being in particular industries such as high tech, or pursuing a brilliant strategy. Yet, research shows there is virtually no connection between industry and success. As Wal-Mart and Southwest Airlines have shown us, an individual business can be very successful in a terrible industry. Similarly, there is little or no connection between success over time and company size or market dominance. Instead, competitive advantage comes from the way business is conducted, and employees are the keys to this. The most successful companies manage their workforce effectively as assets not commodities.

So why are more companies not adopting high-commitment management practices? Why are their executives proclaiming employees to be their most valuable assets, while continuing to treat them as commodities? Perhaps it is a continual cultural emphasis on short run performance and stock prices—an emphasis that makes it seem more profitable to lay off employees or to cut training when times are tough. Perhaps it is a preoccupation with systems that control rather than delegate. Perhaps it is our overwhelming tendency to teach future managers technical tools at the expense of people-management tools. Whatever the reasons, the challenge remains. If a business is able to meet that challenge, the odds are that competitive advantages will follow.

Providing employee voice and influence

By Liz Evans

Employees are the resources of an organization in the same way as material assets but they are also the firm's stakeholders. The concept of **employees as stakeholders** refers to the interest employees have in the success of the company and the fact that actions taken by the organization directly affect the employees (Olson, 2003). Employees' stakes in the company are economic in the fact that their livelihood comes from the firm, psychological in that they derive pride from their work, and political in terms of their rights as employees and citizens. Though employees are the stakeholders who are arguably most visible to management on a day-to-day basis, they do not often command the majority of attention in terms of decision-making influences. The short-term, economic duties to stockholders often command more managerial attention in the decision making process than employee opinion (Peterson, 2005). According to Jones, the best way to incorporate employees' stake to improve firm performance is through employee participation and influence (Employees as Stakeholders, 1997).

Apart from unionization, employees can obtain influence in organizational decisions in several ways. **Grievance and Due Process Systems** allow employees to address grievances and to argue their point if they feel they are wronged by management or another employee. **Participation Systems** provide employees with influence in the organizational or managerial decision making processes. This subchapter will discuss the ways employees are given voice and influence in non-unionized workplaces, with particular attention paid to influence in decision-making and organizational success. This will include the benefits of employee input to the firm, the difference between voice and influence, and the many participation mechanisms management can use to harness employee influence into decision-making.

There are benefits to a firm for providing employee influence. For one, strong employee voice and influence mechanisms are an important part of a **High-Performance Human Resource System** in which the human resources of the firm are coordinated and "designed to maximize the quality of human capital in the organization" (Becker & Huselid, 2001). Voice and influence mechanisms allow employees to give input and to contribute their expertise to business success; these mechanisms allow firms to get the most benefit from the skills of their human capital. Thus, firms with employee influence mechanisms get higher financial return from their employee assets; high-performance HR systems improve the financial bottom line of the firm (Becker & Huselid, 2001).

Despite the many benefits, there are various reasons not to implement voice and influence mechanisms perceived by employees and management. Voice and influence can benefit employees by helping them to protect their rights and most "employees want a voice in their workplace" (Peterson, 2005). However, employees may be hesitant to organize into employee associations or push for voice mechanisms for fear of retribution due to perceived opposition to influence by management (Peterson, 2005). Employers benefit from the increased trust that comes from sharing information and giving employees influence (Pfeffer & Viega, Putting People First for Organizational Success, 1998). However, managers who are used to having control often find it "disconcerting, difficult and even impossible" to share power in the form of influence in exchange for the many organizational benefits (Marken, 2004).

Voice and influence are different, but both are necessary to garner the benefits to the firm. Many managers recognize the importance of giving their employees a **voice**, but often this open communication does not result in authentic employee involvement or influence on the actual decision making process (Golan, 2003). Hearing employee voice is not the same as giving **consideration** to the received information; consideration is what gives employees influence in the organization (Garvin & Roberto, 2001). Visible **action** is as important to influence as consideration (Solnik, 2006). Action provides the follow up that allows management to make it apparent to employees that they have influence; it also allows management to see real change and benefit from the insight provided by employees. Voice without consideration and action creates little benefit for employees or the firm.

Many different participation systems can be implemented to authentically get employee input and to capitalize on the benefits associated with employee influence. **Open book management** empowers employees with the information they need to see the reality of the organizational situation and to give relevant and helpful input (Case, 1997). Similar to open book management are **open-door policies**, where management makes it clear that employees can informally raise issues or give input at any time. The open-door policy page on the Central Parking Corporation website provides an example of such a policy and the procedures employed by the company for submitting and receiving employee input (Central Parking Corporation, 2004). **Feedback programs**, sometimes implemented in the form of employee surveys or through direct employee-management interaction, can be a less expensive way to get feedback from employees concerning specific programs or policies (Solnik, 2006). Surveys are particularly economical, especially when done online using free survey programs such as SurveyMonkey.com (Survey Monkey, 2007). Team mechanisms such as **quality circles, work teams, and total quality management teams** provide employees with the ability to synthesize their individual input into a better solution to organizational problems.

In conclusion, there are many possible benefits to a firm associated with providing employees with voice and influence within the organization. However, in order for these benefits to be realized, management must not only provide employees with an outlet to speak, but must also take the information into consideration and follow up with visible action. In this way, an organization can attend to its most important stakeholders, the employees, and garner return on its investment in its human capital.

Managing differences in organizations

By Hanoi N Soto Garcia and Nora Martin

In today's business environment, an increasing trend towards teamwork, a larger presence of women and ethnic minorities in the workplace, and a greater exposure to international businesses and cultures are constantly challenging employees from a variety of industries in all parts of the world. This posts a greater opportunity for people to learn from cultural and personal differences and create a more productive work environment. Thomas L Friedman, in *The World is Flat*, makes the following comment after one of his trips to Bangalore, India: "It is now possible for more people than ever to collaborate and compete in real time with more people on more different kinds of work from more different corners of the planet and on a more equal footing than at any previous time in the history of the world" (2006). Due to the importance of managing differences effectively in organizations, there is a need to identify the types of differences encompassed in organizations, the effects of differences in work teams, and the importance of understanding and diagnosing differences to maximize organizational performance.

Organizations usually take one of two paths in managing diversity: (1) they encourage people of diverse backgrounds to blend in for the benefit of fairness and equality; or (2) they set them apart in jobs that relate specifically to their backgrounds, assigning them, for example, to areas that require them to interface with clients or customers of the same identity group. African American MBAs often find themselves marketing products to inner-city communities; Latino Americans are frequently positioned to market to Latinos or work for Latin American subsidiaries. In those kinds of cases, companies are operating on the assumption that the main virtue identity groups have to offer is knowledge of their own people. This assumption is limited and detrimental to diversity efforts. Diversity goes beyond increasing the number of different identity-group affiliations on the payroll. Such an effort is merely the first step in managing a diverse workforce for the organization's utmost benefit. Diversity should be understood as the "varied perspectives approaches to work that members of different identity groups bring" (Thomas & Ely, 1996).

Leaders realize that increasing demographic variation does not in itself increase organizational effectiveness. They realize that it is *how* a company defines diversity and *what it does* with the experiences of being a diverse organization that delivers on the promise.

Group diversity refers to the amount of heterogeneity within a group determined by several characteristics derived from informational, visible, and value differences (Hobman, Bordia, & Gallois, 2003). **Informational differences** refer to different professional backgrounds and experiences; **visible differences** refer to things that become more physically apparent, such as age, gender, ethnicity, etc.; and **value differences** are shaped by each individual's set of beliefs, goals, and values. These three categories of differences have a major impact on team performance because they can become the cause for multiple types of conflicts within a team. When approaching tasks, different members of the team will have different behaviors based on their own set of informational, visible, and values characteristics. Employees with different views of the same situation may have totally different ways of responding to it.

After the appearance of conflict, team members can create a true learning environment where they can perform far beyond expectations by leveraging their differences. Hobman, Bordia, and Galois highlight the ways in which group diversity can foster a higher organizational performance, "It has been noted that diversity can lead to higher performance when members understand each other, combine and build on each others' ideas. This suggests that interaction processes within a diverse team are crucial to the integration of diverse viewpoints. For example, Abramson found that organizations that had teams with high diversity and integration had the best performance" (Consequences of Feeling Dissimlar from Others in a Work Team, 2003). Along these lines, diverse groups have a higher ability to overcome initial difficulties by identifying the multiple angles of a problem and generating creative solutions.

The more openly they are recognized and discussed, the better chance there is for differences to become part of organizational success. Tomas and Ely believe in the notion that "a more diverse workplace will increase organizational effectiveness. It will lift morale, bring greater access to new segments of the market place, and enhance productivity" (Making Differences Matter; A New Paradigm for Managing Diversity, 1996). By truly embracing diversity, leveraging the talent within multicultural teams, and approaching diversity as means to higher knowledge and productivity, organizations will effectively manage differences, to achieve competitive advantage successfully.

Table 1: Paradigms of diversity

Paradigm	Focus	Key success factors

Discrimination-and-fairness	• Equal opportunity, fair treatment, recruitment, and compliance with US federal Equal Employment Opportunity requirements • Leaders work towards restructuring the makeup of the organization to reflect more closely that of society	• Effectiveness in its recruitment and retention goals rather than by the degree to which companies allow employees to draw on their personal assets and perspectives to do their work more efficiently
Access-and legitimacy	• Need of a more diverse workforce to help companies gain access to the differentiated segments • Matches the demographics of the organization to those of critical consumer or constituent groups	• Degree to which leaders in organizations understand niche capabilities and incorporate them into differentiated categories aligned to their business strategy
Learning-and-effectiveness	• Incorporates employee's perspectives into the main work of the organization • Enhances work by rethinking primary tasks and redefining markets, products, strategies, missions, business practices, and even cultures	• The promotion of equal opportunity and acknowledgment of cultural differences • Organizational learning and growth fostered by internalizing differences among employees

End goal: Leaders should thrive to shift to the Learning-and-effectiveness paradigm to approach diversity as a means to higher knowledge and productivity.

Recruiting workers

Lukhvinder Rai

Recruitment of talented employees is an essential part of any company's ability to maintain success and ensure the achievement of standards within an organization. Recruiting workers consists of actively compiling a diverse pool of potential candidates which can be considered for employment. A good recruitment policy will do this in a timely, cost-efficient manner. The ultimate goal of any human resources recruitment policy is to develop relationships with potential employees before they may actually be needed while remaining cognizant of the costs of doing so. In different industries, the constant need for talent creates a highly competitive marketplace for individuals, and it is important for any manager to be aware of these factors as they develop recruitment programs and policies. As retirement among baby boomers becomes increasing prevalent, victory in the "war for talent" will depend greatly on recruitment policies.

Methods of recruitment

There are two principal ways to recruit workers: internally and externally. Most companies will actively use both methods, ensuring opportunities for existing employees to move up in the organization while at the same time fielding new talent. Depending on the time frame and the specialization of the position to fill, some methods will be more effective than others. In either case, the establishment of a comprehensive job description for every position for which the company recruits will help to narrow the scope of the search, and offer more qualified candidates, aiding in search efficiency.

Internal recruitment is often the most cost effective method of recruiting potential employees, as it uses existing company resources and talent pool to fill needs and therefore may not incur any extra costs. This is done in two principal ways:

- Advertising job openings internally: This is the act of using existing employees as a talent pool for open positions. It carries the advantage of reallocating individuals that are qualified and familiar with the company's practices and culture while at the same time empowering employees within the organization. It also shows the company's commitment to, and trust in, its current employees taking on new tasks.

- Using networking: This method can be used in a variety of different ways. First, this recruitment technique simply posts the question to existing employees on whether anybody is aware of qualified candidates that they know personally which could fill a position. Known as employee referrals, this method often gives bonuses to the existing employee if the recommended applicant is hired. Another method uses industry contacts and membership in professional organizations to help create a talent pool, through simple word-of-mouth information regarding the needs of the organization.

External recruitment focuses resources on looking outside the organization for potential candidates and expanding the available talent pool. The primary goal of external recruitment is to create diversity among potential candidates by attempting to reach a wider range of individuals unavailable through internal recruitment. Although external recruitment methods can be costly to managers in terms of dollars, the addition of a new perspective within the organization can carry many benefits which outweigh the costs. External recruitment can be done in a variety of ways:

- Traditional advertising: This often incorporates one or many forms of advertising, ranging from newspaper classifieds to radio announcements. It is estimated that companies spend USD 2.18 billion annually on these types of ads (Kulik, 2004). Before the emergence of the Internet, this was the most popular form of recruitment for organizations, but the decline of readership of newspapers has made it considerably less effective (Heathfield, Use the Web for Recruiting: Recruiting Online).

- Job fairs and campus visits: Job fairs are designed to bring together a comprehensive set of employers in one location so that they may gather and meet with potential employees. The costs of conducting a job fair are distributed across the various participants, and can offer an extremely diverse set of applicants. Depending on the proximity to a college or university, campus visits help to find candidates that are looking for the opportunity to prove themselves and have minimum qualifications, such as a college education, that a firm seeks.

- Headhunters and recruitment services: These outside services are designed to essentially compile a talent pool for a company; however they can be extremely expensive. Although this service can be extremely efficient in providing qualified applicants for specialized or highly demanded job positions the rate for the services provided by headhunters can range from 20 to 35 per cent of the new recruit's annual salary if the individual is hired (Heathfield, Recruiting Stars: Top Ten Ideas for Recruiting Great Candidates).

- Online recruitment. The use of the Internet to recruit a talent pool is quickly becoming the preferred way of doing so, due to its ability to reach such a wide array of applicants extremely quickly and cheaply. There are many ways to turn the Internet into a recruitment tool for your company.

First, the use of the company website can allow a business to compile a list of potential applicants which are supremely interested in the company while at the same time allowing them exposure to your company's values and mission. In order to be successful using this recruitment method, a company must ensure that postings and the process for submitting resumes are as transparent and simple as possible.

Another popular use of online recruiting is through career websites (e.g. Monster.com or Careerbuilder.com). These sites charge employers a set fee for a job posting which can remain on the website for an agreed amount of time. These sites also carry a large database of applicants and allow clients to search their database to find potential employees. Although extremely effective, many companies prefer to use their own websites to eliminate the flood of resumes which may result from these services.

Finally, many professional associations may have websites on which a company may post job openings. For instance, the NCAA allows all of its member schools and conferences to post jobs on their website at a minimal cost, allowing for a more specialized selection of candidates. It may also be in a company's interest to contact area schools to see if they offer a career services site for their students for posting openings, further expanding the reach of recruitment efforts.

To learn more about the growth of internet job postings:

http://www.clickz.com/showPage.html?page=3443851

To learn how to create an effective online job posting:

http://www.yourhrexperts.com/posting.html

Evaluating recruiting policies

To evaluate recruitment policies, the concept of a **yield ratio** is often used. This calculates the efficiency of recruitment practices by taking the number of hirable individuals resulting from a recruitment policy divided by the total number of individuals recruited by the same policy (Kulik, 2004). This equation is outlined below:

$$\text{Yield ratio} = \frac{\text{Number of hirable individuals}}{\text{Total number of recruits}}$$

For many companies, this number can vary enormously, depending on the image, size and business of the company. However, it is still an extremely useful measure as it offers insight into the ability of a recruitment policy and whether it needs to be modified. A company like Microsoft may receive thousands of applicants simply based on the image that the firm carries, distorting its yield ratio without telling anything about the effectiveness of their recruitment strategies.

No matter how a company decides to recruit, the ultimate test will remain the ability of a recruitment strategy to produce viable applicants. Each manager will face different obstacles in doing this; however, it is important to remain concise and objective when searching for potential applicants. It is important to remember that recruiting is not simply done at a time of need for an organization but rather is a yearlong process that constantly maintains a talent pool and frequent contact with candidates.

Selective hiring

By Kristen Giacchino and Emily Gray

In recruiting, it is beneficial to attract not only a large quantity of applicants but a group of individuals with the necessary skills and requirements for the position. After obtaining a large, qualified applicant base managers need to identify those applicants with the highest potential for success at the organization. According to Pfeffer and Veiga, selecting the best person for the job is an extremely critical piece of the human resources inflow process (Pfeffer & Viega, Putting People First for Organizational Success, 1998). Selective hiring helps prevent the costly turnover of staff and increases the likeliness of high employee morale and productivity.

In order to evaluate the fit, it is important for managers to create a list of relevant criteria for each position before beginning the recruitment and selection process. Each job description should be associated with a list of critical skills, behaviors or attitudes that will make or break the job performance. When screening potential employees, managers need to select based on cultural fit and attitude as well as technical skills and competencies. There are some companies, such as Southwest Airlines, based out of the United States, who hire primarily based on attitude because they espouse the philosophy that you hire for attitude, train for skill. According to former CEO Herb Kelleher, "We can change skill levels through training. We can't change attitude" (O'Reilly & Pfeffer). After determining the most important qualifications, managers can design the rest of the selection process so that it is in alignment with the other human resource processes.

Managers must strive to identify the best applicants at the lowest cost. Companies have a variety of processes available to screen potential employees, so managers must determine which system will generate the most accurate results. The methods of selection vary both in levels of effectiveness and in cost of application. In addition to biographical information, companies can conduct personal interviews, perform background checks, or request testing. Because of the costs associated with these measures, companies try to narrow down the number of applicants in each round of hiring. In some countries, such as the United States, the selection procedures are subject to Equal Employment Opportunity guidelines (Recruitment). Therefore, the companies also need to ensure that the process is accurate, with a high level of validity, reliable and related to critical aspects of the job. Proactively taking these measures will help companies avoid litigation related to discrimination in the selection process.

Interviews

As mentioned, it is important to first define the skills and attributes necessary to succeed in the specified position, then develop a list of questions that directly relate to the job requirements. The best interviews follow a structured framework in which each applicant is asked the same questions and is scored with a consistent rating process. Having a common set of information about the applicants upon which to compare after all the interviews have been conducted allows hiring managers to avoid prejudices and all interviewees are ensured a fair chance (Smith G.). Many companies choose to use several rounds of screening with different interviewers to discover additional facets of the applicant's attitude or skill as well as develop a more well rounded opinion of the applicant from diverse perspectives. Involving senior management in the interview process also acts as a signal to applicants about the company culture and value of each new hire. There are two common types of interviews: behavioral and situational.

Behavioral interview

In a behavioral interview, the interviewer asks the applicant to reflect on his or her past experiences (Janz, 1982). After deciding what skills are needed for the position, the interviewer will ask questions to find out if the candidate possesses these skills. The purpose of behavioral interviewing is to find links between the job's requirement and how the applicant's experience and past behaviors match those requirements. Examples of behavioral interview questions:

- Describe a time when you were faced with a stressful situation. How did you handle the situation?

- Give me an example of when you showed initiative and assumed a leadership role?

(Free Sample Behavioral Interview Questions).

Situational interview

A situational interview requires the applicant to explain how he or she would handle a series of hypothetical situations. Situational-based questions evaluate the applicant's judgment, ability, and knowledge (Latham & Saari, 1984). Before administering this type of interview, it is a good idea for the hiring manager to consider possible responses and develop a scoring key for evaluation purposes. Examples of situational interview questions:

- You and a colleague are working on a project together; however, your colleague fails to do his agreed portion of the work. What would you do?

- A client approaches you and claims that she has not received a payment that supposedly had been sent five days ago from your office. She is very angry. What would you do?

(Creating Situational Interviews and Rating Scales)

Selection tests

When making a hiring decision, it is critical to understand the applicant's personality style, values, and motivations (Smith G.). Technical aptitude is important, but attitude is often more important. The reality is that technical skills can be learned, but interpersonal work attitudes are usually more difficult to change (Schaefer). Behavioral assessments and personality profiles are a good way for hiring managers to learn how the individual will interact with their coworkers, customers, and supervisors (Smith G.). Tests such as the Myers Briggs and D.I.S.C Profile assessments are popular tools that provide an accurate analysis of an applicant's attitudes and interpersonal skills; however, it is critical that the tests are administered, scored and interpreted by a licensed professional. Other selection tests used in hiring, may include cognitive, which measure general intelligence, work sample tests that demonstrate the applicant's ability to perform specific job duties, and integrity tests, which measure honesty (Kulik, 2004).

Background checks

Background checks are a way for employers to verify the accuracy of information provided by applicants in resumes and applications. Information gathered in background checks may include employment history, education, credit reports, driving records, and criminal records. Employers must obtain written consent from the applicant before conducting a background check, and the information gathered in a background check should be relevant to the job.

Evaluation

Employers may choose to use just one or a combination of the screening methods to predict future job performance. It is important for companies to assess the effectiveness of their selective hiring process using metrics. This provides a benchmark for future performance as well as a means of evaluating the success of a particular method. Companies can continuously improve their selection practices to ensure a good fit for future employees that will successfully accomplish all that the job entails as well as fit into the organizational culture. If companies are not successful in their hiring practices, high turnover or low employee morale, decreased productivity will result. Research shows that the "degree of cultural fit and value congruence between job applicants and their organizations significantly predicts both subsequent turnover and job performance" (Pfeffer & Viega, Putting People First for Organizational Success, 1998). Thus, companies need to assess their hiring in terms of technical success as well as cultural fit. Evaluating the hiring process will help ensure continuing success because human capital is often a company's most important asset.

Employee training

By Peter Wright

For years, employee training was viewed as a necessary evil something unpleasant but needed. However, with time it was realized that training could be used to the advantage of the company. When used effectively, training provides the employee with skill and knowledge with relation to the job tasks, which then creates a competitive advantage for the company (Pfeffer & Viega, Putting People First for Organizational Success, 1998).

Training is generally defined as the act of teaching a skill or behavior. However, what does this mean in business terms? Simply put, training in business is the investment of resources in the employees of a company so that they are better equipped to perform the tasks of their job. The type of resources invested may include time to learn, money to create programs and develop training materials, training effectiveness evaluation systems, etc. (Fukami, Strategic Human Resources: Training, 2007). There are many training methods from which a company may choose; these will be covered in the *Training Methods* section of this article.

Benefits of training

Training can be a source of a competitive advantage for a company. The primary benefit to the company is the result of an accumulation of smaller benefits. Training provides greater skill and knowledge to the employees, which translate into any number of improved job performances. The belief is that providing employees with training will result in increased profits—the improved performance or error reduction of the employees results in cost reduction for the company (Pfeffer & Viega, Putting People First for Organizational Success, 1998). The company is not the only beneficiary of employee training; the employee benefits quite a bit as well.

The well-trained employee creates an advantage for him or herself. By attending training sessions, employees can deepen their existing skill set, increase their overall skill set and increase their understanding of the organization. Additionally, the trained employee becomes more marketable in the event that he or she searches for another job—more and better skills will often lead to better or higher paying jobs (Kulik, 2004).

These are not the only benefits that the company and employee enjoy as a result of utilizing a company's training systems. Below is a list of other benefits that both may enjoy:

- increased job satisfaction and morale among employees

- increased employee motivation

- increased efficiencies in processes, resulting in financial gain

- increased capacity to adopt new technologies and methods

- increased innovation in strategies and products

- reduced employee turnover

- enhanced company image, e.g. conducting ethics training (note that this is **not** a good reason for ethics training!)

- risk management, e.g. training about sexual harassment, diversity training (Duening & Ivancevich, 2003)

Need for training

The need for training varies depending on the type of organization that is being discussed; a manufacturing company has different training needs than an insurance firm. But regardless of the type of company being discussed, appropriate training systems can greatly benefit the company. However, how does one decide on a training system? The answer to this question stems from the example above—it depends on the type of organization that is being discussed as well as what the company wishes to address in the training. The process begins with a training needs assessment. This assessment ought to be a systematic and objective analysis of the training needs in three main areas—organizational, job, and person.

Organizational needs deal mostly with the skills the company is looking for, the labor force, etc. whereas the job needs focus on the skills that the company views as necessary for a specific position. Then there are the person needs, and these are the most variable needs. Often these needs arise after a gap is seen in the expected performance compared to the actual performance of the employee. A large gap needs to be addressed and is often dealt with through training or termination (see the *Termination and Downsizing* section) (Fukami, Strategic Human Resources: Training, 2007). Other reasons for the person issues in regards to training may include training to develop a skill set that is lacking but not affecting performance or that the employee feels a need to develop. Training can also be a part of a young employee's "exploration" stage, where training can be used to focus the employee's interest and development towards a specific area (Kulik, 2004).

Specific circumstances may also create the need for training. These circumstances usually occur rather suddenly and infrequently, creating a need for a specific and highly directed training mechanism. Examples of such circumstance are shifts in an organizations ethics (keeping the employees and organization in alignment), new legal requirements (such as Sarbanes-Oxley compliance in the United States), or during states of change within the organization (Duening & Ivancevich, 2003). If a company, regardless of the circumstances surrounding that need, deems training necessary a method for conducting this training needs to be developed and implemented.

Training methods

Designing and implementing the training systems requires the company to consider a number of things; the method of training, the material the training will deal with, who will provide the training, how to evaluate the effectiveness of the training, etc. (Fukami, Strategic Human Resources: Training, 2007). There are also a number of other items that can impact the training system, things like what the training program is called. Because of the negative view that training has had for so long, some organizations are shying away from the term training and replacing it with things such as "<u>Learning & Development</u>" in order to emphasize the importance of learning for the individual and the organization. In other organizations, the term "Human Resource Development" is used (Training and Development, 2007).

Two of the largest issues that a company faces with developing these training systems are: (1) what type of training to use, and (2) how to evaluate the effectiveness of the training. It is important that these training systems and evaluation procedures remain in-line with the culture and policies of the rest of the company. Below is a partial list of common training systems:

- Lectures: Similar to a school classroom, the session is lead by a "trainer/teacher" who covers a specific topic such as how to use a new computer program.

- Audio-visual media & computer-based training: With the advancement of technology, companies can invest in video, audio and computer based learning such as instructional tapes, recorded lectures or "podcasts", or computer materials such as Flash presentations. The benefit of these methods is that they are relatively inexpensive and can be utilized by the employee at their discretion (Training and Development, 2007).

- On-the-job: a training method that relies on the employee to recognize the skills and knowledge he or she will need as they perform their work, and then develop those skills on his or her own.

- Technical training: specialized training that focuses on a specific need of specific employees. This typically applies to manufacturing based companies in relation to training their employees on the machinery and methods used.

- Mentoring & coaching: Mentoring systems pair a younger or less experienced employee with an individual that has experience and success within the company who can offer guidance, aid and insight to the younger/less experienced employees (Craumer, 2001). Coaching systems are slightly different. They involve the manager offering developmental assistance to the employee through observation, assessment, providing feedback, questioning, etc. (Kram, 1985)

- Outdoor programs: the use of physical and mental activities such as ropes courses or problem-solving tasks that encourage the use of team work.

After the training system has been developed and implemented, the effectiveness of the system needs to be evaluated, and there are multiple ways to do this. Common methods includes surveys given to the employees who have used the system, an ROI analysis and test at the end of the session (Fukami, Strategic Human Resources: Training, 2007).

Training in the context of global business

When examining the need for and type of training in the context of global/international business, training becomes even more necessary. The training of an employee who will be working in a country other than his or her own can be broken into three segments—pre-departure, on-site, and repatriation.

The **pre-departure** training consists of formal language training, training with respect to the local culture (culture sensitivity), education about the country (history, geography, government, etc.), and education about the companies operation in the foreign country. Such training allows for easier assimilation of the employee into the country and the company's office there.

Once on site, training takes the shape of training at any other branch of the company (see "Training methods" section). When the employee abroad returns to his or her home country it is equally important that the company offer some form of repatriation program. Such programs are designed to reduce culture shock upon return and to integrate the experience abroad into the employees overall career plans and development. These programs are often most effectively carried out through mentor programs (Asheghian & Ebrahimi, 2005).

Aligning employee career development with organizational growth

By Rahul Choudaha

Work is such a cozy place that it's sometimes difficult for Google employees to leave the office...

(Lashinsky, 2007).

We all can predict at least one thing about the future of businesses—competition will increase. However, the direction of competition will not only be for customers, but also for talent. Satisfied talent will attract more customers and in turn will keep them satisfied. Losing talent in an era of talent scarcity is the last thing an organization wants. Especially for small and medium enterprises, criticality and dependability on the talent is much higher. Schweyer makes a case for improving the retention strategies within the organization because winning the internal war for talent is as critical as losing a top performer and leads to general employee dissatisfaction. "Successful talent management inside an organization sets in motion a virtuous cycle. Through word of mouth it becomes known as a great place to work. This reduces the external war for talent to mere skirmishes in which talent will almost always choose the top employer" (An Internal War for Talent, 2006).

Recruiting and selecting the right talent is the first stage, and identifying talent which fits into company's needs and values is critical. Subsequently, the challenge for the organization is to keep the talent and consistently motivate them to over deliver. Baruch examines transforming models of career management, arguing that there is a general shift in career trajectories from linear to multidirectional trajectories (Transforming Careers from Linear to Multidirectional Career Paths, 2004). In this new model, workers' experience of career development and progression does not follow a traditional linear model of moving up organizational hierarchies. The multidirectional career model suggests that as the individual career trajectories gain multiple direction and possibilities, workers are exposed to greater diversity of relationships, involving cross-functional, inter- and intra-organizational and multi-level encounters which transform the landscape of relationships involved in career experiences.

Best of East and West

Google was ranked number 1 in the Fortune 100 Best Companies to Work For. Google receives almost 1,300 resumes every day. The biggest challenge for Google is not how to attract the best talent but how to retain them and keep them excited. Google provides innumerable perks at the office like free meals, free professional advice on health and finance, childcare, shuttle services, gym etc. Google provides two key opportunities for career development. First, engineers are required to devote 20 per cent of their time to pursuing projects of their interests which are in alignment with organizational goals. Second, Google is exploring a sabbatical program and mobility within the company for the developing and retaining talent.

TCS was ranked the number 1 technology company in the DQ-IDC India Survey: Best Employers. This is not an easy achievement considering size of TCS and its philosophy of being one of the moderate pay masters. TCS has over 70,000 employees, and earned global revenue of USD 4.3 billion (2006-07). The key to success is the learning culture that the organization promotes. The organization has adopted a two-prong strategy for developing talent. First, continuous learning through technology: TCS has launched iCALMS, an integrated competency and learning management system. Second, providing global assignments to employees and hence enabling a route for professional and financial growth (Dataquest, 2006).

The career development programs should provide excitement and satisfaction at various stages of employee development. Marshall highlighted that leadership development programs for small organizations should identify the talent early on and provide multiple opportunities of learning by job rotation (Leadership Development for Small Organizations, 2002). These development programs should also leverage the internal talent, who are already experts in their fields for creating inspiration and developing the next chain of leaders. Komisar shared his experiences and mentioned that a passion-driven career has major virtues and ample learning opportunities. This is good for the organization as they know that employee is enjoying the work, and finally it provides fluidity and flexibility in the ever-changing landscape of the new economy (Goodbye Career, Hello Success, 2000).

The changing nature of careers and organizations has increased the significance of mentoring. It benefits and strengthens employer-employee relationship. Mentoring can be accomplished by immediate superiors, peers within one's own organization, individuals outside of one's organization, subordinates, and any number of other individuals (Baugh & Sullivan, 2005). Michaels, Handfield-Jones, and Axelrod in their book *The War for Talent* mentions that talent development is critical for organizations and many think development means training, but training is only a small part of the solution (2001). They suggest that development primarily happens through a sequence of stretch jobs, coaching, and mentoring. However, organizations are not leveraging the development opportunities. Companies need to adopt and accelerate development by improving the frequency and candor of feedback and institutionalizing mentoring. Every leader at all levels can and should be responsible for people development.

Hymowitz says that managers are not spending adequate time in understanding their team members and providing them with opportunities to learn and grow on the job (When Managers Neglect to Coach Their Talent, 2007). This is leading to employees feeling alienated, underutilized and ignored, and may be searching for new jobs elsewhere. "Managers who focus on talent assign their employees to jobs that play to their strengths, make sure they have the resources they need to perform well, respect their opinions and push them to advance" (Hymowitz, 2007). The people manager should develop relationships and an environment that is conducive to development. Five skill areas that successful developers of people have mastered are:

- encouraging an open climate for dialogue with employees

- providing employees with on-going feedback regarding performance

- helping employees understand the strategies of the organization

- helping employees identify multiple and realistic options for their career growth and development within the enterprise

- helping employees compile meaningful, business-driven personal development plans (Kaye & Vultaggio, 2004)

"...[I]n the new career model, employees make major shifts within the same company, or exit and reenter the company at different career stages" (Kulik, 2004). Organizations need to realize that talent is precious and dynamic. Organizations need to create action strategies and provide a favorable environment to help talent grow in line with the organizational goals.

Performance appraisal

By Adam Ruberg

Purpose of appraisals

Historically, performance appraisals have been used by companies for a variety of different purposes, including salary recommendations, promotion and layoff decisions, and training recommendations (Kulik, 2004). In general, "performance elements tell employees what they have to do and standards tell them how well they have to do it" (United States Department of the Interior, 2004). This broad definition, however, can allow for appraisals to be ineffective, even detrimental, to employee performance. "Second only to firing an employee, managers cite performance appraisal as the task they dislike the most", and employees generally have a similar disposition (Heathfield, Performance Appraisals Don't Work). One key item that is often forgotten during the appraisal process (by managers and employees alike) is that the appraisal is for improvement, not blame or harsh criticism (Bacal, 1999).

Creating an appropriate appraisal process

One significant problem in creating an appraisal process is that no single performance appraisal method will be perfect for every organization (Kulik, 2004). Establishing an appropriate process involves significant planning and analysis in order to provide quality feedback to the employee. The most crucial task in the process is determining proper job dimensions that can be used to gauge the employee against accepted standards that affect the performance of the team, business unit, or company (Fukami, Performance Appraisal, 2007). Peter Drucker developed a method termed 'Management by Objectives' or MBO, in order to address the creation of such job dimensions. Drucker suggests that the objectives of any employee can be validated if they pass the following six tests (Management by Objectives—SMART, 2007):

- **Specific**

- **Measurable**

- **Achievable**

- **Realistic**

- **Time-related**

If an objective meets these criteria, it is considered a valid dimension on which to gauge performance. The standards on which the objective is compared with should also be validated using the SMART method.

Appraisal methods

Numerous methods exist for gauging an employee's performance, and each provides strengths and weaknesses for given environments. The following outlines some of the more commonly used methods, as well as some recently developed ones that can be useful for various feedback situations:

Graphic rating scales: This method involves assigning some form of rating system to pertinent traits. Ratings can be numerical ranges (1-5), descriptive categories (below average, average, above average), or scales between desirable and undesirable traits (poor ↔ excellent). This method can be simple to setup and easy to follow, but is often criticized for being too subjective, leaving the evaluator to define broad traits such "Leadership ability" or "Conformance with standards" (Kulik, 2004).

Behavioral methods: A broad category encompassing several methods with similar attributes. These methods identify to what extent an employee displays certain behaviors, such as asking a customer to identify the usefulness of a sales representative's recommendation. While extremely useful for jobs where behavior is critical to success, identifying behaviors and standards for employees can often be very time consuming for an organization (Kulik, 2004).

2+2: A relative newcomer in performance appraisal methodology, the 2+2 feedback system demonstrates how appraisals can be used primarily for improvement purposes. By offering employees two compliments and two suggestions for improvement focused around high-priority areas, creators Douglas and Dwight Allen suggest that organizations can become "more pleasant, more dynamic, and more productive" (Formula 2+2, 2004). If the goal of the performance appraisal is employee improvement, this system can provide significant benefits; however, if the goals are more akin to compensation changes and rankings, the system provides little benefit.

Appraisal methodologies depend greatly on the type of work being done; an assembly worker will require a considerably different appraisal system than a business consultant. Significant planning will be required to develop appropriate methods for each business unit in an organization in order to obtain maximum performance towards the appraisal goals.

Performing the appraisal

Performing an appraisal on employees can be nerve racking for both parties if the situation is not handled correctly, and is thus seen as one of the most difficult tasks managers face. There are many acts a manager can perform to make the process easier on both parties, and hopefully, mutually beneficial.

Many assume that performance appraisals are meant to identify weaknesses to be worked on, and exposing these weaknesses can be painful for employees. Martha Craumer suggests that organizations should be leveraging the strengths of each employee rather than focusing on their weaknesses. By "encouraging and developing what people do well naturally...the organization could become more efficient by allowing their people to do what they do best" (Craumer, 2001).

The frequency of appraisal can be a notable factor in ongoing development. Yearly performance reviews are becoming increasingly rare as companies begin to see the benefits of frequent appraisal. Susan Heathfield suggests that quarterly performance development meetings can allow for clear direction towards performance goals (Heathfield, Performance Management is NOT an Annual Appraisal). Constant tuning of performance can be much more effective than annual overhauls.

Any individual administering performance appraisals must realize the two-way conversation that is occurring. Inviting feedback and listening to reactions and concerns from the employee during the appraisal process becomes very important to establishing trust with the employee (United States Department of the Interior, 2004). If the appraiser provides any negative feedback or improvement points, suggestions should be made to help resolve the problem to develop the person's performance. With the suggestions made, follow-up should occur to assist with any problems with the development and to track progress, rather than waiting until the next performance review (Fukami, Performance Appraisal, 2007).

Often being seen as a strictly hierarchical feedback tool, performance appraisals can be less "scary" if employees have the opportunity to appraise their managers as well as their peers. With this 360-degree feedback process, employees and managers will see multiple vantages of their performance and can participate on an even playing field, ultimately providing a greater ability to work together to achieve corporate goals (Kulik, 2004).

Performance appraisals should not be looked upon as a necessary evil, but rather a process that has the ability to develop and improve the people within the company. By taking the time to create appropriate performance measures, and administering them accordingly, the resulting system can provide long-term gain for the company.

For further investigation:

For a discussion of why many people think of feedback as criticism visit:

http://www.selfhelpmagazine.com/articles/growth/feedback.html

For a discussion of differing views on feedback and specific examples on how to give feedback visit:

http://home.att.net/~nickols/feedback.htm

Giving and receiving feedback

By Kristin Hamilton and Tiffani Willis

In a broad sense, **feedback** is simply verbal or nonverbal communication between two or more parties. So, why are so many of us afraid of the word feedback? People often think of feedback as being synonymous with criticism because feedback is given, in most circumstances, when expectations have not been met (Rich). As humans, we all have the desire to fit in with our society's social norms and please those within our community by meeting expectations. As shown in Exhibit 25, we are constantly surrounded by feedback as we see the consequences of our actions and how our actions affect the impressions of those around us (Jossey and Bass, 1995). Feedback is an essential part of our personal life and our work environment, making, giving and receiving feedback successfully critical.

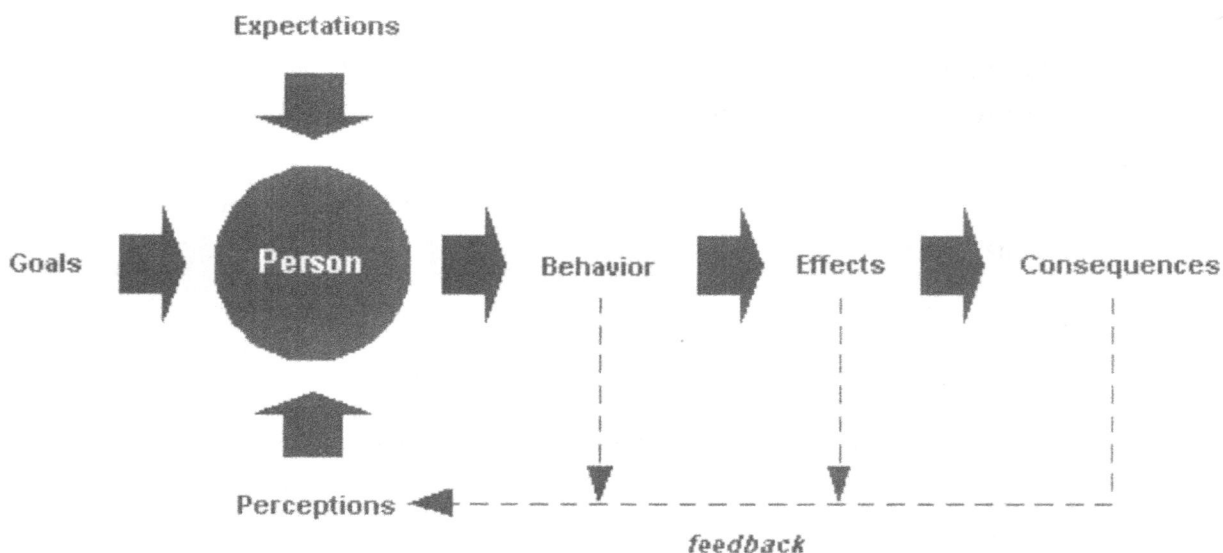

Exhibit 25: Feedback

Giving feedback

Many are not aware that giving successful feedback is affected by more than just the words used to communicate. Words used to tell ideas are only "7 per cent of your communication, your tone of voice comes out to 38 per cent and your gestures are equivalent to 55 per cent of your total communication" (Hathaway). As a result, the effectiveness of communication is related to how well one mirrors the culture and behaviors of the person to which one is talking. Matching a person's voice tone, tempo, body posture, movements, and gestures creates a feedback environment where the ideas being communicated are easily understood.

In addition to mirroring the person you are communicating with, there are nine easy steps that can be followed when giving feedback. First, be clear about what you have to say. Second, emphasize the person's ability to change in a positive way. Third, avoid general comments and clarify pronouns such as "it" and "that" so the person understands exactly what you are attempting to communicate. Fourth, make sure to pick the right time. Fifth, focus on the behavior that can be changed rather than the person or your opinions (Meister). Sixth, be descriptive rather than evaluative. Seventh, own the feedback by using "I statements" that clarify your feelings related to the person you are giving feedback to. Eighth, avoid generalization words such as "all", "never", "always" etc.; rather, use more specific examples of the behavior you are trying to change or encourage in the future. Ninth, to ensure mutual understanding after giving feedback, ask the person you are communicating with to restate their understanding of the issue being discussed (McGill & Beatty, 1994).

When thinking about feedback in an organization, it is likely a person will think of performance reviews. One common problem that managers overlook when reviewing performance is remembering that feedback is not all about forms. Traditional performance reviews have checklists, ratings or reports that are used as tools to analyze feedback in the organization. While these forms are useful in documenting and appraising a person's performance, feedback should not be dictated by the type of form an organization uses. Performance appraisals are often given at benchmarked times throughout the year. As a result, feedback is often delayed. Increased amounts of time that pass between the time the behavior took place and the time the recipient receives the feedback greatly affects the recipients ability to accept the feedback as useful information.

In one's personal life and in the work environment, it is important to understand that feedback is something that can be asked for. As such, the giver and receiver of feedback are equally accountable for communicating the need and desire to give and receive feedback. Finally, it is important to ask for comment on the way one gives feedback because most humans are great at self-delusion. It is much easier to think that our suggestions are useful to another person than to actually understand how our feedback is being interpreted by another. In the end, feedback is a continuous process which ensures goals and expectations are being met through communication between two parties.

Receiving feedback

While giving feedback is extremely important, receiving feedback and changing one's characteristics to reflect that feedback is just as important. Often, employees become defensive when they are receiving feedback on their performance. Ken Blanchard, co-author of *The One Minute Manager* states, "[t]he reason a lot of people get defensive with feedback is they don't distinguish feedback from reaction. While they are listening to the feedback, they have a reaction to the demand for action that your feedback implies" (Blanchard, 1996). For example, when a boss is telling an employee the aspects of the job the employee needs to work on, he may only focus on the negative points and not the positive.

Receiving feedback should not only be looked at from a downward point of view, such as a boss giving his employees critiques; but it should also be studied in an upward way. According to Richard Reilly, James Smither, and Nicholas Vasilopoulos, authors of *A Longitudinal Study of Upward Feedback*, "upward feedback (that is, subordinates rating the performance of their immediate supervisor) is growing in importance as a tool for the individual and organizational development" (1996). Upward feedback allows management to see the effects they have on their employees. It is then up to the managers to act on that feedback. Atwater, Roush and Fischthal found that "follower ratings of student leaders improved after feedback was given to leaders and that leaders receiving 'negative' feedback (defined as self-ratings that were considerably higher than follower ratings) improved the most" (The Influence of Upward Feedback on Self and Follower Ratings of Leadership, 1995). This shows that there is a bigger reaction when the upward feedback is negative instead of positive.

In order to effectively receive feedback, a person has to be ready to understand that they may hear critiques that they do not want to hear. Jan B. King, the former President and CEO of Merritt Publishing states that an individual is ready to receive feedback when he:

- wants to know him as others see him and he is clear that this is their perception, net necessarily what is true about you inside.

- trusts his co-workers to care enough about his development to risk hearing their opinion.

- has a place outside work where you can talk it through.

- Has opportunities for additional feedback so he gets validation of the changes he has made (Receiving Feedback Gracefully is a Critical Career Skill).

If an individual is not ready to constructively receive feedback, then the feedback he does receive will not be effective. King continues to state that individuals must remember this about feedback, "it is one opinion coming from another individual's unique perspective" (Receiving Feedback Gracefully is a Critical Career Skill). Just because one person views another individual in a particular way does not mean that the rest of world views that person in the same way, but it is a good way for an individual to find out what others think of him/her that is not known.

There are several tips that an individual can use when receiving feedback. These tips include:

- Try to show your appreciation to the person providing the feedback. They will feel encouraged and believe it or not, you do want to encourage feedback.

- Even your manager or supervisor finds providing feedback scary. They never know how the person receiving feedback is going to react.

- If you find yourself becoming defensive or hostile, practice stress management techniques such as taking a deep breath and letting it out slowly.

- Focusing on understanding the feedback by questioning and restating usually defuses any feelings you have of hostility or anger.

- If you really disagree, are angry or upset, and want to dissuade the other person of their opinion, wait until your emotions are under control to reopen the discussion (Heathfield, How to Receive Feedback with Grace and Dignity).

These tips are helpful in becoming a better receiver for feedback, but they will only work as long as they are practiced on a regular basis.

With the above facts and figures workers can see that giving and receiving feedback does not have to be scary. As long as people give and receive feedback in a constructive way and practice their feedback skills it will eventually become second nature to the employees. It will also show that feedback provides benefits for both the individuals that work for the company, and the company itself.

For further investigation:

For information on Ken Blanchard, his **Book** *One Minute Manager*, and various facts on feedback visit:

http://www.answers.com/topic/ken-blanchard

For more information on the findings of "A longitudinal study of upward feedback" visit:

http://www.blackwell-synergy.com/ doi/ abs/10.1111/j.1744-6570.1996.tb01586.x

Link your knowledge:

Click on this link to find an exercise to practice effective ways to receive feedback:

http://humanresources.about.com/cs/communication/ht/receivefeedback.htm

Determining base pay

By Cynthia V Fukami

Have you ever wondered how a company decides how much to pay for a particular job? Imagine that you have seen a job posted on the Internet. It reads, "Office Assistant Wanted. Will answer the phone and greet visitors. Some word processing duties. Other duties as assigned. Start at USD 8.00 an hour". How did the manager decide to pay USD 8.00 per hour? Why did she decide that was fair? In this subchapter, we will cover the two types of "fairness" important in designing a base pay system.

Internal equity

The first consideration is that the base pay system needs to be **internally equitable**. This means that the pay differentials between jobs need to be appropriate. The amount of base pay assigned to jobs needs to reflect the relative contribution of each job to the company's business objectives. In determining this, the manager should ask his or herself, "How does the work of the office assistant described above compare with the work of the office manager?" Another question to be asked is, "Does one contribute to solutions for customers more than another?" Internal equity implies that pay rates should be the same for jobs where the work is similar and different for jobs where the work is dissimilar. In addition, determining the appropriate differential in pay for people performing different work is a key challenge. Compensation specialists use two tools to help make these decisions: job analysis and job evaluation.

Job analysis is a systematic method to discover and describe the differences and similarities among jobs. A good job analysis collects sufficient information to adequately identify, define, and describe the content of a job. Since job titles may in and of themselves be misleading, for example, "systems analyst" does not reveal much about the job; the content of the job is more important to the analysis than the title. In general, a typical job analysis attempts to describe the skill, effort, responsibility, and working conditions of each job. **Skill** refers to the experience, training, education, and ability required by the job. **Effort** refers to the mental or physical degree of effort actually expended in the performance of the job. **Responsibility** refers to the degree of accountability required in the performance of a job. **Working conditions** refer to the physical surroundings and hazards of a job, including dimensions such as inside versus outside work, heat, cold, and poor ventilation. A **job description** summarizes the information collected in the job analysis. See http://en.wikipedia.org/wiki/Job analysis for more information about job analysis.

Job evaluation is a process that takes the information gathered by the job analysis and places a value on the job. Job evaluation is the process of systematically determining the relative worth of jobs based on a judgment of each job's value to the organization. The most commonly used method of job evaluation in the United States and Europe is the "point method". The point method consists of three steps: (1) defining a set of compensable factors, (2) creating a numerical scale for each compensable factor, and (3) weighting each compensable factor. Each job's relative value is determined by the total points assigned to it. See <u>http://www.hr-guide.com/jobevaluation.htm</u> for more information about job evaluation and the point system.

The result of the job analysis and job evaluation processes will be a pay structure or queue, in which jobs are ordered by their value to the organization.

External equity

The second consideration in creating a base pay system is external equity. **External equity** refers to the relationship between one company's pay levels in comparison to what other employers pay. Some employers set their pay levels higher than their competition, hoping to attract the best applicants. This is called "leading the market". The risk in leading the market is that a company's costs will generally be higher than its competitors' costs. Other employers set their pay levels lower than their competition, hoping to save labor costs. This is called "lagging the market". The risk in lagging the market is that the company will be unable to attract the best applicants. Most employers set their pay levels the same as their competition. This is called "matching the market". Matching the market maximizes the quality of talent while minimizing labor costs.

An important question in external equity is how you define your market. Traditionally, markets can be defined in one of three ways. One way to define your market is by identifying companies who hire employees with the same occupations or skills. For example, if a company hires electrical engineers, it may define its market as all companies that hire electrical engineers. Another way to define a market is by identifying companies who operate in the same geographic area. For example, if the company is in Denver, Colorado, the market would be defined as all companies in Denver, Colorado. A third way to define a company's market is by identifying direct competitors, that is, those companies who produce the same products and services. For example, Shady Acres Veterinary Clinic may define its market as all other veterinary clinics. Notice that these three characterizations can interact, that is, Shady Acres might define its market as all veterinary clinics in Denver, Colorado that employ veterinary technicians.

Once you have defined your market, the next step is to survey the compensation paid by employers in your market. Surveys can be done in a variety of ways. First, there are publicly available data through the Bureau of Labor Statistics in the United States. Second, there are publicly available data through the Internet, from sites such as <u>www.salary.com</u> or <u>www.haypaynet.com</u>. Third, salary information can be obtained from a third party source, such as an industry group or employer organization, which has collected general information for a geographic region or industry. Fourth, the company can hire a consulting organization to custom design a survey. Finally, one can conduct a survey one's self. See <u>http://www.hr-guide.com/data/G474.htm</u> for more information about salary surveys.

Combining internal and external equity

A company that has performed appropriate research has two sets of data. The first is **pay structure**, the output from the job evaluation. The second is **market data**, the output from the market survey. The next step will be to combine these two sets of data, to create a **pay policy line**. The pay policy line can be drawn freehand, by graphing actual salaries and connecting the dots. Alternatively, statistical techniques such as regression analysis are used to create a pay policy line. **Regression** generates a straight line that best fits the data by minimizing the variance around the line. In other words, the straight line generated by the regression analysis will be the line that best combines the internal value of a job (from job evaluation points) and the external value of a job (from the market survey). You can also enact a policy of "leading" the market by raising the line, and the policy of "lagging" the market by lowering the line.

How do companies decide the pay associated with each job? First, they analyze the content of each job. Second, they assess the value each job contributes to the company. Third, they price each job in the market. Finally, they look at the relationship between what they value internally and what the market values externally. By following each of these steps, a company will have a fair base pay system, which will lead to attracting and retaining the best employees.

Benefits and non-monetary compensation

By Julie Wells

In order for most businesses to function, employees must be provided with a payment in exchange for their services. Cash is one way to compensate employees, but cash alone is rarely enough payment. "Compensation is becoming more variable as companies base a greater proportion of it on stock options and bonuses and a smaller proportion on base salary, not only for executives but also for people further and further down the hierarchy" (Pfeffer, Six Dangerous Myths About Pay, 2000). Benefits and other forms of non-monetary compensation are becoming more appropriate forms of compensation for employees in today's workplace.

A **benefit** is a "general, indirect and non-cash compensation paid to an employee" that is offered to at least 80 per cent of staff (Employee Benefits Definition). On average, 40 per cent of payroll is dedicated to non-cash benefits (Kulik, 2004). In order to attract, retain, and motivate the best employees, benefits and other sources of non-monetary compensation should be considered. There are three things a company must fully consider before determining if and how they will issue employee benefits: the industry structure, the strengths of the company and its competitors, and the wage structure. A company should not issue benefits to employees if they have not considered the implications of these factors, specifically the wage structure. If a company offers employees extremely high wages compared to other businesses in the industry in addition to non-monetary compensation, costs may increase at a faster rate than profit. Benefits are also related to the type of industry in which the company does business. If the company has an understanding of what they can offer to employees and how those offerings will be received in the industry, benefits can increase a company's workforce quality and general happiness of employees.

Table 2: Types of non-monetary compensation

Employee Benefits	Fringe Benefits	Perks (perquisites)
relocation assistance	sick leave	company cars
medical and/or dental insurance plans	income protection	hotel stays
flexible spending accounts	vacation	profit-sharing
retirement plans	profit sharing	leisure activities on work time, in-office exercise facilities
life and long-term insurance	education funding	stationary, business cards,

		personalized office supplies
legal assistance plans		first choice at job assignments
adoption assistance and child care plans		
miscellaneous employee discounts		

The benefit of benefits

Benefits can be required by government, offered willingly by employers, or arise from pressures within the company. In the US, the government requires that businesses deduct Federal Income Contribution Act (**FICA**) taxes from employee paychecks, which pay for Social Security and Medicare (Internal Revenue Service). **Workers' Compensation** is paid to employees if they are injured while performing work necessary for their job function; this can include breaking a bone, getting into a car accident, or payments made to the family of someone killed on the job. **Unemployment insurance** provides wages to unemployed persons, generally only if they are registered as unemployed and actively seeking a job. In Australia, these benefits are paid through the income taxes, but payments are issued by Centrelink, a governmental office that seeks to support unemployed individuals and help them become self-supporting (Centrelink). The Family Medical Leave Act (**FMLA**) allows individuals to leave work for a semi-extended period of time in order to care for an ailing family member, new child, or personal illness. This leave is unpaid, but it guarantees that employees will not lose their jobs if they leave under these circumstances.

Employee benefits that are not required by law are often provided. These are attractive to businesses as well as employees because they provide both with some tax advantages. For example, if a company offers employees a flexible spending account, money that employees receive in this account may be deducted from total earnings on employees' tax returns. Employees can "use pre-tax dollars to pay for eligible health care and dependent care expenses", however any money that remains in the account at the end of the year will be forfeited (SHPS). This is a benefit to employees because individuals will receive a portion of their income tax-free. Employers also benefit from offering these types of programs because they also receive tax benefits and they retain happy employees by providing programs that meet their needs.

Benefits are also offered to employees as incentives. These are designed to attract, keep, and improve life for employees. They are not usually required by the government but companies may receive tax benefits for some types of these non-monetary payments. There are a plethora of services that can be offered, including complementary gym memberships, on-site daycare, company cars, and paid vacations. Companies offer such these benefits in order to create a culture for their employees, which have the ability to promote social interaction, make life easier for working parents, or improve employees' quality of life. Depending on the industry, benefits may be more attractive than salary figures; this could allow companies to pay lower wages to employees, thus reducing the total amount spent in payroll. In situations like these, a company may want to be extremely creative in devising their benefit packages.

Detriments of benefits

Benefits can provide companies with ways to attract high quality employees and help retain them especially if the benefits offered are significantly different or better than the benefits offered by competitors. However, there are negative situations that can arise from offering too many or the wrong kind of benefits to employees. These can be better understood in the context of the following case study.

By attracting employees who desire a strong work/life balance, the SAS Institute has the potential to create an overly homogenous culture. This can lead to a lack of dissent in the company; if someone disagrees with a policy or practice, they may be less likely to voice their opinions for fear of demonstrating different opinions than their friends and co-workers. This can also foster an environment that lacks cultural, ethnic, or social diversity, which can lead to an inability to adopt change within the company.

Case, The SAS Institute

The SAS Institute, based in the southern United States, is a software development company that competes against global software giants, such as Microsoft. In order to attract employees that fit their unique company culture, SAS has developed an extensive employee benefit program that is offered to all employees at the company. Salaries paid to SAS employees are not significantly higher than competitors in the industry, but they do maintain a competitive pay rate. For the ideal employee, however, the benefits more than compensate for an unimpressive salary.

Benefits at SAS include: private offices for all employees; contributions of 15 per cent into employee profit sharing plans; 200 acre natural campus setting with on-site hiking trails and picnic areas, sculptures, and artwork; the latest technology and equipment; 35 hour work week; on-site medical facility (including nurses, doctors, a physical therapist, massage therapist, and mental health practitioner), five minute waiting time for appointments, and free healthcare for employees and their families; health plans that cover most basic needs and offer "cost accountable" services for services that are more extensive; on-site Montessori daycare at 33 per cent of the cost of normal daycare; on-site private junior and senior high schools, open to students from outside of SAS, with high tech laboratories and equipment; free on-site gym for employees and families with a pool, exercise classes, yoga, weight room, etc.; cafeteria with high quality food at low prices, live piano music, and the option of dining with your children if they attend the on-site schools; subsidized memberships offered for health clubs and daycare off property; company owned country club memberships at significantly low costs for employees and their families; and more.

SAS is a unique example of a company that hires employees who desire a strong work/life balance. Not all software engineers would desire this lifestyle, but SAS recognizes that they hire from a unique niche of employees and seek to attract these individuals. This has been very successful; "SAS is certainly among the lowest [turnover] in the industry—less than 4 per cent annually. For a company of more than 5,000 employees, this is quite an achievement, and much of their success can be linked to their unique HRM practices" (SAS).

Pay for performance

By *Bonggi Yim and Chanakiat "Art Samarnbutra"*

Compensation techniques

According to Kulik, it is important for companies to attract "quality job applicants, motivate employees to be high performers, and encourage long-term employee retention" (Human Resources for the Non-HR Manager, 2004). Doing these things can increase companies' competitive power today. Compensation systems usually consist of three categories: "base salary, short-term incentive systems, and long-term incentive systems" (Kulik, 2004). Reward systems really affect work performance.

Reward systems can be applied to employees with different formula. Poorly designed and administered reward systems can do more harm than good. It is important to design reward systems carefully, taking into considerations base salary and incentives according to the different tasks of specific employees.

Companies should have well-designed base salaries. Nowadays, many websites (e.g. <u>salary.com</u>, <u>jobstar.org</u>, <u>wageweb.com</u>) provide detailed information to employees according to company mission (Kulik, 2004). When a company designs a base salary, they have to consider the company's unique aspects: locations and acquisition period of skills and so on. Depending on ranking system of the company, employees need to be evaluated differently. A CEO's evaluation is different from that of management and evaluation of management is different from that of employees.

Companies also provide short term incentives to employees. Most companies' compensation systems include "variable pay" (Kulik, 2004). Depending on work performance, many companies reward their employees without affecting base salary. To achieve a set goal, many companies use bonuses. For example, "Nucor set its base pay at about half of the competition's. By emphasizing a bonus system, Nucor has shifted the risk onto the employee's shoulders" (Kulik, 2004). Companies should have exact evaluation systems that support bonus pay. Many companies such as GE, HP, and Sun Microsystems are using software that directly evaluates employees' behavior with respect to customer service.

Long-term incentives are also a part of reward systems. Stock options and profit-sharing plans are representative long-term reward systems (Kulik, 2004). Even though employees are motivated by these incentives, they do not receive benefits until after few years. For example, employees cannot sell stock options until after a few years after they receive stock options. "In a profit-sharing plan, employees are promised a payment beyond base pay that is based on company profits" (Kulik, 2004).

Components of pay for performance

According to Dr Cynthia Fukami, a professor from the University of Denver, these are the main components of pay for performance (Fukami, Reward Systems, 2007):

1. The company pays the employee beyond his or her job value.

2. Many forms for improving the pay system are available.

3. The company can divide up the pay into 3 levels that are individual, team, and company-wide.

Pay secrecy

Besides the compensation techniques, the companies should consider whether the compensation system should be secret. Historically, employees and businesses both expressed concerns about the public discussion of salary; however, such discussions should not be prohibited (Kulik, 2004). Companies need to conclude what information they should reveal in their pay systems. Some US companies select to announce salary ranges. For example, for each position American Express posts the market pay ranges so that its employees can compare them with their salaries. Some companies disclose the formula and the factors they may use to calculate salaries, such as education and experience.

Good outcomes of paying for performance

Dr Cynthia Fukami notes that reward system is a powerful tool if pay links with performance (Fukami, Reward Systems, 2007):

1. Strategic objectives of the organization will be achieved.

2. The reward system will support the organizational culture.

3. Employees' working performance will be improved from the right pay practice.

4. Competitive advantages have increased continuously.

Folly of reward systems in different organizations

In politics: Politicians are separated from the general population when they speak only of official goals that are purposely vague and generalized. In contrast, the electorate will punish the candidate who frankly informs about the source of fund.

In universities: According to Steven Kerr, "Society hopes that professors will not neglect their teaching responsibilities but rewards them almost entirely for research and publications" (p. 9). While it is easy to recognize those professors who receive awards, quantifying a dedication to teaching is more difficult. To resolve this problem, it is essential that university leadership should emphasize teaching and doing research equally.

In sport: Coaches talk about teamwork, not individuals. Clearly, in a reward system, the best player will receive the biggest reward. Therefore, players normally think of themselves first and their team second. To correct this problem, the team manager needs to reduce the gaps of pay among team players.

Cautions for introducing a pay system

- *Much advice about pay is wrong* (Kerr, 1995).

  Many executives learn that the employees will certainly work more effectively in case that the company gives them higher compensation. Pfeffer said that the executives may not be "spending as much time and effort as it should on the work environment-on defining its jobs, on creating its culture, and making work fun and meaningful" (Six Dangerous Myths About Pay, 2000). Sometimes, companies pay well to create proactive work environment and get new innovative ideas in return. This policy does not surely work, especially when the top executives and employees are lacking of trust with each other.

- *Pay systems need to align with the company culture.*

  The top management should adjust the pay system when it is not fit with the current business strategy. However, changing the internal culture is a wrong idea because it is embedded in the employees' minds. The confusion can make the growth of the company stagnant.

- *Implementing the reward system is hard and takes management time*

Most companies believe that employees will work effectively when they get rewards for their efforts. Because of this concern, the HR managers cannot maintain the policy in compensation. From Mercer survey, "nearly three-quarters of all the companies surveyed had made major changes to their pay plans in just the past two years" (Pfeffer, Six Dangerous Myths About Pay, 2000). In addition, an example of changing reward system occurred in Sears. Sears had to eliminate its commission system because Sears's employees wanted high commission, so they offered unneeded services to customers.

Meaningful job design

By Ryan Brown and Mike McClain

Job design is critical to the success of any organization. For our purposes **job design** is defined as the allocation of specific work tasks to individuals and groups (Schermerhorn, Job Design Alternatives, 2006). Allocating jobs and tasks means specifying the contents, method and relationships of jobs to satisfy technological and organizational requirements as well as the personal needs of jobholders. If successful job design is not implemented, than the companies general strategy and direction will be strongly diverted. Meaningful jobs must also exemplify the company's goals and culture.

Elements to job design

In order to better understand job design it is helpful to define some key elements and their relationship with job design processes. A **task** can be best defined as a piece of assigned work expected to be done within a certain time. It is important to strictly and thoroughly identify tasks that need completion. In addition individuals need to be compelled, excited, and passionate to do their work. Hence, it is essential to design jobs that motivate employees. **Motivation** describes forces within the individual that account for the level, direction, and persistence of effort expended at work (Schermerhorn, Job Design Alternatives, 2006).

In job design it is necessary to identify and structure jobs in a way so that the company's resources are being efficiently used. **Resource Allocation** occurs when organizations decide to appropriate or allocate certain resources to specific jobs, tasks or dilemmas facing the organization. Jobs need to be constructed so that efficiency of the worker or department is maximized. Organizations need to use the resources and creativity of their employees effectively and efficiently. Appropriate resource allocation allows large organizations to foster and develop innovation in their workforce (Dorenbosch, van Engen, & Verhagen, 2005).

Reward systems also play a role in job design. **Reward systems** include compensation, bonuses, raises, job security, benefits, and various other methods of reward for employees. An outline or description of reward packages needs to be established while constructing jobs.

Brief history of traditional approaches to job design

Taylorism, also known as scientific management, is a foundation for management and managerial decisions. Frederick Taylor developed this theory in an effort to develop a "science" for every job within an organization (Taylorism).

Table 3: Taylorism

Taylorism principles

Create a standard method for each job.
Successfully select and hire proper workers.
Effectively train these workers
Support these workers.

Hertzberg's Motivation-Hygiene theory attempts to uncover psychological needs of employees and enhance employee satisfaction. In regards to this theory employers are encouraged to design jobs that enhance and motivate employees beyond simply meeting a daily or weekly quota. This theory highlights the importance of rewards systems and monitoring when and how employees are rewarded. Simple recognition is often enough to motivate employees and increase job satisfaction (Herzberg's Motivation-Hygiene Theory).

More effective jobs can be created when specific goals are established. **Goal setting theory** as described by Edwin Locke mainly focuses on the motivational properties of task goals (Schermerhorn, Job Design Alternatives, 2006). Task goals can be highly motivating when set and managed properly. One of the problems with goal setting theory in job design is that individuals are more strongly motivated by establishing or setting their own personal goals. If organizations set these goals for their employees the effectiveness of this technique is diminished. Moreover, individuals are often times ineffective at setting personal goals (Godwin, Neck, & Houghton, 1999). If a company wants to implement goal setting theory with regards to job design than a reasonable job criteria and description must be established.

Current approaches to job design

Technology and the flattening of the global economy have contributed greatly to the changes we now see in jobs and job content across the world. This shift is a signal for employers to meet changing job demands and expectations (McDonald & Obenchain, 2003). We now recognize that a person presented with quality meaningful work is more likely to do that work well. Because of this insight, job design now presently takes a couple of prominent forms.

The first of which is designed around the evolution from individual work to work-groups. This job design practice is called socio-technical systems (STS) approach. This approach has the following guiding principles:

- The design of the organization must fit its goals.

- Employees must be actively involved in designing the structure of the organization.

- Control of variances in production or service must be undertaken as close to their source as possible.

- Subsystems must be designed around relatively self-contained and recognizable units of work.

- Support systems must fit in with the design of the organization.

- The design should allow for a high quality of working life.

- Changes should continue to be made as necessary to meet the changing environmental pressures (Accel Team)

<u>Click here</u> to read more about soci-technial systems approach to job design.

Another modern job design theory is the Job Characteristics Model (**JCM**), which maintains five important elements that motivate workers and performance: skill variety, task identity, task significance, autonomy, and job feedback. The individual elements are then proposed to lead to positive outcomes through three psychological states: experienced meaningfulness, experienced responsibility, and the knowledge of results (Parker & Turner, 2002).

A further evolution of this theory is **Psychological Empowerment Theory** (Spreitzer, 1995). This theory posits that there is a distinction between empowering practices and cognitive motivational states. When a person is aware of the impact that they are having, they benefit more than if they cannot relate a positive impact to any of their behaviors or practices.

There are many more iterations of job design theory that have evolved from the practices of previous generations, but one general trend can be identified among them; the move towards autonomous work teams and the importance placed upon the meaning derived from the individual.

Steps to effective job design

Key to effectively crafting a meaningful job for an employee is starting the thought process by looking at the values and strategy of the organization. By framing the job in these contexts the job design process is more likely to align potential employees with the purpose of the company. Once you have this context the <u>following steps</u> will ensure both meaningful and effective job design:

1. Assess skills, needs, abilities, and motivations of employees and the organization.

2. Design the job to meet those needs, abilities and motivations.

3. Implement the new job design.

4. Audit the success of the job design and begin with step one periodically as well as when problems have been identified.

How meaningful job design can impact an organization

The goal of job design is to positively affect the performance of an organization. "It (job design) affects how well employees coordinate their work, the degree to which they are committed to the goals of the organization, the extent to which their abilities are tapped, and the extent to which their psychological and ergonomic needs are met" (Beer, Spector, Lawrence, Mills, & Walton, 1984). As this quote shows, job design is the base element for producing effective work organizations, and without meaningful job design, an organization will never operate to its potential.

Termination

By James Frasche

The termination of an employee is an uncomfortable event for all parties involved. Obviously, the employee losing his or her job will be distraught for many reasons, and in many cases the manager responsible for making the termination decision and the employee have formed a personal relationship during the employee's tenure, thereby making the manager's responsibility of "letting someone go" an undesirable one. However, there are ways that a manager can lessen the unpleasantness of the termination process.

5. Selecting and managing your team

There are many factors to take into consideration when terminating an employee. First and foremost, an employer must take into account the nature of the relationship that exists between the organization and the employee in order to assess the legality of the termination. In the United States, approximately 70 per cent of employers and employees maintain an 'at will" relationship with one another, that is, an employee may quit their job for any reason, at any time, or an employer may fire an employee for any reason, at any time. The other 30 per cent of the workforce is employed under individual employment contracts or union contracts that specify the "length of an employment relationship, how the relationship can be severed, and how the relationship can be extended" (Kulik, 2004).

An "at will" relationship may give the impression that a termination decision may never be challenged. Indeed, firing an employee "for cause" is made even easier when an "at will" relationship is present. Broadly speaking, an employer can typically fire an employee "for cause" when their behavior falls under the following categories (Falcone, 2002):

1. Policy and procedure violations

2. Substandard job performance

3. Inappropriate workplace conduct

4. Attendance/tardiness problems

However, there are some instances in which employees can be wrongfully discharged or fired for reasons that are not legitimate, typically either because they are unlawful or because they violate the terms of an employment contract (Lectric Law Library). Some of the illegitimate reasons for terminating employees include, among many others, discrimination and violations of public policy. For a more complete list of illegitimate reasons for terminating employees in the US, visit: http://smallbusiness.findlaw.com/employment-employer/employment-employer-ending/employment-employer-ending-wrongful-reasons(1).html.

There are several laws that have been enacted in the United States in order to protect employees from unfair termination in the workplace based on discrimination, the most prevalent of which are Title VII of the *Civil Rights Act of 1964*, the *Age Discrimination and Employment Act of 1967* (**ADEA**) and the *Americans with Disabilities Act of 1990* (**ADA**). Title VII, the broadest of these statutes, protects employees, applicants, and union members from termination and discrimination in the workplace based on race, color, religion, gender, and national origin, regardless of the nature of the employment relationship (at will, union, etc.) (Clarkson, 2004). For instance, if an African American or Muslim individual can prove in a court of law that he or she was fired because of race or religious preferences, that employee is entitled to both compensatory and punitive damages under Title VII. Organizations that employ 100 people or less are liable for USD 50,000 and organizations that employ 100 or more employees are liable for USD 300,000 in punitive and compensatory damages under Title VII (Clarkson, 2004). For more information on Title VII, including the claims process, bona fide occupational qualification defense, and who is protected, visit the Equal Employment Opportunity Commission's (**EEOC**) website at: http://www.eeoc.gov/policy/vii.html.

According to West's Business Law, it is quite possible that discrimination based on age is the most widespread form of discrimination, being that anyone, regardless of gender, national origin, etc. may find themselves a victim at some point in their life (Clarkson, 2004). The practice of "laying-off" older employees and hiring younger, less expensive ones in order to cut costs is a common occurrence amongst organizations that operate in the United States. Sec. 621 (Section 2) of the ADEA states, "in the face of rising productivity and affluence, older workers find themselves disadvantaged in their efforts to retain employment, and especially to regain employment when displaced from jobs". In an effort to promote employment of older persons based on their ability rather than age, Congress enacted the ADEA, which "prohibits employment discrimination on the basis of age against individuals *forty years of age* or older" (The US Equal Employment Opportunity Commission). In order for the ADEA to apply to a specific employer (under federal law), that employer must employ twenty or more people, and the employer must engage in interstate commerce.

Should a plaintiff successfully prove that age discrimination has occurred, the remedies under the ADA stipulate that the employee may be awarded back pay, attorney's fees, liquidated damages (when a willful violation has been proven), front pay (which is designed to compensate the victim for future losses), and injunctive relief (which may include reinstatement). Unlike Title VII, punitive and compensatory damages are not awarded under the ADEA (Clarkson, 2004). To view the ADEA in its entirety, visit the EEOC's website at: http://www.eeoc.gov/policy/adea.html.

According to the US Congress, 43,000,000 Americans have one or more mental or physical disabilities. In 1990, Congress enacted the *Americans with Disabilities Act*, which made it illegal for private employers, state and local governments, employment agencies, labor organizations, and labor-management committees to discriminate against individuals based on a disability (The US Equal Employment Opportunity Commission). Furthermore, the ADA was specifically enacted in order to "(1) provide a clear and comprehensive mandate for the elimination of discrimination against individuals with disabilities, (2) provide clear, strong, consistent, enforceable standards addressing discrimination against individuals with disabilities, (3) to ensure that the Federal Government plays a central role in enforcing the standards established in this Act on behalf of individuals with disabilities, and (4) to invoke the sweep of congressional authority, including the power to enforce the fourteenth amendment and to regulate commerce, in order to address the major areas of discrimination faced day-to-day by people with disabilities" (US Department of Labor).

As of 1994, the ADA is applicable to companies that employ 15 or more employees and prohibits such companies from discriminating based on a disability in all employment practices such as recruitment, pay, hiring, firing, promotion, benefits, etc. For more information on the ADA including remedies under the act and the plaintiff's burden of proof, visit the US Department of Labor's website at: http://www.dol.gov/esa/regs/statutes/ofccp/ada.htm.

Most states in the US prohibit employers from "firing an employee in violation of public policy, that is, for reasons that most people would find morally or ethically wrong such as terminating an employee for (1) refusing to commit an illegal act such as refusing to falsify insurance claims or lie to government auditors (2) complaining about an employer's illegal conduct such as the employer's failure to pay minimum wage, or (3) exercising a legal right such as voting or taking family leave" (FindLaw.com).

The manner in which an organization terminates an employee can send a powerful message to the organization's remaining staff (Heathfield, How to Fire an Employee). Managers must be aware that seemingly unfair or harsh terminations may cause some of the organizations best workers to become less effective or seek new employment for fear of the same treatment. In some cases, it is appropriate for managers to engage in progressive discipline before terminating an under performing employee. Progressive discipline is "a process for dealing with job-related behavior that does not meet expected and communicated performance standards. The primary purpose for progressive discipline is to assist the employee to understand that a performance problem or opportunity for improvement exists" (Heathfield, Discipline (Progressive Discipline)). By attempting to assist an employee in fixing any problems that they are experiencing in the workplace before terminating them, the organization communicates a strong commitment to its employees, which can go a long way in regards to retention, turnover, and other areas of concern.

Should the decision be made to move forward with the termination process after all other options have been exhausted, it is important for managers to know how, when, and where to break the news to the employee. Supervising managers should generally be responsible for terminating an employee, and it is generally improper to pass this responsibility off to upper management or to the human resources department. Most managers postpone telling an employee about their termination until the end of the week. However, this may be a grave mistake, as the employee will have the entire weekend to complain about their treatment to their coworkers and friends, thereby tarnishing the reputation of the organization. An alternative is for managers to break the news of termination to employees at the beginning of the week. This will give the employee time to "cool off" and think about their next move before they have the opportunity to socially interact with former coworkers during the weekend (Kulik, 2004).

The termination interview is an important aspect of the exit process. The following are guidelines for the termination interview provided by the experts at Hay Associates as seen in Framework for Human Resource Management.

- *Plan the interview carefully.*
    - Make sure the employee keeps the appointment time.
    - Never inform an employee over the phone.
    - Allow 10 minutes as sufficient time for the interview.
    - Use a neutral site, never your own office.
    - Have employee agreements, the human resources file, and a release announcement (internal and external) prepared in advance.
    - Be available at a time after the interview in case questions or problems arise.
    - Have phone numbers ready for medical or security emergencies.
- *Get to the point.* As soon as the employee enters the meeting, give the person a moment to get comfortable and then inform him or her of your decision.
- *Describe the situation.* Briefly explain why the person is being fired. Remember to describe the situation rather than attack the employee personally.

- *Listen*. Continue the interview until the person appears to be talking freely and reasonably calmly about the reasons for termination.

- *Review all elements of the severance package*. Describe severance payments, benefits, access to office support people, and the way references will be handled. However, under no conditions should any promises or benefits beyond those already in the support package be implied.

- *Identify the next step*. The terminated employee may be disoriented and unsure of what to do next. Explain where the employee should go next, upon leaving the interview.

Note: The above is a brief summary of some of the issues surrounding the termination process in the United States and, due to space constraints, in no way takes into account all of the factors that managers should consider while terminating an employee. Readers are encouraged to explore the outside reference material noted above as well as other literature that will provide more insight into the termination process, as well as consulting with appropriate legal counsel.

Downsizing

By Logan Price

The goal of any company is to supply a product or service that customers are willing to pay for. If a company provides a good that consumers are willing to pay a lot of money for, the company will similarly earn a lot of money. As long as the amount of money the company brings in is more than the amount they spend to make the good the company will profit and grow. To fuel this growth companies must invest in additional resources and must increase its number of workers. During times of growth few employees are laid off and the company is making money.

However, a company's product or service may no longer be desired by consumers over time. Some reasons this might occur are because the good has gone out of date or a competitor may have created a better product or may offer a better service. Loss of demand happens all the time in a competitive business environment. With so many companies trying to sell their products or services it becomes essential for companies to continually improve upon existing offerings so they do not fall behind competitors. But companies do fall behind, and as a result growth and profits quickly turn to layoffs and losses. Sometimes losses are so bad that the company cannot survive and simply closes down. Other times the lost revenue is not enough to shut down the company. In this instance the company cuts some resources and workers in order to survive the downturn in business. When companies decide to do this it is called **downsizing**.

To downsize, as defined by the Merriam-Webster Dictionary, is "to fire (employees) for the purpose of <u>downsizing</u> a business". The reasons for downsizing businesses vary, but the main reason for doing this is because the product(s) or service(s) that the company offers is not as successful as it once was. As a result revenues decrease, and expenses (costs like materials and employees) must be cut to counter the lost revenue. Obviously, employees do not like it when they get laid off. However, downsizing is something that neither the company nor the employees want to see happen. Since both sides suffer (the company loses money and the worker loses a job) downsizing is often not met with strong resistance from employees. One reason for this lack of resistance is that employees understand that they are not being fired for doing a bad job. Employees tend to be more understanding if a company is forced to reduce its labor force. Also, the employees that are laid off during a downturn are normally the first ones to be rehired if business picks back up. Business will always have companies that are growing and companies that are dying, and downsizing and layoffs are a natural part of that cycle. Since downsizing is a normal part of business it can often be seen as necessary and reasonable.

There is one other main reason why companies would downsize. If a company observes that they could be getting the same amount of output from fewer workers it makes economic sense to let the excess workers go. As an example, imagine a job that it would take three workers an hour to do. Now, if a fourth worker was added the job area would get crowded so everyone worked slowly and it took the four of them over an hour to complete. Clearly, the fourth worker is not adding value to the job and the company should downsize by firing the fourth worker. This practice is somewhat common, as most businesses continually review their processes to look for areas of the business that could run more efficiently with fewer expenses. For example, by evaluating and changing a manufacturing process could be streamlined resulting in reduced labor, material, and/or time costs while producing the same output.

In order to continue growth and avoid the need for downsizing, products and services must constantly be made better, cheaper, and/or faster than what is being offered by the competition. A company that does this successfully will enjoy increased revenues and most likely growth. Companies that fail to offer products and services that are better, cheaper, and/or faster than their competition will not succeed. Companies are constantly battling with each other for market share, and downsizing and growth are two results of how effectively companies create demand for their good.

HR Metrics

By Ronald Tam

For any company that is implementing new human resource programs or adjusting existing ones, these changes can quickly become a substantial company project. The roles of human resource programs are to manage the employees of companies to increase the **human capital** in a company. However, the specific goals or strategies that HR seeks to achieve may be different for each company or situation. Therefore, there is no set standard for measuring the success of HR.

"The business world is dominated by people who look at metrics, and the HR world needs to play in that space... if you can measure manufacturing efficiency with Six Sigma, why not use similar analytics to measure human capital performance" (Grossman, 2006). It is suggested that the business world is focused on metrics in determining success. Similar approaches must be taken to value HR in order for it to be widely accepted, "but were the HR policies and practices really worth the time and effort? HR thought so, based on overall company performance. But Poses, who also had served as a financial analyst at AlliedSignal, wanted more. He wanted substantive proof, validation that his HR investments were paying off" (Grossman, 2006). This is the most common view of companies when it comes to HR, so the metrics sought out here is a financial measure.

The first approach to HR metrics would be the approach in measuring the financial success of the company as a result of the HR implementations. Evaluations can be viewed as company projects or investments in this case. The first measurement is just a simple ratio of change in profits due to new HR divided by cost of the new HR. This measure will give an idea of how well the new changes paid off relative to how much was spent on it. Another measure is payback period, "The payback period of an investment is the period of time required for the cumulative cash inflows (net cash flows) from a project to equal the initial cash outlay (net investment)" (Moyer, McGuigan, & Kretlow, 2006). The payback period is measured by the net investment divided by the annual cash inflows as a result of that investment; this measure will give a company an idea of how long it takes the project to earn by its cost. The final measure for financial metrics of HR is a net present value, "The net present value of a capital expenditure project is defined as the present value of the stream of net (operating) cash flows from the projects minus the project's net investment" (Moyer, McGuigan, & Kretlow, 2006). This is done by taking the present value of all future expected cash flows from the HR change and subtracting it from the cost of the project. This will put the value of the HR project in monetary terms like any other investment for the company. These are all measures that can be used to express the HR program or changes in terms of a relationship between its financial returns and costs. There are no specific standards for determining whether an HR project was a good investment or not, but the company should relate their results with industry results or historic results.

The other approach to HR metrics is more towards operations aspect of the company. "The old HR measures, such as head count, the cost of compensation and benefits, time to fill, and turnover, no longer cut it in this new world of accountability. They don't go far enough to create shareholder value and align people decisions with corporate objectives" (Schneider, 2006). Since the purpose of HR is to improve an operational aspect of the company, it should also be measured in that context. "Many companies are forging ahead on efforts to create a new set of metrics that the traditional HR functions like recruiting, training, and performance review [relate] to overall corporate goals" (Schneider, 2006). Measurements here can include a variety of traditional measurements such as employee turnover, average stay of employees, efficiency of employees, etc. These measures all affect the operation aspects of a company and are standardized information currently. A new measure that can be introduced is the measurement of human capital; "human-capital metrics can provide meaningful correlations that help predict behavior and human-capital investment demands well ahead of the annual budget". Another new HR metric can be directly related to the operational aspects of the company. "HR metrics might measure efficiency, or the time and cost of activities; human-capital metrics measure the effectiveness of such activities. Time to fill becomes time to productivity; turnover rate becomes turnover quality; training costs become training return on investment" (Schneider, 2006). The take from non-financial HR metrics is that there is no limit to any measurements or techniques. They can range from something simple and standard such as employee turnover to something creative that measures the effects of human capital increases, customer satisfaction increases, etc.

Human resources should be treated like any other projects that a company can undertake. It can be measured both with financial results or operational results. The financial results are measures to compare the cost against the return from HR. The operational measure can look at standards or more complex and creative measures. Ultimately HR metrics are valued and judged against the goals or strategies of the company and how well they are aligned with the results. Therefore, a company should not limit themselves on how they are evaluating their HR success and build techniques around how they feel they feel they should value it.

Discussion questions

> Provide three reasons for a company to implement a high-commitment work system.

> Name and describe three examples of mechanisms a company could use to increase employee participation.

5. Selecting and managing your team

> ➤ Discuss the four different categories of diversity. Give one reason why each would be important to a company.

> ➤ Discuss the pros and cons of internal and external recruiting. Which one do you prefer, and why?

> ➤ Should tests be used to select employees? Why? Why not?

> ➤ What are the primary benefits of training employees?

> ➤ What is the relationship between career development systems and employee retention?

> ➤ Identify the critical parts of an effective performance appraisal.

> ➤ Provide two lessons for giving, and for receiving, feedback effectively.

> ➤ Define internal and external equity in establishing a base pay system.

> ➤ Provide three reasons to provide employees compensation in the form of benefits.

> ➤ Name and describe two examples of each: short-term incentives and long-term incentives.

> ➤ Name the five characteristics of the JCM approach to job design, and provide an example of each.

> ➤ What are the four main reasons why an employee is terminated?

> ➤ How can a company avoid downsizing?

> ➤ Identify two ways to measure the effectiveness of your Human Resource Management policies.

Exercise

1. Read the description of SAS Institute in the section on Employee Benefits. Do some research on SAS Institute. Based on the description and your research, be prepared to debate the following issue:

Is SAS smart to provide these abundant benefits to its employees, or, are they spending too much money on their employees?

References

Accel Team. (n.d.). *Job Design*. Retrieved May 17, 2007, from Accel Team: http://www.accel-team.com/work_design/wd_03.html

Adams, S. (2002). *Dilbert*. Retrieved May 18, 2007, from http://pag.csail.mit.edu/~adonovan/dilbert/show.php?day=17&month=03&year=2002

Allen, D., & Allen, D. (2004). *Formula 2+2*. San Francisco: Berrett-Koehler Publishers, Inc.

Asheghian, P., & Ebrahimi, B. (2005). *Global Business: Environments, Strategies, and Operations*. San Bernardino, CA: Globe Academic Press.

Atwater, L., Roush, P., & Fischthal, A. (1995). The Influence of Upward Feedback on Self and Follower Ratings of Leadership. *Personnel Psychology*, 35-59.

Bacal, R. (1999). *Ten Stupid Things Managers Do to Screw Up Performance Appraisal*. Retrieved May 18, 2007, from Work911.com: http://www.work911.com/performance/particles/stupman.htm

Baruch, Y. (2004). Transforming Careers from Linear to Multidirectional Career Paths. *Career Development International*, 58-73.

Baugh, S., & Sullivan, S. (2005). Mentoring and Career Development. *Career Development International*, 425-428.

Becker, B., & Huselid, M. (2001). The Strategic Impact of HR.

Beer, M., Spector, B., Lawrence, P., Mills, D., & Walton, R. (1984). *Managing Human Assets.* New York: The Free Press.

Blanchard, K. (1996). Feedback Facts. *Incentive* , 59.

Canadian Centre for Occupational Health & Safety. (2002). *What is "Job Design?".* Retrieved May 17, 2007, from CCOHS: http://www.ccohs.ca/oshanswers/hsprograms/job_design.html

Case, J. (1997). What Can You Learn from Open-Book Management? *Harvard Management*, 3-5.

Center for Advanced Human Resource Studies. (1999). Waging the War for Talent. *HR Spectrum*, 1-4.

Central Parking Corporation. (2004). *Communication Policy.* Retrieved May 17, 2007, from Central Parking: http://www.parking.com/people/communicationpolicy.aspx

Centrelink. (n.d.). *Centrelink.* Retrieved May 2007, from Centrelink: http://www.centrelink.gov.au/

Clarkson, K. (2004). *West's Business Law.* Mason: Thompson Learning.

Craumer, M. (2001). How to Coach Your Employees. *Harvard Management Communication Letter* .

Creating Situational Interviews and Rating Scales. (n.d.). Retrieved May 15, 2007, from http://www.hrtoolkit.gov.bc.ca/staffing/staffing_steps/assess_methods/oral_interviews/situational_sa mples.htm

Dataquest. (2006). *The Top 10: 1-TCS: A Giant on Top.* Retrieved May 3, 2007, from Dataquest: http://dqindia.ciol.commakesections.asp/06090619.asp

Dessler, G. (2004). *Framework for Human Resource Management.* Upper Saddle River: Pearson Prentice Hall.

Dorenbosch, L., van Engen, M., & Verhagen, M. (2005). On-the-Job Innovation: The Impact of Job Design and Human Resource Management Through Production Ownership. In *Creativity and Innovation Management* (pp. 129-141). Blackwell Publishing Limited.

Duening, T., & Ivancevich, J. (2003). *Managing Organizations.* Cincinnati, OH: Atomic Dog Publishing.

Employee Benefit. (n.d.). Retrieved May 2007, from Wikipedia: http://en.wikipedia.org/wiki/Employee_benefit

Employee Benefits Definition. (n.d.). Retrieved 2007, from BusinessDictionary.com: http://www.businessdictionary.com/definition/employee-benefits.html

Employee Benefits Magazine. (n.d.). Retrieved May 2007, from http://www.employeebenefits.co.uk/

5. Selecting and managing your team

Employee Recruitment: How to Hire the Right People. (1999). Retrieved 14 2007, May, from http://www.truckstoptravelplaza.com

Employment Case Law Headlines. (n.d.). Retrieved May 19, 2007, from EEO News: http://www.eeonews.com/news/adea/index.html

Falcone, P. (2002). *The Hiring and Firing Question and Answer Book.* New York: AMACOM.

FindLaw.com. (n.d.). *Illegal Reasons for Firing Employees.* Retrieved May 18, 2007, from FindLaw: http://smallbusiness.findlaw.com/employment-employer/employment-employer-ending/

Free Sample Behavioral Interview Questions. (n.d.). Retrieved May 15, 2007, from QuintCareers.com: http://www.quintcareers.com/sample_behavioral.html

Friedman, T. (2006). *The World is Flat.* New York: Farrar, Straus, and Giroux.

Fukami, C. (2007, May 1). Performance Appraisal. *Lecture.* Denver, CO, USA: University of Denver; Daniels College of Business.

Fukami, C. (2007). Reward Systems. *Lecture.* Denver, CO, USA: University of Denver; Daniels College of Business.

Fukami, C. (2007, April). Strategic Human Resources: Training. *Class Lectures.* Denver, CO, USA: University of Denver—Daniels College of Business.

Garvin, D., & Roberto, M. (2001). What You Don't Know About Making Decisions. *Harvard Business Review.*

Ghemawat, P. (2007). Managing Differences; The Central Challenge of Global Strategy. *Harvard Business Review,* 59-68.

Godwin, J., Neck, C., & Houghton, J. (1999). The Impact of Thought Self-Leadership on Individual Goal Performance. *Journal of Management Development, 18,* 153-170.

Golan, P. (2003). All Talk But No Voice: Employee Voice at the Eurotunnel Call Centre. *Economic and Industrial Democracy,* 509-541.

Graham, S. (2006). *Diversity: Leaders not Labels.* New York: Free Press.

Grossman, R. (2006, December). Measuring the Value of H. *HR Magazine,* pp. 44-49.

Hathaway, P. (n.d.). *Powerful Communication Skills that Get Results!* Retrieved May 21, 2007, from http://www.thechangeagent.com/communication.html

Heathfield, S. (n.d.). *Discipline (Progressive Discipline).* Retrieved May 18, 2007, from About.com: http://humanresources.about.com/od/discipline/a/discipline.htm

Heathfield, S. (n.d.). *How to Fire an Employee.* Retrieved May 18, 2007, from About.com: http://humanresources.about.com/od/discipline/a/fire_employee.htm

Heathfield, S. (n.d.). *How to Receive Feedback with Grace and Dignity.* Retrieved May 16, 2007, from About.com: http://humanresources.about.com/cs/communication/ht/receivefeedback.htm

Heathfield, S. (n.d.). *Performance Appraisals Don't Work.* Retrieved May 21, 2007, from About.com: http://humanresources.about.com/od/performanceevals/a/perf_appraisal.htm

Heathfield, S. (n.d.). *Performance Management is NOT an Annual Appraisal.* Retrieved May 21, 2007, from About.com: http://humanresources.about.com/od/performanceevals/a/perf_appraisal.htm

Heathfield, S. (n.d.). *Recruiting Stars: Top Ten Ideas for Recruiting Great Candidates.* Retrieved from About.com: http://humanresources.about.com

Heathfield, S. (n.d.). *Use the Web for Recruiting: Recruiting Online.* Retrieved from About.com: http://humanresources.about.com

Herzberg's Motivation-Hygiene Theory. (n.d.). Retrieved May 2007, from ChangingMinds.org: http://instruct1.cit.cornell.edu/courses/dea453_653/ideabook1/thompson_jones/Taylorism.htm

Hobman, E., Bordia, P., & Gallois, C. (2003). Consequences of Feeling Dissimlar from Others in a Work Team. *Journal of Business and Psychology,* 301-325.

Human Resources. (n.d.). Retrieved April 15, 2007, from Wikipedia: http://en.wikipedia.org

Hymowitz, C. (2007, March 20). *When Managers Neglect to Coach Their Talent.* Retrieved May 3, 2007, from The Wall Street Journal Online: http://www.careerjournal.com/columnists/inthelead/20070320-inthelead.html

Internal Revenue Service. (n.d.). *What are Employment Taxes?* Retrieved May 2007, from Internal Revenue Service: http://www.irs.gov/businesses/small/article/0,,id=98858,00.html

Janz, T. (1982). Initial Comparisons of Patterned Behavior Description Interviews Versus Unstructured Interviews. *Journal of Applied Psychology,* 577-580.

Jones, D. (1997). Employees as Stakeholders. *Business Strategy Review,* 21-24.

Jossey and Bass. (1995). *Feedback About Feedback.* Retrieved May 21, 2007, from http://home.att.net/~nickols/feedback.htm

Kaye, B., & Vultaggio, P. (2004). *The Development-Minded Manager.* Retrieved May 3, 2007, from http://www.careersystemsintl.com/Word per cent20Files/The per cent20Development-Minded per cent20Manager.doc

Kerr, S. (1995). An Academy Classic: On the Folly of Rewarding A, While Hoping for B. *Acadmy of Management Executives,* 7-14.

King, J. (n.d.). *Receiving Feedback Gracefully is a Critical Career Skill.* Retrieved May 16, 2007, from http://www.sideroad.com/Career_Advice/receiving-feedback.html

Komisar, R. (2000). Goodbye Career, Hello Success. *Harvard Business Review,* 160-174.

Kram, K. (1985). *Mentoring at Work: Developmental Relationships in Organizational Life.* Glenview, IL: Scott, Foresman.

5. Selecting and managing your team

Kulik, C. (2004). *Human Resources for the Non-HR Manager*. New Jersey: Lawrence Erlbaum Associates, Inc.

Lashinsky, A. (2007, January 29). Google's Employment Roster. *Fortune* .

Latham, G., & Saari, L. (1984). Do People Do What They Say? More Studies of the Situational Interview. *Journal of Applied Psychology*, 569-573.

Lectric Law Library. (n.d.). Retrieved May 21, 2007, from Lectric Law Library: http://www.lectlaw.com/def2/w025.htm

Lockwood, N. (2005). Workplace Diversity: Leveraging the Power of Difference for Competitive Advantage. *HR Magazine* .

Management by Objectives—SMART. (2007, May 1). Retrieved May 18, 2007, from Values Based Management: http://www.valuebasedmanagement.net/methods_smart_management_by_objectives.html

Marken, G. (2004). *Collaboration: Managers Who Share Power, Have More Power*. Retrieved 18 2007, May, from Enterprise Networks and SErvers: http://www.enterprisenetworksandservers.com/monthly/art.php?694

Marshall, T. (2002). Leadership Development for Small Organizations. *T+D*, 52-55.

McDonald, G., & Obenchain, K. (2003). How does information technology affect communication, decision making, job design, and power within an organization? In D. Laube, & R. Zammuto, *Business Driven Information Technology: Answers to 100 Critical Questions for Every Manager*. Stanford: Stanford Business Books.

McGann, R. (2004). *Online Job Sites Overshadow Newspaper Classifieds*. Retrieved May 14, 2007, from Clickz.com: http://www.clickz.com

McGill, & Beatty. (1994). *Action Learning: A Practitioner's Guide*. London: Kogan.

Meister, M. (n.d.). *How to Give Feedback*. Retrieved May 21, 2007, from FastCompany: http://www.fastcompany.com/magazine/80/sgodin.html

Michaels, E., Handfield-Jones, H., & Axelrod, B. (2001). *The War for Talent*. Boston: Harvard Business School Press.

Moyer, . R., McGuigan, J., & Kretlow, W. (2006). *Financial Management*. Thompson South-Western.

Olson, D. (2003, April 22). *Stakeholder*. Retrieved May 17, 2007, from Six Sigma: http://www.isixsigma.com/dictionary/Stakeholder-127.htm

O'Reilly, C., & Pfeffer, J. *Southwest Airlines: Using Human Resources for Competitive Advantage*. Stanford University Graduate School of Buiness.

Parker, S., & Turner, N. (2002). Organizational Design and Organizational Development as Preconditions for Good Job Design and High Job Performance. In S. Sonnentag, *Psychological Management of Individual Performance*. Indianapolis: John Wiley & Sons, LTD.

Peterson, R. (2005, April 21). *Who Speaks For Employees? It's Certainly Not Management*. Retrieved May 19, 2007, from The Seattle Times: http://seattletimes.nwsource.com/html/opinion/2002247724_peterson21.html

Pfeffer, J. (2000). Six Dangerous Myths About Pay. *Harvard Business Review* .

Pfeffer, J., & Viega, J. (1998). *Putting People First for Organizational Success.*

Recruitment. (n.d.). Retrieved May 15, 2007, from Wikipedia: http://en.wikipedia.org/wiki/Recruitment

Reilly, R., Smither, J., & Vasilopoulos, N. (1996). A Longitudinal Study of Upward Feedback. *Personnel Psychology* , 599-612.

Rich, P. (n.d.). *Giving and Receiving Feedback*. Retrieved May 21, 2007, from http://www.selfhelpmagazine.com/articles/growth/feedback.html

Ritberger, C. (2007). Tips on Managing the Differences Among Payroll Staff. *Payroll Manager's Report*, pp. 11-14.

SAS. (n.d.). *Careers*. Retrieved May 2007, from SAS: http://www.sas.com/jobs/corporate/index.html

Schaefer, P. (n.d.). *How to Avoid Hiring Failures: Assess Interpersonal Skills and Motivation Levels*. Retrieved May 15, 2007, from http://www.businessknowhow.com/manage/hiring-failure.htm

Schermerhorn, J. (2006). Job Design Alternatives. In S. Elbe, *Personal Management 8th Edition*. Hoboken: John Wiley and Sons, Inc.

Schermerhorn, J. (1993). *Taylorism?* Retrieved May 19, 2007, from Management for Productivity: http://instruct1.cit.cornell.edu/courses/dea453_653/ideabook1/thompson_jones/Taylorism.htm

Schneider, C. (2006, February). The New Human-Capital Metrics. *CFO*, pp. 22-27.

Schweyer, A. (2006). *An Internal War for Talent*. Retrieved May 3, 2007, from Inc: http://www.inc.com/resources/recruiting/articles/20050401/talentwars.html

Shim, J., Siegel, J., & Simon, A. (2004). *The Vest Pocket MBA*. London: Penguin Books.

SHPS. (n.d.). *Program Information*. Retrieved May 2007, from FSAFEDS: https://www.fsafeds.com/fsafeds/literature.asp

Smith, G. (n.d.). *How to Interview and Hire Top People Each and Every Time*. Retrieved May 15, 2007, from Business Knowhow.com: http://www.businessknowhow.com/manage/hiretop.htm

Smith, S., & Mazin, R. (2004). *The HR Answer Book*. New York: Division of American Management.

Solnik, C. (2006, April 14). *Employee Input is Key to Improving Workplace*. Retrieved May 17, 2007, from Long Island Business News: http://findarticles.com/p/articles/mi_qn4189/is_20060414/ai_n16167375

5. Selecting and managing your team

Spreitzer, G. (1995). Psychological Empowerment in the Workplace: Dimensions, Measurement, and Validation. *Academy of Managment Journal , 38*, 1442-1465.

Srohm, O. (2002). Organizational Design and Organizational Development as Preconditions for Good Job Design and High Job Performance. In S. Sonnentag, *Psychological Management of Individual Performance*. Indianapolis: John Wiley & Sons, LTD.

Survey Monkey. (2007). *Survey Monkey*. Retrieved May 21, 2007, from http://www.surveymonkey.com

Taylorism. (n.d.). Retrieved May 2007, from Cornell University: http://instruct1.cit.cornell.edu/courses/dea453_653/ideabook1/thompson_jones/Taylorism.htm

The U.S. Equal Employment Opportunity Commission. (n.d.). *The ADA: Your Responsibilities as an Employer*. Retrieved May 19, 2007, from EEOC: http://www.eeoc.gov/facts/ada17.html

Thomas, D., & Ely, R. (1996). Making Differences Matter; A New Paradigm for Managing Diversity. *Harvard Business Review*, 1-13.

Thomas, R. J. (20014). *Harvard Business Review on Managing Diversity*. Boston: Harvard Business School Publishing Corporation.

Tips for Creating an Effective Online Job Posting. (n.d.). Retrieved April 17, 2007, from http://yourhrexperts.com

Training and Development. (2007). Retrieved May 19, 2007, from Wikipedia: http://en.wikipedia.org/wiki/Training_ per cent26_Development

U.S. Department of Justice. (n.d.). *ADA Home Page*. Retrieved October 18, 2006, from http://www.usdoj.gov/crt/ada/adahom1.htm

U.S. Department of Labor. (n.d.). *The Americans With Disabilities Act of 1990*. Retrieved October 15, 2006, from The American's With Disabilities Act of 1990

United States Department of the Interior. (2004). *Performance Appraisal Handbook*. Retrieved from http://www.doi.gov/hrm/guidance/370dm430hndbk.pdf

Wilson, T. (2000, Fall). What's Hot and What's Not: Key Trends in Total Compensation. *Wilson Group Newsletter*.

6. Marketing on a global scale

Editor: Dr John Burnett (Daniels College of Business, University of Denver, USA)

Reviewer: Dr Asit Sarkar (University of Saskatchewan, Canada)

Learning objectives

As you read this chapter, you should develop an understanding of the following key marketing concepts:

- the important role marketing can play in the success of an organization

- the various kinds of marketing

- the strategic workings of marketing components

- understand the various bases for market segmentation

- understand the role of marketing research

- understand the behavior of the individual consumer in the marketplace

- understand the primary tools available to marketers and how they are used

Defining marketing

Noted Harvard Professor of Business Theodore Levitt, states that the purpose of all business is to "find and keep customers". Furthermore, the only way you can achieve this objective is to create a competitive advantage. That is, you must convince buyers (potential customers) that what you have to offer them comes closest to meeting their particular need or want at that point in time. Hopefully, you will be able to provide this advantage consistently, so that eventually the customer will no longer consider other alternatives and will purchase your product out of habit. This loyal behavior is exhibited by people in the US who drive only Fords, brush their teeth only with Crest, buy only Dell computers, and have their plumbing fixed only by "Samson Plumbing—On Call 24 hours, 7 days a week". Creating this blind commitment—without consideration of alternatives—to a particular brand, store, person, or idea is the dream of all businesses. It is unlikely to occur, however, without the support of an effective marketing program. In fact, the specific role of marketing is *to provide assistance in identifying, satisfying, and retaining customers.*

While the general tasks of marketing are somewhat straightforward, attaching an acceptable definition to the concept has been difficult. A textbook writer once noted, "Marketing is not easy to define. No one has yet been able to formulate a clear, concise definition that finds universal acceptance". Yet a definition of some sort is necessary if we are to layout the boundaries of what is properly to be considered "marketing". How do marketing activities differ from non-marketing activities? What activities should one refer to as marketing activities? What institutions should one refer to as marketing institutions?

Marketing is advertising to advertising agencies, events to event marketers, knocking on doors to salespeople, direct mail to direct mailers. In other words, to a person with a hammer, everything looks like a nail. In reality, marketing is a way of thinking about business, rather than a bundle of techniques. It is much more than just selling stuff and collecting money. It is the connection between people and products, customers and companies. Like organic tissue, this kind of connection—or relationship—is always growing or dying. It can never be in a steady state. And like tissue paper, this kind of connection is fragile. Customer relationships, even long—standing ones, are contingent on the last thing that happened.

Tracing the evolution of the various definitions of marketing proposed during the last thirty years reveals two trends: (1) expansion of the application of marketing to non-profit and non-business institutions; e.g. charities, education, or health care; and (2) expansion of the responsibilities of marketing beyond the personal survival of the individual firm, to include the betterment of society as a whole. These two factors are reflected in the official American Marketing Association definition published in 1988.

"Marketing is the process of planning and executing the conception. pricing, promotion, and distribution of ideas, goods, and services to create exchanges that satisfy individual (customer) and organizational objectives." 1

While this definition can help us better comprehend the parameters of marketing, it does not provide a full picture. Definitions of marketing cannot flesh out specific transactions and other relationships among these elements. The following propositions are offered to supplement this definition and better position marketing within the firm.

1. The overall directive for any organization is the mission statement or some equivalent statement of organizational goals. It reflects the inherent business philosophy of the organization.

2. Every organization has a set of functional areas (e.g. accounting, production, finance, data processing, marketing) in which tasks that are necessary for the success of the organization are performed. These functional areas must be managed if they are to achieve maximum performance.

3. Every functional area is guided by a philosophy (derived from the mission statement or company goals) that governs its approach toward its ultimate set of tasks.

4. Marketing differs from the other functional areas in that its primary concern is with exchanges that take place in markets, outside the organization (called a *transaction*).

5. Marketing is most successful when the philosophy, tasks, and manner of implementing available technology are coordinated and complementary.

The role of marketing in the firm: a basis for classification

Marketing is an individualized and highly creative process. Despite the availability of high-powered computers and sophisticated software capable of analyzing massive amounts of data, marketing is still more of an art rather than a science. Each business must customize its marketing efforts in response to its environment and the exchange process. Consequently, no two marketing strategies are exactly the same.

This requirement of marketing to play slightly different roles, depending upon some set of situational criteria, has in turn provided us with a division of marketing into a number of different categories. This is not to imply, however, that there are not general marketing principles that work in most businesses—there are. There is a right and wrong way to design a package. There are certain advertising strategies that tend to work more often than others. Rather, we are saying that because of certain factors, a business's approach toward marketing and the ensuing strategy will require some modification from the basic plan.

Shown in Table 4 are the most common types of marketing categories. Since these various types of marketing will be discussed throughout this text, a brief introduction is provided at this point.

Macromarketing versus micromarketing

The division of marketing into macromarketing and micromarketing is a fairly recent one. Initially, the division was a result of the controversy concerning the responsibility of marketing. Should marketing be limited to the success of the individual firm, or should marketing consider the economic welfare of a whole society? Accepting the later, or "macro", point of view dramatically changes the way marketing is carried out. In this light, every marketing decision must be evaluated with regard to how it might positively or negatively affect each person and institution operating in that society. In 1982, Bunt and Burnett surveyed the academic community in order to define more precisely the distinction between macro- and mircomarketing.4 Their findings suggest that the separation depends upon "what is being studied", "whether it is being viewed from the perspective of society or the firm", and "who receives the consequences of the activity". Examples of macromarketing activities are studying the marketing systems of different nations, the consequences on society of certain marketing actions, and the impact of certain technologies on the marketing transaction.

The use of scanners in supermarkets and automatic teller machines in banking illustrates the last example. Micromarketing examples include determining how Nikon Steel should segment its market, recommending how Denver Colorado's National Jewish Hospital in the US should price their products, and evaluating the success of the US "Just Say No" anti-drug campaign.

Service marketing versus goods marketing

The distinction between services and goods products is not always clear-cut. In general, service products tend to be intangible, are often consumed as they are produced, are difficult to standardize because they require human labor, and may require the customer to participate in the creation of the service product.

Goods products tend to be just the opposite in terms of these criteria. Consequently, marketers of service products usually employ a marketing strategy quite different from that of goods marketers. For example, a local family physician creates tangibility by providing an environment: waiting room examination rooms, diplomas on the walls, that convinces patients that they are receiving good health care. Conversely, coffee producers create intangibility in order to appear different from competitors. This is done through colorful packaging and advertisements showing people who are successful because they start each day with a cup or two or ten of Starbuck's coffee.

Table 4: Kinds of marketing

Classification	Example	Factors
Macromarketing	The devaluation of the yen	Emphasis of study
Micromarketing	A pricing strategy for Wal-Mart	Perspective, receiver of consequences
Goods Marketing	Nabisco International	Tangibility, standardization, storage, production, involvement
Service marketing	Chase Manhattan Bank	
For-profit marketing	Otis Elevator	Concerns for profits
Nonprofit marketing	New York Museum of Art	Tax status
Mass marketing	Sony	Nature of contact
Direct marketing	Time Magazine	Information
Internet marketing	trip.com	Process for purchasing and delivery
Local marketing	Imperial Garden Restaurant	Proximity of customers
Regional marketing	Olympia Brewery	Geographic area
National marketing	American Red Cross	Extent of distribution
International marketing	Ford Motor Company	Network, marketing
Global marketing	Qwest	variation commitment to country
Consumer goods marketing	Kraft Foods	Nature of consumer
Business-to-business marketing	IBM	Product function

For-profit marketing versus nonprofit marketing

As the terms connote, the difference between for-profit and nonprofit marketing is in their primary objective. For-profit marketers measure success in terms of profitability and their ability to pay dividends or pay back loans. Continued existence is contingent upon level of profits.

Nonprofit institutions exist to benefit a society, regardless of whether profits are achieved. Because of the implicit objectives assigned to non-profits, they are subject to an entirely different additional set of laws, notably tax laws. While they are allowed to generate profits, they must use these monies in specific way in order to maintain their non-profit status. There are several other factors that require adjustments to be made in the marketing strategies for nonprofits.

Mass marketing, direct marketing, and Internet marketing

Mass marketing is distinguished from direct marketing in terms of the distance between the manufacturer and the ultimate user of the product. Mass marketing is characterized as having wide separation and indirect communication. A mass marketer, such as Nike, has very little direct contact with its customers and must distribute its product through various retail outlets alongside its competitors. Communication is impersonal, as evidenced by its national television and print advertising campaigns, couponing, and point-of-purchase displays. The success of mass marketing is contingent on the probability that within the huge audience exposed to the marketing strategy there exist sufficient potential customers interested in the product to make the strategy worthwhile.

Direct marketing establishes a somewhat personal relationship with the customer by first allowing the customer to purchase the product directly from the manufacturer and then communicating with the customer on a first-name basis. This type of marketing is experiencing tremendous growth. Apparently, marketers have tired of the waste associated with mass marketing and customers want more personal attention. Also, modern mechanisms for collecting and processing accurate mailing lists have greatly increased the effectiveness of direct marketing. Catalogue companies (Spiegel, J.C. Penney), telecommunications companies (Sprint), and direct mail companies (Publishers Clearing House) are example of direct marketers. A modified type of direct marketing is represented by companies that allow ordering of product by calling a toll-free number or mailing in an order card as part of an advertisement.

Although (officially), Internet marketing is a type of direct marketing, it has evolved so quickly and demanded the attention of so many companies that a separate section here is warranted. Essentially, Internet technology (which changes by the moment) has created a new way of doing business. In the Internet age, the way consumers evaluate and follow through on their purchase decisions has changed significantly. "Call now!" is no longer an effective pitch. Consumers have control over how, when, and where they shop on the Internet. The Internet has all but eliminated the urgency of satisfying the need when the opportunity is presented.

Local, regional, national, international, and global marketers

As one would expect, the size and location of a company's market varies greatly. Local marketers are concerned with customers that tend to be clustered tightly around the marketer. The marketer is able to learn a great deal about the customer and make necessary changes quickly. Naturally, the total potential market is limited. There is also the possibility that a new competitor or environmental factor will put a local marketer out of business.

Regional marketers cover a larger geographic area that may necessitate multiple production plants and a more complex distribution network. While regional marketers tend to serve adjoining cities, parts of states, or entire states, dramatic differences in demand may still exist, requiring extensive adjustments in marketing strategy.

National marketers distribute their product throughout a country. This may involve multiple manufacturing plants, a distribution system including warehouses and privately owned delivery vehicles, and different versions of the marketing "mix" or overall strategy. This type of marketing offers tremendous profit potential, but also exposes the marketer to new, aggressive competitors.

International marketers operate in more than one country. As will become clear later in this book, massive adjustments are normally made in the marketing mix in various countries. Legal and cultural differences alone can greatly affect a strategy's outcome. As the US market becomes more and more saturated with US-made products, the continued expansion into foreign markets appears inevitable.

Global marketing differs from international marketing in some very definite ways. Whereas international marketing means a company sells its goods or services in another country, it does not necessarily mean that the company has made any further commitments. Usually the product is still manufactured in the home country, sold by their people, and the profits are taken back to that country. In the case of Honda Motors, for example, it means building manufacturing plants in the US, hiring local employees, using local distribution systems and advertising agencies, and reinvesting a large percentage of the profits back into the US.

Consumer goods marketing and business-to-business (industrial) marketing

Consumer goods marketers sell to individuals who consume the finished product. Business-to-business marketers sell to other businesses or institutions that consume the product in turn as part of operating the business, or use the product in the assembly of the final product they sell to consumers. Business-to-marketers engage in more personal selling rather than mass advertising and are willing to make extensive adjustments in factors such as the selling price, product features, terms of delivery, and so forth.

For the consumer goods marketer, the various marketing components are relatively fixed. In addition, consumer goods marketers might employ emotional appeals and are faced with the constant battle of getting their product into retail outlets.

Defining international marketing

Now that the world has entered the next millennium, we are seeing the emergence of an interdependent global economy that is characterized by faster communication, transportation, and financial flows, all of which are creating new marketing opportunities and challenges. Given these circumstances, it could be argued that companies face a deceptively straightforward and stark choice: they must either respond to the challenges posed by this new environment, or recognize and accept the long-term consequences of failing to do so. This need to respond is not confined to firms of a certain size or particular industries. It is a change that to a greater or lesser extent will ultimately affect companies of all sizes in virtually all markets. The pressures of the international environment are now so great, and the bases of competition within many markets are changing so fundamentally, that the opportunities to survive with a purely domestic strategy are increasingly limited to small-and medium-sized companies in local niche markets.

Perhaps partly because of the rapid evolution of international marketing, a vast array of terms have emerged that suggest various facets of international marketing. Clarification of these terms is a necessary first step before we can discuss this topic more thoroughly.

Let us begin with the assumption that the marketing process outlined and discussed in Chapters 1-4 is just as applicable to domestic marketing as to international marketing. In both markets, we are goal-driven, do necessary marketing research, select target markets, employ the various tools of marketing (i.e. product, pricing, distribution, communication), develop a budget, and check our results. However, the uncontrollable factors such as culture, social, legal, and economic factors, along with the political and competitive environment, all create the need for a myriad of adjustments in the marketing management process.

At its simplest level, *international marketing* involves the firm in making one or more marketing decisions across national boundaries. At its most complex, it involves the firm in establishing manufacturing and marketing facilities overseas and coordinating marketing strategies across markets. Thus, how international marketing is defined and interpreted depends on the level of involvement of the company in the international marketplace. Therefore, the following possibilities exist:

- *Domestic marketing*. This involves the company manipulating a series of controllable variables, such as price, advertising, distribution, and the product, in a largely uncontrollable external environment that is made up of different economic structures, competitors, cultural values, and legal infrastructure within specific political or geographic country boundaries.

- *International marketing*. This involves the company operating across several markets in which not only do the uncontrollable variables differ significantly between one market and another, but the controllable factor in the form of cost and price structures, opportunities for advertising, and distributive infrastructure are also likely to differ significantly. Degree of commitment is expressed as follows:

  (a) *Export marketing*. In this case the firm markets its goods and/or services across national/political boundaries.

  (b) *Multinational marketing*. Here the marketing activities of an organization include activities, interests, or operations in more than one country, and where there is some kind of influence or control of marketing activities from outside the country in which the goods or services will actually be sold. Each of these markets is typically perceived to be independent and a profit center in its own right.

  (c) *Global marketing*. The entire organization focuses on the selection and exploration of global marketing opportunities and marshals resources around the globe with the objective of achieving a global competitive advantage. The primary objective of the company is to achieve a synergy in the overall operation, so that by taking advantage of different exchange rates, tax rates, labor rates, skill levels, and market opportunities, the organization as a whole will be greater than the sum of its parts.[1]

Thus Toyota Motors started out as a domestic marketer, eventually exported its cars to a few regional markets, grew to become a multinational marketer, and today is a true global marketer, building manufacturing plants in the foreign country as well as hiring local labor, using local ad agencies, and complying to that country's cultural mores. As it moved from one level to the next, it also revised attitudes toward marketing and the underlying philosophy of business.

Ultimately, the successful marketer is the one who is best able to manipulate the controllable tools of the marketing mix within the uncontrollable environment. The principal reason for failure in international marketing results from a company not conducting the necessary research, and as a consequence, misunderstanding the differences and nuances of the marketing environment within the country that has been targeted.

Standardization and customization

In 1983, Harvard marketing professor Theodore Levitt wrote an article entitled, "The Globalization of Markets", and nothing about marketing has been the same since.2 According to Levitt, a new economic reality-the emergence of global consumer markets for single standard products-has been triggered in part by technological developments. Worldwide communications ensure the instant diffusion of new lifestyles and pave the way for a wholesale transfer of goods and services.

Adopting this global strategy provides a competitive advantage in cost and effectiveness. In contrast to multinational companies, standardized (global) corporations view the world or its major regions as one entity instead of a collection of national markets. These world marketers compete on a basis of appropriate value: i.e. an optimal combination of price, quality, reliability, and delivery of products that are identical in design and function. Ultimately, consumers tend to prefer a good price/quality ratio to a highly customized but less cost-effective item.

Levitt distinguished between products and brands. While the global product itself is standardized or sold with only minor modifications, the branding, positioning, and promotion may have to reflect local conditions.

Critics of Levitt's perspective suggest that his argument for global standardization is incorrect and that each market strategy should be customized for each country. Kotler notes that one study found that 80 per cent of US exports required one or more adaptations. Futhermore, the average product requires at least four to five adaptations out of a set of eleven marketing elements: labeling, packaging, materials, colors, name, product features, advertising themes, media, execution, price, and sales promotion.3 Kotler suggests that all eleven factors should be evaluated before standardization is considered.

To date, no one has empirically validated either perspective. While critics of Levitt can offer thousands of anecdotes contradicting the validity of standardization, a more careful read of Levitt's ideas indicate that he offers standardization as a strategic option, not a fact. Although global marketing has its pitfalls, it can also yield impressive advantages. Standardized products can lower operating costs. Even more important, effective coordination can exploit a company's best product and marketing ideas.

Too often, executives view global marketing as an either/or proposition-either full standardization or local control. But when a global approach can fall anywhere on a spectrum-from tight worldwide coordination on programming details to loose agreements on a product ideas-there is no reason for this extreme view. In applying the global marketing concept and making it work, flexibility is essential. The big issue today is not whether to go global, but how to tailor the global marketing concept to fit each business and how to make it work.

Reasons for entering international markets

Many marketers have found the international marketplace to be extremely hostile. A study by Baker and Kynak,4 for example, found that less than 20 per cent of firms in Texas with export potential actually carried out business in international markets. But although many firms view in markets with trepidation, others still make the decision to go international. Why?

In one study, the following motivating factors were given for initiating overseas marketing involvement (in order of importance):5

    1. large market size

2. stability through diversification

3. profit potential

4. unsolicited orders

5. proximity of market

6. excess capacity

7. offer by foreign distributor

8. increasing growth rate

9. smoothing out business cycles

Other empirical studies over a number of years have pointed to a wide variety of reasons why companies initiate international involvement. These include the saturation of the domestic market, which leads firms either to seek other less competitive markets or to take on the competitor in its home markets; the emergence of new markets, particularly in the developing world; government incentives to export; tax incentives offered by foreign governments to establish manufacturing plants in their countries in order to create jobs; the availability of cheaper or more skilled labor; and an attempt to minimize the risks of a recession in the home country and spread risk.6

Reasons to avoid international markets

Despite attractive opportunities, most businesses do not enter foreign markets. The reasons given for not going international are numerous. The biggest barrier to entering foreign markets is seen to be a fear by these companies that their products are not marketable overseas, and a consequent preoccupation with the domestic market. The following points were highlighted by the findings in the previously mentioned study by Barker and Kaynak, who listed the most important barriers:7

1. too much red tape

2. trade barriers

3. transportation difficulties

4. lack of trained personnel

5. lack of incentives

6. lack of coordinated assistance

7. unfavorable conditions overseas

8. slow payments by buyers

9. lack of competitive products

10. payment defaults

11. language barriers

It is the combination of these factors that determines not only whether companies become involved in international markets, but also the degree of any involvement.

The stages of going international

Earlier in our discussion on definitions, we identified several terms that relate to how committed a firm is to being international. Here we expand on these concepts and explain the rationale behind this process. Two points should be noted. First, the process tends to be ranked in order of "least risk and investment" to "greatest involvement". Second, these are not necessarily sequential steps, even though exporting is apparently most common as an initial entry.

Firms typically approach involvement in international marketing rather cautiously, and there appears to exist an underlying lifecycle that has a series of critical success factors that change as a firm moves through each stage. For small-and medium-sized firms in particular, exporting remains the most promising alternative to a full-blooded international marketing effort, since it appears to offer a degree of control over risk, cost, and resource commitment. Indeed, exporting, especially by the smaller firms, is often initiated as a response to an unsolicited overseas order-these are often perceived to be less risky.

Exporting

In general, exporting is a simple and low risk-approach to entering foreign markets. Firms may choose to export products for several reasons. First, products in the maturity stage of their domestic life cycle may find new growth opportunities overseas, as Perrier chose to do in the US. Second, some firms find it less risky and more profitable to expand by exporting current products instead of developing new products. Third, firms who face seasonal domestic demand may choose to sell their products to foreign markets when those products are "in season" there. Finally, some firms may elect to export products because there is less competition overseas.

A firm can export its products in one of three ways: indirect exporting, semi-direct exporting, and direct exporting. *Indirect exporting* is a common practice among firms that are just beginning their exporting. Sales, whether foreign or domestic, are treated as domestic sales. All sales are made through the firm's domestic sales department, as there is no export department. Indirect exporting involves very little investment, as no overseas sales force or other types of contacts need be developed. Indirect exporting also involves little risk, as international marketing intermediaries have knowledge of markets and will make fewer mistakes than sellers.

In semi-direct exporting, an American exporter usually initiates the contact through agents, merchant middlemen, or other manufacturers in the US. Such semi-direct exporting can be handled in a variety of ways: (a) a combination export manager, a domestic agent intermediary that acts as an exporting department for several noncompeting firms; (b) the manufacturer's export agent (MEA) operates very much like a manufacturer's agent in domestic marketing settings; (c) a Webb-Pomerene Export Association may choose to limit cooperation to advertising, or it may handle the exporting of the products of the association's members and; (d) piggyback exporting, in which one manufacturer (carrier) that has export facilities and overseas channels of distribution handles the exporting of another firm (rider) noncompeting but complementary products.

When *direct exporting* is the means of entry into a foreign market, the manufacturer establishes an export department to sell directly to a foreign film. The exporting manufacturer conducts market research, establishes physical distribution, and obtains all necessary export documentation. Direct exporting requires a greater investment and also carries a greater risk. However, it also provides greater potential return and greater control of its marketing program.

Licensing

Under a licensing agreement, a firm (licensor) provides some technology to a foreign firm (licensee) by granting that firm the right to use the licensor's manufacturing process, brand name, patents, or sales knowledge in return for some payment. The licensee obtains a competitive advantage in this arrangement, while the licensor obtains inexpensive access to a foreign market.

A licensing arrangement contains risk, in that if the business is very successful, profit potentials are limited by the licensing agreement. Alternatively, a licensor makes a long-term commitment to a firm and that firm may be less capable than expected. Or, the licensee may be unwilling to invest the necessary resources as needed to be successful. Licensing may be the least profitable alternative for market entry. Scarce capital, import restrictions, or government restrictions may make this the only feasible means for selling in another country.

Franchising represents a very popular type of licensing arrangement for many consumer products firms. Holiday Inn, Hertz Car Rental, and McDonald's have all expanded into foreign markets through franchising.

Joint ventures

A *joint venture* is a partnership between a domestic firm and a foreign firm. Both partners invest money and share ownership and control of partnership. Joint ventures require a greater commitment from firms than licensing or the various other exporting methods. They have more risk and less flexibility.

A domestic firm may wish to engage in a joint venture for a variety of reasons; for example, General Motors and Toyota have agreed to make a subcompact car to be sold through GM dealers using the idle GM plant in California. Toyota's motivation was to avoid US import quotas and taxes on cars without any US-made parts.

Direct investment

Multinational organizations may choose to engage in full-scale production and marketing abroad. Thus, they will invest in wholly owned subsidiaries. An organization using this approach makes a *direct investment* in one or more foreign nations. Organizations engaging in licensing or joint ventures do not own manufacturing and marketing facilities abroad.

By establishing overseas subsidiaries, a multinational organization can compete more aggressively because it is "in" the marketplace. However, subsidiaries require more investment as the subsidiary is responsible for all marketing activities in a foreign country. While such operations provide control over marketing activities, considerable risk is involved. The subsidiary strategy requires complete understanding of business conditions, customs, markets, labor, and other foreign market factors.

US commercial centers

Another method of doing business overseas has come in the form of *US Commercial Centers*8. A Commercial Center serves the purpose of providing additional resources for the promotion of exports of US goods and services to host countries. The Commercial Center does so by familiarizing US exporters with industries, markets, and customs of host countries. They are facilitating agencies that assist with the three arrangements just discussed.

US Commercial Centers provide business facilities such as exhibition space, conference rooms, and office space. They provide translation and clerical services. They have a commercial library. They have commercial law information and trade promotion facilities, including the facilitation of contacts between buyers, sellers, bankers, distributors, agents, and government officials. They also coordinate trade missions and assist with contracts and export and import arrangements.

Trade intermediaries

Small manufacturers who are interested in building their foreign sales are turning to trade intermediaries to assist them in the sale and distribution of their products. These entrepreneurial middlemen typically buy US-produced goods at 15 per cent below a manufacturer's best discount and then resell the products in overseas markets. These trade intermediaries account for about 10 per cent of all US exports9. The trade intermediary provides a valuable service to small companies, which often do not have the resources or expertise to market their products overseas. The trade intermediaries have developed relationships with foreign countries; these relationships are time-consuming and expensive to develop.

Alliances

Heineken, the premium Dutch beer, is consumed by more people in more countries than any other beer10. It is also the number-one imported beer in America. Miller and Budweiser, the two largest American beer producers, have entered into global competition with Heineken, partly because the American beer market has been flat. They are doing so by forming alliances with global breweries such as Molson, Corona, and Dos Equis. Heineken has responded to the challenge, heavily promoting products such as Amstel Light and Murphy's Irish Stout. Heineken has also begun developing an alliance with Asia Pacific Breweries, the maker of Tiger Beer.

The international marketing plan

It should be apparent by now that companies and organizations planning to compete effectively in world markets need a clear and well-focused international marketing plan that is based on a thorough understanding of the markets in which the company is introducing its products. The challenge, then, of international marketing is to ensure that any international strategy has the discipline of thorough research, and an understanding and accurate evaluation of what is required to achieve the competitive advantage. As such, the decision sequence in international marketing (see Exhibit 26) is much larger than that of domestic markets. As noted in the next Integrated Marketing box, it is also more complicated. See below.

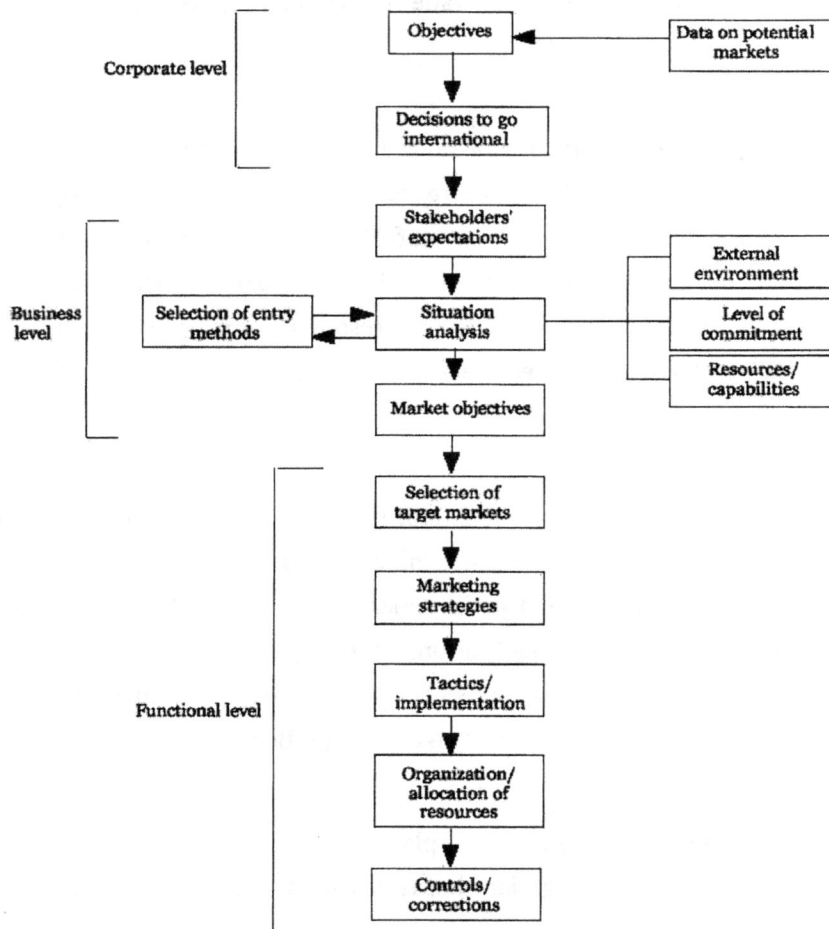

Exhibit 26: The decision sequence in international marketing

The corporate level

We begin at the corporate level, where firms decide whether to become involved in international markets and determine the resources they are willing to commit. Thus, this stage is primarily concerned with the analysis of international markets. Decisions here will be dependent on matching the results of that analysis with the company's objectives. These objectives, in turn, will be determined by the many motivating factors we have discussed in the earlier sections. The level of resources that the company is willing to commit should be determined by the strategy that is needed to achieve the objectives that have been set.

The business level

Business-level considerations begin with the assessment of the stakeholders involved in the business. It is important to clearly identify the different stakeholder groups, understand their expectations, and evaluate their power, because the stakeholders provide the broad guidelines within which the firm operates. In the case of international marketing, it is particularly important to address the concerns of the stakeholders in the host company.

The situation analysis concerns a thorough examination of the factors that influence the businesses' ability to successfully market a product or service. The results lead to a realistic set of objectives. Conducting a situation analysis in an international setting is a bit more extensive. It not only includes the normal assessment of *external environmental* factors and *resources/capabilities*, it also includes a determination of the *level of commitment* exhibited by the business, as well as possible methods of entry. These last two factors are interrelated in that a company's level of commitment to international markets will directly influence whether they employ exporting, a joint venture, or some other method of entry.

In turn, level of commitment and method of entry are influenced by the evaluation of environmental factors as well as resources and capabilities. The latter audits not only the weaknesses of the company, but also the strengths of the company, which are often taken for granted. This is particularly important in international markets; for example, customer brand loyalty may be much stronger in certain markets than others, and products may be at the end of their life in the domestic market but may be ideal for less sophisticated markets.

It is important, too, to evaluate the capacity of the firm to be flexible, adaptable, and proactive, as these are the attributes necessary, for success in a highly competitive and rapidly changing world.

Undoubtedly, environmental factors have received the most attention from marketers considering international markets.

Marketing objectives

Having identified stakeholder expectations, carried out a detailed situation analysis, and made an evaluation of the capabilities of the company, the overall marketing goals can be set. It is important to stress that there is a need for realism in this, as only too frequently corporate plans are determined more by the desire for short-term credibility with shareholders than with the likelihood that they will be achieved.

The process adopted for determining long-term and short-term objectives is important and varies significantly, depending on the size of the business, the nature of the market and the abilities and motivation of managers in different markets. At an operational level, the national managers need to have an achievable and detailed plan for each country, which will take account of the local situation, explain what is expected of them, and how their performance will be measured. Examples of objectives might be:

- financial performance, including return on investment and profitability

- market penetration, including sales (by volume and value), market share by product category

- customer growth, by volume and profitability

- distribution, including strength in supply chain, number of outlets

- brand awareness and value

- new product introductions and diffusion

- company image, including quality and added value (or service)

The functional level

Having set the objectives for the company, both at the corporate level and the business level, the company can now develop a detailed program of functional activities to achieve the objectives. Following the integrated approach employed throughout this text, each of the functional elements (e.g. finance, human resources, research) must be considered jointly. The international marketing strategy is doomed to failure if human resources can not find and train the appropriate employees, or research can not modify the product so that it is acceptable to consumers in another country. Ultimately, this coordination between business functions is contingent on the market entry strategy employed as well as the degree of standardization or customization deemed.

Having integrated at the function level, we next consider integration of the marketing mix elements.

Product/promotion

Keegan11 has highlighted the key aspect of marketing strategy as a combination of standardization or adaptation of product and promotion elements of the mix and offers five alternative and more specific approaches to product policy:

1. *One product, one message, worldwide:* While a number of writers have argued that this will be the strategy adopted for many products in the future, in practice only a handful of products might claim to have achieved this already.

2. *Product extension, promotion adaptation:* While the product stays the same this strategy allows for the adaptation of the promotional effort either to target new customer segments or to appeal to the particular tastes of individual countries.

3. *Product adaptation, promotion extension:* This strategy is used if a promotional campaign has achieved international appeal, but the product needs to be adapted because of local needs.

4. *Dual adaptation:* By adapting both products and promotion for each market, the firm is adopting a totally differentiated approach.

5. *Product invention:* Firms, usually from advanced nations, that are supplying products to less well-developed countries adopt product invention.

Another critical element that is closely aligned with the product and promotion is the brand. Anthony O'Reilly, Chairman of H.J. Heinz, believes that the communications revolution and the convergence of cultures have now set the stage for truly global marketing. The age of the global brand is at hand. For example, Heinz was looking to expand its 9 Lives cat food brand and Morris the Cat logo into Moscow. Although it is a stable and successful brand in the US, testing and research done by Dimitri Epimov, a local marketing manager in Moscow, led Heinz executives to make a marketing change to ensure the product's success in Russia. Namely, a fatter-looking Morris was created for packaging. Another discovery: While Americans tend to treat their kitties with tuna, Russian cat-lovers prefer to serve beef-flavored food.

As discussed earlier, product positioning is a key success factor and reflects the customer's perceptions of the product or service. However, in countries at different stages of economic development, the customer segments that are likely to be able to purchase the product and the occasions on which it is bought may be significantly different. For example, while KFC and McDonald's restaurants aim at everyday eating for the mass market in the developed countries, in less-developed countries they are perceived as places for special-occasion eating, and are beyond the reach of the poorest segments of the population. The product positioning, therefore, must vary in some dimensions. In confirming the positioning of a product or service in a specific market or region, it is therefore necessary to establish in the consumer perception exactly what the product stands for and how it differs from existing and potential competition by designing an identity that confirms the value of the product.

Pricing

Pricing products in foreign nations is complicated by exchange rate fluctuations, tariffs, governmental intervention, and shipping requirements. A common strategy involves a marketer setting a lower price for their products in foreign markets. This strategy is consistent with the low income levels of many foreign countries, and the lower price helps to build market share. Pricing strategies are also strongly influenced by the nature and intensity of the competition in the various markets.

For these reasons, it is important to recognize at the outset that the development and implementation of pricing strategies in international markets should follow the following stages:

1. analyzing the factors that influence international pricing, such as the cost structures, the value of the product, the market structure, competitor pricing levels, and a variety of environmental constraints

2. confirming the impact the corporate strategies should have on pricing policy

3. evaluating the various strategic pricing options and selecting the most appropriate approach

4. implementing the strategy through the use of a variety of tactics and procedures to set prices

5. managing prices and financing international transactions

Perhaps the most critical factor to be considered when developing a pricing strategy in international markets, however, is how the customers and competitors will respond. Nagle 12 has suggested nine factors that influence the sensitivity of customers to prices, and all have implications for the international marketer. Price sensitivity reduces:

The more distinctive the product is:

• the greater the perceived quality

• the less aware consumers are of substitutes in the market

• if it is difficult to make comparisons

• if the price of a product represents a small proportion of total expenditure of the customer

• as the perceived benefit increases

• if the product is used in association with a product bought previously

• if costs are shared with other parties

• if the product cannot be stored

Finally, there are several inherent problems associated with pricing in international markets. Often companies find it difficult to coordinate and control prices across their activities in order to enable them to achieve effective financial performance and their desired price positioning. Simply, how can prices be coordinated by the company across the various markets and still make the necessary profit? Difficulty answering this question has led to two serious problems. *Dumping* (when a firm sells a product in a foreign country below its domestic price or below its actual costs) is often done to build a company's share of the market by pricing at a competitive level. Another reason is that the products being sold may be surplus or cannot be sold domestically and are therefore already a burden to the company. When companies price their products very high in some countries but competitively in others, they engage in a gray market strategy. A *gray market*, also called *parallel importing*, is a situation where products are sold through unauthorized channels of distribution. A gray market comes about when individuals buy products in a lower-priced country from a manufacturer's authorized retailer, ship them to higher-priced countries, and then sell them below the manufacturer's suggested price through unauthorized retailers.

Considerable problems arise in foreign transactions because of the need to buy and sell products in different currencies. Questions to consider are: What currency should a company price its products? How should a company deal with fluctuating exchange rates?

Finally, obtaining payment promptly and in a suitable currency from less developed countries can cause expense and additional difficulties. How should a company deal with selling to countries where there is a risk of nonpayment? How should a company approach selling to countries that have a shortage of hard currency?

Distribution and logistics

Distribution channels are the means by which goods are distributed from the manufacturer to the end user. *Logistics*, or physical distribution management, is concerned with the planning, implementing, and control of physical flows of materials and final goods from points of origin to points of use to meet customer needs at a profit.

Essentially there are three channel links between the seller and buyer. The first link is the seller's headquarters organization, which is responsible for supervising the channel, and acts as part of the channel itself. Channels between countries represent the second link. They are responsible for getting products to overseas markets and payment in return. Finally, the third link is the channel structure (logistics) within countries, which distributes the products from their point of entry to the final consumer.

Distribution strategies within overseas markets are affected by various uncontrollable factors. First, wholesaling and retailing structure differs widely from one nation to the next. So, too, does the quality of service provided. Differences in the size and nature of retailers are even more pronounced. Retailers more closely reflect the economic conditions and culture of that country; many small retailers dominate most of these countries.

Physical distribution to overseas markets often requires special marketing planning. Many countries have inadequate docking facilities, limited highways, various railroad track gauges, too few vehicles, and too few warehouses. Managing product inventories requires consideration of the availability of suitable warehousing, as well as the costs of shipping in small quantities.

The budget

Marketing mix components must be evaluated as part of an overall marketing strategy. Therefore, the organization must establish a marketing budget based on the required marketing effort to influence consumers. The marketing budget represents a plan to allocate expenditures to each of the components of the marketing mix. For example, the firm must establish an advertising budget as part of the marketing budget and allocate expenditures to various types of advertising media—television, newspapers, magazines. A sales promotion budget should also be determined, allocating money for coupons, product samples, and trade promotions. Similarly, budgets are required for personal selling, distribution, and product development.

How much should be spent? Consider the following example. A common question that marketers frequently ask is, "Are we spending enough (or too much) to promote the sale of our products?" A reasonable answer would revolve around another consideration: "What do we want to accomplish? What are our goals?" The discussion should next turn to the methods for achievement of goals and the removal of obstacles to these goals. This step is often skipped or avoided.

Usually, when the question is asked, "Are we spending enough?" an automatic answer is given, in terms of what others spend. Knowing what others in the same industry spend can be important to an organization whose performance lags behind the competition or to an organization that suspects that its expenditures are higher than they need to be. But generally, knowing what others spend leads to an unproductive "keeping-up-with-the-Joneses" attitude. It also assumes that the others know what they are doing.

Evaluating results

No marketing program is planned and implemented perfectly. Marketing managers will tell you that they experience many surprises during the course of their activities. In an effort to ensure that performance goes according to plans, marketing managers establish controls that allow marketers to evaluate results and identify needs for modifications in marketing strategies and programs. Surprises occur, but marketing managers who have established sound control procedures can react to surprises quickly and effectively.

Marketing control involves a number of decisions. One decision is what function to monitor. Some organizations monitor their entire marketing program, while others choose to monitor only a part of it, such as their sales force or their advertising program. A second set of decisions concerns the establishment of standards for performance; e.g. market share, profitability, or sales. A third set of decisions concerns how to collect information for making comparisons between actual performance and standards. Finally, to the extent that discrepancies exist between actual and planned performance, adjustments in the marketing program or the strategic plan must be made.

Once a plan is put into action, a marketing manager must still gather information related to the effectiveness with which the plan was implemented. Information on sales, profits, reactions of consumers, and reactions of competitors must be collected and analyzed so that a marketing manager can identify new problems and opportunities.

The international marketing environment

A number of factors constitute the international environment: social, cultural, political, legal, competitive, economic, plus technology. Each should be evaluated before a company makes a decision to go international.

The social/cultural environment

The cultural environment consists of the influence of religious, family, educational, and social systems in the marketing system. Marketers who intend to market their products overseas may be very sensitive to foreign cultures. While the differences between our cultural background in the United States and those of foreign nations may seem small, marketers who ignore these differences risk failure in implementing marketing programs. Failure to consider cultural differences is one of the primary reasons for marketing failures overseas.

This task is not as easy as it sounds as various features of a culture can create an illusion of similarity. Even a common language does not guarantee similarity of interpretation. For example, in the US we purchase "cans" of various grocery products, but the British purchase "tins". A number of cultural differences can cause marketers problems in attempting to market their products overseas. These include: (a) language, (b) color, (c) customs and taboos, (d) values, (e) aesthetics, (f) time, (g) business norms, (h) religion, and (i) social structures. Each is discussed in the following sections.

Language

The importance of language differences cannot be overemphasized, as there are almost 3,000 languages in the world. Language differences cause many problems for marketers in designing advertising campaigns and product labels. Language problems become even more serious once the people of a country speak several languages. For example, in Canada, labels must be in both English and French. In India, there are over 200 different dialects, and a similar situation exists in China.

Colors

Colors also have different meanings in different cultures. For example, in Egypt, the country's national color of green is considered unacceptable for packaging, because religious leaders once wore it. In Japan, black and white are colors of mourning and should not be used on a product's package. Similarly, purple is unacceptable in Hispanic nations because it is associated with death.

Consider how the following examples could be used in development of international marketing programs:

- In Russia, it is acceptable for men to greet each other with a kiss, but this custom is not acceptable in the US.
- Germans prefer their salad dressing in a tube, while Americans prefer it in a bottle.
- In France, wine is served with most meals, but in America, milk, tea, water, and soft drinks are popular.

McDonalds's Corporation has opened 20 restaurants in India. Since 80 per cent of Indians are Hindu, McDonald's will use a nonbeef meat substitute for its traditional hamburger. The likely beef substitute will be lamb, a very popular meat in India. In anticipation of its restaurant openings, McDonald's conducted extensive market research, site selection studies, and developed a relationship with India's largest chicken supplier. McDonald's has opted to market its product in India, largely because India's population of more than 900 million represents one sixth of the world's population.

Values

An individual's values arise from his/her moral or religious beliefs and are learned through experiences. For example, in America we place a very high value on material well-being, and are much more likely to purchase status symbols than people in India. Similarly, in India, the Hindu religion forbids the consumption of beef, and fast-food restaurants such as McDonald's and Burger King would encounter tremendous difficulties without product modification. Americans spend large amounts of money on soap, deodorant, and mouthwash because of the value placed on personal cleanliness. In Italy, salespeople call on women only if their husbands are at home.

Aesthetics

The term *aesthetics* is used to refer to the concepts of beauty and good taste. The phrase, "Beauty is in the eye of the beholder" is a very appropriate description for the differences in aesthetics that exist between cultures. For example, Americans believe that suntans are attractive, youthful, and healthy. However, the Japanese do not.

Time

Americans seem to be fanatical about time when compared to other cultures. Punctuality and deadlines are routine business practices in the US. However, salespeople who set definite appointments for sales calls in the Middle East and Latin America will have a lot of time on their hands, as business people from both of these cultures are far less bound by time constraints. To many of these cultures, setting a deadline such as "I have to know next week" is considered pushy and rude.

Business norms

The norms of conducting business also vary from one country to the next. Here are several examples of foreign business behavior that differ from US business behavior:

- In France, wholesalers do not like to promote products. They are mainly interested in supplying retailers with the products they need.

- In Russia, plans of any kind must be approved by a seemingly endless string of committees. As a result, business negotiations may take years.

- South Americans like to talk business "nose to nose". This desire for close physical proximity causes American business people to back away from the constantly forward-moving South Americans.

- In Japan, businesspeople have mastered the tactic of silence in negotiations. Americans are not prepared for this, and they panic because they think something has gone wrong. The result is that Americans become impatient, push for a closure, and often make business concessions they later regret.

These norms are reflected in the difficulty of introducing the Web into Europe (see the next Integrated Marketing box).

Religious beliefs

A person's religious beliefs can affect shopping patterns and products purchased in addition to his/her values, as discussed earlier. In the United States and other Christian nations, Christmastime is a major sales period. But for other religions, religious holidays do not serve as popular times for purchasing products. Women do not participate in household buying decisions in countries in which religion serves as opposition to women's rights movements.

Every culture has a social structure, but some seem less widely defined than others. That is, it is more difficult to move upward in a social structure that is rigid. For example, in the US, the two-wage earner family has led to the development of a more affluent set of consumers. But in other cultures, it is considered unacceptable for women to work outside the home.

The political/legal environment

The political/legal environment abroad is quite different from that of the US. Most nations desire to become self-reliant and to raise their status in the eyes of the rest of the world. This is the essence of nationalism. The nationalistic spirit that exists in many nations has led them to engage in practices that have been very damaging to other countries' marketing organizations. For example, foreign governments can intervene in marketing programs in the following ways:

- contracts for the supply and delivery of goods and services

- the registration and enforcement of trademarks, brand names, and labeling

- patents

- marketing communications

- pricing

- product safety, acceptability, and environmental issues

Political stability

Business activity tends to grow and thrive when a nation is politically stable. When a nation is politically unstable, multinational firms can still conduct business profitably. Their strategies will be affected however. Most firms probably prefer to engage in the export business rather than invest considerable sums of money in investments in foreign subsidiaries. Inventories will be low and currency will be converted rapidly. The result is that consumers in the foreign nation pay high prices, get less satisfactory products, and have fewer jobs.

Monetary circumstances

The *exchange rate* of a particular nation's currency represents the value of that currency in relation to that of another country. Governments set some exchange rates independently of the forces of supply and demand. The forces of supply and demand set others. If a country's exchange rate is low compared to other countries, that country's consumers must pay higher prices on imported goods. While the concept of exchange rates appears relatively simple, these rates fluctuate widely and often, thus creating high risks for exporters and importers.

Trading blocs and agreements

US companies make one-third of their revenues from products marketed abroad, in places such as Asia and Latin America. The North American Free Trade Agreement (NAFTA) further boosts export sales by enabling companies to sell goods at lower prices because of reduced tariffs. Regional trading blocs represent a group of nations that join together and formally agree to reduce trade barriers among themselves. NAFTA is such a bloc. Its members include the US, Canada, and Mexico. No tariffs exist on goods sold between member nations of NAFTA. However, a uniform tariff is assessed on products from countries not affiliated with NAFTA. In addition, NAFTA seeks common standards for labeling requirements, food additives, and package sizes.

One of the potentially interesting results of trade agreements like NAFTA is that many products previously restricted by dumping laws, laws designed to keep out foreign products, would be allowed to be marketed. The practice of *dumping* involves a company selling products in overseas markets at very low prices, one intention being to steal business from local competitors. These laws were designed to prevent pricing practices that could seriously harm local competition. The laws were designed to prevent large producers from flooding markets with very low priced products, gain a monopoly, and then raise prices to very high levels. In 1993, about 40 nations, counting the European Community as one, had anti-dumping legislation. Those in favor of agreements argue that anti-dumping laws penalize those companies who are capable of competing in favor of those companies that are not competitive.

Almost all the countries in the Western hemisphere have entered into one or more regional trade agreements. Such agreements are designed to facilitate trade through the establishment of a free trade area customs union or customs market. Free trade areas and customs unions eliminate trade barriers between member countries while maintaining trade barriers with nonmember countries. *Customs Unions* maintain common tariffs and rates for nonmember countries. A *common market* provides for harmonious fiscal and monetary policies while free trade areas and customs unions do not. Trade agreements are becoming a growing force for trade liberalization; the development of such agreements provides for tremendous opportunities for US companies doing business in Latin America and North America.

The creation of the single European market in 1992 was expected to change the way marketing is done worldwide. It meant the birth of a market that was larger than the United States, and the introduction of European Currency Units (Euros) in place of the individual currencies of member nations. Experience in multilingual marketing would help non-European companies succeed in this gigantic market. With new technologies such as multilingual processing programs, it would be possible to target potential customers anywhere in Europe, in any language, and in the same marketing campaign.

Progress toward European unification has been slow-many doubt that complete unification will ever be achieved. However, on 1 January 1999, 11 of the 15 member nations took a significant step toward unification by adopting the Euro as the common currency. These 11 nations represent 290 million people and a USD 6.5 trillion market. Still, with 14 different languages and distinctive national customs, it is unlikely that the EU will ever become the "United States of Europe".

Tariffs

Most nations encourage free trade by inviting firms to invest and to conduct business there, while encouraging domestic firms to engage in overseas business. These nations do not usually try to strictly regulate imports or discriminate against foreign-based firms. There are, however, some governments that openly oppose free trade. For example, many Communist nations desire self-sufficiency. Therefore, they restrict trade with non-Communist nations. But these restrictions vary with East-West relations.

The most common form of restriction of trade is the tariff, a tax placed on imported goods. Protective tariffs are established in order to protect domestic manufacturers against competitors by raising the prices of imported goods. Not surprisingly, US companies with a strong business tradition in a foreign country may support tariffs to discourage entry by other US competitors.

Expropriation

All multinational firms face the risk of expropriation. That is, the foreign government takes ownership of plants, sometimes without compensating the owners. However, in many expropriations there has been payment, and it is often equitable. Many of these facilities end up as private rather than government organizations. Because of the risk of expropriation, multinational firms are at the mercy of foreign governments, which are sometimes unstable, and which can change the laws they enforce at any point in time to meet their needs.

The technological environment

The level of technological development of a nation affects the attractiveness of doing business there, as well as the type of operations that are possible. Marketers in developed nations cannot take many technological advances for granted. They may not be available in lesser developed nations. Consider some of the following technologically related problems that firms may encounter in doing business overseas:

- Foreign workers must be trained to operate unfamiliar equipment.

- Poor transportation systems increase production and physical distribution costs.

- Maintenance standards vary from one nation to the next.

- Poor communication facilities hinder advertising through the mass media.

- Lack of data processing facilities makes the tasks of planning, implementing, and controlling marketing strategy more difficult.

The economic environment

A nation's economic situation represents its current and potential capacity to produce goods and services. The key to understanding market opportunities lies in the evaluation of the stage of a nation's economic growth.

A way of classifying the economic growth of countries is to divide them into three groups: (a) industrialized, (b) developing, and (c) less-developed nations. The *industrialized nations* are generally considered to be the United States, Japan, Canada, Russia, Australia, and most of Western Europe The economies of these nations are characterized by private enterprise and a consumer orientation. They have high literacy, modem technology, and higher per capita incomes.

Developing nations are those that are making the transition from economies based on agricultural and raw materials production to industrial economies. Many Latin American nations fit into this category, and they exhibit rising levels of education, technology, and per capita incomes,

Finally, there are many *less developed* nations in today's world. These nations have low standards of living, literacy rates are low, and technology is very limited.

Usually, the most significant marketing opportunities exist among the industrialized nations, as they have high levels of income, one of the necessary ingredients for the formation of markets. However, most industrialized nations also have stable population bases, and market saturation for many products already existing. The developing nations, on the other hand, have growing population bases, and although they currently import limited goods and services, the long-run potential for growth in these nations exists. Dependent societies seek products that satisfy basic needs-food, clothing, housing, medical care, and education. Marketers in such nations must be educators, emphasizing information in their market programs. As the degree of economic development increases, so does the sophistication of the marketing effort focused on the countries.

The competitive environment

Entering an international market is similar to doing so in a domestic market, in that a firm seeks to gain a differential advantage by investing resources in that market. Often local firms will adopt imitation strategies, sometimes successfully. When they are successful, their own nation's economy receives a good boost. When they are not successful, the multinational firm often buys them out.

Japanese marketers have developed an approach to managing product costs that has given them a competitive advantage over US competitors. A typical American company will design a new product, then calculate the cost. If the estimated cost is too high, the product will be taken back to the drawing board. In Japan, a company typically starts with a target cost based on the price that it estimates the market is most willing to accept. Product designers and engineers are then directed to meet the cost target. This approach also encourages managers to worry less about product costs and more about the role it should play in gaining market share. Briefly, at Japanese companies like NEC, Nissan, Sharp, and Toyota, a team charged with bringing a product idea to market estimates the price at which the product is most likely to appeal to the market. From this first important judgment, all else follows. After deducting the required profit margin from the selling price, planners develop estimates of each element that make up the product's cost: engineering, manufacturing sales, and marketing. US firms tend to build products, figure how much it costs to build the product, and then ask whether the product can be sold at a profitable price. US companies tend not to assess what the market will be willing to pay.

Discussion questions

> What is a competitive advantage? How does marketing contribute to the creation of a competitive advantage?

> Describe the reasons for studying marketing.

> What adjustments are necessary as you apply marketing principles to various cultures/countries?

> List the steps in the market segmentation process.

> What is the value in conducting formal marketing research?

> Discuss several reasons why marketers continue to have a difficult time understanding, predicting, and explaining consumer behavior.

> Present a diagram of the consumer decision process. What is the role of marketing in each stage of this process.

> Briefly describe the major strategies a firm might use to enter a foreign market.

> How does the cultural environment affect international marketing activities?

> Why is marketing critical to the success of a business?

References

1 *Dictionary of Marketing Terms*, Peter D. Bennett, Ed., American Marketing Association, 1988 p. 54.

2 "A New Recipe for the Family Dinner," *Adweek*, April 27. 1992, p. 46.

3 Theodore Levitt, "Marketing Myopia," *Harvard Business Review*, July-August, 1960, pp. 45-66.

4 Shelby D. Hunt and John J. Burnett, "The Macromarketing/Micro marketing Dichotomy: A Taxonomical Model," Journal of Marketing, Summer. 1982 pp. 11-26.

More references

[1]Isobel Doole, Robin Lowe, and Chris Phillips, *International Marketing Strategy*, International Thompson Business Press: London, 1999, pp. 14-15.

[2]Theodore Levitt. "The Globalization of Markets." *Harvard Business Review*. May-June 1983, pp. 92-102.

[3]Philip Kotler, "Global Standardization-Courting Danger," *Journal of Consumer Marketing*, Vol. 3, No.2, Spring, 1986, pp. 13-20.

[4]S. Barker and E. Kaynak, "An Empirical Investigation of the Differences Between Initiating and Continuing Exporters," *European Journal of Marketers*, Vol. 26, No.3, 1992.

[5]Ibid.

[6]Anne Chen and Malt Hicks, "Going Glob Avoid Culture Clashes," *PC Week*, April 3, 2000, pp. 68-69.

[7]Barker and Kaynak, op. cit.

[8]Eileen Cassidy Imbach, "US Commercial Centers: The Future of Doing Business Abroad," *Business America*, November, 1994, pp.25-26.

[9]Michael Selz, "More Small Firms Are Turning to Trade Intermediaries," *The Wall Street Journal*, February 2, 1995, p. B2.

[10]Julia Flunn and R A. Melcher, "Heineken's Battle to Stay Top Bottle," *Business Week*, August 1, 1998, pp. 60-62.

[11]Warren J. Keegan, "Conceptual Framework for Multinational Marketing," *Columbia Journal of World Business*, Vol. 7, November 1973, p.67.

12 TT Nagle, The Strategies and Tactics of Pricing, Prentice-Han, Inc. Englewood Cliffs, N.J., 1999.

7. Operations management

Editor: Michael J Pesch (St Cloud University, USA)

Reviewer: Ronald F Farina (Daniels College of Business, University of Denver, USA)

Learning objectives:

- understand the role of operations management in organizations

- differentiate between strategic and tactical operations decisions

- describe the key operations management decisions faced by managers

- understand three of the most important operations management practices: Total Quality Management, Supply Chain Management, and Just-in-Time/Lean Operations

What is operations management?

Operations management is the management of processes that transform inputs into goods and services that add value for the customer. The goal of operations management is to maximize efficiency while producing goods and services that effectively fulfill customer needs. For example, if an organization makes furniture, some of the operations management decisions involve the purchasing of wood and fabric, the hiring and training of workers, the location and layout of the furniture factory, and the purchase of cutting tools and other fabrication equipment. If the organization makes good operations decisions, it will be able to produce affordable, functional, and attractive furniture that customers will purchase at a price that will earn profits for the company.

In another example, the owners of a restaurant must make important decisions regarding the location, layout, and seating capacity of the restaurant, the hiring, training, and scheduling of chefs and servers, the suppliers of fresh food at the right prices, and the purchase of stoves, refrigerators, and other food preparation equipment. If the restaurant owners make good operations decisions, they will be able to meet their customers' needs for delicious and affordable food that is served in a pleasing atmosphere. The owners in turn will be able to charge a price that earns a profit and allows the restaurant to stay in business.

One of three strategic functions

Operations is one of the three strategic functions of any organization. This means that it is a vital part of accomplishing the organization's strategy and ensuring its long-term survival. The other two areas of strategic importance to the organization are *marketing* and *finance*. For example, a company that makes team jerseys for sport teams must have strong *marketing* ability to identify groups of customers, understand their needs, and communicate with them to win their business. The company must also manage its *finances* so it can pay for building and equipment expenses, bank loans, worker wages, and supplies. Finally, the company must have strong *operations* skills so it can provide customized team jerseys that are attractive, durable, affordable and delivered on time to the customer.

The operations strategy should support the overall organization strategy. For example, JetBlue airlines is a successful airline that has an organization strategy of providing high-value air transportation service to travelers. JetBlue strives to provide fun, comfortable, and safe air service to popular destinations at a price that middle-income passengers can afford. Given JetBlue's organization strategy, JetBlue features an operations strategy that focuses on low costs, competent and service-oriented employees, and reliable aircraft.

JetBlue's operations strategy is driven by its organization strategy. For example, JetBlue locates ("location" is an operations decision area) its main transportation hub in New York City, a city of 19 million people that helps ensure that JetBlue's planes fly at full capacity. In the area of equipment decisions, JetBlue operates only one type of aircraft, the Airbus 330. The Airbus 330 has high passenger carrying capacity (to maximize revenue), provides good fuel economy and requires only two pilots (versus three) to operate. Having one type of aircraft reduces training costs for pilots and mechanics, reduces investments in parts inventories, and enables JetBlue to negotiate greater discounts on high-volume purchases from Airbus. In another key operations area, JetBlue pays careful attention to hiring, training, and compensating employees who can deliver excellent service, loyalty, and high levels of productivity.

In addition to an operations strategy, JetBlue also has financial and marketing strategies that support its organization strategy. One part of its financial strategy is securing sufficient amounts of capital to help the start-up airline establish reliable service and gain a loyal clientele. JetBlue's marketing strategy keeps advertising costs under control by attracting free media publicity that emphasizes its fun and affordable airline service.

Strategic versus tactical operations decisions

Operations decisions include decisions that are **strategic** in nature, meaning that they have long-term consequences and often involve a great deal of expense and resource commitments. **Strategic** operations decisions include facility location decisions, the type of technologies that the organization will use, determining how labor and equipment are organized, and how much long-term capacity the organization will provide to meet customer demand.

For example, the leaders of a new hospital must decide where to locate the facility to be accessible to a large number of potential patients. Hospital administrators must evaluate the performance and cost of a wide variety of health equipment. Administrators must also assess and purchase information technologies to keep patient records, fulfill government regulations, provide accurate and timely communications, and track financial performance. Doctors, nurses, and staff must be hired and various departments (x-ray, lab, pharmacy, physical therapy, etc.) must be arranged to maximize both efficiency and effectiveness in patient care.

Tactical operations decisions have short to medium term impact on the organization, often involve less commitment of resources, and can be changed more easily than strategic decisions. Tactical decisions include workforce scheduling, establishing quality assurance procedures, contracting with vendors, and managing inventory. In the hospital example, scheduling the workforce to match patient admissions is critical to both providing quality care and controlling costs. Selecting a food service vendor is important to serving both employees and patients. Ensuring that the right drugs and supplies are on hand is achieved by working closely with vendors in the supply chain.

Operations management provides competitive advantage!

Strategic and tactical operations decisions determine how well the organization can accomplish its goals. They also provide opportunities for the organization to achieve unique competitive advantages that attract and keep customers.

For example, United Parcel Service, an international package delivery service, formed a partnership with its customer, Toshiba computers. Toshiba needs to provide a repair service to its laptop computer customers. The old approach of providing this service was cumbersome and time-consuming: (1) Customers had pick up their computers, (2) delivered the computers to Toshiba, (3) Toshiba repaired the computers, (4) picked up the repaired computers and delivered them back to the customers. Under this traditional approach, the total time to get a laptop computer repaired was two weeks—a long time for people to be without their laptop! Then they came up with an innovative idea for Toshiba to provide better service to its customers. United Parcel Service hired, trained, and certified its own employees to repair Toshiba laptop computers. The new repair process is much more efficient: (1) picks up computers from Toshiba owners, (2) repairs the computers, (3) delivers the computers back to their owners. The total time to get a computer repaired is now about two days. Most Toshiba customers think that Toshiba is doing a great job of repairing their computers, when in fact Toshiba never touches the computers! The result of this operations innovation is better service to Toshiba customers and a strong and profitable strategic partnership between and its customer, Toshiba.

The input/output transformation model

Operations management transforms inputs (labor, capital, equipment, land, buildings, materials and information) into outputs (goods and services) that provide added value to customers. Exhibit 27 summarizes the transformation process. The arrow labeled "Transformation System" is the critical element in the model that will determine how well the organization produces goods and services that meet customer needs. It does not matter whether the organization is a for-profit company, a non-profit organization (religious organizations, hospitals, etc.), or a government agency; all organizations must strive to maximize the quality of their transformation processes to meet customer needs.

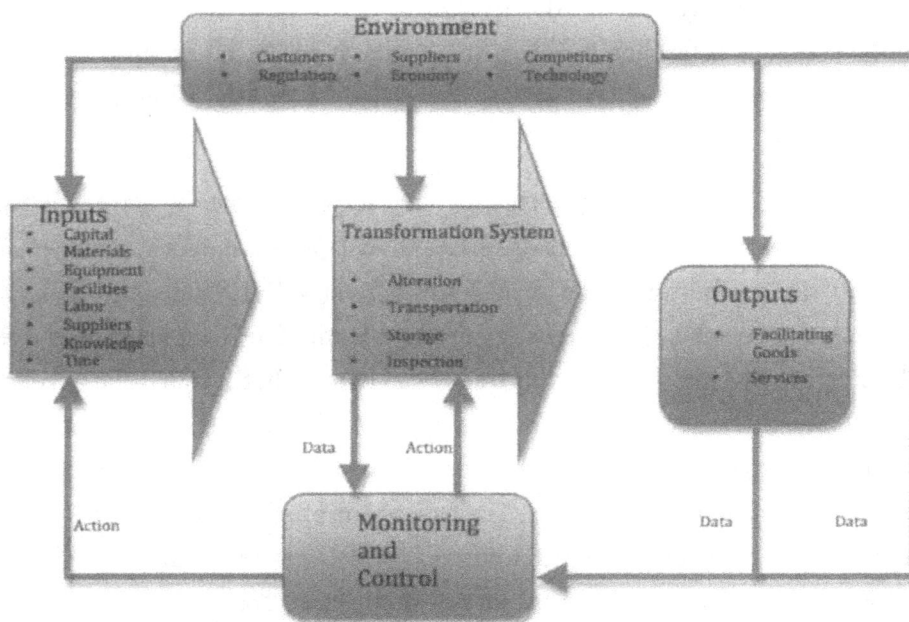

Exhibit 27: Example of typical transformation process

The 3M Company is a good example of the strategic importance of transforming inputs into outputs that provide competitive advantage in the marketplace. 3M manufactures a top-quality adhesive tape called "Magic Tape". Magic Tape is used for everyday taping applications, but it offers attractive features that most other tapes do not, including smooth removal from the tape roll, an adhesive that is sticky enough to hold items in place (but not too sticky that it can not be removed and readjusted if necessary!), and a non-reflective surface. For several decades, 3M has enjoyed a substantial profit margin on its Magic Tape product because 3M engineers make the manufacturing equipment and design the manufacturing processes that produce Magic Tape. In other words, 3M enjoys a commanding competitive advantage by controlling the transformation processes that turn raw material inputs into the high value-added Magic Tape product. Controlling the transformation process makes it extremely difficult for competitors to produce tape of the same quality as Magic Tape, allowing 3M to reap significant profits from this superior product.

An opposite example of the strategic implications of the input/output transformation process is 3M's decision in the 1980s to stop manufacturing VHS tape for video players and recorders. In the VHS tape market 3M had no proprietary manufacturing advantage, as there were many Asian competitors that could produce high-quality VHS tape at lower cost. Since 3M had no proprietary control over the transformation process for VHS tape that would allow the company to protect its profit margins for this product, it dropped VHS tape from its offerings. The two 3M examples of Magic Tape and VHS tape show how important the transformation process and operations management can be to providing and protecting an organization's competitive advantage.

A service example of the strategic importance of the transformation process is ING Bank, a banking company that conducts all banking transactions through the Internet, phone, and mail. ING maintains no traditional bank facilities, except for the buildings that house the employees that execute remote transactions with ING's customers. This strategy results in tremendous cost savings and competitive advantage to ING by not having to spend capital resources on land and buildings that traditional banks must spend. Consequently, ING can offer its customers higher interest rates on savings accounts and lower interest rates on loans.

Operations decisions

Countless operations decisions that have both long-term and short-term impacts on the organization's ability to produce goods and services that provide added value to customers must be made. If the organization has made mostly good operations decisions in designing and executing its transformation system to meet the needs of customers, its prospects for long-term survival are greatly enhanced. Major operations decisions areas include inventory, capacity, quality, scheduling, process type, technology, location, layout, and supply chain management. Each of these nine decision areas will be discussed in this section.

Inventory decisions

The key question that must be answered for inventory is "How much?" Understanding the best inventory levels to carry is critical to the organization because too much inventory and too little inventory are both costly to the organization. Inventory that exceeds what is needed to satisfy customer demand imposes unnecessary costs such as storage, deterioration, obsolescence, theft, and money tied up in inventory that cannot be used for other purposes. Too little inventory means the organization cannot meet 100 per cent of its customer demand and sales revenues are delayed or lost.

For example, a restaurant that specializes in serving fresh fish needs to make careful purchasing decisions so it has enough fresh fish each day to serve its customers, but not so much that unsold fish must be severely discounted or discarded at the end of the day. Computer companies such as Dell must carefully manage its computer chip inventory so it can meet current customer orders, but not be stuck with too much inventory if a new computer chip comes out or if vendors reduce prices.

Capacity decisions

The question managers must answer for the capacity decision area is the same as the question for inventory: "How much?" Determining the organization's capacity to produce goods and services involves both long-term and short-term decisions. *Long-term* capacity decisions involve facilities and major equipment investments. In 2007, Airbus introduced its Super Jumbo Jet that carries up to 850 passengers and costs USD 3 billion. The Super Jumbo provides huge amounts of passenger carrying capacity, but before an airline purchases this jet, it needs to decide if it has enough passengers to generate the revenue to pay for the plane and earn profits for the airline. A large single airplane like the Super Jumbo may not be the right capacity decision for an airline that serves numerous medium sized cities. On the other hand, an airline that serves passengers traveling between New York City, USA and Shanghai, China might find the Super Jumbo to be a perfect choice for meeting demand because of the large populations in each city.

Capacity decisions also involve *short-term* situations. In a grocery store, the number of customers that need to pay for their groceries at any one point during the day will vary significantly. To provide good customer service, managers must make sure that sufficient cash registers and employees are on hand to meet check-out demand. Similarly, hotels must make sure that they have enough employees to register arriving guests, to clean hotel rooms, and to provide food and beverages to customers. These decisions must be made carefully to avoid excessive labor costs from having too many employees for the number of customers being served.

Quality decisions

The decision relating to quality is not "how much" quality to have. If asked whether they support high quality in their organization, virtually all managers will respond enthusiastically that they fully support high quality! Rather, the quality of goods and services is determined by *numerous* decisions throughout the organization that have both long-term and short-term consequences for the organization's quality performance.

For example, while all managers may say they support quality, how many will support the capital expenditure to purchase new equipment that can meet tighter tolerance requirements more consistently? How many managers will spend money to send their engineers out into the field to talk to customers to better understand necessary product performance standards? How many managers will send teams of quality engineers to supplier facilities to assist suppliers with their quality programs? How much attention and resources does management give to employee skill development and training in the use of quality tools and in the philosophy of defect prevention? The outcome of these decisions will most certainly affect an organization's ability to produce outstanding quality in products and services.

For example, in the air transportation industry, the prevention of crashes is obviously something that everyone supports. Yet, for the past two decades in the United States, the press has reported on the weaknesses and neglect of the US air traffic control technology that plays a critical role in air travel safety. One might conclude that although everyone supports safety in air travel, more investment in modern technology and better decision making is needed to ensure the long-term safety of air transportation. Virtually all organizations are faced with similar decision-making scenarios when it comes to the factors that determine quality performance.

Another example is in the health care industry where one critical measure is the number of surgeries where foreign objects (sponges, instruments, etc.) are left in surgery patients. Such incidents are considered to be a serious oversight and totally unacceptable. In recent years, hospitals have developed processes for preventing these mistakes. In one approach, a member of the surgical staff tracks every object that enters the body cavity during surgery, then checks that object off when it is removed from the cavity. Any object that can not be accounted for triggers an inspection of the cavity, and perhaps an x-ray to help find the item before the incision is closed.

Quality improvement efforts require a great deal of analysis and teamwork, as well as a determined effort to make quality a top priority in the organization. Improving quality requires everyone to adopt a "continuous improvement" philosophy, where everyone approaches their work with the view that there are always opportunities to improve on the organization's key performance measures. Continuous improvement efforts are complex, multidimensional, and require partnerships among workers, management, suppliers, and customers.

Scheduling decisions

Scheduling is an operations decision that strives to provide the right mix of labor and machines to produce goods and services at the right time to achieve both efficiency and customer service goals. For example, a hotel must anticipate the peaks and valleys in demand that may occur during a day, during the week, and at different times of the year. Labor (front desk clerks, room service personnel, housekeepers, bellhops, etc.) must be scheduled carefully to meet customer demand at any given time, without scheduling excess employees that would impose unnecessary costs on the hotel. In a hospital setting, scheduling surgeries is a very important activity. Surgeons, nurses, support staff, equipment, supplies, and operating rooms must be scheduled carefully so patient surgeries can be conducted effectively and efficiently. At colleges and universities, scheduling the right courses with the right number of classroom seats at the right times is critical to allowing students to graduate on time.

Process decisions

Managers must decide how to organize equipment and labor to achieve the competitive goals of the organization. There are two basic choices for organizing the workplace to produce goods and services: (1) intermittent processes, and (2) repetitive processes.

Intermittent processes organize labor and equipment into departments by similarity of function to serve a wide variety of production requirements. For example, a health care clinic must cater to the individual needs of every patient who enters the clinic for treatment. One patient may have a broken ankle, while another patient may be a pregnant woman who needs a prenatal care checkup. One patient may be a baby with a fever, while another patient may be getting a prescription medication refilled. The primary organizational goal for a health clinic is *effectiveness* in treating the individual needs of each patient, and an intermittent process is often the most suitable way to organize labor and equipment to provide customized treatment for each individual patient. X-ray equipment and technicians are organized into an 'X-ray Department". Other departments are created for pediatrics, lab, gynecology, pharmacy, physical therapy, and many more. Patients are routed only to the departments that are needed for their particular treatment requirements. This production process is called an "intermittent" process, because the activity of each department happens intermittently at irregular intervals, depending on the particular needs of different patients (customers) at different points in time.

Intermittent processes are also used in manufacturing operations where a wide variety of products are manufactured, or where products are made to customer specifications. Equipment and labor can be organized into departments such as drilling, punch press, lathe, machining, painting, heat treating, molding, etc. Raw materials and components are routed through the facility according to the type and order of manufacturing activities necessary to produce the finished items. Exhibit 28 illustrates how two different products, "A63" and "B5" make their way through an intermittent process layout.

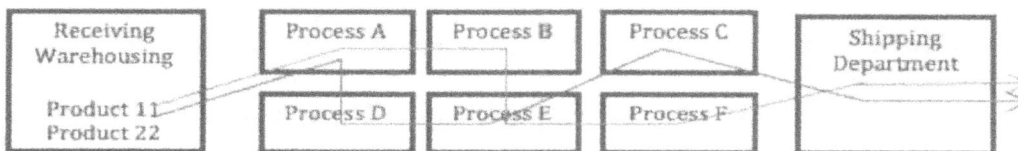

Exhibit 28: Intermittent process flows

Repetitive processes are used to produce identical or very similar products in high volumes. Equipment and labor are organized in a line flow arrangement to meet very specific customer or product processing requirements. Examples include assembly lines that produce products such as computers, cars, hamburgers, automatic car washes, and cafeteria lines. In all of these cases, the products or customers follow the same production steps to produce a standardized outcome. Since the production requirements to produce each unit of output are so well understood, there are many opportunities to achieve high levels of efficiency in repetitive process environments. *Efficiency* is a key goal in repetitive process environments. Investments in automation and technology are financially justified because the high volume of production spreads out the investment cost over more items/customers.

A paper mill is a good example of a repetitive process. The manufacturing requirements are well-understood, capital investment in automation is high, and production volume is extremely high to keep unit production costs as low as possible.

Exhibit 29 represents an example of a repetitive process for producing a product such as a small appliance, where raw materials and components are assembled to each unit at different stages of production. The units flow through the facility in a uniform pattern until they are completed and shipped to the customer.

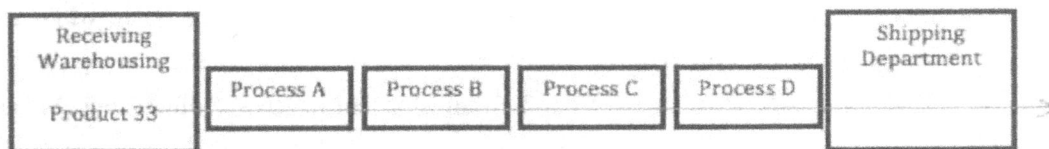

Exhibit 29: Product flow in a repetitive process

The two main differences between the intermittent and repetitive processes are product variety and product volume.

Intermittent processes are very flexible in meeting the individual requirements of different products or customers, but they tend to be very inefficient, with high amounts of waiting time, work in process inventories, and space requirements. Repetitive processes are very efficient at reducing unit production costs, waiting time, and inventories, but they are not very flexible in accommodating high product/customer variety. A compromise solution is the **cellular** process layout that captures the advantages of both intermittent and repetitive processes.

A cellular process arranges dissimilar machines and equipment together in a line that is dedicated to producing a specific family of products that have similar processing requirements. By setting up multiple dedicated cells, the facility can efficiently produce a wide variety of products (Exhibit 30). Since the products within a family have similar production requirements, equipment setup times, inventories, and lot sizes can be kept to a minimum. The cellular approach allows each product to be sent through the manufacturing process one piece at a time, according to the immediate set of customer orders. It provides workers the flexibility to change a product or customize it in some way in response to specific customer requirements. The cells are usually arranged in a U shape. This enables one worker to view multiple machines simultaneously and puts all machines within easy reaching distance. Cellular processes minimize cycle times and enable the organization to maintain higher levels of product volumes, variety, and customization.

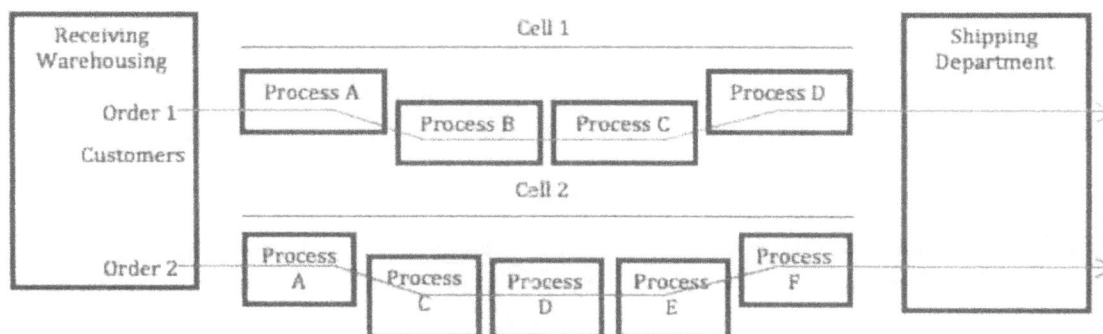

Exhibit 30: Cellular Layouts

Technology decisions

There are many benefits that technology can bring to an operations environment. Automated machinery, programmable equipment, and management information systems can provide speed, low unit processing costs, labor cost savings, increased accuracy and consistency, and sophisticated tracking and decision support systems to increase operations efficiency and effectiveness for both manufacturing and service environments. The main drawback in many technology decisions is the high fixed cost of purchasing and implementing the new systems. If mistakes are made in technology purchases, it can severely impact the fortunes of the company.

Managers are often biased in favor of adopting leading edge technology, especially if they see their competitors adopting it. Financial justifications for purchasing new technology are often overly optimistic in estimations of payback periods, the costs of implementation, and the actual gains in overall productivity the firm will enjoy.

The challenge for managers in technology is selecting the right technology for the right application. For example, if a manufacturing company believes that automation will increase the firm's flexibility to adapt to a changing competitive environment, questions should be asked, such as:

- What type of flexibility does the company need to thrive?

- Does it need to quickly switch production across a wide variety of products (product mix flexibility)?

- Does it need to quickly produce new products for a rapidly changing marketplace (product development flexibility)?

- Does it need to be able to quickly ramp up production during times of high demand, and quickly scale down production when cyclical or seasonal demand hits downturns (volume flexibility)?

Deere & Co manufactures machinery for the highly cyclical agricultural and construction industries. One of the reasons for Deere's success over the many decades is its ability to keep its technology expenditures under control so it can weather the inevitable declines in demand for its products. Deere managers use a mix of low technology/labor intensive production methods and automated/programmable technologies in its manufacturing plants. Careful technology decision making is a major reason why Deere & Co continues to thrive in spite of its highly volatile markets.

Location decisions

There are many factors that can determine where an organization will locate its facilities. For any given situation, some factors become more important than others in how facility location affects an organization's efficiency and effectiveness.

- **Proximity to sources of supply:** Firms that process bulk raw materials usually locate close to the source of supply to reduce transportation costs. Paper mills locate close to forests, canneries are built close to farming areas, and fish processing plants are located close to the harbors where the fishing vessels dock.

- **Proximity to customers:** There are several reasons why an organization would locate close to end customers. Service firms need to be close to customers to be convenient, as is the case for grocery stores, gas stations, fast food restaurants, and hospitals. Transportation costs can also require proximity to customers, as in the case of concrete manufacturing. Perishable products often require that they be produced close to the final market, as is the case for bakeries and fresh flowers.

- **Community factors:** Communities may offer a number of incentives to entice companies, including waiving or reducing taxes, and providing access roads, water and sewer connections, and utilities. Community attitudes can also play a role in an organization's location decision. Some communities may actively discourage companies that might bring more pollution, noise, and traffic to the area. Some communities may not want a prison to be located in their community. Other communities may welcome such firms because of the jobs, tax revenues, and economic diversity they promise.

- **Labor factors:** Research shows that the majority of location decisions are largely based on labor factors, since labor is a critical variable for many firms. Labor factors include the prevailing wage rate in a community for similar jobs, the supply of qualified workers, and the average education level of the local population (percentage of high school graduates, etc.). Other labor factors can include the degree of union organizing and the general work ethic of a community, as well as other measures of absenteeism and worker longevity in a job can play strong roles when a firm makes a location decision.

- **Other factors:** Many other factors can play a role in the location decision, including quality of life (crime rates, good schools, climate, and recreation options), access to major transportation arteries, construction costs, proximity of the competition, and opportunities for future expansion. As mentioned earlier, the importance of any location factor can vary greatly, depending on the circumstances of the decision.

In the 1990s, MCI, a major US telecommunications company, decided to relocate its engineering services division from MCI's headquarters in Washington DC to Colorado Springs, Colorado to reduce labor and facility costs. The decision was largely unsuccessful due to the high costs of employee relocation and the fact that much of the ethnically diverse engineering workforce did not want to live in Colorado Springs. Unlike Washington DC, Colorado Springs did not have cultural diversity to match with its diverse and highly educated workforce, it lacked employment options for spouses, and the work ethic was more relaxed due to the beautiful natural setting that provided unlimited options for outdoor recreation. In short, if MCI had put more effort into researching how well the Colorado Springs location matched its strategic requirements, it probably could have saved itself millions of dollars and a great deal of internal disruption to the organization.

Chapter summary

Operations management is a strategic function of the organization that produces the goods and services that are offered to the customer. Operations decisions determine how well these goods and services meet the needs of the organization's target market, and consequently, whether the organization will be able to survive over the long term.

This chapter concludes with discussions of three "Special topics" in operations management that deserve special attention because they are widely acknowledged as "best practices" for successful organizations. They include Total Quality Management, Supply Chain Management, and Just-In-Time/Lean Operations.

Special topic: Total Quality Management

Total Quality Management (TQM) is the organization-wide management of quality that includes facilities, equipment, labor, suppliers, customers, policies, and procedures. TQM promotes the view that quality improvement never ends, quality provides a strategic advantage to the organization, and zero defects is the quality goal that will minimize total quality costs. While this special topic on TQM is not a comprehensive discussion of all aspects of TQM, several key concepts will be discussed.

Quality costs

An important basis for justifying TQM practice is understanding its impact on total quality costs. TQM is rooted in the belief that preventing defects is cheaper than dealing with the costs of quality failures. In other words, total quality costs are minimized when managers strive to reach zero defects in the organization. The four major types of quality costs are prevention, appraisal, internal failure, and external failure.

Prevention costs are the costs created from the effort to reduce poor quality. Examples are designing the products so that they will be durable, training employees so they do a good job, certifying suppliers to ensure that suppliers provide quality in products and services, conducting preventive maintenance on equipment, and documenting quality procedures and improvements. In a traditional organization that does not practice TQM, prevention costs typically comprise the smallest percentage of total quality costs.

A good example of good product design occurs in all Honda products. Honda produces a wide variety of items including automobiles, ATVs, engines, generators, motorcycles, outboard motors, snow blowers, lawn and garden equipment, and even more items. To say the least, Honda engines last a long time. For example, Honda Accords typically run for well over 200,000 miles.

Employee training is also a very important prevention cost. For instance, employees in a vegetable/fruit packaging warehouse need to know what a bad vegetable/fruit looks like, since customers will not want to find spoiled produce in the store. Lifeguards at a swimming pool must know proper procedures for keeping swimmers safe. In many circumstances in both manufacturing and service businesses, the training of employees can make an enormous difference in preventing defects.

Supplier selection and certification are critical prevention activities. A product or service is only as good as the suppliers who partner with an organization to provide the raw materials, parts and components, and supporting services that make up the final products and services that the end customers receive. For example, a home furnishings store might use an outside subcontractor to install carpeting, but if the subcontractor fails to show up on time, tracks mud into the customer's home, or behaves in a rude manner, the store's reputation will suffer.

Similarly, a car manufacturer who purchases defective tires from a supplier risks incurring high costs of recalls and lawsuits when the defects are discovered.

Preventive maintenance is necessary for preventing equipment breakdowns. Many manufacturing companies use sophisticated software to track machine usage, and determine optimal schedules for regular machine maintenance, overhauls, and replacement.

Documenting quality is a necessary prevention cost because it helps the organization track quality performance, identify quality problems, collect data, and specify procedures that contribute to the pursuit of zero defects. Documentation is important to communicating good quality practice to all employees and suppliers.

Appraisal costs are a second major type of quality cost. Appraisal costs include the inspection and testing of raw materials, work-in-process, and finished goods. In addition, quality audits, sampling, and statistical process control also fall under the umbrella of appraisal costs.

Inspection and testing of raw materials is very important, since substandard raw materials lead to substandard products. Raw materials used for a bridge determine the strength of the bridge. For example, soft steel will erode away faster than hardened steel. Moreover, the concrete bridge decking needs to be solid, as concrete with air pockets will erode and crumble faster creating an unsafe bridge.

Finished goods and work-in-process inventory also need inspecting and testing. For example, worker error is quite common in the home construction industry, and this is why inspections occur frequently on newly constructed homes during and after the construction process is complete. Building inspectors ensure that the house has the proper framing, electrical, plumbing, heating, and so forth.

Quality audits and sampling are also important appraisal costs. Quality audits are checks of quality procedures to ensure that employees and suppliers are following proper quality practices. With sampling, a company can ensure with confidence that a batch of products is fit for use. For example, a wooden baseball bat manufacturer may test 10 out of every 100 bats to check that they meet strength standards. One weak bat can signal that quality problems are present.

Statistical process control (SPC) is the final type of appraisal cost. SPC tracks on-going processes in manufacturing or service environments to make sure that they are producing the desired performance. For example, a restaurant might statistically track customer survey results to make sure that customer satisfaction is maintained over time. In manufacturing windshields for automobiles, SPC might be used to track the number of microscopic air bubbles in the glass to make sure the process is performing to standard.

Internal failure costs are a third category of quality costs. This cost occurs when quality defects are discovered before they reach the customer. Examples of internal failure costs include scrapping a product, reworking the product, and lost productivity due to machine breakdowns or labor errors. Internal failure costs are typically more expensive than both prevention and appraisal costs because a great deal of material and labor often has been invested prior to the discovery of the defect. If a book publisher prints 10,000 books, then discovers that one of the chapters is missing from every copy, the cost of reworking or scrapping the books represents a major loss to the company. It would have been much cheaper to have procedures in place to prevent such a mistake from happening in the first place.

In the case of internal failure cost due to machine failures, FedEx, and other courier services cannot keep up with demand when a conveyor belt breaks down in the package distribution center. Major delays and costs occur when such incidents occur. Other examples include a road construction company having a road grader break down, a tool and die shop having a CNC machine break down, and a farmer having a combine break down during harvest time.

External failure costs are the fourth major cost of quality. External failure costs when the defect is discovered after it has reached the customer. This is the most expensive category of quality costs. Examples include product returns, repairs, warranty claims, lost reputation, and lost business. One spectacular example of external failure cost was when the Hubbell telescope was launched into space with mirrors that were ground improperly. When the telescope was turned on, instead of a magnificent view of stars, planets, and galaxies, the scientists could see only blurred images. The price of correcting the problem was over USD 1 billion.

External failure costs also occur when the wrong meal is delivered to a restaurant customer, when a computer breaks down shortly after it was purchased, when the wrong kidney is removed from a patient, and when a poorly designed automobile causes the death of drivers and passengers. Because of the enormous costs of internal and external failures, all companies should strive for zero defects. Successful TQM practice dictates that pursuing zero defects will result in the minimization of total quality costs by spending more on prevention and appraisal activities in order to reduce the much higher costs of internal and external failure.

TQM's seven basic elements

Successful practice of Total Quality Management involves both technical and people aspects that cover the entire organization and extend to relationships with suppliers and customers. Seven basic elements capture the essence of the TQM philosophy: customer focus, continuous improvement, employee empowerment, quality tools, product design, process management, and supplier quality.

- **Customer focus:** Decisions of how to organize resources to best serve customers starts with a clear understanding of customer needs and the measurement of customer satisfaction. For example, the Red Cross surveys its blood donors to determine how it can make the blood donation experience more pleasant and convenient. It collects information on the place, date and time donors came in, and asks donors questions of whether the donation time was convenient, whether they were treated with respect and gratitude, how long they had to wait to donate, and whether parking was adequate. By understanding donors' needs and experiences, Red Cross managers can determine strengths and weaknesses of the donation service process and make adjustments if necessary.

- **Continuous improvement:** An organizational culture that promotes continuous learning and problem solving is essential in the pursuit of zero defects. The Toyota Production System (TPS) is a universal continuous improvement system that has been effectively applied to many different types of organizations, including the health care industry. Essential elements of the TPS culture include studying process flow, collecting data, driving out wasteful non-value-added activities, and making everyone responsible for quality improvement. In the case of health care, the TPS approach enabled one hospital to analyze the causes of patient infections from catheters and pneumonia in patients on ventilators. With simple changes in procedures that prevented patients from getting these secondary illnesses, the hospital was able to save USD 40,000 per patient in these cases.

- **Employee involvement:** Employees in a TQM environment have very different roles and responsibilities than in a traditional organization. They are given responsibility, training, and authority to measure and control the quality of the work they produce, they work together in teams to address quality issues, they are cross-trained to be able to perform multiple tasks and have a greater understanding of the total production process, and they have a more intimate understanding of the operation and maintenance of their equipment. Employees are essential to the building of a continuous improvement organization.

- **Quality tools:** Discussion of the details of quality tools extends beyond the scope of this chapter, but there are seven basic quality tools that are used by front-line workers and managers in monitoring quality performance and gathering data for quality improvement activities. These tools include: cause-and-effect (fishbone) diagrams, flowcharts, checklists, control charts, scatter diagrams, Pareto analysis, and histograms. The beauty of these tools is that they are easy to understand and apply in on-going quality efforts.

- **Product design:** Product design is a key activity to avoid costly internal and external failure costs. For example, when a dental office designs the service process, it might have patients fill out a form that covers important information on general health issues, allergies, and medications. This helps to avoid future complications and problems. Staff, hygienists, and dentists are highly trained to follow proper procedures, the facility is both functional and pleasant, and the equipment and tools are state of the art to ensure that the patient's desired outcome is achieved. In a manufacturing setting, products should be designed to maximize product functionality, reliability, and manufacturability.

- **Process management:** "Quality at the Source" is an important concept in TQM. It means that managers and employees should be focused on the detailed activities in a process where good or bad quality is created. For example, in a Toyota plant in the United States in Georgetown, Kentucky, one of the work stations was responsible for installing seat belts and visors in every vehicle that came along the assembly line. There were 12 possible combinations of visors and seat belts that would go into any particular vehicle and the worker had to select the right combination and install the items in the vehicle in 55 seconds. Even the best workers made several errors during a shift on this activity. After studying the process, the workers came up with an idea to put all the items for a particular vehicle model in a blue plastic tote. With this change, the worker only had to make one decision per vehicle. Almost all the errors from the previous system were eliminated with this simple solution.

- **Supplier quality:** The focus on quality at the source extends to suppliers' processes as well, since the quality of a finished product is only as good as the quality of its individual parts and components, regardless of whether they come from internal or external sources. Sharing your quality and engineering expertise with your suppliers, having a formal supplier certification program, and including your suppliers in the product design stage are important measures to take to ensure that quality at the source extends to the supplier network.

Quality awards and standards

There are several quality awards and standards that are available for organizations to access. The large majority of organizations that use these programs use them as tools to help improve their quality processes and move toward implementing and successfully practicing TQM. The Malcolm Baldrige Award is a United States quality award that covers an extensive list of criteria that are evaluated by independent judges if an organization chooses to compete for the award. In many cases, organizations use the Baldrige criteria as a guide for their internal quality efforts rather than compete directly for the award. The criteria can be accessed from the Internet at: http://www.baldrige.nist.gov/rnet.

The International Organization for Standardization (ISO) sponsors a certification process for organizations that seek to learn and adopt superior methods for quality practice (ISO 9000) and environmentally responsible products and methods of production (ISO 14000). These certifications are increasingly used by organizations of all sizes to compete more effectively in a global marketplace due to the wide acceptance of ISO certification as a criterion for supplier selection. ISO 9000 and ISO 14000 are described on the ISO web page at: http://www.iso.org/iso/home.htm .

> *"The ISO 9000 family addresses "quality management". This means what the organization does to fulfill:*
>
> *the customer's quality requirements, and*
>
> *applicable regulatory requirements, while aiming to*
>
> *enhance customer satisfaction, and*
>
> *achieve continual improvement of its performance in pursuit of these objectives.*
>
> *The ISO 14000 family addresses "environmental management". This means what the organization does to:*
>
> *minimize harmful effects on the environment caused by its activities, and to*
>
> *achieve continual improvement of its environmental performance."*

Another popular quality award is the Deming Prize, which is a Japanese quality award for which organizations from any country can apply. The Deming Prize was named after W. Edwards Deming, an American statistician, author, and consultant who helped improve United States production capabilities during World War II, but is best known for his work in post-war Japan. He is widely credited with assisting the Japanese in rebuilding their nation's production infrastructure in the areas of product design, product quality, and testing through the application of statistical methods. Florida Power and Electric was the first American company to win the Deming Prize, due to its meticulous use of formal approaches to quality improvement, data-based decision making, quality improvement teams, and the careful documentation of processes and procedures. More information on the Deming Prize can be found at:

http://www.juse.or.jp/e/deming/index.html

7. Operations management

Special topic: supply chain management

Supply chain management is the business function that coordinates and manages all the activities of the supply chain, including suppliers of raw materials, components and services, transportation providers, internal departments, and information systems. Exhibit 31 illustrates a supply chain for providing packaged milk to consumers.

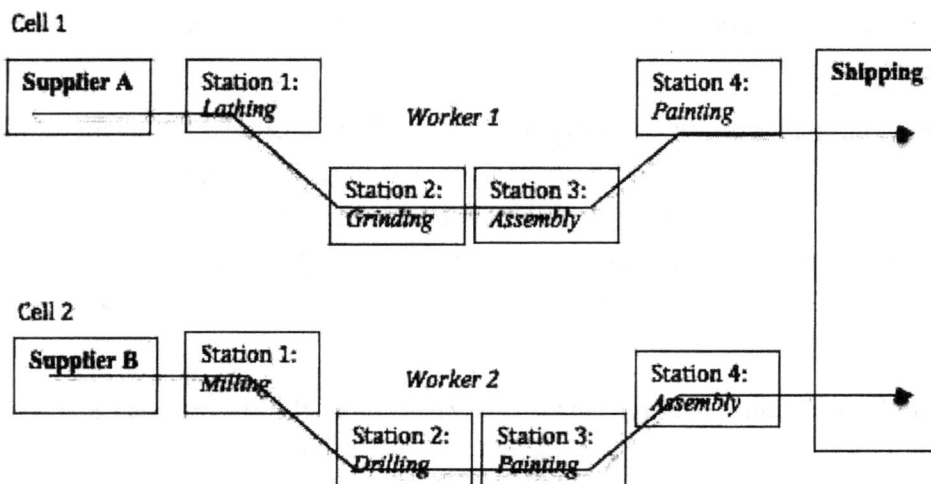

Exhibit 31: Illustration of a supply chain

In the manufacturing sector, supply chain management addresses the movement of goods through the supply chain from the supplier to the manufacturer, to wholesalers or warehouse distribution centers, to retailers and finally to the consumer. For example, Apple, Inc uses sophisticated information systems to accept orders for custom-built computers from individual customers all over the world. Apple assembles the computers in Shanghai, China, to the customers' specifications. It uses parts and components that are provided by outside suppliers who can deliver the right parts in the right quantity in a timely way to satisfy the immediate production schedule. The completed computers are flown from Shanghai by FedEx, reaching the end-user customers only a few days after the orders were placed. Apple's supply chain allows it to provide fast delivery of high-quality custom computers at competitive prices.

Supply chain concepts also apply to the service sector, where service firms must coordinate equipment, materials, and human resources to provide services to their customers in a timely manner. For example, a retail store that sells electronic products may contract with an outside business to provide installation services to its customers. In many cases, the customer does not even know the installation was done by an outside contractor. Information and communication technologies such as global positioning systems (GPS), barcode technology, customer relationship management (CRM) databases, and the Internet allow service businesses to coordinate external and internal service suppliers to efficiently and effectively respond to customer demand.

The supply chain is not just a one way process that runs from raw materials to the end customer. Although goods tend to flow this way, important data such as forecasts, inventory status, shipping schedules, and sales data are examples of information that is constantly being conveyed to different links in the supply chain. Money also tends to flow "upstream" in the supply chain so goods and service providers can be paid.

Bullwhip effect

A major goal in supply chain management strategy is to minimize the bullwhip effect. The bullwhip effect occurs when inaccurate or distorted information is passed on through the links in the supply chain. As the bad information gets passed from one party to the next, the distortions worsen and cause poor ordering decisions by upstream parties in the supply chain that have little apparent link to the final end-item product demand. As information gets farther from the end customer, the worse the quality of information gets as the supply chain members base their guesses on the bad guesses of their partners. The results are wasteful inventory investments, poor customer service, inefficient distribution, misused manufacturing capacity, and lost revenues for all parties in the supply chain.

For example, Open Range Jeans (a fictitious company) are sold in a popular retail store chain. The retail chain decides to promote Open Range Jeans and reduce the price to boost customer traffic in its stores, but the chain does not tell the Open Range manufacturer of this promotion plan. The manufacturer sees an increase in retail orders, forecasts a long-term growth in demand for its jeans, and places orders with its suppliers for more fabric, zippers, and dye.

Suppliers of fabric, zippers and dye see the increase in orders from the jeans manufacturer and boost their orders for raw cotton, chemicals, etc. Meanwhile, the retail chain has ended its Open Range promotion, and sales of the jeans plummet below normal levels because customers have stocked up to take advantage of the promotion prices. Just as end-customer demand falls, new jeans are being manufactured, and raw materials are being sent to the jeans factory. When the falling end-customer demand is finally realized, manufacturers rush to slash production, cancel orders, and discount inventories.

Not wanting to get burned twice, manufacturers wait until finished goods jean inventories are drawn down to minimal levels. When seasonal demand increases jeans purchases, the retail stores order more Open Range jeans, but the manufacturers cannot respond quickly enough. A stockout occurs at the retail store level just as customers are purchasing jeans during the back-to-school sales season. Retail customers respond to the stockout by purchasing the jeans of a major competitor, causing long-term damage to Open Range's market share.

Causes of the bullwhip effect

The bullwhip effect is caused by demand forecast updating, order batching, price fluctuation, and rationing and gaming.

- **Demand forecast updating** is done individually by all members of a supply chain. Each member updates its own demand forecast based on orders received from its "downstream" customer. The more members in the chain, the less these forecast updates reflect actual end-customer demand.

- **Order batching** occurs when each member takes order quantities it receives from its downstream customer and rounds up or down to suit production constraints such as equipment setup times or truckload quantities. The more members who conduct such rounding of order quantities, the more distortion occurs of the original quantities that were demanded.

- **Price fluctuations** due to inflationary factors, quantity discounts, or sales tend to encourage customers to buy larger quantities than they require. This behavior tends to add variability to quantities ordered and uncertainty to forecasts.

- **_Rationing and gaming_** is when a seller attempts to limit order quantities by delivering only a percentage of the order placed by the buyer. The buyer, knowing that the seller is delivering only a fraction of the order placed, attempts to "game" the system by making an upward adjustment to the order quantity. Rationing and gaming create distortions in the ordering information that is being received by the supply chain.

Counteracting the bullwhip effect

To improve the responsiveness, accuracy, and efficiency of the supply chain, a number of actions must be taken to combat the bullwhip effect:

- Make real-time end-item demand information available to all members of the supply chain. Information technologies such as electronic data interchange (EDI), bar codes, and scanning equipment can assist in providing all supply chain members with accurate and current demand information.

- Eliminate order batching by driving down the costs of placing orders, by reducing setup costs to make an ordered item, and by locating supply chain members closer to one another to ease transportation restrictions.

- Stabilize prices by replacing sales and discounts with consistent "every-day low prices" at the consumer stage and uniform wholesale pricing at upstream stages. Such actions remove price as a variable in determining order quantities.

- Discourage gaming in rationing situations by using past sales records to determine the quantities that will be delivered to customers.

Other factors affecting supply chain management

In addition to managing the bullwhip effect, supply chain managers must also contend with a variety of factors that pose on-going challenges:

- Increased demands from customers for better performance on cost, quality, delivery, and flexibility. Customers are better informed and have a broader array of options for how they conduct business. This puts added pressure on supply chain managers to continually improve performance.

- Globalization imposes challenges such as greater geographic dispersion among supply chain members. Greater distances create longer lead times and higher transportation costs. Cultural differences, time zones, and exchange rates make communication and decision-making more difficult. Boeing and Airbus have discovered the downside of sourcing from global suppliers. Much smaller suppliers of kitchen galleys, lavatories, and passenger seats have been unable to fulfill orders from Boeing and Airbus, leaving the latter unable to deliver planes to its airline customers.

- Government regulations, tariffs, and environmental rules provide challenges as well. For example, many countries require that products have a minimum percentage of local content. Being environmentally responsible by minimizing waste, properly disposing of dangerous chemicals, and using recyclable materials is rapidly becoming a requirement for doing business.

Supplier selection

Choosing suppliers is one of the most important decisions made by a company. The efficiency and value a supplier provides to an organization is reflected in the end product the organization produces. The supplier must not only provide goods and services that are consistent with the company's mission, it must also provide good value. The three most important factors in choosing a supplier are price, quality, and on-time delivery.

A company must not only choose who it wants as a supplier, it must also decide how many suppliers to use for a given good or service. There are advantages to using multiple suppliers and there are advantages to using one supplier. Whether to single-source or multiple-source often depends on the supply chain structure of the company and the character of the goods or services it produces.

If a company uses a single supplier, it can form a partnership with that supplier. A partnership is a long-term relationship between a supplier and a company that involves trust, information sharing, and financial benefits for both parties. When both parties benefit from a partnership, it is called a "win-win situation". It is easy to see how choosing suppliers is one of the most important decisions a company makes.

There are advantages and disadvantages to using one supplier. One advantage is that the supplier might own patents or processes and be the only source for the product. With one supplier, pricing discounts may be granted because purchases over the long-term are large and unit production costs for the supplier are lower. The supplier may be more responsive if you are the only purchaser of an item, resulting in better supplier relations. Just-in-time ordering is easier to implement, and deliveries may be scheduled more easily. Finally, using a single supplier is necessary to form a partnership. One disadvantage is that if that one supplier experiences a disaster at its warehouse like a fire or a tornado, or its workers go on strike, there is no other ready source for the product. Another possible disadvantage is that a single supplier may not be able to supply a very large quantity if it is suddenly needed. Also, sometimes the government requires the use of multiple suppliers for government projects.

There are also advantages and disadvantages to using multiple suppliers. Suppliers might provide better products and services over time if they know they are competing with other suppliers. Also, if a disaster happens at one supplier's warehouse, other suppliers can make up the loss. If a company uses multiple suppliers, there is more flexibility of volume to match demand fluctuations. One disadvantage with multiple suppliers is that it is more difficult to forge long-term partnerships. Information sharing becomes riskier, lower volumes for each supplier provide fewer opportunities for cost savings, and suppliers tend to be less responsive to emergency situations.

Partnerships are long-term relationships between a supplier and a company that involve trust and sharing and result in benefits for both parties. A good example of a partnership is the partnering between a Deere & Co. farm equipment factory and its suppliers. Deere decided to outsource its sheet metal, bar stock, and castings part families.

When Deere sent requests for bids to 120 companies, 24 companies responded to say they were interested. Deere then sent a team of engineers, quality specialists, and supply chain managers to evaluate each company. One supplier was chosen for each of the three part families. All three of the suppliers that were chosen were located less than two hours of driving time from the Deere plant.

For many years, all three suppliers have continued to provide outstanding quality, delivery, and cost performance to Deere. The suppliers benefited by gaining a long-term customer with a large amount of profitable business. Deere realized a 50 per cent drop in production costs on the three part families and was able to better focus on its mission of manufacturing farm equipment.

Conclusion

Supply chain management concerns the development of communication and information systems to link suppliers together in cooperative partnerships that promote advantage for all participants. Benefits include faster response times, reduced inventory costs, increased accuracy, and improved quality.

Special topic: just-in-time and lean systems

Just-in-time (JIT) is a management philosophy that originated in the 1970s. Taiichi Ohno is credited with developing JIT and perfected it for Toyota's manufacturing plants in Japan. The main goal of JIT is to eliminate anything that does not add value from the customer's perspective. Non-value-added activities are referred to as "waste" in JIT. Examples of waste include:

- overproduction beyond what is needed to satisfy immediate demand

- waiting time (work-in-process, customer waiting)

- unnecessary transportation (material handling, customer travel through a facility, etc.)

- processing waste (yield rates, start-up costs)

- inventory storage waste (space, deterioration, obsolescence, etc.)

- unnecessary motion and activity (waste in work techniques, etc.)

- waste from product and service defects (rework, scrap, warranty, etc.)

There are three essential elements that contribute to the successful practice of JIT:

- JIT manufacturing principles

- Total Quality Management (TQM)

- employee empowerment

JIT manufacturing principles

In a manufacturing setting, there are six major ways to pursue JIT goals: inventory reduction to expose waste, use of a "demand-pull" production system, quick setups to reduce lot sizes, uniform plant loading, flexible resources, and cellular flow layouts.

Inventory reduction to expose waste

Inventory covers up a lot of wasteful practices (poor equipment, weak vendors, bad quality, long setup times, etc.). By gradually lowering inventory, the weaknesses of the production system can be revealed and addressed one by one. Machines can be replaced or better maintained, vendors quality and delivery can be improved, machine setup procedures can be streamlined, quality practices can be implemented, and labor and equipment can be laid out more efficiently. These improvements permit the organization to operate with less inventory, less costs, and faster response times in meeting customer needs.

Demand-pull production system

The traditional approach to manufacturing management promotes a strong focus on machine and labor utilization. The view was that if managers make sure that workers and machines are always busy, then surely the factory will be productive and efficient. This approach is called the "push" system of manufacturing, where raw material and work-in-process is continuously pushed through the factory in the pursuit of high utilization. The problem with this approach is that it usually produces high levels of inventories, long lead times, overtime costs, high levels of potential rework, and workers who are competing with one another rather than working cooperatively.

In contrast to the push system, JIT espouses a "demand-pull" system that operates on the rule that work should flow to a work center only if that work center needs more work. If a work center is already occupied with work activity, the upstream work center should stop production until the downstream work center communicates a need for more material. The emphasis on maintaining high utilization is removed in a JIT environment. The focus of a JIT environment is on addressing the challenges that affect the overall effectiveness of the factory (setup time reduction, quality improvement, enhanced production techniques, waste elimination, etc.) in meeting its strategic goals, rather than allowing excess inventory to cover up inefficiencies that reduce the factory's competitiveness.

Quick setups to reduce lot sizes

The longer it takes, and the more expensive it is to setup equipment and labor to produce an item, the greater the quantity of items that have to be produced in a given production run. Traditional production management philosophy promoted the notion that long production runs of the same item were the key to driving down unit costs. The problem was that large production runs created large quantities of WIP and finished goods inventory that far exceeded the demand. These items would consequently cause high levels of inventory costs, long lead times, high potential rework, low flexibility in responding to customer needs, etc.

Driving down setup costs and setup times are key to dramatically improving factory competitiveness in a JIT environment. In the 1980s, the 3M company converted a factory that made a few adhesive products in long production runs into a factory that made over 500 adhesive products in small production runs. To keep unit production costs under control, 3M studied the setups on its coating machines. Since the cost of chemical waste disposal was a major part of the cost of changing over a coating machine to make another product, 3M shortened the length of hoses that needed purging and redesigned the shape of the adhesive solution holding pan on the coating machine to be shallower. 3M also used quick-connect devices, disposable filters, and work teams to speed up setups. The result was that 3M could maintain low unit costs on its coating machines while producing small lots of hundreds of products to meet market demand quickly.

Uniform plant loading

The successful practice of JIT means having the right quantities of the right products in the right place at the right time. Driving down setup times enables the company to produce the product mix and quantities that are demanded in the present time period.

Flexible resources

The enemy of JIT is uncertainty. A JIT environment thrives on predictability in customer demand, production processes, suppliers, and workers. Of course, uncertainty cannot be completely eliminated in most organizational environments.

The defense against uncertainty that cannot be driven out is to implement flexible resources that can adapt easily to changing circumstances. General-purpose, moveable equipment that can fulfill a wide variety of production requirements is one way to improve flexibility. For example, drilling machines with quick-change bits which can be wheeled into position to form new work cells allows the factory to maximize efficiency while producing exactly what is needed to satisfy immediate demand. Another example is Toyota's use of paint canisters that attach to paint sprayers. Any car can be painted any color without having to purge hoses in switching from one color to another.

Multifunctional workers are another way to bring flexibility to the work environment. At Honeywell's heating and cooling controls plant, workers are trained to operate all the machines on their work line. The flexibility that comes from multifunctional workers changes the nature of how work gets done. Instead of workers being trained on one machine and working independently of one another, multifunctional workers have a "big picture" view of the production line, where every worker understands all aspects of the line and how to work together to meet quality and schedule goals regardless of the circumstances.

Line/cellular flow layouts

Earlier in this chapter, we described the efficiencies that repetitive process layouts provide. Repetitive process layouts are perfectly suited for driving out non-value-added activities and transitioning to a JIT environment. Intermittent layouts feature dozens or even hundreds of different paths through the facility. They are filled with complexity, uncertainty, and low visibility. Workers tend to have specialized skills, work independently of other departments, and have little sense of "ownership" of the products they work on.

In contrast, cell layouts promote JIT goals by featuring unidirectional product flows, high visibility, and fast throughput times. Workers with multifunctional skills are assigned to individual cells and have responsibility and control of the products they produce. Workers in a cell environment tend to have a greater sense of ownership and pride in their work because they have a "big picture" view of the product as it is converted from raw material to a finished good. This deeper understanding of the production process increases the opportunities for workers to contribute ideas for process improvements.

Total Quality Management

TQM was discussed in detail earlier. TQM goes hand in hand with the JIT philosophy because quality is a major source of uncertainty and non-value-added activities in an organization with poor quality practices. TQM promotes continuous improvement, doing it right the first time, designing quality into products and processes, and establishing an overall focus on prevention as the primary quality activity.

Employee empowerment

Front-line employees play a critical role in successful JIT practice. They work in partnership with management and each other in the continuous pursuit of excellence. There are several ways in which front-line employees contribute to JIT success:

- Employees work together in problem-solving teams to gather data and build consensus on how to improve work processes.

- Employees are responsible for understanding the quality measures of their work and what they need to do to meet the needs of internal and external customers.

- Each employee is empowered to take action to correct problems.

- Employees have cross-functional skill sets that allow them to be assigned to areas which need help, and to help them adopt a broader ("big picture") view of the production process.

- Unlike a traditional "push" environment where line workers are relatively independent of one another in their work activities, JIT employees are connected by the "demand pull" discipline, where work is not produced unless the downstream work center needs it. Demand-pull promotes the inter-connectedness of workers.

- Front-line employees are responsible for the basic maintenance of their machines. This helps employees have a better understanding of the condition of their equipment and its ability to meet quality and production requirements.

Management works with employees by being coaches and facilitators rather than authoritative supervisors. Managers are charged with hiring employees who can work in a proactive team environment, and provide the training and incentives to build a work culture that is focused on continuous improvement.

Conclusion: The evolution of JIT into "lean operations"

The JIT philosophy has evolved from a manufacturing-focused management approach to a set of management principles that can be applied to any organization. "Lean operations" is a term that is replacing JIT, especially in service environments. "Lean operations" captures the true essence and power of how a culture built around continuous improvement and the pursuit of value-added activities leads directly to competitive advantage in the marketplace. Lean operations is a management philosophy for any organization to achieve higher quality, increased productivity, improved delivery speed, greater responsiveness to changing markets, and increased customer satisfaction.

8. Securing and managing external relationships

Editor: Steven D Sheetz (Virginia Tech, USA)

Contributors: Kimberly Watkins, Sarah ElShawarby, Nicholle Depaz (Virginia Tech, USA)

Reviewer: Robin S Russell (Virginia Tech, USA)

Learning objectives

- understand the fundamental elements of external relationships

- know the type of common relationships and the phases of developing relationships

- use the characteristics of the business situation to choose the right type of relationship

- understand the relationship between types of external relationship and business strategies

- understand the risks associated with various business strategies

Introduction to external relationships

In today's business world, organizations increasingly depend upon developing external relationships to remain competitive. This trend occurs for two reasons. First, organizations have come to realize that they cannot be first-rate in every phase of their business (e.g. marketing, production, information systems, etc). Instead, they recognize that a better strategy is one in which they focus on core competencies, or the things they do best, and establish relationships with other companies to perform those functions where they do not have outstanding capabilities. For example, <u>Amazon.com</u> offers a wide variety of products and even recommends personalized suggestions to its customers. It realizes, however, that other companies such as FedEx and UPS have world-class competence in delivering goods. That is why Amazon.com customers have their purchases delivered by FedEx, UPS or a country's postal service. You do not see Amazon delivery trucks and likely never will. Secondly, information and communication technologies make it much easier to operationally create seamless relationships. Instant communications between two separate companies enable them to manage a business process as if the two companies were a single company. Both companies and the customers benefit from relationships that work. The entire business process of ordering and delivering is world class for Amazon.com. Additionally, FedEx or UPS receives more business, and customers benefit from receiving superior service.

External relationships provide access to additional information and financial resources, which ideally results in increased profitability and success. Yet, forming relationships involves associated risks, and debate continues about how to best realize benefits and minimize costs (Street and Cameron, 2007). Nevertheless, many managers now agree that strategies for establishing and managing external relationships are necessary for all organizations in the current and future global business environment.

This chapter describes the components of external relationships to provide the background needed to understand and form the right relationships for organizations of all sizes. These include the types of common relationships, the phases of relationship development, critical factors for successful relationships and the skills needed to perform these essential tasks. Leveraging external relationships requires a strategic perspective that ranges from obtaining reliable supplies of raw materials for internal production processes to outsourcing entire business processes. Exhibit 32 shows that developing the right relationships depends on implementing explicit strategies that are built upon an understanding of relationship fundamentals.

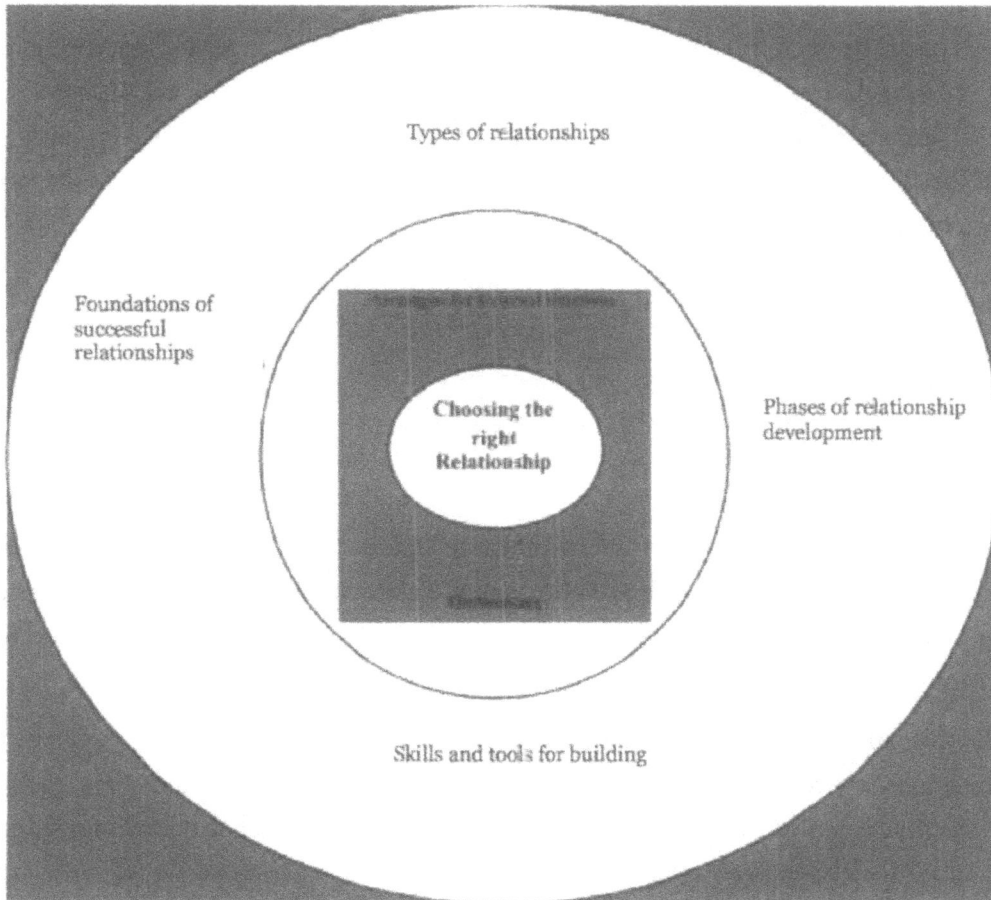

Exhibit 32: Developing relationships

An external relationship is defined as a commercially oriented link between two business institutions with the intent of increasing tangible and/or intangible benefits for one or both of the organizations involved (Street and Cameron, 2007). Two common types of external relationships are market exchanges and partnerships, which we will discuss later in this chapter.

Trends in management

The global business environment requires managers to integrate outside sources and business partners to increase efficiency. Technology has been proven to be a key factor in improving good relationships, while also providing capabilities to evaluate and eliminate poor relationships (Scannell and Sullivan, 2000). Companies are partnering together to form virtual organizational units, which work to the benefit of core businesses as we illustrated with the Amazon.com example in the introduction to this chapter. Managers must have business management skills, technical skills, and a thorough knowledge of external relationship management in order to take optimal advantage of opportunities and leverage the skills and knowledge of other organizations to maximize returns on investment.

Trust: the foundation for a successful relationship

One of the most important elements in developing a successful, long-term relationship is trust. Trust affects the quality of every relationship, every communication, and every project. **Trust** can be defined as the belief that one party will fulfill its obligations. According to Jim Burke, former chairman and CEO of Johnson & Johnson, "You can't have success without trust. The word trust embodies almost everything you can strive for that will help you to succeed" (Covey, 2006). This key factor must be mutual between all organizations involved, whether they are suppliers of materials or providers of outsourcing capabilities. If mutual trust is established early on, all organizations will benefit through a greater willingness to share ideas, goals, and work together to solve problems Exhibit 33 reveals trust is a function of five different dimensions.

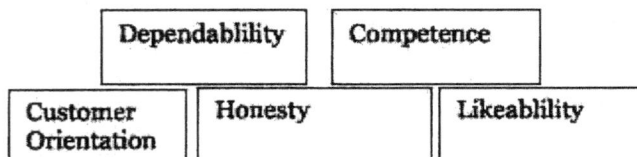

Dependablility	Competence	
Customer Orientation	Honesty	Likeablility

Exhibit 33: Dimensions of trust

- **Dependability:** Is one party making and fulfilling promises to another (Covey, 2006). Dependability can also be exemplified via third party confirmations. For example, a credible source can vouch for a firm when dependability has been proven through past experiences. Product demonstrations and plant tours are other ways companies can illustrate the capability to be dependable.

- **Competence:** Is when an organization appears knowledgeable. Demonstrating competence can be the fastest way to increase trust (Covey, 2006). A thorough understanding of suppliers, customers, products, competitors, and the industry demonstrates competence. If a manager understands the relationships they develop, the organization will be perceived as competent.

- **Relationship orientation:** Is the degree to which the company puts the partner first (Weitz, Castleberry, and Tanner, 2005). A company cannot be successful if managers are only concerned about their own profits within a transaction. The company has to make their partner feel valued and can accomplish this by tailoring a product or service specifically for its partner. Creating a feeling of individuality usually results in a loyal, reliable partner.

- **Honesty:** Incorporates truthfulness, sincerity, and dependability. For example, if a seller has established a dependable reputation, the company is usually perceived to be honest. However, illustrating honesty has many other facets as well. A good partner organization should provide all aspects of the truth, whether it is positive or negative information. Creating a relationship based on a foundation of lies is one of the biggest mistakes an organization can make. Partners typically discover the lies, which may result in the loss of critical supplies and/or highly profitable opportunities. One way to combat this is to create a culture that values and encourages honesty. Studies have, in fact, shown that telling the truth strengthens team-building efforts and increases morale and productivity (Smith, 2007).

- **Likeability:** Is finding a common, friendly ground between the partners. The relationships you select should be ones where you would like to increase trust, and where, by improving trust, you would get far better results professionally (Covey, 2006). This is likely the least important of the five dimensions of trust; however it is still noteworthy in the formation of an external relationship.

Marketing exchanges and partnerships

In 2005, Barton A Weitz, Stephen B Castleberry, and John F Tanner published their book "Selling: Building Relationships" in which they discuss many of the aspects of modern business relationships, including market exchanges and partnerships. According to their book, a market exchange is defined as a relationship where each party is only concerned with their own welfare. A partnership, conversely, is based on creating a mutually beneficial affiliation for both of the organizations. Market exchanges and partnerships both generate commercially oriented connections, which classifies the two relationships as external (Weitz, Castleberry, and Tanner, 2005).Market exchange:

A **market exchange** is a type of relationship between a buyer and seller in which each party is only concerned about that particular party's benefit (Weitz, Castleberry, and Tanner, 2005).

Seller: concerned with making a sale vs **Buyer:** concerned with lowest prices

Exhibit 34: Market exchange

A **solo exchange** is a transaction that occurs between the buyer and seller where each pursues' their own individual self-interest (Weitz, Castleberry, and Tanner, 2005). Suppose you are traveling to visit relatives in a nearby town on a warm and sunny Saturday morning. As you pass a small store that is having a sale you see a wooden bench, much like one your grandmother had, with a USD 25 selling price. At this point you might pay the USD 25 for the bench, haggle for a lower price, or walk away from the transaction. You decide to make the seller an offer of USD 10 for the bench. After minimal negotiations the bargain price of USD 15 is agreed upon.

This transaction is an example of a solo exchange. The two parties are not interested in or concerned about the well-being of the other party. Neither you, nor the seller, expect to engage in future transactions, and both parties are successful in pursuing their individual goals. The consumer receives the bench for the lowest possible price, while the seller charges the highest acceptable price. A solo exchange should not be considered an ethical decision, merely an uncomplicated, one-time choice.

Two basic relationship types

The two basic relationship types of market exchange and partnerships are divided further based on eight factors shown in column 1 of Table 5. Varying values of these factors represent situations where the organizations reach greater levels of integration and provide greater returns to both sides of the relationship.

Table 5: Types of relationships

	(1) Market exchanges		(2) Partnerships	
Factors involved in the relationship	Solo exchange	Functional relationship	Relational partnership	Strategic partnership
Time horizon	short term	long term	long term	long term
Concern for the party	low	low	medium	high
Trust	low	low	high	high
Investment in relationship	low	low	low	high
Nature of relationship	conflict, bargaining	cooperation	accommodation	coordination
Risk in relationship	low	medium	high	high
Potential benefits	low	medium	high	high

Functional relationship

A **functional relationship** is a long-term market exchange characterized by loyalty (Weitz, Castleberry, and Tanner, 2005). This type of relationship portrays the buyer purchasing a product out of routine or pattern. In a functional relationship, previous purchases will often influence later purchases. Typically, the buyer will continue to purchase from their selected seller as long as the price and the product stay relatively consistent to the original transaction. Buyers often illustrate this loyalty for several reasons. One reason a buyer remains loyal is simply convenience. It is easier for the buyer to avoid the arduous task of searching and negotiating for a product every time a recurring purchase needs to be made, especially when they are likely to come to the same conclusion and buy again from the previous supplier.

For example: A buyer for a school is in charge of purchasing all items that will be necessary for the cafeteria to function. Assume the school in question is a small elementary school with only about one hundred students. The buyer must purchase snacks, candy, meat, and drinks, just to name a few. This particular buyer uses a wholesaler to purchase all necessary items. This wholesaler has no desire to establish a partnership with the school; it merely wishes to sell as many items as possible. Similarly, the success of this relationship will not make or break the school's success as an educational institution. This affiliation is established out of convenience. However, if the vendor begins to have poor service or inflated prices, the purchaser will simply choose a comparable wholesaler with little anxiety.

With a functional relationship, both parties are interested in their own profits, therefore, price is usually the most important factor in the decision making process. The relationship established between the buyer and seller is not permanent. Buyers will often change suppliers to try and get the best possible deal; however, when deciding on a supplier other factors are often weighed into the equation such as quality, reliability, trust, and commitment.

Partnerships

A **partnership** is two parties concerned about the welfare of each other in developing a win-win relationship (Mohr, 1994). There are two types of partnerships: a relational and strategic partnership.

Relational partnership

A **relational partnership** is a partnership that develops on the premise of a close, personal relationship built on trust (Mohr, 1994). With this type of partnership there is an open line of communication, and the parties work together in order to overcome any potential problems. Both sides of the partnership are trying to make money, but the more important factor is developing a long-term, working relationship that will continue to generate money over time. When relational partnerships are successful, it is often not necessary to have more than minimal negotiations about price. In addition, minor details will not be allowed to derail or end the relationships because the goal is to establish an ongoing mutually beneficial exchange.

Relational partnerships may develop because of personal ties, but more often they occur due to professional necessity. For example, every year large US businesses recruit new employees using booths at career fairs across the country. Such a career fair program is not significant enough for the company to enter into a strategic partnership with an employment service to perform hiring at career fairs, but finding employees with the necessary skills is still very important. Regional managers will likely be responsible for this job and they may form a relational partnership with the organizations that host the job fairs in their area to ensure that when the job fairs are planned the representative company will be included. A relational partnership is more similar to a friendship than to a market exchange. Rather than showing concern only for their own self interests, partners will offer their time and resources to continue the relationship, because of the expected future benefits of continuing interactions. James Cash Penney, the founder of the US department store chain JCPenney, believed that "all great businesses are built on friendship". If this ideal is applied, a strong foundation can be formed through relational partnerships.

Strategic partnership

A **strategic partnership** is a long-term business relationship in which the partner organizations make significant investments to improve the profitability of both parties (Mohr, 1994). Strategic partnerships are created to uncover and exploit joint opportunities while minimizing joint weaknesses. Both parties will contribute financially, and consequently take significant risks in order to provide the partnership with a strategic advantage. This type of partnership is founded on the basis that both members are dependent on each other. The partners will have the same goals, as well as agree on the best course of action to achieve those goals. In order to achieve the target objective, partnerships must be based on an open-door policy; the partnership cannot be successful if information is kept confidential or there is a lack of willingness to accept risk equally.

An example of a strategic partnership was evident in 2007 when Time Warner's AOL strengthened their strategic partnership with Google. Google invested one billion dollars for a five per cent stake in AOL. The agreement created a global online advertising partnership, which has made more of AOL's industry leading content available to Google users. These strategic partnerships tend to be very successful because products and services are created that are not offered by competitors.

Before entering into any particular type of partnership, each company should consider all of the potential benefits and consequences. The next section of this chapter will help weigh the various costs and benefits related to choosing a relationship.

Choosing the right relationship

Managers are responsible for establishing the type of relationship that is appropriate for each situation. Every situation should be considered inherently different. The dynamics of every relationship are unique and managers must customize their agreements to the situation. Therefore, before deciding what type of relationship to develop several factors need to be considered (Weitz, Castleberry, and Tanner, 2005). These factors include market issues (e.g. maturity, size, and barriers), the potential returns of the relationship, and the capabilities provided by the partners (e.g. experience with technology or access to innovations). In addition, managers must assess the likelihood of success and other risks. These items include both quantitative and qualitative measures that require a manager's complete attention when designing relationships.

In the previous example, the strategic partnership formed between Time Warner's AOL and Google was justified, because the company expects a return great enough to justify the investment. Time Warner's AOL was a suitable partner for Google because the company was large enough to meet Google's product demands. Conversely, Google would not have entered into a strategic partnership with a small, local Internet provider, because a smaller company would not have enough production capability to meet Google's demand. The idea is that as partnerships are successful, the companies will make more money, i.e. Google believes benefits will exceed costs as does Time Warner's AOL.

Strategic partnerships may be established in order to gain access into a specific niche or market. The relationship between Google and AOL may be an example of this type of relationship. Other partnerships may be formed in an effort to improve a company's image. For example, large oil companies receive a significant amount of bad press due to pollution and environmental concerns. Therefore, it may be in their best interest to partner with companies attempting to develop alternative energy sources, e.g. solar or wind power, to gain goodwill among consumers.

A partnership may be developed in order to gain access to technological innovation. A company may find a relationship with a lead user beneficial. A **lead user** is someone who has invented or resolved a customer issue months or even years ahead of competitors in the marketplace. They provide information and give companies the ability to co-develop novel products, which provide a competitive edge over other market participants.

The key to every successful partnership is communication and, as a result, technology should be used as a means of increasing communication lines. This may mean using e-mail to interact with customers, or in a much more complex manner, using ongoing data exchange enabled by information technologies designed to increase efficiency. Wal-Mart is a perfect example of a company using technology in a highly sophisticated manner. Wal-Mart has created a competitive advantage through managing their inventory system. Their inventory is systematically programmed to replenish common items as they reach a minimum level. This inventory control system has been central to Wal-Mart maintaining low operating costs and providing competitive advantage through product availability.

Foundations of successful relationships

Earlier we discussed the importance of trust in a relationship. Trust, however, is only one building block of several involved in the creation of strategic partnerships. This section will briefly introduce five foundational elements and present how they form long-term, successful relationships.

These elements include:

- mutual trust

- open and truthful communication

- measurable mutual goals

- organizational support

- commitment to mutual gain

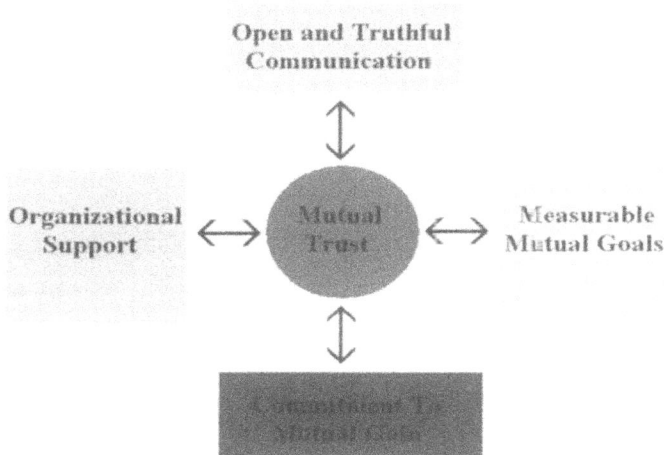

Exhibit 35: Elements of successful relationship

Mutual trust: Not all building blocks are created equally; the most important of the five foundational elements is mutual trust. As previously mentioned, **trust** is the confidence one party has in another to perform an action as agreed. In order for a partnership to be successful, trust must be mutual. As mutual trust grows between partners, parties will not limit themselves to contractual requirements but actually go to great lengths in order to satisfy the other partner, as well as strengthen the relationship.

Open and truthful communication: An additional element in building long-term, successful, relationships is establishing open and truthful communication lines. Parties that communicate openly and truthfully have a better understanding of each others' visions, missions and goals in the relationship. One way this can be accomplished is by always creating environments where each party feels comfortable speaking up. Once both partners gain a strong understanding of what motivates the other partner, dealing with changing business conditions becomes significantly easier. Communications often include the exchange of measures of the efficiency of shared business processes.

Measurable, mutual goals: A key element necessary for relationships to be successful is having both parties share measurable, mutual goals. Mutual goals allow parties to pool together company resources and strengths. In order to ensure goals are being met, they must be measurable and quantifiable. Some examples of measurable mutual goals include sales revenue, return on assets, or some performance indicator of customer satisfaction. Measures may also include production levels, error-rates, or other items that enable integration of the businesses processes of the partners. Agreeing on the items to be measured and establishing a continuous measurement program is necessary to provide optimal cooperation among partners and a substantive contributor to establishing mutual trust.

Organizational support: The support of employees throughout the organization is another key element in creating successful relationships. The organization as a whole, from front line members to local and corporate offices, must support the idea of a partnership. Structure and culture are the underlying roots that create organizational support. Although it is expected that employees support management decisions, it is necessary for managers to objectively understand and evaluate the structure and culture of the organization when designing partnership relationships. Proposed partnerships perceived as contrary to the existing structure or cultures are candidates for enhanced scrutiny. Once a partnership is entered into it is necessary to develop programs such as training and rewards to establish the desired partnership behaviors. Establishing these types of programs will increase the frequency of and improve the dynamics within the interactions of both partners. Training teaches behaviors which are needed to achieve partnership goals and rewards encourage the support of the previously taught behaviors.

Commitment to mutual gain: The final building block in the foundation of successful relationships relates to the level of commitment each partner has in creating mutual gain. Simply put, partners look out for one another and do not take advantage of each other. If one party has more resources or more efficient operating procedures than the other, this should not impact the relationship. If problems arise within the partnership, both parties need to consider the mutual investment each has contributed to the relationship. **Mutual investments**, or **relationship-specific assets**, are the tangible investments and resources that are specific to the relationship in nature. Although mutual investments strengthen mutual gain, they cannot be easily transferred if a partner wishes to leave the relationship. Thus, it is important to evaluate the level of intrinsic gain that has been established through the partnership. Ideally, such an analysis is performed before entering the partnership, although it requires the manager to make a substantial number of assumptions.

These foundations of relationships comprise the broad range of factors managers must consider when developing and implementing durable relationships. In addition, developing relationships consist of a series of phases that explains how they are identified through how the partners become committed to continuous improvement of the relationship. The next section presents these phases of relationship development.

Phases of relationship development

Strategic partnerships experience four major developmental phases and Exhibit 36 represents the life cycle of such a relationship. The length of phases and transitions between phases will vary due to cultural and/or social differences. Managers should be aware of the current phase of the relationship and evaluate decisions based upon how they impact the development of the relationship. Dissolution can occur at any time when incompatibilities exist between partners as the relationship develops.

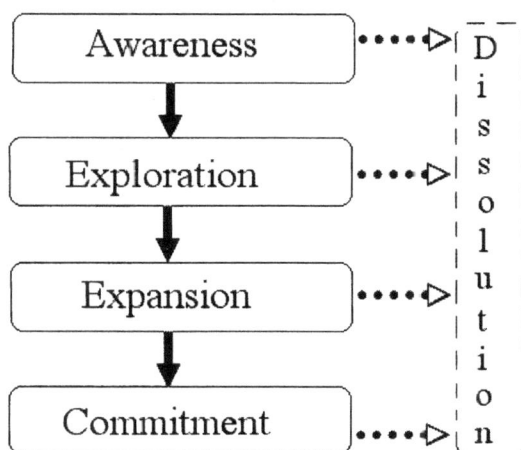

Exhibit 36: The relationship development process

The awareness phase begins before any transactions actually occur. During this phase, partners are locating, identifying and qualifying various prospects. Since no transactions take place, company image and reputation are weighed heavily during this phase. Awareness means assessing the business relationships needed to advance organizational goals, evaluating potential areas that would benefit from a partnership, and identifying potential partners. Partnerships can have various types of relationships; some areas may only need to be functional, whereas others may seek to be strategic. Consequently, identifying which type of relationship would most benefit the firms is imperative and a primary responsibility of managers

The exploration phase is considered the test for both parties. During this phase, parties engage in exchanges to explore potential partnership costs and benefits. Although neither side has committed to a relationship at this point, each transaction between the two parties tests each of their capabilities. Managers evaluate the transactions in terms of the foundations of relationships discussed above, e.g. identifying potential measures that indicate successful transactions or estimating the impact on organizational culture should the relationship become established. After both parties prove that they are capable of performing as needed, the partnership will move to the expansion phase. In this phase, additional business interactions focused on a long-term relationship are investigated. The expansion phase may be time consuming because it requires extensive research to be conducted both internally and externally. The primary activity of this phase is comparing the results of a series of financial analyses of various possible interactions and relationship types.

A contract, or at least a verbal commitment, for a certain period of time must take place for the commitment phase to begin. This stage is usually the final and most complex stage of a strategic relationship. During this phase, the details of the transactions are decided, including initial investments that will be made into the partnership and specification of how returns will be divided among the partners. The dissolution phase is the decision to end the partnership. This may occur during any of the various phases of the relationship development process. Dissolution may arise for a number of reasons, including rising costs, poor performance, or changes in corporate goals. The decision to end the partnership should not be taken lightly, but when all other options have been exercised it may be the correct choice. While relationships will follow this development life cycle, a manager's skills will substantially impact how the relationship develops and the success of the agreements for the organization. Training and development programs for managers should explicitly include skills for developing relationships.

Skills for building positive relationships

Two key skills that promote positive relationships are negotiation and facilitation. **Negotiation skills** can assist with problem solving and conflict resolution with partner organizations. **Facilitation skills** deal with the understanding of group processes and feedback.

Negotiation skills are necessary for managers to ensure they understand the goals and tactics of others. Negotiation involves understanding goals and the impacts of the range of possible outcomes on an organization. Adept negotiators must be able to identify compromises such that both partners are supportive of the resulting agreements.

Facilitation involves listening to the views of all parties and ensuring that critical issues are heard, regardless of their origin. Active facilitation brings objectivity to group processes and results in shared understandings of potential opportunities and the costs of pursuing those opportunities. Technology can aid managers in facilitating group discussions and recording group interactions. In some situations, professional facilitation may be appropriate if either side has reached a point where reaching a mutual understanding is difficult.

Strategies for external relationships

The rapid change in technology and the development of the Internet has changed the traditional definitions of manufacturers, suppliers, and customers. **Supply Chain Management** (SCM) is the integration of key business processes that add value for customers and other stakeholders. This added value is created through the integration of networks of suppliers that provide products, services, and information. Supply chain management allows this network of cooperating agents to perform one or more supply chain functions, potentially reducing costs and resulting in a competitive advantage for the organization.

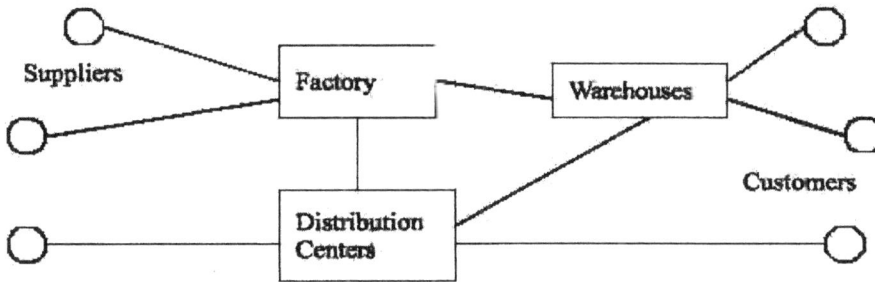

Exhibit 37: Movement through a supply chain

The above figure illustrates the movement of products through a supply chain network. The supply chain begins when suppliers send raw materials to a factory. The factory may use the materials in a number of ways. They can either manufacture subcomponents or assemble the materials into finished products to be sent to the warehouse or distribution center where customers can get the products.

In order for the supply chain to be successful, organizations must recognize that they are but one player in the long chain that starts with suppliers and also includes transporters, distributors, and customers. The organizations must interact cooperatively with their channel partners (Gandhi, 2003). An important issue relating to the development of a collaborative supply chain is following specified ordering and replenishment policies. An example of Collaborative Supply Chain Planning (CSCP) is Vendor Managed Inventory (VMI).

Vendor Managed Inventory allows the supplier to receive electronic data to maintain constant information about the manufacturer's sales and stock levels. The supplier is then responsible for creating and managing the inventory replenishment schedule. VMI is defined as a process where the supplier generates orders for customers based on demand information sent by the customer (Gandhi, 2003). VMI leads to changes in both the buyers' and suppliers' inventory management activities. VMI has not become a standard way of managing the replenishment process in the supply chain due to some practical issues that have slowed down its implementation in many organizations. One problem may exist because the supplier and manufacturer are unwilling to share information because of a lack of trust. In order for VMI to be effective, it has to produce observable benefits, especially in the reduction of inventory costs.

Some of the benefits of VMI include:

- lower customer inventories

- better forecasts

- reduced costs

- improved services

- strengthening competitive advantage

- strengthening buyer-supplier relationships

Similar to SCM and VMI, Collaborative Planning, Forecasting, and Replenishment (CPFR) was developed to allow better communication of control information, which enables coordination and optimization of shared business processes. CPFR is defined as an initiative among all participants in the supply chain intended to improve the relationship among them through jointly managed planning processes and shared information (Seifert, 2003). When successful, it also improves relationships between producers and retailers.

One of the first CPFR projects was initiated by Wal-Mart and Warner-Lambert, which merged with Pfizer in 2000. This project was intended to reduce inventories across the supply chain. It provided comparisons of sales and order forecasts of each trading partner and highlighted any visible forecast differences early enough for the partners to resolve any potential issues. Warner-Lambert applied CPFR to the Listerine mouthwash products by sharing of forecasts and responding to inconsistencies between the collaboration partners' forecasts. In Warner-Lambert's case, Wal-Mart's promotions created large swings in consumer demand, which Warner-Lambert was unaware of prior to CPFR. Warner-Lambert maintained substantial inventory as a hedge in order to prevent supplies from running out of stock. Wal-Mart and Warner-Lambert independently calculated the demand they expected six months in advance. The partners shared this information, as well as the weekly forecast, and they worked together to resolve variations between their forecasts on a weekly basis. Wal-Mart began placing orders six months in advance, instead of nine days, so that Warner-Lambert was able to construct a smoother production plan. This allowed Warner-Lambert to maintain production based on consumer demand for Listerine rather than maintaining sufficient stock. Wal-Mart's in-stock position improved and sales increased, while inventories dropped. Additionally, Warner-Lambert's supply management improved substantially. Optimal applications of CPFR occur when, for example, many other retailers join Wal-Mart in sharing their projected demand with Warner-Lambert. Combining demand forecasts from many retail customers makes it possible for Warner-Lambert's production plans to be much better aligned with total market demands.

Benefits of using CPFR are:

- drastically improved reaction times to consumer demand

- higher precision of sales forecasts

- direct and lasting communication

- improved sales

- inventory reduction

- reduced costs

The CPFR process model is divided into three phases: planning, forecasting, and replenishment. The exhibit below provides an overview of the phases and activities in the CPFR model.

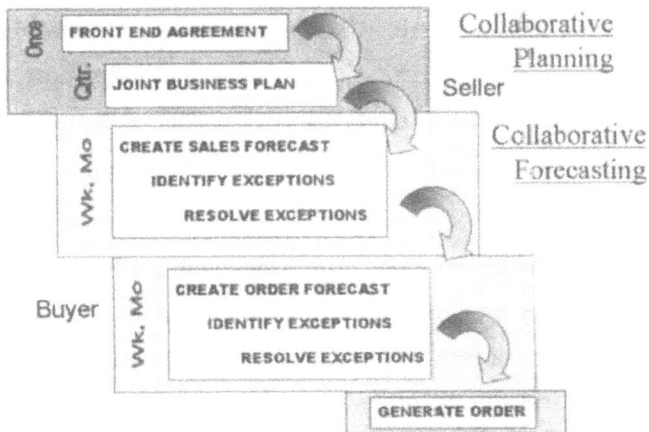

Exhibit 38: PFR Process Model

Source:

http://www.scdigest.com/images/misc/Original-CPFR-Model.jpg. Accessed 30 December 2008

Planning consists of identifying an opportunity for collaboration, then developing an agreement to collaborate, as well as forming a collaborative business plan. Forecasting is the most important part of the model. It provides the mechanism through which needs are determined. It is improvement of this aspect of the supply chain through which all of these strategies provide advantages over more traditional methods. Replenishment involves making and delivering the product consistent with the needs schedule developed by the forecast. More accurate forecasts lead to production of only the needed products, which smooths the production schedule and results in price stability. This allows for existing capacity to be used to enable other products or to develop markets for additional production.

Many of the processes replaced by SCM, VMI, and CPFR strategies involve merely producing "the average of this month over the last 3 threes plus a small percentage". Such ad hoc strategies, although widely employed, contain substantial inefficiencies. Exploiting these inefficiencies is the incentive for pursuing these programs. Another reason such programs are popular with managers is that savings realized go directly to the bottom line as customer needs are met while using less organizational resources.

An effective supply chain management program is one that develops processes shared among all the supply chain members in order to minimize the waste of time and enable fast and reliable reactions to changes in demand. Technology has exponentially increased the transfer of information between organizations, resulting in improved supply chain performance. Two common practices, Just-In-Time (JIT) and agile inventory approaches, are used to allow suppliers to react more quickly to changes in customer demand.

Just-In-Time emphasizes minimizing inventory and smoothing the flow of materials to ensure adequate and prompt delivery of components. Products and materials are ordered and delivered "just in time" as they are needed reducing inventory costs and ensuring unneeded materials are not ordered. JIT began at Toyota Motor Company but it evolved into a system for continuous improvement of all aspects of the manufacturing operations.

Lean production is a philosophy based upon a collection of management methods and techniques (Russell, 2006). Workers and machines are multifunctional in lean systems. Workers are required to perform various tasks and help in the improvement process. The machines are arranged in small, U-shaped work cells; this structure enables parts to be processed in a continuous flow. Workers produce parts one at a time and transport them between the cells in small lots. The only schedules prepared are for the final assembly line. This schedule "pulls" sub-components through production by making requests to stations that cascade to production lines. Nothing is done until requested by the next station.

The system is best implemented when suppliers are few in number and are reliable. The suppliers' manufacturing system must be flexible, because multiple deliveries may be requested of the same item in the same day. Lean production produces items in necessary quantities at necessary times. Consequently, quality must be extremely high, as there is little buffer inventory between workstations and production schedules include only requested products.

Lean systems can produce high quality service quickly at a low cost. Also, the system responds to changes in customer demand. Many retailers use lean systems such as Zara and Blockbuster.

Benefits of using lean production are:

- reduced inventory
- improved quality
- lower costs
- reduced space requirements
- shorter lead time
- increased productivity
- greater flexibility
- better relations with suppliers
- simplified scheduling and control activities
- increased capacity
- better use of human resources
- greater product variety

Outsourcing

Outsourcing is a contractual relationship where an external organization takes responsibility for performing all or part of a company's functions (Vita, 2006). Outsourcing is the term used to designate a relationship in which a partner company performs business functions. Common examples of outsourced functions for companies in the developed world are software development and call centers. The principle justification for outsourcing functions like these from, for example, the US to India is that prevailing wage rates for these kinds of tasks are much lower than in the US and the Indian partner companies hire and train employees who speak English and are skilled at their jobs. There's a difference between outsourcing and off-shoring. When a vendor in another country performs an outsourced function, off-shoring is the correct terminology for describing the relationship. The jobs being outsourced in an organization do not necessarily have to be outsourced to another country. Off-shoring can result in significant savings due to wage and currency discrepancies among countries. However, quality controls must be maintained to ensure that the products and services provided are returning the expected results. **Outsourcing** is typically done by organizations who outsource non-core processes that are inefficient, difficult to manage, or too costly. Choosing a supplier to meet an organization's outsourcing needs depends on the business process being outsourced, the scope of the project to be outsourced, as well as geographic factors. Business processes that are often considered good candidates to outsource include, but are not limited to:

- administration (audit, tax)

- asset and property management

- finance (accounting, billing, accounts payable, accounts receivable)

- human resources (benefits administration, payroll)

- information systems (development and operations)

- miscellaneous (energy services, customer service, mailroom, food processing)

- procurement/logistics

Business process outsourcing is becoming increasingly important. The management of one or more processes or functions by a third party is a means for the organization to reduce costs. The key benefits of outsourcing are realized by organizations that outsource business processes by transferring the entire function out-of-house. This enables access to specialized knowledge and expertise in the area; sharing of new methodologies, technologies and other resources; and standardizing processes across the organization.

An organization needs to outline the benefits and risks of outsourcing when deciding whether to outsource. The benefits need to outweigh the risks in order for outsourcing to be efficient and effective (Halvey, 2000). A typical benefit/risk analysis is:

Benefits:

- cost savings

- increased flexibility

- better customer or employee service

- higher productivity

- ability to concentrate on the core business

- implementation of wide initiatives

- movement of assets off books

- more resources

- variety of skills

- access to new methodologies and technologies

- training expense reduction

- greater flexibility

Risks:

- loss of control

- difficulty in managing costs

- additional liability

- difficulty in bringing the business process back in-house

- reduced flexibility

Uncertainty in outsourcing occurs when an organization is not sure which business process function to outsource. Organizations should be overly inclusive with what needs to be outsourced. Including an unbundled requirement where the vendor provides separate pricing for certain functions can be helpful. Also, deciphering through the complexity of outsourcing can be easier once determining where the services will be provided.

The next step in assessing outsourcing is to identify potential vendors that have the desired resources, capabilities, and experience. The following will provide beneficial information to help make an informed decision:

- vendor information from industry reports/survey

- looking at industry publications

- talking to other outsourcing customers

- sharing goals and concerns with chosen vendors

Potential external relationship obstacles

Outsourcing offers a number of potential benefits for companies; however they cannot ignore the obstacles that come along with outsourcing. Some countries have not achieved the desired benefits from outsourcing, because they have not realized the expected cost reductions anticipated from outsourcing their business processes to a third party. The lack of capable suppliers and service providers is a major problem. Losing control over the outsourced process is not uncommon. Additionally, problems and issues may emerge due to the integration of services and systems provided by the vendor.

Problems within the networked organization usually arise due to the failure in identifying all stakeholders and network partners. All nodes and partners in the networked organization have to know and recognize all the stakeholders involved. Another potential problem can result from having dominant nodes, which must be eliminated in the early stages of the relationship. All nodes within a relationship must fully understand the mission and goals. Having incompatible missions and goals will destroy a relationship and no benefits will be achieved. Also, problems may arise from clashing company cultures. Therefore, when choosing a supplier or a partner in the networked organization, having similar goals, missions, and similar ways of performing the business processes are vital for the success of the relationship.

Chapter summary

This chapter presents the basics necessary for developing relationships among organizations. These include the common types of external relationships, phases of relationship development, the building blocks of successful relationships, and the skills necessary for developing a variety of relationships. Several strategies for managing external relationships were presented that focus on the integration of the processes of multiple organizations to create "virtual suppliers" that benefit from rapid information exchange and just-in-time adjustment of sales forecasts and production capacities.

Managers must consider the many factors of each situation and design a unique relationship or set of relationships that enable the organization to accomplish its goals in the most efficient manner possible. Yet efficiency is not enough, as the needs for flexibility and quality assurance lead to ever more integrated networks of organizations, which require strategic perspectives for maximizing profitability. It is expected that every organization be involved in a variety of external relationships, where each relationship is justified according to cost and quality.

Exercises

List and describe the four dynamics that should be considered in order to choose the right relationship.

1. What are the two basic relationship types?

2. What is the difference between a functional relationship and a strategic partnership?

3. List the five foundational elements involved in the development of long-term, successful relationships.

4. Is any element more significant than another? If so, which one and why?

5. List the four major phases involved in the relationship development process.

6. When in the relationship development process does dissolution occur?

7. Define Supply Chain Management and state its goals.

8. Select a company and determine the different suppliers it has. What criteria does the company most probably use for its suppliers?

9. Describe how Wal-Mart has used VMI to improve its supply chain management?

10. On what basis does a company decide whether to outsource or not?

11. What are some potential risks to outsourcing?

References

De Vita, Glauco and Catherine L. Wang. "Development if Outsourcing Theory and Practice." Idea Group Inc., 2006.

Gandhi, Ujval. "Vendor Managed Inventory: A New Approach to Supply Chain Management." Virginia Polytechnic Institute and State University. 2003.

Halvey, John and Barbara Melby. "Business Process Outsourcing: Process, Strategies, and Contracts." <u>John Wiley & Sons, Inc.</u> 2000.

Mohr, Jakki. "Characteristics of Partnerships Success: Partner Attributes, Communication Behavior, and Conflict Resolution Techniques." Strategic Management Journal 15.1994 135-152. 12 Dec 2007.

Russell, Roberta and Bernard W. Taylor III. "Operations Management: Quality and Competitiveness in a Global Environment." <u>John Wiley & Sons, Inc</u>. 2006.

Scannell, Ed and Tom Sullivan . "Reining in external relationships." <u>Info World Media Group</u> 18 SEP 2000 20. 29 SEP 2007 <u>http://infotrac.galegroup.com.ezproxy.lib.vt.edu:8080/itw/infomark/797/834/13524898w18/purl=rc1 BIM 0 A65286562&dyn=33!xrn 14 0 A65286562&bkm 34 14</u>

Seifert, Dirk. "Collaborative Planning, Forecasting, and Replenishment: How to Create a Supply Chain Advantage." AMACOM Books. 2003.

Smith, Michael. "Honesty as a core value." Practical Strategies Newsletter 12 Dec 2007 <<u>http://www.michaelhsmithphd.com/honesty.html</u>>.

Street, Christopher and Ann-Frances Cameron. "External relationships and the small business: a review of small business alliance and network research." <u>Journal of Small Business Management.</u> Apr 2007 239-254. 09 SEP 2007.

9. Financial and managerial accounting; financing your organization

Editor: Donald J McCubbrey (Daniels College of Business, University of Denver, USA)

Reviewer: Roger K Baer (CPA, LLC; and Former Partner, Arthur Andersen & Co., USA)

Learning objectives

- to appreciate the importance of an accounting system

- to differentiate between financial accounting and managerial accounting

- to understand the basic types of accounts and their characteristics

- learn to set up a chart of accounts for your organization

- understand the advantages of double-entry bookkeeping; types of ledgers and basic reports

- to learn how to select and use accounting software

- to understand common options for funding a start-up

Introduction

In this chapter, we will discuss the principles of accounting as well as some of the options you have for designing and installing an accounting system for your business. There are many computer-based accounting systems available now, for relatively low cost, that make it easier for an entrepreneur to use software on a PC or the Internet to run an accounting system. We discuss some of the software options you may want to consider in Chapter 10, "Leveraging with information technology". Although it is possible to keep essential accounting records manually, or perhaps on a series of spreadsheets, you will find that it is much easier and more reliable to simply use accounting software from the beginning.

You may need the advice of an accounting professional to work with you in setting up your accounting records and helping you select and implement a suitable accounting package. On the other hand, you may be able to handle the task yourself. In any event, starting your business with a well-designed accounting system tailored to the needs of your business will be worth the effort.

Why an accounting system is important

Professional accountants look at the accounting records and reports of a business from two perspectives. The term they use to describe these two perspectives is **financial accounting** and **managerial accounting**. Wikipedia has good definitions of both perspectives in order to help you understand the difference between the two.

9. Financial and managerial accounting; financing your organization

"Financial accountancy (or financial accounting) is the field of <u>accountancy</u> concerned with the preparation of <u>financial statements</u> for decision makers, such as <u>stockholders</u>, <u>suppliers</u>, <u>banks</u>, employees, <u>government agencies</u>, owners, and other stakeholders. The fundamental need for financial accounting is to reduce <u>principal-agent problem</u> by measuring and monitoring agents' performance and reporting the results to interested users.

"Financial accountancy is used to prepare accounting information for people outside the organization or not involved in the day to day running of the company".

"In short, Financial Accounting is the process of summarizing financial data taken from an organization's accounting records and publishing in the form of annual (or more frequent) reports for the benefit of people outside the organization.

"Financial accountancy is governed by both local and international accounting standards". (Wikipedia 2009a). In addition, financial accounting records and financial statements are essential sources of information for the preparation of tax returns.

"Management (or managerial) accounting, on the other hand, is concerned with the provisions and use of accounting information to managers within organizations, to provide them with the basis to make informed business decisions that will allow them to be better equipped in their management and control functions.

In contrast to financial accountancy information, management accounting information is:

- usually confidential and used by management, instead of publicly reported
- forward-looking, instead of historical
- pragmatically computed using extensive management information systems and internal controls, instead of complying with accounting standards

This is because of the different emphasis: management accounting information is used within an organization, typically for decision-making". (Wikipedia 2009b)

You will not need to be terribly concerned about financial accounting when your business is just beginning, inasmuch as the kinds of information you will need falls into the category of internal management information rather than information for external stakeholders. Also, note that financial accounting reports must be prepared in accordance with national and international accounting standards. In the United States the Financial Accounting Standards Board (FASB) has been the designated independent entity for established accounting reporting standards since 1973. Independent auditors of an organization's financial statements must provide written assurance in their report that such statements were prepared in accordance with Generally Accepted Accounting Principles (GAAP). While, in theory, there can be many supportable ways of presenting accounting information on such topics as business combinations, subsequent events after the date of an audit, the fair value of financial instruments and the like, FASB will typically specify the ways such information should be reported. You can find more information on FASB on their website at http://www.fasb.org.

Since so many organizations are global in scope, a relatively new entity, the International Accounting Standards Board (IASB) has come upon the scene. According to their website, their mission "is to develop, in the public interest, a single set of high quality, understandable and international financial reporting standards (IFRSs) for general purpose financial statements" (IASB 2009). Finally, when your business reaches the point where you need to issue financial statements to external stakeholders, (e.g. banks, stockholders, regulatory agencies, etc.), your accountant will need to be familiar with and, ideally a member of, the national association of accountants in your country. The reason for this is that there may be national standards for generally accepted standards that are, in some ways, unique to your country. Examples of national associations are the Institute of Certified Public Accountants of Kenya (<u>http://www.icpak.com/</u>), the Malaysian Institute of Certified Public Accountants (<u>http://www.micpa.com.my/</u>), and the South African Association of Chartered Accountants (<u>https://www.saica.co.za</u>).

Accordingly, the balance of this chapter is focused on how you can use a well-designed accounting system as the basis for generating useful information to help you run your business.

Basic types of accounts

The six basic types of accounts used in a typical accounting system, according to Wikipedia are:

- asset accounts

- liability accounts

- equity accounts

- revenue or income accounts

- expense accounts

- contra accounts

Each type of account is discussed below (adapted from Wikipedia 2009c). In subsequent sections of this chapter we will discuss how they are used in an accounting system.

- **Asset accounts:** represent the different types of economic resources owned by a business, common examples of asset accounts are cash, cash in bank, equipment, building, inventory, prepaid rent, goodwill, accounts receivable. Assets are usually broken down into three categories: Current assets, fixed assets, and intangible assets. Current assets are assets which could be converted to cash fairly quickly if necessary, certainly in less than a year. Examples of current assets include cash, cash in bank, inventory, prepaid rent, and accounts receivable. Fixed assets are assets of a more permanent nature like manufacturing equipment, buildings owned, and the like. Intangible assets, like goodwill, are monetary values assigned to intangibles like a brand name. It is typically used when accountants need to justify the purchase price of one company by another when the price cannot be justified by the monetary value of the purchased company's assets minus liabilities. Intangible assets are beyond the scope of this chapter as they apply more to larger corporations than to a start-up business.

- **Liability accounts:** represent the different types of economic obligations by a business, such as accounts payable, bank loan, bonds payable, accrued interest. Current liabilities are liabilities which are scheduled to be paid within a short period of time, usually less than a year. Examples of current liabilities include accounts payable to creditors, like suppliers, current amounts payable to employees (payroll) and interest due on short term loans. Long-term liabilities (sometimes called fixed liabilities) are liabilities of a more permanent nature like loans that are not due in the current year (long-term debt), and the like.

- **Equity accounts:** represent the residual equity of a business (after deducting from assets all the liabilities). In the case of a start-up company totally financed by the founder, it is often called owner's equity and represents the capital provided by the owner. If the company is a corporation and stock has been issued to the owner and to others, it is often called stockholders' equity.

- **Revenue accounts or income:** represent the company's gross income before expenses are deducted. Common examples include sales, service revenue, commissions, and interest income.

- **Expense accounts:** represent the company's expenditures to enable itself to operate. Common examples are employee costs (payroll and fringe benefits), supplies, software, telephone bills, electricity and water, rentals, depreciation, bad debt, interest, and insurance.

- **Contra-accounts:** from the term ciccia, meaning to deduct, these accounts are opposite to the other five above mentioned types of accounts. For instance, a contra-asset account is accumulated depreciation. This label represents deductions to a relatively permanent asset like a building. It accumulates an annual charge in recognition that a fixed asset like a building is not used up over the course of a year, but that it has a useful life measured in multiple years. Since in certain countries and under certain economic conditions real estate tends to steadily rise in price, perhaps a better example is a truck purchased for use in the business. Its value is more likely to continue to decrease over the years. Even though the market value of a building might increase rather than decrease over the years, accountants will still reduce its value by an annual depreciation charge each year. This is a good example of how financial accounting differs from managerial accounting from the owner's perspective. Depreciation on a building or a truck reduces income for tax purposes in most countries, so it is to the owner's advantage to reflect depreciation charges in the company's accounting records. On the other hand, you can bet that the owner knows the true market value of the building when it comes time to sell it!

Chart of accounts

Setting up an appropriate chart of accounts will take some careful thought on your part because you want to be sure that accounts are set up in each category (i.e. assets liabilities, etc.) that will enable you to accumulate accounting transactions in a meaningful way. As a starting point, you should consider the kinds of information you will need in order to run your business. You may then go on to consider other types of information that may be required for financial reporting, as we discussed earlier. Setting up a chart of accounts is best understood if we walk through an example. Let us suppose a young entrepreneur plans to start a men's clothing store and needs to develop a chart of accounts. Typically, accounts in a chart of accounts each have an account number. This is no different than you having a unique account number for companies you deal with, such as a bank or a telephone company. A number uniquely identifies you from another customer that might have exactly the same name and is easier to use in a computerized customer accounting system. In the same way, an account number in a chart of accounts uniquely identifies an account and is easier to use in a computerized general accounting system. It is common to assign a range of numbers to each type of account. One common way is illustrated in Table 6:

Table 6: Range of account numbers in a sample chart of accounts

Account Type	Account Number Range
Asset accounts	100-199
Liability accounts	200-299
Equity accounts	300-399
Income accounts	400-499
Expense accounts	500-599
Contra accounts	600-699, or in the range to which they relate

The next step is to decide the breakdown of accounts you need so that you set up an account for the detailed information you need for each account type. For example, starting with the asset account category, you may decide that you need to begin your business with at least the following accounts:

Table 7: Examples of current asset accounts in a chart of accounts

Account Number	Account Name
100	Cash on Hand (Petty cash)
105	Cash in Bank
110	Accounts Receivable
115	Inventory for resale
120	Office equipment

The same process is followed with all of the account types until your chart of accounts is complete, and contains all of the categories you believe will be needed in order to accumulate accounting information in meaningful categories.

Fortunately, there are many sources where you can obtain *sample* charts of accounts by type of business that you can use as a guide and starting point. One source of such information can be the national associations (or institutes) of professional accountants we referred to previously in this chapter. Another source is the providers of accounting software we will discuss later in this chapter and in Chapter 10. One other option is to do an Internet search for a sample chart of accounts for your type of business. For example, we did a simple Google search for a "Bed and Breakfast" (B&B) sample chart of accounts and found a 98 page document that discusses almost every issue someone who wants to start a B&B needs to know, including a sample chart of accounts, beginning on page 90 (Buchanan and Espeseth 2009).

Basic financial statements

Later in this chapter we will discuss some of the other types of reports you will want to be able to produce in order to plan and control your business finances, but for now, let us concentrate on the two most fundamental statements of all: The Income Statement and the Balance Sheet. The Income Statement is important because it will tell you if your business was profitable or not for any given period of time. The Balance Sheet will show you the financial condition of your business, what you own, what you owe, and the owners' financial interest. You will sometimes hear the Income Statement referred to as the Profit and Loss Statement and the Balance Sheet called the Statement of Financial Condition.

Here's a simple example of an Income Statement:

Income Statement – Bill's Bicycle Shop – Year 2009	
Sales	$20,000
Cost of goods sold	-8000
Gross Margin	$12,000
Payroll costs	-6000
Rent	-2000
Other expenses	-1000
Net Income	$3,000.00

The only items that need additional explanation are "*Cost of goods sold*" and "*gross margin*". The cost of goods sold is the total cost the owner of a business paid for products sold. If the owner of Bill's Bicycle Shop simply buys bicycles from the manufacturer and has them shipped to the shop, the cost of a bicycle is whatever bill paid the manufacturer plus the cost of shipping it to the shop and any labor cost that might be involved in assembling the bicycle before putting it on display for customers to see. The Cost of goods sold shown on the Income Statement (USD 8,000) is the total costs associated with all of the bicycles sold by Bill in the year 2009. This is the accounting concept of "matching". (The Sales figure of USD 20,000 is the total of the prices paid by all of the customers who bought bicycles from Bill during the year).

Gross margin is simply the difference between Sales and the Cost of goods sold. It is an important figure for owners to watch, and you will sometimes hear business owners talk about their margins or "managing their margins". The greater the gross margin is the more profitable a business is likely to be. For example, see if you can determine what Bill's gross margin and profit would be if he had to sell his bicycles at a discount because of competitive pressure and his sales revenue for the year amounted to USD 17,000 instead of USD 20,000.

This is, of course, a relatively simple example to illustrate the general outline of an Income Statement, but it should give you an appreciation of why the Income Statement is important to the owner of any business. Am I making money or not? And if not, why not?

Here's a simple example of a Balance Sheet:

Table 8: Balance Sheet –Bill's Bicycle Shop– 31 December 2009

Assets	
Cash on hand and in bank	USD 8,000
Accounts Receivable	3000
Inventory – New Bicycles	12000
Parts Inventory	4000
Office Equipment	2000
Repair Equipment	1000
Total Assets	**USD 30,000**
Liabilities	
Accounts Payable	USD 10,000
Loan from Bank	15,000
Total Liabilities	**25000**
Owner's Equity	**5000**
Total Liabilities and Owner's Equity	**USD 30,000**

You can see why it is called a Balance Sheet. It is because the sum of the asset accounts must equal the sum of the liability and owner's equity accounts. In other words, they must be in balance. You can also see why it is sometimes called a statement of financial position. It shows the condition of the business, in financial terms, as of a specific date.

Next, we will discuss a short history of accounting and the invention of double-entry bookkeeping, a technique that is of great assistance to accountants and bookkeepers in assuring the accuracy of accounting records and the reports that are prepared from them.

A short history of accounting and double entry bookkeeping

There are many stories of how accounting began, but most writers agree that it has a long history, going back 5,000 years or so. Legend has it that wealthy individuals, wanting to keep track of their possessions (cattle, stores of grain, gold ornaments and so forth), hired scribes to keep records of additions and deletions to their lists of possessions as they bought, sold, or traded them. One supposes that that they wanted to be sure that any changes were legitimate; that losses were not due to theft, and that if 100 cattle were purchased that the herd increased by 100. From time to time, a count of possessions would be made and compared to the records maintained by the scribe. Any unexplained losses would be a signal that something was amiss and worthy of investigation.

Modern bookkeeping is generally thought to have been invented during the Italian Renaissance (around 1494 AD, according to one version:

> "Formal accounting was invented by a Franciscan friar named Luca Pacioli in 1494 in his paper "Summa de Arithmetica, Geometria, Proportioni et Proportionalita" ("Everything About Arithmetic, Geometry and Proportion")."The treatise described double-entry bookkeeping—that for every credit

entered into a ledger there must be a debit, a concept created by Florentine merchants and hailed by Goethe as "one of the most beautiful discoveries of the human spirit". "Three traits shared by successful merchants, Mr. Pacioli wrote, were access to cash, a constantly updated accounting system and a good bookkeeper. His contemporary Christopher Columbus apparently knew that: On his voyage to the New World, he took a royal accountant to track his "swindle sheet when he started to figure the cost of gold and spices he would accumulate", according to Alistair Cooke's 1973 book "America."" (Executive Caliber 2009)

In my opinion, Goethe was exaggerating when he called double entry bookkeeping "one of the most beautiful discoveries of the human spirit". I can think of many other discoveries that are more beautiful, but as the old saying goes: "Beauty lies in the eye of the beholder" and perhaps Goethe was a bookkeeper at heart. At any rate, the discovery of double-entry bookkeeping was undeniably important, because, as Wikipedia explains:

"Double-Entry Bookkeeping is a system that ensures the integrity of the financial values recorded in a financial accounting system. It does this by ensuring that each individual transaction is recorded in at least two different (sections) nominal ledgers of the financial accounting system and so implementing a double checking system for every transaction. It does this by first identifying values as either a Debit or a Credit value. A Debit value will always be recorded on the debit side (left hand side) of a nominal ledger account and the credit value will be recorded on the credit side (right hand side) of a nominal ledger account. *A nominal ledger has both a Debit (left) side and a Credit (right) side. If the values on the debit side are greater than the value of the credit side of the nominal ledger then that nominal ledger is said to have a debit balance".*

"Each transaction must be recorded on the Debit side of one nominal ledger and that same transaction and value is also recorded on the Credit side of another nominal ledger hence the expression Double-Entry (entered in two locations) one debit and one credit" (Wikipedia 2009d).

Here is a simple example to give you a feel for the way that double entry bookkeeping works:

Let us assume that the owner of Bill's Bicycle Shop, which we discussed above, bought some new bicycles on credit, for inventory. This is how the accounts would be affected:

Debit the inventory – new bicycles account: USD 2,000

Credit the accounts payable account: USD 2,000

Next let us assume that the owner had some extra cash and decided to pay down some of our bank loan. This is how the accounts would be affected:

Debit the loan from bank account: USD 1,000

Credit the cash account: USD 1,000

Note two things. First, a single transaction affects two accounts (a double-entry). Secondly, note that a debit to an asset account increases the value of the account and a debit to a liability (or owner's equity) account decreases its value. So, when USD 1,000 is paid to the bank, the debit to the loan from bank account reduces the amount we owe to the bank, and the credit to cash decreases the balance in our cash account.

Ledgers

The version quoted above states that debits and credits must be entered into a *ledger,* so it is important that you understand what this term means, as it may be new to you. As you will see from some of the additional sources we quote, oftentimes *journal* and *ledger* are used to describe the same thing.

So, what is a ledger? A ledger is simply a collection of the accounts of your business where transactions are recorded using the double-entry bookkeeping method. If you are operating with a completely manual system, your ledgers (you will have more than one, as discussed in a moment) are on paper, usually in a bound volume pre-printed in a special way to accommodate the recording of transactions. If you are using a pre-coded application software package on a PC for your accounting system, your ledgers will be on the computer.

Types of ledgers

Most organizations operate with two types of ledgers, the General Ledger and one or more subsidiary ledgers. The General Ledger contains a minimum of one page for <u>each account in the chart of accounts.</u> According to one authoritative source:

"It is also known as G/L and The Final Book of Entry. It is a collection of all balance sheet, income, and expense accounts used to keep the accounting records of a company. A General Ledger is a perpetual record of the activity and balances of the accounts. Each company has only one General Ledger" (Universal Accounting 2009)

However, some accounts, like accounts receivable or accounts payable, are comprised of the sum of a number of individual amounts. Let us look at accounts receivable as an example. Suppose we have a balance (i.e. total) amount of USD 3,250 in our accounts receivable account in the General Ledger. Remember, accounts receivable are amounts our customers owe us. Therefore, the USD 3,250 balance we have in our accounts receivable is the sum total of amounts owed to us by several individual customers. For the sake of convenience, we keep a subsidiary ledger of individual accounts receivable as illustrated in Exhibit 39 below.

Customer Name:

Customer Address:

Customer City/State:

Customer Telephone Number:

Customer email address:

Date	Invoice Number	Sales Amount	Payment Amount	Payment Reference Number	Balance
June 27, 2009	870345980	USD 200			USD 200.00
July 6, 2009	870346001	USD 20			USD 220.00
July 15, 2009	870346125		USD 200.00	6589	USD 20.00
July 20, 2009	870346198	USD 15			USD 35.00
July 28, 2009	870346225	USD 25			USD 60.00
August 9, 2009			USD 60.00		USD 0.00
August 24, 2009	870346552	USD 55			USD 55.00

Exhibit 39: Accounts Receivable Subsidiary Ledger example

The Accounts Receivable Subsidiary Ledger has one page for each customer who has earned the right to be extended credit, and is expected pay off their outstanding balance each month. The sum of the customer balances in the Accounts Receivable Subsidiary Ledger must equal the Accounts Receivable balance in the company's General Ledger.

In the case of the Accounts Receivable example, when a sale is entered in the ledger, a corresponding entry is made in a Sales Journal. And, when a payment is received and posted to a customer's account in the Accounts Receivable ledger, a corresponding entry is made in a Cash Receipts Journal.

Similar subsidiary ledgers are created any time there is a sufficient number of detail accounts to warrant it. Detailed accounts may be employee accounts for payroll, or product numbers for inventory, for example. Setting up subsidiary ledgers and journals for special purposes like this shields the General Ledger from an excessive amount of detail and, at the same time, preserves the principle of double-entry accounting, makes reconciliations easier and, in general, promotes accuracy in a company's accounting records. In real life, of course, things can get more complicated, but this is the basic approach that is followed.

In Chapter 10, we discuss the many opportunities that small businesses have to use computer software to set up and maintain records of all sorts for their business, from accounting, payroll, customer relationship management, inventory control and the like. Going much beyond this is beyond the scope of this chapter. You can expect the most popular accounting software packages to assume you do not know a lot about accounting. Therefore, most offerings will lead you through the process of setting up a chart of accounts that is appropriate for your business and help you decide which basic reports you should have. Over and above that, most will permit you to prepare the advanced reports and analyses discussed in the following section, as well as custom reports tailored to your specific needs.

There are several sources on the Internet that compare the functions, features, and prices of software packages for accounting to help you make the proper selection. One especially good one is "Accounting Software Review 2009 – TopTenREVIEWS" (Accounting Software Review 2009).Quoting from their website:

"Opening a small business in today's fast-paced economic climate can be an exciting, complicated and expensive endeavor. On the surface, it seems simple—just make sure you're selling your goods for more than it costs to produce them, right? Wrong. Without proper bookkeeping, your blooming company can take an abrupt dive towards bankruptcy.

"This is why accounting is a key component in any small business's success. It should play a role in every financial decision you make—from purchasing vehicles, equipment and supplies to increasing production, stocking inventory and determining salaries.

"But if you, like most people, lack an extensive background in accounting, where do you begin? Today's accounting software has the solution—giving you the tools and the information you need to keep your financial records in check, while aiding you in making the most of your company's cash flow.

"Unfortunately, there are about as many software packages for accounting as there are types of small businesses and determining which one best meets the needs of your company can be a tricky transaction—but that's where we can help.

"Within this site, you'll find articles on accounting and comprehensive reviews to help you make an informed decision on which accounting software is right for your business. At TopTenREVIEWS, we do the research so you don't have to!™" If you have access to the Internet, we highly recommend exploring this site for ideas on how to move forward with your accounting system.

Here is an excerpt from the website where they compare ten software packages feature by feature. In the table reproduced here, we only show the names of the packages and their prices. For more detail you will need to visit the Accounting Software Review 2009 website itself (see the end of chapter references for the link).

9. Financial and managerial accounting; financing your organization

Table 9: 2009 Accounting Software Review Product Comparisons

Package Name	Overall Ranking	Price in US Dollars
Peachtree Complete	Excellent	$249.99
MYOB Business Essentials	Very Good Plus	$99.00
Quickbooks Pro	Very Good	$178.95
NetSuite Small Business	Very Good	$1188.00
Cougar Mountain	Very Good	$1499.00
Bookkeeper	Very Good	$29.99
Simply Accounting	Good Plus	$149.99
CYMA IV Accounting for Windows	Good Plus	$595.00
DacEasy	Good Plus	$499.99
Bottom Line Accounting	Good	$399.00

As you can see, there is a wide range of prices, from USD 29.99 to USD 1499.00, and the package which sells for USD 29.99 is rated the same as the one that sells for USD 1499.00. Clearly, this shows that some analysis is necessary before settling on a specific accounting software package. You may need to engage the service of a professional accountant or, at least, a colleague who has studied accounting and accounting software packages to help you make the right selection for your business. Here is some good advice from the Accounting Software Review 2009 website:

"With all the accounting software available, it's hard to know which program is the best fit for your business finances. Below are the criteria TopTenREVIEWS used to evaluate small business accounting software.

- **Ease of Use** – We look for finance software that is simple to install, set up, and understand. The best accounting programs make navigating intuitive, so you never have to guess where you are or what to do next.

- **Accounting Modules** – Accounting modules are categories required to successfully maintain your business finances (such as Accounts Payable and Accounts Receivable). Does the accounting software have all the basic accounting modules you'll need? All the bells and whistles of the software aren't relevant if the basics aren't covered. Will the finance software grow with your company? We look for accounting software that lets you grow and customize your system to fit your individual business needs.

- **Reporting Categories** – Consider accounting software that offers a wide range of reports. You should be able to print at least one kind of report for every module. Reporting features are often built into each section, but it's better if you can create reports from anywhere in the program. Customizable reports save you time; look for accounting software that will let you set your own criteria. With detailed financial reporting, you can analyze what is and isn't working for your business.

- **Help Documentation** – Look for email and phone support; toll-free phone and live support, online help is a bonus. Online, we look for indexed help topics that can be searched easily. You'll want quick access for both technical help and accounting help for your software. Accounting software companies should have qualified people (both technicians and accountants) answering these tough questions.

"With the right accounting software, you will be able to manage your company books quickly and easily". (Accounting Software Review 2009)

Advanced reports and analyses

This section discusses some of the more common reports prepared from an accounting system that have, over the years, proven to be valuable tools for managing a business.

Cash flow forecasts

There is a saying in business that "Cash is King". One of the worst things that can happen to a company is to run short of cash unexpectedly. This can make it difficult to pay suppliers and employees without scurrying around to raise needed cash quickly, and when you must raise cash quickly you often find it a difficult and expensive task. Business owners are not always successful in raising cash quickly and in the worst cases, must go bankrupt. This is why cash flow forecasts are prepared. They are easy to prepare and can be quickly done using a spreadsheet program. They can also be prepared manually. What a cash flow forecast does is estimate cash inputs and outputs over a period of time, usually at least 90 days in order to give you assurance that your business will have the cash necessary to meet its obligations to others. If the cash flow forecast shows, for example, that you are in a deficit position two months out, you will have time to raise the necessary cash you need and avoid a sudden cash crisis. Cash flow forecasts are often prepared for longer periods of time as well, depending on circumstances. In addition, they are often prepared using various assumptions about the future (e.g. general economic conditions, sales growth, increased expenses, etc).

As one authoritative website states: "By knowing your cash position now and in the future, you can:

- Make certain you have enough cash to purchase sufficient inventory for seasonal cycles;

- Take advantage of discounts and special purchases;

- Properly plan equipment purchases for replacement or expansion;

- Prepare for adequate future financing and determine the type of financing you need (short term credit line, permanent working capital, or long-term debt).

- Show lenders your ability to plan and repay financing.

"For a new or growing business, the cash flow projection can make the difference between succeeding and failure. For an ongoing business, it can make the difference between growth and stagnation".

Preparing a cash flow projection is a something like preparing your budget and balancing your checkbook at the same time. Unlike the income statement, a cash flow statement deals only with actual cash transactions. Depreciation, a non-cash transaction, does not appear on a cash flow statement. Loan payments (both principal and interest) will appear on your cash flow statement since they require the outlay of cash.

Cash is generated primarily by sales. But in most businesses, not all sales are cash sales. Even if you have a retail business and a large percentage of your sales are cash, it is likely that you offer credit (charge accounts, charge cards, term payments, layaway, trade credit) to your customers. Thus, you need to have a means of estimating when those credit sales will turn into cash-in-hand. (Smallbusinessnotes.com 2009)

Working capital analyses

Working capital is commonly defined as the funds a business needs to support its normal operations. In some ways, a working capital analysis is similar to a cash flow forecast, but it differs in its focus on the operating cycle of the business.

Quoting from the website Entrepreneur.com, "the operating cycle analyzes the accounts receivable, inventory and accounts payable cycles in terms of days. In other words, accounts receivable are analyzed by the average number of days it takes to collect an account. Inventory is analyzed by the average number of days it takes to turn over the sale of a product (from the point it comes in your door to the point it is converted to cash or an account receivable). Accounts payable are analyzed by the average number of days it takes to pay a supplier invoice.

"Most businesses cannot finance the operating cycle (accounts receivable days + inventory days) with accounts payable financing alone. Consequently, working capital financing is needed. This shortfall is typically covered by the net profits generated internally or by externally borrowed funds or by a combination of the two.

"Most businesses need short-term working capital loans at some point in their operations. For instance, retailers must find working capital to fund seasonal inventory buildup between September and November for Christmas sales. But even a business that is not seasonal occasionally experiences peak months when orders are unusually high. This creates a need for working capital to fund the resulting inventory and accounts receivable buildup". (Entrepreneur.com 2009) A working capital analysis is prepared in a manner similar to what we described for a cash flow forecast in that assumptions are made about the impact on working capital as a result of activities during the forecast period in order to provide the business owner with assurance that adequate working capital to support operations will be generated by normal business operations. If not, alternative sources of working capital must be lined up, and the earlier such a need is recognized, the better.

Break-even analysis

A break even analysis is designed to show you how much revenue must be generated to cover your fixed and variable costs. Revenue below the breakeven point means the business is losing money and revenue above the breakeven point means the business is profitable.

Let us look at a simple example, one that assumes your business is selling only one product. In order to calculate the breakeven point you will need to know three things:

- Your fixed costs

- Your variable cost

- Your unit selling price

Once the breakeven point is passed and revenue continues to rise, your business will be profitable. This is why knowing your breakeven point in terms of unit sales is so important. The website About.com:Entrepreneurs contains an easy to understand formula for calculating your breakeven point:

To conduct your breakeven analysis, take your fixed costs, divided by your price minus your variable costs. As an equation, this is defined as:

Breakeven Point = Fixed Costs/(Unit Selling Price - Variable Costs)

This calculation will let you know how many units of a product you will need to sell to break even. Once you have reached that point, you have recovered all costs associated with producing your product (both variable and fixed).

Above the breakeven point, every additional unit sold increases profit by the amount of the unit contribution margin, which is defined as the amount each unit contributes to covering fixed costs and increasing profits. As an equation, this is defined as:

Unit Contribution Margin = Sales Price - Variable Costs

Recording this information in a spreadsheet will allow you to easily make adjustments as costs change over time, as well as play with different price options and easily calculate the resulting breakeven point. You could use a program such as Excel's Goal Seek, if you wanted to give yourself a goal of a certain profit, say USD 1 million, and then work backwards to see how many units you would need to sell to hit that number. (This online tutorial will show you how to use Goal Seek.)"(About.com: Entrepreneurs 2009).

Profitability analyses (e.g. by customer, product, region)

There are many types of analyses that managers prepare in order to gain a deeper insight into the operations of their businesses. One of the most important of these is profitability analyses. Managers, know, intuitively, that some customers are more profitable than others, that they make more gross margins on some products than others, and if the business has more than just local coverage, that some geographical regions are more profitable than others. While it is good to know such things intuitively, it is better to know them for sure. And knowing them for sure requires that systematic analyses be prepared.

According to Wikipedia, "Customer profitability (CP) is the difference between the revenues earned from and the costs associated with the customer relationship in a specified period".

"Although CP is nothing more than the result of applying the business concept of profit to a customer relationship, measuring the profitability of a firm's customers or customer groups can often deliver useful business insights.

"Quite often a very small percentage of the firm's best customers will account for a large portion of firm profit. Although this is a natural consequence of variability in profitability across customers, firms benefit from knowing exactly who the best customers are and how much they contribute to firm profit.

"At the other end of the distribution, firms sometimes find that their worst customers actually cost more to serve than the revenue they deliver. These unprofitable customers actually detract from overall firm profitability. The firm would be better off if they had never acquired these customers in the first place" (Wikpedia 2009e).

"The biggest challenge in measuring customer profitability is the assignment of costs to customers. While it is usually clear what revenue each customer generated, it is often not clear at all what costs the firm incurred serving each customer". So, accountants try and develop some sort of reasonable method of allocating fixed and variable costs to customers. A typical method is to analyze each cost and try to determine the proportion attributable to each customer. A simple and clear-cut example is a situation where a store has both walk-in and on-line customers. The costs of renting and maintaining the physical store could reasonably be allocated to the customers who purchase goods in person, based on the number of visits or more likely on the amount of sales to each customer. On-line customers could have the costs of developing and maintaining the website allocated to them. With this information in hand, a customer profitability analysis can be prepared. It is usually prepared in descending order by customer profitability, as illustrated in Exhibit 40:

Your Restaurant Supply Company Year to Date 2009

Customer Name	Gross Sales	Allocated Costs	**Profit**
Rose's Restaurant	USD 12000	USD 7000	USD 5000
Bill's Bar B Q	USD 10000	USD 5500	USD 4500
Cal's Coffee Shop	USD 8000	USD 3500	USD 4500
Alice's Cafe	USD 5000	USD 3000	USD 2000
Paul's Pizza Hut	USD 4000	USD 3500	USD 500
Total	USD 39000	USD 22500	USD 16500

Exhibit 40: Customer Profitability Analysis

Assume you are the owner of the restaurant supply company illustrated in the exhibit. What kinds of useful information can you gather from an analysis such as this?

Many companies prepare a similar type of analysis at the gross margin level and skip the step of trying to allocate costs to individual customers. In this case, cost of goods sold is substituted for "allocated costs" in column three of Exhibit 40, and column four will show gross margin by customer instead of profitability by customer. For many managers, gross margin by customer gives them the essential information they need without going through the additional step of trying to allocate costs to customers, which is clouded by its inherent inaccuracies.

Budgets, forecasts, and alternative scenarios
Budgets

Earlier, we discussed cash flow forecasts and how they are used. An extension of the cash flow forecast concept is the operating budget. Most organizations have them. A budget is the financial expression of an organization's operating plan for a period of time, usually at least a year. Prior to the beginning of the year, managers prepare a plan for what they hope to accomplish in the coming year in terms of revenue, expenses, and net profit.

A more formal definition of a budget is:

"A **budget** is a financial document used to project future income and expenses. The budgeting process may be carried out by individuals or by companies to estimate whether the person/company can continue to operate with its projected income and expenses.

A budget may be prepared simply using paper and pencil, or on computer using a spreadsheet program like Excel, or with a financial application like Quicken or QuickBooks.

The process for preparing a monthly budget includes:

- Listing of all sources of monthly income

- Listing of all required, fixed expenses, like rent/mortgage, utilities, phone

- Listing of other possible and variable expenses". (Biztaxlaw.about.com 2009)

Then, as the year unfolds, actual income and expenses are posted to the accounting records, and compared to what was budgeted, and a variance from budget for each item budgeted (e.g. sales, selling expenses, advertising costs, etc) is calculated. Managers responsible for the various income and expense items then examine each variance and, if it is substantial, search for an explanation. For example, it is one thing if electricity costs are 20 per cent higher than what was budgeted for one month because workmen were using power tools to repair the roof. In that case, we can expect costs to return to normal when the repair work is completed. It is quite another thing if costs are higher because the electric company raised its rates. In that case, we can expect that costs will be at least 20 per cent higher in the future.

Forecasts

Most organizations take budget variance to date into consideration each month, and then prepare a *revised budget (or forecast)* for the balance of the year. This step is particularly important if variances to date vary from the original budget in a major way. For example, if sales are less than projected because market conditions are less favorable than anticipated when the budget was prepared, managers may look for ways to increase sales or reduce expenses in order to avoid a loss for the year.

Scenarios

There are many other forecasts that managers ask for in order to try and anticipate what the future might hold so they can prepare contingency plans in case of unforeseen events. Examples of unforeseen events that may well affect future outcomes are the arrival of a new competitor, a change in the overall economic outlook which could affect costs and/or revenues either positively or negatively, or even the arrival of a new company in another line of business that could raise prevailing wage rates in your region.

So, what managers like to do is to develop forecasts of sales, costs, cash, profits, interest rates and the like using different assumptions which, of course, result in different outcomes, some good and some bad. Another word for such forecasts is *scenarios*. For example, let us assume that a forecast of the income statement for a business at the end of the year assumes that sales will grow by 8 per cent over the previous year and costs will grow by 6 per cent. A manager might ask for an alternative scenario where sales increase by 12 per cent and costs increase by 9 per cent and another scenario where sales decrease by 3 per cent and costs increase by 1 per cent.

The Wall Street Journal had a story recently on how businesses use scenarios for planning purposes. Quoting from it: "Each spring, executives at JDS Uniphase Corp. plan for three potential sales scenarios for the coming fiscal year, which begins in July. Last year, rattled by financial-market turmoil, they included an extremely pessimistic sales outlook and outlined potential cost cuts.

"The planning proved useful when the economy stalled and customers began delaying orders later in the year. "We knew what levers to pull", says Dave Vellequette, chief financial officer at the Milpatis, Calif., maker of fiber-optic telecommunications equipment.

"The experience highlights the value of scenario planning, or preparing responses to imagined changes in conditions. "It's not about predicting the future", says Peter Schwartz, a partner at Monitor Group, a Cambridge, Mass. Consulting firm. "Scenario planning is a tool for learning" and making better decisions." (Wall Street Journal 2009).

Sources of financing for your organization

Once you have your accounting system established, you can take your plans for the initial months and years of operation of your organization, and prepare scenarios of the financial results of operations for your own peace of mind or as documents to discuss with potential investors. Keep in mind that potential investors are interested in something they call the "path to profitability" or P2P. In other words, while they expect that your organization will not be profitable immediately, they will want some assurance that it will be profitable relatively soon before they help you get started. While potential investors may like you as an individual, they want to be sure they will get a return on their investment. The way you do this is to go over your business plan with them, including the financial analyses that shows them the path to profitability. They will ask you questions to make sure your assumptions are reasonable, so make sure you do your "homework" in advance, anticipate their questions, and have good answers ready for them. The author of Chapter 2 discussed several possible sources you can explore to obtain the start-up financing you will need:

- savings
- friends and family
- micro-financers
- governmental support
- barter
- bank loans
- networking
- online network
- memberships

Savings: If you have been saving your money and have accumulated enough to provide the funds you need to finance your start-up, this is the best way for you to go. It can be difficult to convince third parties that your start-up is a good investment, and, in some cases, you may have to relinquish some degree of ownership (and management control) over your business to an investor. This can lead to disagreements which, if serious enough, could cause your investor to demand his or her money returned to them at an inconvenient time.

However, only a small percentage of entrepreneurs are fortunate enough to be able to fund their start-up costs with personal funds, so most are forced to seeking funding elsewhere. Many entrepreneurs in the US, for example borrow from their credit cards or take out a higher mortgage on their homes to avoid having to get funds from others. While this is common, it can result in personal financial disaster if the start-up fails.

Friends and family: Asking friends and families to invest is another common way that start-ups are funded. Often the potential entrepreneur is young, energetic, and has a good idea for a start-up, but does not have much in the way of personal savings. Friends and family may be older and have some money set aside. While your parents, or other family members should not risk all of their retirement savings on your start-up, they may be willing to risk a small percentage of it to help you out. Sometimes friends your own age are willing to work for little or no wages until your cash flow turns positive. The term "sweat equity" is often used for this type of contribution as the owner will often reward such loyalty with a small percentage ownership of the organization in lieu of cash. A variation on this is **barter** or trade. As mentioned in Chapter 1, this is a method by which you could provide a needed service such as consulting/management advice in return for the resources needed for your start up. This needs to be accounted for in your accounting records also.

Networking, online networks, and memberships all can be ways of meeting managers who have either successfully launched a star-up or who are in the process of moving their organization forward on the "path to profitability". Adding to some of the examples given in Chapter 1, you may wish to consider your local chamber of commerce, a Rotary Club, or a local organization comprised of entrepreneurs. For example, if your start-up is located in Africa, the Africa Business Communities portal could be a good source for you to locate networking opportunities in your community. According to their website:

"The African continent is enjoying a period of unprecedented economic growth. The idea that business is the key to sustainable development in Africa is gaining ground rapidly worldwide.

"Africa Business Communities is a portal website that brings the visitor into the heart of the African economy, by granting access to African entrepreneurs. Currently Africa Business Communities hosts 35 Africa business networks, in the future that will be hundreds". (African Business Communities 2009).

Bank loans (as stated in Chapter 1) "are not usually available to early-stage entrepreneurs unless you have a track record of a previous success and/or the assets to put up (as collateral) such as a home you own in return for securing the bank loan".

Angel investors, venture capitalists: Venture capitalists are usually not interested in start-ups. They tend to invest in young companies after they have demonstrated that they are clearly on a path to profitability and they need additional capital to help them grow quickly. Angel investors, on the other hand, are interested in start-up companies and, unlike venture capitalists who tend to seek control of the organization, angel investors like to leave management of the organization to its founder(s). Angel investors are always available to provide advice and counsel, however. This can be extremely valuable to a young entrepreneur as angel investors are usually successful entrepreneurs themselves. For example, a recent article in Business Week magazine describes a USD 300 million angel investment firm co-founded by Marc Andreessen, of Netscape Communications fame. Named Andreessen Horowitz, the firm's investors (in addition to Andreessen's business partner Ben Horowitz) include "prominent tech industry players including Reid Hoffman, founder of the social networking site LinkedIn, and Peter Thiel, former CEO of the payment service PayPal". The article goes on to say that "Andreessen Horowitz is expected to concentrate on making investments in technology, with an emphasis on corporate services and Internet businesses that cater to consumers. Investors who have heard the firm's pitch say it is adopting a "super angel" strategy in which a modest-size venture firm invests morsels of money into many startups. "They want to sprinkle as many seeds in the ground as possible," says one investor who was approached to invest in the firm but declined".

"There's a twist though: While most super angels finance the first round of a startup and work closely with the company to launch a product, the investor says Andreessen and Horowitz told him they intend to take a more hands-off approach: They'll invest in 70 or 80 companies with minimal involvement in most, and then double or triple down on the dozen or so winners that emerge. The strategy will allow Andreessen to back many more startups than the average venture firm, but with less control" (BusinessWeek.com 2009).

Micro-financers If you do the Google search suggested in Chapter 1 you will find a number of organizations that give small loans to budding entrepreneurs in developing economies. One such example is Microfinancing Partners in Africa. Here is a quote from their website where they describe their program:

"Microfinancing Partners in Africa (MPA) develops sustainable businesses and economically viable communities. We work with community-based organizations to create and support funding systems that furnish small, collateral-free, low-interest business loans. Grants are given to organizations that provide business, health and nutrition classes.

"Very often, all that is required are loans as small as $20 to bring a business into full production. Realistic microfinancing terms, comprehensive training and the development of a community-based support network result in a high percentage of on-time repayments. This funding system provides the financial basis for the provision of additional training, loans and business creation.

"Ultimately, these thriving business communities provide the economic foundation for community development projects, including schools, health centers, power sources, etc." (Microfinancing Partners in Africa 2009)

The one aspect of microfinancers is that their loans are truly "micro". They may be too small to be helpful in getting your business started. But, you never know. Microfinancing organizations can be a good place to start, and if your needs exceed their normal limits they may be able to refer you to other sources of funding. There may be microfinancing resources available through UN programs, Rotary.org and other sources.

Finally, **governmental support** is also a possibility. As an example, here is a quote from a website describing government grants available to start-ups in the US, along with some of the reasons why the US government is allocating federal funds to private business start-ups:

"Economic development is very important for every country. The economic conditions are unpredictable and volatile and so every country needs all the help it can get to improve its overall standing. Businesses are the major contributors to the success of the economy and so the government is always willing to extend the needed financial aid.

"Some entrepreneurs are hesitant to get assistance from the government. But if you're one of those entrepreneurs with capital problems, don't hesitate to ask for help from the government. The government has a huge fund allocation for the grants. If you want to know more about the government grants, you can simply log on to the internet and search for these entrepreneur grants.

"Before an entrepreneur decides to put up a business, he conducts a lot of studies to determine if the business is feasible or not. If he can prove the feasibility of his business proposal, the government will immediately provide the needed capital assistance through the entrepreneur grants.

"If the working capital that you've raised from family, relatives, and friends are insufficient, try to contact the local government and ask for the requirements in order to avail the government entrepreneur grant. You can either do this online or you can visit the physical office of the local government of your state or country". (BusinessStartUpAssistance.com 2009)

Does your country have a program of assistance for entrepreneurs?

Chapter summary

In this chapter we discussed the importance of having a well-designed accounting system for your organization as well as the distinction between financial and managerial accounting. While both financial and managerial accounting statements and reports are required and important, managerial accounting statements and reports are more likely to contain the kinds of information you will need to help manage the operations of your organization.

We explained the six different types of accounts, their characteristics, and how they are used to create a detailed chart of accounts which is tailored to the specific needs of your organization. Next we covered the advantages of the system of double-entry bookkeeping and how, together with ledgers and other accounting records, it enhances the accuracy of information maintained in an accounting system, whether it is manual or computer-based.

Next, since the cost of computers and software has dropped to the point where even many small organizations can afford them, we covered some of the accounting software packages that are available, their costs, criteria for selection, and the advantages of using them.

Finally, we discussed the common options for obtaining funds for your start-up organization, some of the pros and cons of each, and the advantage you will have in approaching lenders or investors with accounting reports that demonstrate a clear path to profitability.

Discussion questions

➢ Explain the difference between financial accounting and managerial accounting. Which one is most important to owner/managers of a start-up organization and why?

➢ List and give examples of the six basic types of accounts. What are the characteristics of each?

➢ Why is it important to have a chart of accounts that is tailored to particular types of organizations rather than one chart of accounts that applies to all types of organizations?

➢ Where can you find sample charts of accounts that apply to your type of organization?

➢ Explain the advantages of double-entry bookkeeping. Do you agree with Goethe's description of double-entry bookkeeping as Goethe as "one of the most beautiful discoveries of the human spirit"?

9. Financial and managerial accounting; financing your organization

> Please discuss the advantages and disadvantages of using computer software packages for your accounting system.

> What sort of difficulty can you imagine the manager of an organization would be in if the organization did not routinely prepare cash flow forecasts and working capital analyses?

> Why is it important for managers to understand the concept of a break-even point?

> Please give examples of how information from a customer profitability report could be used?

> Why is it important for an organization to prepare and use a budget (or financial plan)?

> Please give examples of alternative scenarios an organization should prepare and how they might be used.

References

(About.com: Entrepreneurs 2009) http://entrepreneurs.about.com/od/businessplan/a/breakeven.htm, accessed July 5, 2009.

(Accounting Software Review 2009) http://accounting-software-review.toptenreviews.com/, accessed July 4, 2009.

(African Business Communities 2009) http://www.africabusinesscommunities.com/, accessed July 7, 2009.

(Biztaxlaw.about.com 2009) http://biztaxlaw.about.com/od/glossaryb/g/Budget.htm, accessed July 6, 2009.

(Buchanan and Espeseth 2009) "Developing a Bed and Breakfast Business Plan 2009", North Central Regional Extension Publication 273, http://web.aces.uiuc.edu/vista/pdf_pubs/b&b.pdf, accessed June 22, 2009.

(BusinessStartUpAssistance.com 2009) http://www.businessstartupassistance.com/a-government-entrepreneur-grant--its-easier-then-you-think.php, accessed July 7, 2009.

(BusinessWeek.com 2009) http://www.businessweek.com/magazine/content/09_28/b4139032324083.htm, accessed July 7, 2009.

(Entrepreneur.com 2009) http://www.entrepreneur.com/money/moneymanagement/financialanalysis/article21940.html#ixzz0KJKa21Vk&D, accessed July 4, 2009.

(Executive Caliber 2009) http://www.executivecaliber.ws/sys-tmpl/historyofaccounting/, accessed June 23, 2009.

(IASB 2009) http://www.iasb.org/, accessed June 20, 2009.

(Microfinancing Partners in Africa 2009) http://www.microfinancingafrica.org/, accessed July 7, 2009.

(Smallbusinessnotes.com 2009) http://www.smallbusinessnotes.com/operating/finmgmt/financialstmts/cashprojection.html, accessed July 4, 2009.

(Universal Accounting 2009) <u>http://www.know-accounting.com/glossary/index.php?terml=g&termid=90</u> accessed June 25 2009.

(Wall Street Journal 2009). Tuna, Cari, "Pendulum is Swinging Back on "Scenario Planning", *The Wall Street Journal,* July 6, 2009, page B6.

(Wikipedia 2009a) <u>http://en.wikipedia.org/wiki/Financial_accounting</u>, accessed June 20, 2009.

(Wikipedia 2009b) <u>http://en.wikipedia.org/wiki/Managerial_accounting</u>, accessed June 20, 2009.

(Wikipedia 2009c) <u>http://en.wikipedia.org/wiki/Chart_of_accounts</u>, accessed June 20. 2009.

(Wikipedia 2009d) <u>http://en.wikipedia.org/wiki/Double-entry_bookkeeping_system</u>, accessed June 23, 2009.

(Wikpedia 2009e) <u>http://en.wikipedia.org/wiki/Customer_profitability</u>, accessed July 5, 2009.

10. Leveraging with information technology

Editors: Donald J McCubbrey (Daniels College of Business, University of Denver, USA) and Garry Woods (CommerceNext LLC, USA)

Reviewer: Richard A Scudder (Daniels College of Business, University of Denver, USA)

Learning objectives

- define the four components of an information system

- identify how information systems can assist a start-up

- understand how to create a web presence for your organization

- learn how to use information systems to gain a competitive advantage

- understand how companies identify their information needs and set priorities

- acquire an appreciation of why it is important to manage is risks

Introduction

This chapter explores how Information Systems (IS) can be used by managers to better develop their business idea, launch and sustain their businesses. It will also examine how IS forms the foundation for operations management, customer relationship management and financial and managerial accounting.

While you may be familiar with the term "this is the information age" it can mean different things to different people. In his famous book, *The World is Flat*, (Friedman 2005) Thomas Friedman explains how IS has changed the way the world works. He calls the World Wide Web a "Global network for collaboration" and gives many examples of how many forms of knowledge work can now be done anywhere in the world, that individuals from different countries can collaborate on projects without having to travel to distant cities to meet each other face-to-face, and that projects can be worked on by contributors from anywhere in the world. Examples of these three possibilities are listed below, in order to give you a better appreciation for what is possible:

- Knowledge work can be done anywhere. Perhaps the most common example of this is software development. Software engineers in developing economies can develop programs under contract from companies in the developed world at much lower cost. Known as "outsourcing", this is effective because universities in many developing economies such as India, China, Brazil, and Eastern Europe have well-trained programmers who are willing to work for wages above the prevailing wage levels in their home countries, but less than what a trained programmer earns in a developed country.

- Colleagues can collaborate on projects without having to travel great distances. Videoconferencing has reached the point where individuals can meet "face-to-face" over the Internet and have discussions related to a project they are working on together. These products can range from very sophisticated (and expensive) products like Cisco's "Telepresence" conferencing tool (Cisco 2009) to relatively inexpensive (or even free) software tools like Skype (Skype 2009).

The best examples of a large number of individuals collaborating on a common project is the so-called "open" movements: Open source programs like Linux and others we discuss later in this chapter, Open access to research journals, and the Open Educational Resources (OER) initiative which provide free educational resources over the Internet developed by volunteers from all over the world, of which the textbook you are reading from the Global Text Project is a prime example.

IS tools for the start-up organization

Before we begin our discussion of IS tools for a start-up organization, it is important to note that it may not be necessary to use a computer-based information system when you first go into business. You may be able to satisfy your information processing and record-keeping needs with manual systems. However, as the price of computers drop and your business expands, you may find it wise, as many small business owners do, to invest in computer-based information systems. Many people use Information Systems and Information Technology as if they meant the same thing. They are different, and it is important for you to understand the difference between them. As illustrated in Exhibit 41, an Information System is comprised of two sub-systems, a Social sub-system and a Technology sub-system.

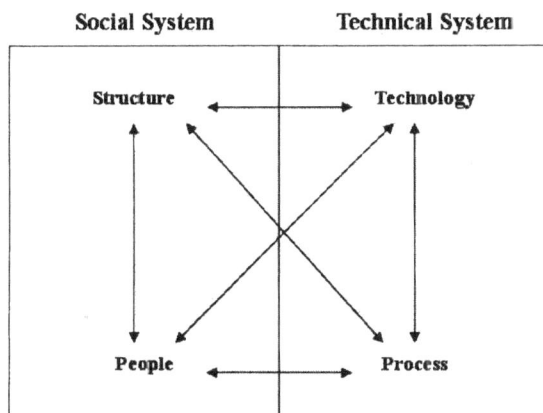

Exhibit 41: An information system

The discussion of the four components of information systems as well as Exhibit 41 above has been extracted from another book in the Global Text library (Information Systems 2008).

The technology sub-system

An information system may not need the use of computers to make the accumulation, organization, and reporting of information easier, faster, or more reliable. In your organization early stages, you may find it simple enough to just keep paper records and communicate face-to-face or by telephone rather than use email. However, modern organizations increasingly rely on information technology as the core of their information systems and part of the reason is that the cost of using computers has decreased as technology improves. We define information technology to include hardware, software and telecommunication equipment that is used to capture, process, store and distribute information.

Hardware is the physical equipment—such as a personal computer, a laptop, a portable computing device, and even a modern cell phone—used to process information. Software is the set of coded instructions (programs) that direct the hardware to perform the required tasks. A typical example is Google Docs—a word processing program designed to instruct a computer to create text documents. Telecommunication systems are the networking equipment enabling users and devices to communicate. An example of a telecommunication system is a telephone network, which allows two callers to interact by voice over a distance.

These three elements—hardware, software and telecommunication systems—comprise the technology component of an information system.

The process sub-system

As discussed in Chapter 7, a process is the set of steps employed to carry out a specific business or organizational activity. In other words, a process maps the set of actions that an individual, a group or an organization must enact in order to complete an activity. Consider the job of a grocery store manager and the process he engages in when restocking an inventory of goods for sale. The store manager must:

- check the inventory of goods for sale and identify the needed items

- call individual suppliers for quotations and possible delivery dates

- compare prices and delivery dates quoted among several suppliers for the same goods

- select one or more suppliers for each of the needed items based on the terms of the agreement (e.g. availability, quality, delivery)

- call these suppliers and place the orders

- receive the goods upon delivery, checking the accuracy and quality of the shipped items; pay the suppliers

Note that there are multiple viable processes that an organization can design to complete the same activity. In the case of the grocery store, the timing and form of payment can differ dramatically, from cash on delivery to direct transfer of the payment to the supplier's bank account within three months of the purchase. The critical insight here is that the design of the process must fit with the other components of the information system and be adjusted when changes occur. It must also meet the unique needs of the organization. For example, imagine the grocery store manager purchasing a new software program that enables her to get quotations from all of the suppliers in the nearby regions and place orders online. Clearly the preceding process would need to change dramatically, and the store manager would need to be trained in the use of the new software program—in other words, changes would also affect the people component.

People

The people component of an information system encompasses all those individuals who are directly involved with the system. These people include the managers who define the goals of the system, and the users. The critical insight here is that the individuals involved in the information system come to it with a set of skills, attitudes, interests, biases, and personal traits that need to be taken into account when the organization designs the information system. Very often, an information system fails because the users do not have enough skills, or have a negative attitude toward the system. Therefore, there should be enough training and time for users to get used to the new system.

For example, when implementing an automated payroll system, training on how to enter employees' account information, how to correct wrong entries, and how to deposit the salaries into each account should be provided to the human resources staff. The benefits of the system should be communicated to both the human resources staff and the employees in order to build up positive attitudes towards the new system.

Structure

The structure (or organizational structure) component of information systems refers to the relationship among the individuals in the people component. Thus, it encompasses hierarchical and reporting structures, and reward systems. Many of these issues are discussed in Chapter 5. The structure component plays a critical role in an information system, simply because systems often fail when they are resisted by their intended users. This can happen because individuals feel threatened by the new work system, or because of inherent human resistance to change. When designing a new information system the organization needs to be cognizant of the current and future reward system in order to create incentives to secure its success.

Relationships between the four components

At this point it should be clear how information systems, while enabled by IS, are not synonymous with IS. Each of the four components discussed above can undermine the success of an information system—the best software application will yield little result if users reject it and fail to adopt it. More subtly, the four components of information systems must work together for the systems to perform. Thus, when the organization decides to bring in a new technology to support its operation, the design team must adjust the existing processes or develop new ones. The people involved must be trained to make sure that they can carry out the processes. If the skills of these individuals are such that they can not perform the required tasks or be trained to do so, a different set of individuals need to be brought in to work with the system. Finally, the design team must evaluate whether the organizational structure needs to be modified as well. New positions may need to be created for additional responsibilities, and old jobs may need to be eliminated. The transition from the old way of doing things to the new system needs to be managed, ensuring that appropriate incentives and a reward structure is put in place.

Some practical advice for start-ups

- Do not invest in IS solutions until you can see that they will provide you with real benefits. They will require an investment of valuable time and money that you could perhaps use more effectively in other areas of your business.

- Installing IS systems often takes longer and costs more than originally estimated. You should have someone with IS skills available to help you get past the troubling points.

- Remember that it is usually a mistake to be one of the first to use a new technology. It can be risky, and it is even more important that you have access to personnel with strong IS skills.

At the same time, it can be a mistake to wait too long to gain business benefits from carefully chosen IS applications, particularly if your competition is taking advantage of IS for efficiency, effectiveness, and innovation.

Moving forward with information systems

When you decide it is time to move forward with leveraging your organization with information systems, you will appreciate the effort spent on developing a systems plan. The plan will state the kind of hardware, software, and communications technologies you need, as well as the sectors of your organization which should receive your attention first.

Many small organizations begin operations with manual systems to keep track of their operations. They may have simple lists on paper for customer, vendor, and employee information and keep a set of accounting records on paper as well. This was the way business information was kept by all organizations, large and small, before the advent of computers. When PCs became available, their cost was such that the power of the computer was made available at low cost and so today, most organizations of any size have at least one PC or laptop. You may well start out with keeping records manually, but before too long, you will appreciate how much easier it is to keep records on a computer and how well-designed software applications can provide you with valuable information quickly, in many different ways, whenever you need it.

One issue you will need to address early is your sourcing options, i.e. where will you obtain your hardware, software, and human resources to help you acquire and manage the IS resources you need. In Chapter 8, we discussed the ways that organizations partner with other organizations to perform essential business functions. It is very common for organizations to partner with another company to supply them with the specialized knowledge needed to acquire the right combination of hardware, software, and communications services to meet the needs of the organization. We will discuss these issues later in this chapter when we discuss the ways organizations develop a systems plan. Suffice it to say at this point, that you will have many options:

For example:

- You can hire an IS professional if your needs require a full-time employee to manage your IS processes (and if you can afford it). Organizations that do not need a full-time employee and do not have IS expertise available in-house or even on a part-time basis typically make arrangements for part-time support from an IS consulting firm. Sometimes the consulting firm is a sole proprietorship.

- You can acquire your own hardware (e.g. PCs) or you can buy time on another organization's hardware to run your software applications. In developed economies, there are companies like Google and Amazon that offer so-called "cloud computing" services. They have developed so much expertise in managing server farms (i.e. data centers) that they now sell hardware capacity on-demand to other companies. Similar options are available in other parts of the world.

- As with hardware, you have similar options with software. Up until recently, if you needed a software package to do the accounting for your organization, for example, you had to buy a package and install it on your own computer. Now, many software packages can be accessed with a simple Internet connection and a web browser. The software package resides not on your computer, but on the vendor's computer (or perhaps another computer "in the clouds").

All of the options have their advantages and disadvantages and we discuss them later in this chapter.

While it is certainly possible for you to hire a programmer and have him or her develop the software programs your organizations need, it is rare when a start-up company needs to do this as there are so many software programs available for you to use (and some of them are free). In all likelihood, you will begin to move your organization into the "information age" in one of two ways, either (1) acquiring a suite of commonly-used programs designed for meeting the needs of both individuals and organizations, or (2) acquiring software programs designed specifically to meet most needs of a small organization. Each of these options is discussed below:

Acquiring a suite of commonly-used programs

Perhaps the best-known suite of commonly used programs is Microsoft Office. A basic version of Office, Microsoft Office Standard 2007 includes four programs:

1. Microsoft Word, used for preparing documents

2. Microsoft Excel, used for preparing spreadsheets (most commonly used for accounting analyses but also useful for basic record-keeping such as customer lists or checkbooks)

3. PowerPoint, used for making presentations

4. Microsoft Outlook, used for managing email (Microsoft 2009)

There are several other open-source options available as well, typically at no cost to you. Some of these are:

1. OpenOffice (OpenOffice.org 2009)

2. Google Docs (Google 2009)

3. Zoho (Zoho 2009)

In addition to being free, the open source options have the ability to read and write computer file and is format compatible with the more widely used Microsoft products.

When to think about using database management software

As your business grows and you need to keep accurate records on a computer beyond what is reasonable to do with a spreadsheet program, you should consider adding database management software.

Karen Stille placed a good comparison of the features of database and spreadsheet software a website, QCISolutions. In summary, she states that:

"As a general rule of thumb, databases should be used for data storage and spreadsheets should be used to analyze data.

"In a nutshell we use a database if...

- the information is a large amount that would become unmanageable in spreadsheet form and is related to a particular subject.

- you want to maintain records for ongoing use.

- the information is subject to many changes (change of address, pricing changes, etc.).

- you want to generate reports based on the information.

Use a spreadsheet if...

- you want to crunch numbers and perform automatic calculations.

- you want to track a simple list of data.

- you want to easily create charts and graphs of your data.

- you want to create "What-if" scenarios.

"In most cases, using the combination of a database to store your business records and a spreadsheet to analyze selected information works best". (Stille 2009)

Microsoft's widely-used database management software is called ACCESS, and versions of Microsoft Office that use ACCESS are available for purchase. More information is available on the Microsoft site (Microsoft). On the other hand, open source database management software is also available at no cost to you. You may wish to examine one of the following open source packages to see if one of them meets your needs:

- MySQL (MySQL 2009)

- Zoho Creator (Zoho 2009)

One of the prevailing issues with using open source software rather than software you purchase is the level of support you can expect from the software's creator. If you pay for software, you have a right to expect excellent documentation and support. If the software is free, sometimes documentation and support do not meet the same standards. Much of the support you get is from the community of users. As of this writing, the worldwide community for ACCESS is much larger, and there are many books written about it. The open source databases are just as useful, but finding information and support can be a more tedious process. However, according to the Gartner Group, a highly-respected technology research company based in the US, open source database management software is becoming more attractive. In a report released in November 2008, they made the following observations:

"During 2008, since our last note about open-source database management systems (DBMSs), we have seen an increase in the interest and use of open-source DBMS engines in a production environment. As this trend continues to gain speed, the cost benefits of using an open-source DBMS is increasing and the risk of using it is decreasing.

Key findings:

- Lower total cost of ownership (TCO), compared to commercial DBMSs, can be realized for non-mission-critical applications.

- There are large third-party software vendors looking to certify open-source DBMSs as a platform for existing applications, including SAP.

- The major open-source DBMS products are now available for installation as a package, without involving the source code, including tools to help support the DBMS environment.

- If the technical capabilities of the staff are strong, use of an open-source DBMS in mission-critical environments is possible now.

Recommendations:

- Open-source DBMS engines can be used today for non-mission-critical applications with reduced risk over several years ago.

- Only use an open-source DBMS engine supplied by a vendor who controls or participates in the engineering of the DBMS and always purchase subscription support when used in production environments.

- If open source is part of your overall IS strategy, plan for the use of open-source DBMS engines in mission-critical environments in two to five years." (Gartner 2008)

- Acquiring software programs designed specifically to meet most needs of a small organization

- In the same way that Office Suites are available which can perform many of the basic information systems tasks of a small organization, there are suites of programs available to perform specific functions like accounting, payroll, customer relationship management, inventory control and the like. Recall that we discussed computer-based accounting systems in considerable detail in Chapter 9.

- (Enterprise Resource Planning (ERP) systems are the analogous software solutions for large and medium-sized companies.) Examples of small business "suites" include the following:

Microsoft has a site devoted to software suite solutions for small businesses at:

http://www.microsoft.com/business/peopleready/

NetSuite (www.netsuite.com) NetSuite is in a category of software called "software as a service" (SaaS). In the SaaS model, the software resides on the servers of the software provider rather than on the using the organization's computer. The advantages of this model are that users never have to worry about software and data backups or software updates. These functions are provided at the software company's data centers. Some SaaS models charge users by the month, others charge them at a variable rate, based on the number of transactions per month and/or the size of their databases. The downside for some users with SaaS is that the information is not kept "in-house". Although hosted solutions are considered very secure, some users worry about security and privacy issues. The website, www.2020software.com, compares several small business software suites, and has links to the companies' sites.

There are a number of open source initiatives for small business software you may wish to investigate. One such example is xTuple (http://www.xtuple.org/). A comprehensive list of options is available at SourceForge (www.sourceforge.net). Our previous cautions on the use of open source software products apply here as well.

Creating a Web presence

Having a website is now considered as necessary as a phone or fax number even an email address for corresponding with customers. Since the site will be a reflection of your organization, its product or service, the most important step is to research and plan. For most businesses, a Web site can serve as a resource for information and to promote the organization, its brand, and the value of the product or services being offered. But many times, businesses as well as individuals create a site for the sake of having one, without taking time to understand what customers and the business expect from a site. When you set down to create your site, consider the following first:

- Decide on a budget.

- Decide on a name (Domain Name or URL). Check <u>http://www.whois.com</u> to see if the name is already taken.

- Register the name (Domain Name or URL). Login to a registrar like <u>http://www.godaddy.com</u> and follow their instructions for registration.

- Decide how the site will be designed and maintained (who will handle this).

- What will be the content of the site?

- Decide on a hosting company for the site. There are hundreds, if not thousands of hosting companies will host your website for as little as USD 3.95 per month. A simple Google search will turn up many candidates for you in your locale. To get an appreciation of the kinds of hosting services that are available from US-based companies, go to <u>http://hostingreview.com</u>.

- Decide whether you will hire someone to build the site for you or if you want to use one of the many template-driven software packages to build it yourself.

Finding out what kinds of information your customers want, and then designing and developing your site to provide up-to-date, ongoing resource materials can help you better position your products or services and serve as a credible "go-to spot". A web site can go from a simple one-page site with your name and mission statement to a site with multiple pages that include on-line sales, newsletters and discussion forums.

Know what your customers want

Remember that your Web site should be a dynamic communication tool. Users today are conditioned to use the Web as a where-to-turn resource, where they expect up-to-date news, information and tips related to your product or services. Users will also use the information provide to compare you with others, specifically your competition. For you, it is also another opportunity where you can promote your services and serve the community. There is nothing gained by having a website that posts dry, out-of-date content. Keep a pulse on what kind of information about your product/services customers are looking for, and how and where they expect to find it. Do not be too quick to list the areas where you feel you are strongest—remember to put yourself in your customer's shoes and ask what they want to ask: "What is in it for me (WIIFM) to visit this website?"

An effective site should:

- Recognize the needs of all who will use your site, vendors, customers and yes even employees, and direct each to the content that will interest them most.

- Be easy to access, read and use with well-thought-out content, useful links, e-mail addresses or phone numbers.

- Provide helpful information on how to keep customers coming back

Make your visitors feel confident about choosing your organization as a provider for the product or services for which they are looking.

Give your customer a positive experience

Knowing what your customer wants to see on your website is only half the challenge. In today's quick to find, instant gratification environment, your customers not only want to find information on your services and product quickly, the want to share it and have a positive customer experience when they do. A positive experience is one that not only gives your customer their needed information but one, that provokes positive feedback from your customer when he or she contacts you via a Web chat or Internet phone. This gives customers an incredible ability to quickly and easily influence others as well as providing instant feedback into your customers buying patterns and feelings about your site and company.

If you can better understand your customer, their needs and objectives you will better understand how to measure and track the "voice of the customer". Why? This will foster a better customer relationship and will provide you with two outcomes: (1) having your customer extend your marketing without additional cost and (2) having customer based testimonies on their experiences that will increase your companies' reputation of the products or services you offer.

Know the basics

Whether you already have a site that is an offshoot of a current business you have done work with, or it is a stand-alone site (brochureware)—or whether you are considering creating a Web site, the information you provide is key. Looking at some of the best known websites, several sites stand out for their information, creativity, usefulness and easy to use. One such site, video how-to site http://www.Howcast.com, is a gem. At one time or another we have all tried to do things without reading the instructions. Howcast.com not only addresses this, but provides video as well.

The key elements of any site are a user-friendly, clean appearance and consistently improving content. As you determine your needs for a website, one of the important goals should be to allow your customers to access your site and avoid the time-consuming process of surfing the Web for similar products or services. They can visit your site and be taken to useful, informative sites.

The have-to's of an effective site:

- An introduction of your products or services: what is it, who uses it and why to buy it

- Basic information up front: contact information, product or services information, etc.

- Listing of products or services, grouped together by topic

- News: Post the latest information about how your organization is changing, how your products or services are being accepted or who is buying them. Consider an e-newsletter in PDF form with tips readers can hold onto

- Articles: Post in PDF form product information and marketing material by your marketing or product development team on what is new or what is coming

- A contact mechanism—a way for customers to ask a question, request information, register for warranty of your product or services, get your newsletter or get a referral

The next layer of your site:

- where and how to send a customer information they are seeking

- printable/downloadable forms for transmitting

- product/services tips and tools

- product updates

- upcoming events, such as industry or company seminars, with an agenda and how to register or request information

- community outreach information that shows how your organization is helping members of the community

- periodic satisfaction surveys that poll customers

The enhanced, "special customer" layer to your site:

- Password-protected forms

- password-protected customer sensitive data

- credit card encryption

- personal data (i.e. date of birth, social security number, contact info, etc.)

- enhanced articles and updates

- special programs and communications

eMarket your website

Register your website with search engines, some registration domain sites may have this available (check their pages and see if they do this) and what it will cost you to have your web site pulled to the front of the list. The more search engines that you register with the more the site will be displayed to those looking for products or services you offer. Note: a number of these sites are fee based, the more times your site comes up in a search the more it may cost you. At a minimum, you should consider registering your web page with both Google and Yahoo (instruction with registering on these search engines can be found on there respective sites). Both of these sites as well as MSN.com are the most commonly used web search engines sites globally.

In this process, when you view your web page, at the bottom you will a see box called Meta Tags (Meta tags are text within the source code of a web page. It provides information to search engines about the content of a specific page or site) This is where you put in key words or phrases that the search engines will pick up on when someone does a search.

Examples:

- Fish Store: Fish, Fresh Water, Fish Food, Guppies, Angel, etc.

- Pet Store: Dog, Cat, Hamster, Dog Food, Cat Food, etc.

- Computer Store: Computer, Hard Disk, CD, Hard Drive, DVD, etc.

If you are in a business that does not sell on the Internet, you may want to hold off on paying for this option as local people will go to your site from advertising, word of mouth or local Web searches.

As noted earlier, having a web presence is a very important part of a business today. You must make sure to take the time to plan and design your site so that it has the professional look and a certain "panache" or style that will help your business distinguish it from others. A site that not only will encourage visitors to return, but offers the information they are seeking the first time they visit. With careful and thoughtful planning and decision making you can create a small business site that can and will compete with larger companies, enhance your business and increase your margins and profits.

Using information technology competitively

Competitive advantage

When you are starting your business, very likely you will just be interested in substituting computer-based information systems for keeping the basic records of your business and preparing the reports you need to be an effective decision-maker. As your business grows, however, you should start to think of the potential benefit of going beyond the basics, as larger companies do, and look for ways to use information systems for competitive advantage. Many people use the term "technology-enabled innovation" to describe this process. Since it is never too early for you to start thinking about such innovation, we will cover the topic now.

Just about all businesses have competitors and customers have choices as to which businesses they decide to patronize. For example, you, as a customer, may have several restaurants to choose from if you want to buy a meal. Each restaurant, therefore, has other restaurants as competitors. A restaurant will try to offer its customers a better meal at a better price so that their business is successful in comparison with the competition. This is what is meant by gaining a competitive advantage. Of course, if a restaurant is the only one in a small town, its owner does not have to worry so much about competition (unless someone else decides to open a restaurant and compete for its customers. Businesses that can gain an advantage over their competitors are the ones who will be successful and, as we saw in Chapter 4, most small businesses that start up are doomed to fail. So, competitive advantage is important.

Porter and competitive advantage

In Chapter 3, you were introduced to the ideas of Professor Michael Porter, whose ideas on how to achieve a competitive advantage, first introduced in the 1980s[29] have stood the test of time. Recall that Porter's model consisted of three main categories:

- The Five Forces Model

- Three Generic Strategies

- The Value Chain

---

29 The information on Michael Porter needs to be cited.

In this section we will discuss how the creative use of information technology and communications technologies (IS) can help organizations gain a competitive advantage. These ideas were first expressed in two separate Harvard Business Review articles[30]

Use IS to alter the five forces in your favor. The five forces are illustrated Exhibit 42.

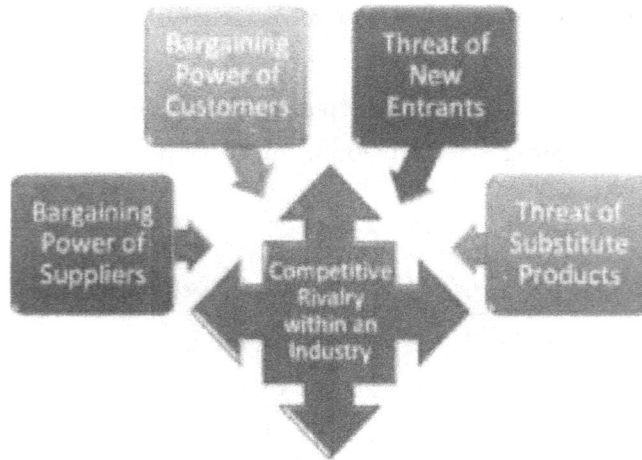

Exhibit 42: Porter's Five Forces Model Source

Source:

http://en.wikipedia.org/wiki/Porter_5_forces_analysis

Buyer power can be reduced by using IS in ways that tend to restrict buyers' choices. A good example is the frequent flyer programs that are offered by most commercial airlines around the world. When they enroll in the program, air travelers are awarded "miles" for every flight they take on, for example, British Airways. Their accumulated miles are maintained by a computer system. Travelers can obtain tickets for free flights once as certain number of miles has been accumulated in their account. This encourages travelers to always use the same airline so they can qualify for rewards more quickly. Frequent flyer programs, of course, have to keep track of a lot of information on the activities of thousands of travelers and would not be possible to manage without computer systems. An airline without a frequent flyer program is at a competitive disadvantage to airlines which have them.

Supplier power is high when a business must rely on just a few suppliers. For example, if there is just one store in a town which stocks office supplies, businesses have nowhere else to buy supplies they need and may be forced to pay higher than normal prices. On the other hand, if a local business is connected to the Internet, it can choose from many other suppliers and possibly find cheaper prices, even when the cost of shipping is considered.

The threat of new entrants can be reduced when IS is used to erect "entry barriers". Entry barriers are offerings that a business must make available to its customers if it expects to do business in a certain sector simply because most or all of its competitors offer a certain feature to their customers. An example is ATM machines offered by banks. ATM machines would not be possible without the use of computers and communications networks. If you had to choose between a bank that offered ATM machines and one that did not, which one would you choose? Most likely the one with ATM machines. ATM machines are a barrier to enter the banking sector in a particular locale.

30 Cite McFarlane and Porter/Millar.

The threat of substitute products can usually be reduced by using IS to bind customers more closely to a business and create what is called "switching costs". This means that the IS systems offered by a business are so appreciated by the customer that customers are reluctant to switch to a substitute product. For example, there are many free open content software products that equally competitive with the costly brands. Zoho, Google Docs, Thinkfree, are examples. One of the reasons many PC users do not switch to them is that they would have to learn how to use a new package. Even though the free packages are easy to learn, there is a switching cost involved that binds users to Microsoft Office: The time it would take to learn even a relatively simple package is enough of an obstacle to many users that they conclude that switching is not worth the effort.

The Intensity of Intra-Industry Competition can often be increased by IS-enabled innovations. For example, the global reach of the Internet means that competitors for many products and services can be located anywhere in the world. For example, tax accounting specialists may now find themselves competing with accounting specialists in low-cost countries. This is becoming a common practice as companies conclude that IS makes it possible for many forms of knowledge work to be performed anywhere in the world.

Use IS to reinforce your basic strategic positioning.

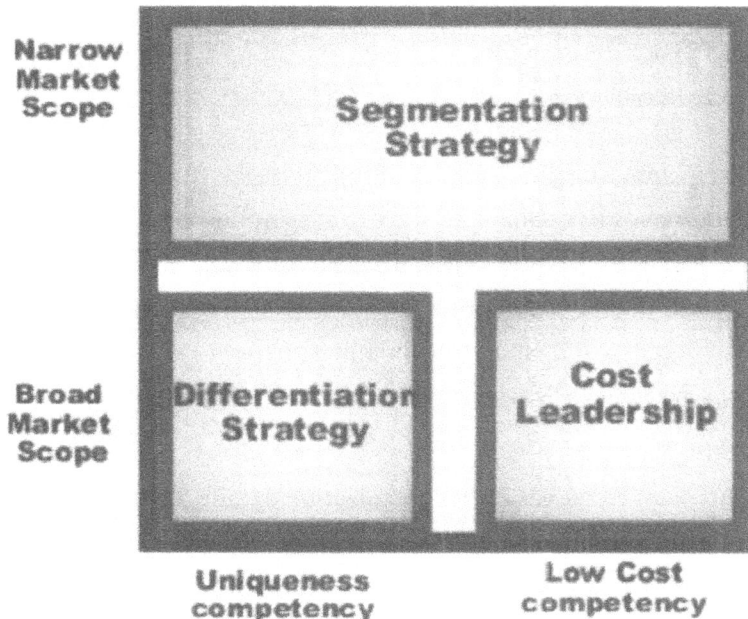

Exhibit 43: Porter's three generic strategies

Source: http://en.wikipedia.org/wiki/Porter_generic_strategies

Porter suggests that a business cannot be all things to all people. It must choose between three generic strategies As illustrated in Exhibit 43, a business can choose to be a cost leader, it can pursue a differentiated strategy for which consumers are willing to pay more, or it can target a segment of the market with either a low-cost or a differentiated strategy. For example, if we consider brands of automobiles, the Tata targets a broad market for low-priced cars, and the Subaru targets a broad differentiated market for low-priced allwheel drive cars. The Mazda Miata targets a segmented market for low-priced sports cars, while Rolls Royce targets a segmented (high-priced) market for sedans.

Information systems can assist a business in implementing one of Porter's three generic strategies by using IS to create operational efficiencies, thus lowering manufacturing costs, for example. Also, IS can create a differentiated model by having a website that permits customers to design a personalized version of an automobile and order it online, much the same way that we can buy personal computers online.

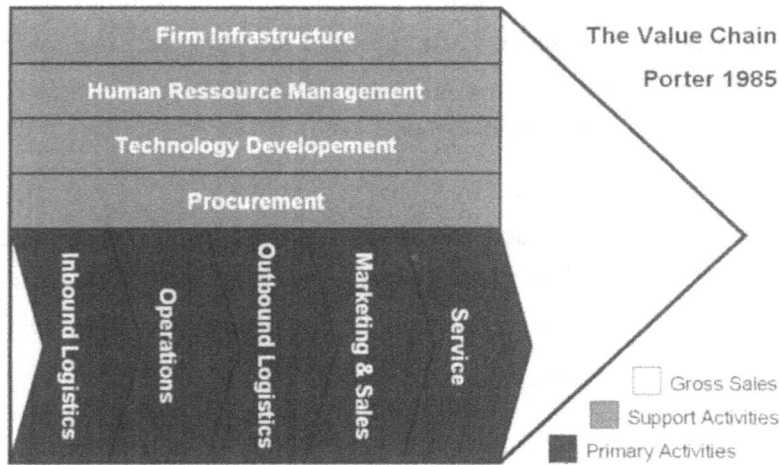

Exhibit 44: Porter's value chain

Source: http://kookyplan.pbwiki/f/ValueChain.ong

As discussed in Chapter 3, the Value Chain is a graphical representation of the processes (or activities) involved in most organizations. Analysts use the value chain framework to look for ways to streamline costly activities or add value to certain activities through the use of IS. As just one example, an organization could use IS to outsource a call center service to a lower cost location or, it could use IS to provide a well-designed website to offer a differentiated experience to customers who need to contact the organization, and embody a personalized call center service for issues that cannot be resolved by the customer just by using website features.

Identify your information systems needs

It is almost always the case that there are insufficient resources for an organization to take advantage of all of its opportunities to use IS to obtain business benefits. Such resources can be in the form of personnel in an internal IS Department or cash to hire outside consultants or both. Because of this, it is important that organizations be sure they are using their resources on IS projects that have the greatest value to the organization. A time-tested way of doing this is to have a process for setting IS development priorities that are consistent with and aligned with organizational priorities. In the literature, this is typically called "strategic alignment". There are three general approaches that organizations take to setting priorities for information systems projects. (Some practitioners say "there is no such thing as an IS project; there are only business projects". Such a perspective emphasizes the importance of obtaining business benefits from an investment in IS). The three general approaches to setting priorities (also known as developing a strategic plan for the IS function) are:

1. Have the IS department set priorities

2. Have a cross-functional steering committee set priorities

3. Conduct a systems planning project

Each of these approaches is discussed in more detail in the following paragraphs.

Have the IS department set priorities

The person in charge of the IS functions, particularly in larger organizations is called the Chief Information Officer or CIO. The CIO is responsible for new system development, systems operations, and maintenance of existing systems. Ideally, the CIO has a solid understanding of the organization's overall strategy and tactics as well as a good understanding of IS issues. A competent CIO should be able, therefore, to do a good job of setting priorities for the IS function. All too often, however, the CIO is more comfortable with technical issues and undertakes projects that are interesting from a technical standpoint, but offer little in the way of business benefits. On the other hand, some CIOs have an insufficient command of technical issues and therefore overlook opportunities to use IS to make their organization more efficient, effective, and innovative. Finding a person with the right blend of business and technical savvy has proven to be difficult, and, thus, CIO has come to be known, in some circles as "Career is Over".

Have a cross-functional steering committee set priorities

Many organizations use a cross-functional steering committee to discuss and agree on overall priorities for the IS function. All major areas of the company are represented, including, for example, accounting, finance, human resources, operations, and sales and marketing. Having all areas involved provides some assurance that the organization's needs and opportunities are addressed in the proper priority sequence. The shortcomings of this approach, in practice, however is that some heads of areas may not be as supportive of IS as they should be, and the process can become complicated when organizational politics intervene.

For example, the organization's best opportunity for obtaining business benefits could lie with a new information system to track how well sales are performing in order to be sure that customer demands will be met But this opportunity may not be understood or appreciated by the sales manager. Without the support from the sales manager, the IS project in his or her area would be unlikely to succeed, so the organization's best opportunity is lost. On the other hand, it could be the case that the operations manager has a strong and persuasive personality, and by force of argument in steering committee meetings is able to convince others that operations projects should get the highest priority.

Develop a formal plan for information systems

Even small companies will benefit from taking a relatively short time to develop a formal plan for the information systems function. In Chapter 1, and elsewhere in this book, we have emphasized the value of having a formal business plan to guide the organization. Many organizations take their business plan down another level and have formal plans for individual departments, such as sales and marketing, operations, and human resources. It is particularly important to have a written plan for the information systems function as top management, must be assured that the benefits of IS are being applied in accordance with the overall goals of the organization. IS professionals call the end result of an IS planning process "strategic alignment", which simply means that the strategic goals of the IS function are aligned with the strategic goals of the organization.

In a very small organization an information systems plan can be developed by one or two individuals. In larger organizations, it is usually developed by a project team, sometimes with the assistance of outside consultants. The important thing is that resources devoted to developing an information systems plan have knowledge of current and emerging information and communications technologies as well as a solid understanding of the organization's strategic plan. Development of a formal plan usually involves interviewing managers in each organizational unit to obtain their perspectives on issues such as:

- the overall strategic plan or direction of the organization

- plans of individual organizational units developed in support of the organization's plan

- industry trends, competitors' strategies and common practices

- legal and regulatory record-keeping and reporting requirements

- current problems and opportunities with operational processes

- information needs for planning and decision-making

Identifying business entities (e.g. customers, products, employees, etc) and data (i.e. attributes) required to describe each entity.

Once this is done, possible IS projects can be determined by identifying natural groupings of process and data and/or unmet information needs of managers. Possible projects must then be ranked in priority sequence.

Technical issues must be considered next, because there are several applications that the organization eventually uses that often share a common technical platform (e.g. PCs, networked PCs, etc). As we discussed earlier in this chapter, another option is to adopt the "software as a service" (SaaS) approach when it is available and appropriate. Technical issues may cause a reassessment of the priority sequence of possible projects. For example, it may be easier or more logical to install the organization's first application which uses database management software on a smaller project to let personnel get familiar with the software before moving on to a larger, more risky project. More details on current technical concept and issues are available in Global Text's Information Systems Text, Chapter 7, available at <u>http://docs.globaltext.terry.uga.edu:8095/anonymous/webdav/Information%20Systems/Information %20Systems.pdf.</u> You may also like to scan the table of contents of the IS Text for additional readings as it covers many of the topics we discuss here in much greater detail.

Once a plan is agreed, it is implemented. Most organizations find it useful to update the plan yearly at least as business and technical issues can change quickly.

What is IS risk management?

The IS risk is the business risk associated with the use, ownership, operation, involvement, influence, and adoption of information/technology solutions (Application, Hardware, Network and People) within an organization. IS risk consists of IS-related events that could potentially impact the business. It is also the management of uncertainty within the functions of IS so as to provide the organization with assurance that:

- the possibility of a threat occurring is reduced or minimized

- the impact, direct and consequential, is reduced or minimized

To provide this assurance, threats must be identified and their impact on the organization evaluated so that appropriate control measures can be taken to reduce the possibility or frequency of a threat occurring and to reduce or minimize the impact on the business.

Information is a key business resource which, in order to be of value, must be correct, relevant and applicable to the business process and delivered in a timely, consistent and usable manner; it must be complete and accurate and provided through via the best use of resources (planned or unplanned), and if sensitive it must have its confidentiality preserved. Information is the result of the combined application of data, application systems, technology, facilities, and people. IS Risk Management ensures that the threats to these resources are identified and controlled so that the requirements for information are met.

Project management risks

Despite the fact that sound system design and installation methodologies have been well known for decades, the IT profession is still plagued by troubled or failed projects, colloquially called "an Ox in the ditch". Studies like the Chaos Reports published by the Standish Group over the years have documented the extent of IT project successes and failures. For example, the latest publicly available report, "CHAOS Summary 2009" states:

> "This year's results show a marked decrease in project success rates, with 32 per cent of all projects succeeding which are delivered on time, on budget, with required features and functions" says Jim Johnson, chairman of The Standish Group, "Forty-four per cent were challenged which are late, over budget, and/or with less than the required features and functions and 24 per cent failed which are cancelled prior to completion or delivered and never used."

"These numbers represent a downtick in the success rates from the previous study, as well as a significant increase in the number of failures", says Jim Crear, Standish Group CIO, "They are low point in the last five study periods. This year's results represent the highest failure rate in over a decade" (Standish 2009). Businesses have to be aware of figures like these before you give the go-ahead for an IT project. Failed IT projects can be disastrous to an organization, even forcing them to go out of business.

Some of the reasons IT projects fail are:

- An inadequate understanding of what functions and features (i.e. requirements) the organization needs in the new system. It would be like trying to build a building before its design has been completed.

- Poor project planning, task identification, and task estimation. Usually this means that essential tasks have been overlooked or under-estimated meaning the project's time and cost estimates are too optimistic.

- Lack of proper skills on the project team. This would be like assigning carpentry tasks to an electrician. Some IT professionals think they can do anything and this is almost always not true.

- Failure to address problems and/or project champion. Just about every IT project has problems. If they are not dealt with on a timely basis they do not go away by themselves, they just get worse. It is helpful in addressing problems if a highly-placed executive is a "champion" of the project and can step in and get problems solved if the project team is struggling.

- Inadequate testing. All too often, a new system is put into operation before it has been adequately tested to be sure it handles all conditions it is likely to encounter. A system failure after conversion can cause normal business processes (like accepting customer orders, for example) to fail.

- No fall-back plan. Before converting to a new system, the project team should have a tested fall-back plan they can revert to in order to keep business processes working while the new system is adjusted.

- Executive champions should be aware that IT project risks are all too often known to the IT professionals but are not always shared with others. Therefore, you should always ask that a formal project risk assessment be done at the beginning of a project and that plans are in place to keep risks at a minimum.

Security risks

The biggest challenge companies face in tackling IS security risks is the growing sophistication of hackers and other cyber-criminals. Organizations must now contend with a range of hi-tech attacks orchestrated by well-organized, financially-motivated criminals. While large organizations often have independent IS security staffs, it is likely that your start-up can focus on just a couple of basic items, such as:

- Identifying the value of information stored on your computer(s) and making sure that access to such information is restricted to employees who need to use for legitimate business purposes. For example, your customer database and customer profitability analyses should be protected as you would not want such information to fall into the hands of a competitor as the result of actions taken by a disloyal employee.

- Computers sometimes break down ("crash"). This is why it is important to have a procedure of backing up critical files on a daily basis, and have written, tested procedures to recover needed information from backup files quickly. Organizations have gone out of business as a result of failed computer systems that were not properly backed-up.

If you have a website, you will need to be sure that it is adequately protected from both internal and external threats. We discuss Internet risks in the next section.

Internet risks

Companies considering a website or Internet-based services need to be aware of the various risks and regulations that may apply to these services. Over the past few decades, the Internet has become critical to businesses, both as a tool for communicating with other businesses and employees as well as a means for reaching customers. Each day of the week and every month, there are new Internet threats. These threats range from attacks on networks to the simple passing of offensive materials sent or received via the Internet. The risks and particular regulations that apply may vary depending on the types of services offered. For example, institutions offering informational websites need to be aware of the various consumer compliance regulations that may apply to the products and services advertised online. Information needs to be accurate and complete to avoid potential liability. Security of the website is also an important consideration. Companies and some individuals traditionally have relied on physical security such as locks and safes to protect their vital business information now face a more insidious virtual threat from cyber-criminals who use the Internet to carry out their attacks without ever setting foot in an establishment or someone's home. More often than not, these crimes are conducted from outside the United States. Security measures should protect the site from defacement and malicious code.

It is clear that no single risk management strategy can completely eliminate the risks associated with Internet use and access. There is no one special technology that can make an enterprise completely secure. No matter how much money companies spend on cyber-security, they may not be able to prevent disruptions caused by organized attackers. Some businesses whose products or services directly or indirectly impact the economy or the health, welfare or safety of the public have begun to use cyber risk insurance programs as a means of transferring risk and providing for business continuity.

Summary of IS risk management

Managing IS risk is a daily decision making process aimed at reducing the amount of losses and threats to a company. It is a pro-active approach to reducing exposure to data/information loss and ensuring the integrity of the applications used day-to-day. An IS security plan should include at minimum a description of the various security processes for specified applications, procedural and technical requirements, and the organizational structure to support the security processes. A risk assessment should be performed first. Identifying risks provides guidance on where to focus the security requirements. Security requirements and controls should reflect the business value of the information assets involved and the consequence from failure of security. Security mechanisms should be "cost beneficial", i.e. not exceed the costs of risk. It should also include expectations for risk within the overall IS security plan.

Chapter summary

Many people use information systems and information technology as if they meant the same. They are different, and it is important for you to understand the difference between them. As we illustrated in Exhibit 41, an Information System is comprised of two sub-systems, a social subsystem and a technical subsystem. The social subsystem has two parts: people and organizational structure. The technical subsystem also has two parts: technology and business processes. The reason it is important to understand this is that all four parts of an Information system must work effectively if the system is to meet the needs for which it was designed and installed.

Information systems can be very powerful tools to help you run your organization. On the other hand, in a start-up, be sure you need the support of information systems before you invest in them. It may be that you can handle your operations manually for a time and avoid the cost and time investing in a computer-based IS requires.

If you do decide to move forward with computer-based information systems it is wise to develop a plan first, and make sure you are proceeding in an orderly manner. There are three general approaches to developing an IS plan. You will also find that you have many options available for hardware and software, and the options can vary widely in initial purchase price and the kind of support provided by the vendor. If you see value in having a website there are some generally-accepted principles you should follow to make your website effective.

Many organizations have found ways to use IS for competitive advantage. Michael Porter's frameworks, the five forces model, the three generic strategies, and value chain have proven to be useful tools in coming up with ideas for innovative information systems.

Finally, when an organization has valuable information stored in computers, it is exposed to risks from errors and from various internal and external threats. It is important for managers to evaluate the risks and come up with cost-effective measures to be sure the organization is adequately protected from loss or damage to valuable information.

Discussion questions

- ➤ Describe the four components of an information system. Why is it important to consider each of them when designing and installing an information system?

- ➤ Under what circumstances might it be wise for a start-up entrepreneur to postpone investing in computer-based information systems for the organization?

- ➤ What are the major options you have for obtaining hardware, software and support from IS professionals?

- ➤ Define a "software suite". What are the advantages of using a software suite instead of a number of stand-alone software applications?

- ➤ When should you consider using database management software instead of a spreadsheet?

- ➤ Discuss the advantages and disadvantages of open source software applications for a start-up organization

- ➤ What are the objectives of a Website? Who benefits the most from your organization's web presence?

- ➤ When having a web presence what is the single most important objective? What is the greatest risk to a website?

- ➤ Give at least three examples of organizations that have used IS in innovative ways to gain competitive advantage. For each example, which of Porter's framework elements does it illustrate?

- ➤ What are the three general approaches for setting an organization's IS priorities? What are the advantages and disadvantages of each?

- ➤ Why is important for start-up entrepreneurs to pay attention to IS risk management?

- ➤ How do managers decide how much attention and resources they should devote to IS risk management?

References

(Friedman 2005) Friedman, Thomas, "The World is Flat" 1st edition, Farrar, Straus and Giroux, 2005, ISBN 0-374-29288-4.

(Gartner 2008) Feinberg, Donald "The Growing Maturity of Open-Source Database Management Systems" http://mediaproducts.gartner.com/reprints/sunmicrosystems/volume1/article2/article2.html Accessed January 31, 2009.

(Google 2009) http://www.google.com/intl/en/options/

(Information Systems 2008) Information Systems 2008, Global Text.

(Microsoft 2009) http://store.microsoft.com/microsoft/Office-Suites/

(MySQL 2009) http://www.mysql.com/

(Openoffice 2009) http://www.openoffice.org/

10. Leveraging with information technology

(Standish 2009) http://www1.standishgroup.com/newsroom/chaos_2009.php, accessed July 27, 2009

(Stille 2009) http://www.qcisolutions.com/dbinfo1.htm

(Zoho 2009) http://zoho.com/

11. Competitive intelligence

Editor: James W Bronson (The University of Wisconsin, USA)

Contributors: Kellie Goldfien, Ryan Wolford

Reviewer: William A Drago, (University of Wisconsin, USA)

Learning objectives

At the conclusion of this chapter, you should be able to:

- define competition and competitive intelligence

- differentiate between parallel products and substitute products

- state the goals of competitive intelligence

- discuss public sources of information for competitive intelligence

- understand the role of industry structure in competitive intelligence

- complete a competitor analysis

Introduction

Chances are competition for your firm's product is already well established. Other firms can be in direct competition with you when they offer a similar product and target the same customers. They can be indirectly competing with you by offering a similar product or service, but targeting a different demographic. Competition can come from overseas. Competition can come from another firm in the same city. Competitors are all around you whether you choose to be aware of it or not. Recognizing and dealing with competition is necessary to your business success.

What every firm is competing for are buyers or customers. Customers are the final evaluator of your product. If they prefer your product above those of competitors, you will receive their business and the sales which will keep you in business. Even a great business idea will fail unless it attracts buyers.

Definition

Competing firms offer functionally interchangeable products to the same buyers. **Competition** occurs when competing firms attempt to attract buyers by offering products with greater perceived benefit. Common benefits include price, service, reputation, and image, but may include virtually anything else associated with a product that the buyer values. A buyer's perceptions of what constitutes a benefit may vary widely based on the nature of the product. Since the actions taken by one competitor to attract buyers are likely to affect the performance of other competitors, competing firms are said to be **interdependent.**

Coke and Pepsi are interdependent. An attempt by Pepsi to attract buyers (increase sales) through an advertising campaign will decrease the sales of Coke. Coke may counter this advertising campaign with its own advertising or it may elect to take another competitive action such as a temporary reduction in the price of Coke. How Coke chooses to react to Pepsi will be based on an analysis of how the firms have acted in past situations. The industry's **competitive dynamics** is the ongoing series of competitive actions and competitive responses that take place as Coke and Pepsi compete for customers.

Competitive intelligence is the systematic collection and analysis of publicly available information about competitors. Intelligence about competitors is key to understanding the actions they are currently taking to attract buyers. Competitive intelligence may also allow the firm to predict a competitor's future actions and take measures to preempt or minimize the impact of those actions. The objective of a firm's competitive intelligence is to understand its competitors.

Exercise

It should be easy to envisage Coke and Pepsi as interdependent competing firms. Can you come up with five more examples of interdependent competing firms, e.g. Honda and Toyota, Boeing and Airbus,...

Why you have competitors (or how buyers have managed to survive without your product and why you need buyers more than buyers need you)

Entrepreneurs commonly underestimate the impact of competition. Entrepreneurs who do underestimate the impact of competition are failing to consider the fact that potential buyers are currently managing without the entrepreneur's product. There are three arguments for why potential buyers are managing without the entrepreneur's product or service:

1. parallel products exist in the market

2. reasonable substitutes exist in the market

3. parallel products and substitutes do not exist, but the public does not perceive, or is not aware, of the benefits offered by the entrepreneur's product or service

Parallel products are those that are functionally interchangeable with the entrepreneur's products, but vary just enough on the product's perceived benefits to exist in the marketplace. For example, many communities have areas where a number of restaurants exist in close proximity to one another. These restaurants all offer the customer a prepared meal, but may vary as to nationality or type of cuisine, complexity and originality of preparation, level of service, seating, and other dimensions for which the buying public perceives a benefit.

An entrepreneur opening a new restaurant in proximity to existing restaurants may be offering a heretofore unavailable national cuisine, but the entrepreneur still has many competitors. In this market of parallel competitors, the entrepreneur will be successful only if buyers perceive that the new restaurant offers desirable benefits that are unavailable from existing restaurants. The new restaurant must generate enough sales to generate a profit. In reality, what often happens is that the new restaurant will initially generate a strong trade as buyers try the restaurant's novel offerings. However, in a few months the new restaurant will fail unless it has found the means of offering a mix of perceived benefits not available in competing restaurants. This suggests that the entrepreneur must learn enough about what buyers or customers need or want and enough about how competitors are attempting to meet those needs, that the entrepreneur can offer enough perceived benefits to keep customers returning indefinitely. Learning about buyers and competitors is the role of competitive intelligence.

Substitutes often exist for the entrepreneur's product. **Substitutes** are products that fill the same function but originate in different industries. Buyers may have a preference for a substitute due to the substitute's greater perceived benefit. For example, the basic construction material for houses varies greatly on a geographic basis. Wood housing tends to be favored where wood is abundant and relatively inexpensive, and a similar argument can be made for the wood substitutes, brick and stone. The entrepreneur is unlikely to be more than marginally successful if s/he attempts to sell bricks where wood remains abundant and cheap. S/he may be marginally successful because wood housing often has brick fixtures and trim. However, in a market where wood is becoming more costly due to a lack of abundance, brick may become an attractive substitute for wood. Understanding substitutes place in the market is the role of competitive intelligence.

Perhaps the most difficult situation for an entrepreneur exists where there currently exists no functionally interchangeable product. It may appear that a complete lack of competition would be to the entrepreneur's advantage, but this is seldom the case. In those instances where firms offering similar products can be found in other markets, the most likely explanation for a lack of competitors is a market that will not sustain the firm. The market may be too small, or too seasonal, or the customer demographic may be skewed, etc. The entrepreneur should proceed cautiously when a superficial inspection suggests a potential market lacking an established competitor. A more thorough investigation will often reveal failed attempts to establish a market for the product. This investigation is one of the roles of competitive intelligence.

In the rare instance where the entrepreneur has discovered or invented a unique product, s/he typically faces a truly daunting task. Potential buyers must be educated as to the existence and benefit of the new product. Educating buyers and establishing a market for a new product is expensive. Unfortunately for the entrepreneur, it is often the follow-on firms that are successful. In the electronics industry, the originators of the personal computer, video game console, and personal data assistant provided the infrastructure for successful follow-on firms, but were unable to capitalize on their own innovative products.

Exercise

A business that faces both parallel products and substitutes is likely to have a difficult time in the marketplace. Example of businesses that have both parallels and substitutes include grocery stores. Parallels include grocery stores with slightly varying themes, warehouse stores, e.g. Sam's club and Costco, and natural food stores. Substitutes include specialty food stores, e.g. bakeries, dairy stores, and butcher shops; restaurants; and take-out shops. Not surprisingly grocery store profit margins are low. What other businesses are characterized by competition that includes both parallel product and substitutes? Is the average profit margin for these businesses low, i.e. < 5 per cent of sales?

Importance and goals of competitive intelligence

Detecting competitive threats

Detecting competitive threats is crucial to every business. Microsoft has concerns with Google's growing market share. Ford attempts to avoid losing market shares to Toyota. A local supermarket is concerned with another supermarket opening up in the area and taking its customers away. When businesses are able to detect a competitive threat, they are better equipped to handle that threat. Steps may be taken to ensure that the impact of the new threat is minimized.

Competition is the effort of two or more firms, acting independently, to obtain the business of a buyer by offering the most favorable benefits. Competitive intelligence is the purposeful and coordinated monitoring of competitors, wherever and whoever they may be, within a specific marketplace. Competitive intelligence allows the firm to make informed decisions about the outcomes of its actions in the marketplace. For example competitor A, through the scanning of new building permits in the local newspaper, discovers that competitor B has taken out a permit for the construction of a new building on B's property. From this information, and other legal sources, competitor A may draw some conclusions as to the purpose of competitor B's new building and take actions designed to minimize the impact of B's new building. The goal of competitive intelligence is to detect threats originating from competitors in all their forms.

Eliminating or lessening surprises

A firm needs to closely monitor the actions of its competitors. Detecting competitive threats early allows the firm to take actions to mitigate the threat. Competitive threats may come from a number of different sources, including new entrants, substitutes, competitors, and even suppliers in the form of a price increase. For example, if a local competitor is building a new retail outlet that will capitalize on the industry's latest trends, the firm will have to decide whether to follow suit. Perhaps a competitor has traditionally held a major sale on a particular holiday, the firm will need to decide whether to follow suit, or give up sales while its competitor holds the sale.

Enhancing competitive advantages by lessening reaction time

A firm that has planned for most common threats will be prepared to move quickly in the face of a threat. Preparedness allows the firm to move past its less well prepared competitors as they devote valuable time and other resources reacting to the threat. While competitors are reacting, the firm can move to increase its competitive advantage over the competition.

For example, a trucking company might plan for an escalation in fuel prices. The trucking company can do this in various ways, but the most common is to "buy" a contract that guarantees the firm the right to purchase fuel at a fixed price for some specified period of time. Should fuel prices increase during the period the contract is in effect, the trucking firm is protected by its fuel contracts. The fuel contracts in turn allow the trucking firm to honor existing quotations and contracts with its customers. By honoring its quotations and contracts in the face of escalating fuel prices the trucking firm's reputation and good will with its customers increases, furthering the trucking firm's competitive advantage.

Finding new opportunities

Ultimately, a firm must be able to grow in order to survive in the business world. The ability to grow is only limited by the imagination of the decision makers of the company. New ideas turned into patents for new products, buying a competitor in order to increase market share and economies of scale, and establishing a sales force in a neighboring country are just a few of the ways that a company can continue to grow.

There are three principle avenues employed by businesses to develop new opportunities for growth.

1. Find ways to increase the sales of existing products to existing customers. Businesses can accomplish this goal by finding new applications for the use of existing products by current customers. This process is known as **market penetration**.

2. **Market development** is the process of finding new customers for the firm's existing products. There are two choices for market development, the firm can look to new geographic markets or the firm can turn to a new demographic market. For example, a firm that sold exercise equipment that traditionally targeted the 18-34 year-old male demographic might find that they could sell the same equipment to a 16-32 year-old female demographic. The only new cost the firm would incur is the cost of marketing existing products to the new demographic.

3. **Product development** is the process of creating new products for customers. Product development is often accomplished by asking customers what types of products would make their job easier. Once a viable need is established, the firm can develop a product to meet that need.

Very few firms can afford to stand still for long. Competitors are constantly looking for opportunities and those opportunities missed by your firm, will not be missed by all your competitors. Complacency in today's business environment will quickly lead to years of dedicated work being usurped by competitors.

Information collection methods

Information or data on products, suppliers, competitors, and industries has never been more available. The Internet permits access to information and data from a wide range of sources. Often, there is simply too much data, and data of dubious quality. When accessing data the entrepreneur needs to evaluate data on its timeliness, source, and relevance.

Internet

Internet search engines make it possible to quickly access information on seemingly any subject. Unfortunately, because anyone can establish and then fail to maintain a website, Internet data is often dated, unreliable, and of dubious value. This places a burden on the entrepreneur to check Internet data carefully before using it. Nonetheless, there is much useful information to be found on the Internet at government, organization, and corporate websites. The information from these sources generally consists of reliable facts and figures. Frequently, these facts and figures will need to be manipulated by the entrepreneur in order to be rendered in a useful form.

In today's market, there are few products and services that are not rated by a third party, e.g. consumer organizations, magazines, commercial sellers, and blogs. However, the qualifications and impartiality of third party raters may be questionable. The entrepreneur should not rely on a single source for product reviews and exercise due diligence by checking multiple sources for product ratings. The entrepreneur should bear in mind that his/her firm and products will eventually be rated on the Internet and check to see that the firm's rating is favorable.

Human intelligence

Human intelligence can yield the most timely and accurate information, but it is the most resource intensive form of information to collect. Human intelligence often tends to take the form of opinion rather than the facts and figures found in documents. This leaves the entrepreneur in the position of evaluating the veracity of opinions. Like product reviews, which can also be a matter of opinion, the entrepreneur should rely on multiple sources. The entrepreneur's network should be the source of his/her human intelligence. The network can be augmented by introductions from network members to others closer to the information objective. Participants in trade shows and trade organizations are excellent sources of information as are suppliers, customers, and employees.

Fee based companies

Fee based companies, such as Hoovers, LexisNexis, and the credit reporting companies are in the business of collecting and compiling information on businesses and individuals. Their revenue is earned through the sale of the information they collect. For the most part, they make no attempt to assess the specific validity of the information they sell. Rather, they tend to rely on the fact that on average, their information is quite reliable. The overall trend for fee based information is that reliability tends to increase with price. Fee based companies can be a useful source of information on competitors that might not be otherwise available. For example, credit reports are available for competing firms and credit reports can yield a good deal of information about a firm's financial condition.

Public documents

Public documents can be an excellent source of information on competitors. Many types of public documents are available over the Internet, while others may only be available at records offices. For example, building permits are typically reported in newspapers and can often be accessed online, while building plans are usually available only through a visit to the public planning office. A visit to the planning office may be warranted if a competitor is building a new plant. The plans will yield a good deal about the project from which a knowledgeable competitor can deduce plant and warehouse capacity. Similarly, the annual report that a public company files with the government is another example of a document that may yield a good deal of information about a competitor.

There are a number of organizations that are concerned with the collection and use of competitive data. Internet sites with a focus on competitive intelligence include:

http://cio.com/

http://www.scip.org/

http://www.brint.com/

http://fuld.com/

Exercise

Select a publicly traded company of interest to you. Using the Internet as an access point, find the following for the previous year: (1) annual sales, (2) profits as a percentage of sales, e.g. profits/sales, (3) number of employees, (4) sales per employee, e.g. sales/employees, and (5) best selling product or service.

The industry environment
What is an industry?

The term **industry** loosely refers to any group of businesses that share a particular type of commercial enterprise. This grouping of firms is also likely to generate profits in a similar manner, or at least share related activities. In the business world, it is common to hear managers discuss particular industries as a whole, for example, 'the automobile industry' or 'the magazine industry'.

In a more formal sense, the North American Industry Classification System (NAICS, http://www.census.gov/epcd/www/naics.html) defines hundreds of different industries. The NAICS is a commonly used system to group businesses. The NAICS typically identifies an industry with a six digit code, with each additional digit narrowing the definition of the industry. Similar classification systems include the International Standard Industrial Classification (ISIC, http://unstats.un.org/unsd/cr/registry/regcst.asp?Cl=17) from the United

Nations and the General Industrial Classification of Economic Activities with the European Communities (NACE, <u>http://www.ltck.se/PrjY1/nacekod/nacecode.htm</u>). Data is gathered and reported for the industry based on the six digit code. Data typically reported includes demographic measures for the industry including employment, number of business, and total sales. Data is not reported for individual firms. Many different agencies and businesses use these categories for statistical studies, business comparisons, and benchmarks. Locating the industry for a business through the NAICS or similar classification scheme can be a useful exercise in gathering competitive intelligence. For example, the average number of employees and sales of firms in the industry can be found and from this information critical benchmarks like sales per employee may be calculated.

Industry structural characteristics

Industries have specific structures and the entrepreneur needs to learn and understand the significance of the structure for his/her industry. Industry structure includes size measures, e.g. industry sales, number of firms, and number of employees. Rate of growth and the industry growth curve are an important element of industry structure as is the extent to which an industry is unionized. There may be many more elements of industry structure. Industry structure is one determinant of competition. For example, competition in an industry comprised solely of union employers will be quite different than in an industry comprised of both union and non-union firms. Competition is also affected by the extent to which the government is a large buyer, or perhaps the only buyer, as in the defense industry.

Concept of strategic groups

Strategic groups exist within most industries. A **strategic group** is a set of firms within an industry that employ similar practices in order to achieve comparable goals. An example of a strategic group within the food service industry would be fast-food chains. The fast-food chains differentiate themselves from other restaurants by offering quick-service, popular foods, and relatively low prices. Within the same industry we can find a number of other strategic groups such as family restaurants, vegetarian restaurants, and coffee houses. Although fast-food chains and vegetarian restaurants both accomplish the same purpose, i.e. providing a prepared meal, their target audience, their methods of marketing, and other methods of doing business are decidedly different. Competition between firms within a strategic group is more direct than competition between firms located in different strategic groups.

Competitive rivalry amongst firms in the same strategic group can be very intense, especially since they are usually competing for the same customers. Consider Pepsi and Coca-Cola versus fruit juice. Pepsi and Coca-Cola are competing for cola drinkers, and they market their products competitively against each other. Although the customer could just as easily have a glass of fruit juice, Pepsi and Coca-Cola are not aggressively marketing against the juice industry. The fruit juice customer has different wants and needs than the cola customer, so the two strategic groups do not compete directly for the same clientele.

Key success factors in an industry

Key success factors (KSF) are areas of critical performance necessary for success in a specific industry. A firm cannot expect to be competitive in its industry without an understanding of the industry's key success factors. Key success factors are a function of both customer needs and competitive pressures. KSFs are typically identified by completing a list in response to two questions:

1. What do customers in my industry want?

2. How do successful firms survive the industry's competitive pressures?

Grocery Store KSF	
Customer	Competition
Cleanliness	Bargaining power over suppliers
Freshness	Number of local competitors
Selection, including take-out	Location relative to competitors
Competitive prices	
Location & parking	
Service & pleasant experience	

The entrepreneur must be aware of the key success factors (KSF) in his/her industry. Resources should be directed to activities that increase competitiveness on KSF and not wasted on activities that are not critical to KSFs.

Exercise

Since we all have decided preferences, it follows that a table of KSFs constructed by one person is likely to omit, or overstate, an industry's KSFs. Select a common type of business-industry with which you have some familiarity, e.g. floral arrangements, coffee house, or bicycle sales.

Construct a table of Key Success Factors by asking yourself the questions: What do customers in my business-industry want? How do successful firms survive the industry's competitive pressures?

Now ask the questions of two other people who have been customers of the business-industry. Are you getting agreement on your list of KSFs, or will you need to ask more people for their opinions to establish a clear list of KSFs?

Porter's 5 forces and the analysis of competitors

Porter's five forces, first covered in Chapter 3 as a methodology for assessing industry attractiveness, plays an important role in competitor analysis. The five forces perspective of competitor analysis views each force as a determinant of the level of competition in the industry. The level of competition in turn determines the firm's ability to operate profitably in the industry.

Bargaining power of buyers

A firm's buyers or customers have varying needs and wants. Meeting customers' needs represents a cost to the firm. When the firm can easily meet the customer's needs the firm's cost is relatively low. Because the firm can easily give the customer what he/she values, the firm is in a strong bargaining position and sales are likely to generate healthy profits. When the customer's needs are not easily met, the cost to the firm increases. Because the firm's product is less attractive to the customer, the firm must lower prices or take other steps to entice the customer to make a purchase. Under these conditions the firm's profits are likely to be low. Consequently, the firm can be seen as always bargaining with customers for the firm's potential profits. The firm is in the strongest bargaining position when it understands its buyer's needs. Understanding buyer needs is the role of marketing and may be viewed as a form of competitive intelligence.

Buyers are in a particularly strong bargaining position when they can easily switch from the firm's product to a competitor's equivalent product. For example, a firm that has many competitors offering a similar product will have customers with significant bargaining power. If the customer is not happy with the product offered by one firm, they can simply choose to go to another firm that provides the same item. For this to be a powerful bargaining tool for the customer, the switch from one firm to another must be cost-efficient and easy. Conversely, if a firm has desirable products and competing products are perceived as less desirable, customers will have reduced bargaining power. If it is expensive or burdensome to switch products, customers will also lose bargaining power. A good example of a firm in this coveted position is Apple with their iPod product. While other MP3 players are on the market, none have the market share and desirability enjoyed by iPod.

Customers almost always have choices and they will vote for their chosen firms with their purchases. Customers will vote against firms by simply walking away. It is important to balance the needs of the customer with the goals of the firm.

Bargaining power of suppliers

Like buyers, suppliers are competing for the firm's profits. Suppliers want to charge the firm more for inputs and the firm wants to pay the supplier less for those same inputs. Consequently, competitive intelligence extends to suppliers and it is in the firm's interest to know as much as possible about their suppliers. Suppliers may offer exclusive territories, financing, advertising, display, and other incentives to the firm to encourage the use or sale of the supplier's product. The firm should evaluate and select its suppliers carefully in order to take full advantage of any and all cost savings offered by suppliers.

In many industries it is common for buyers to form cooperatives in order to increase their bargaining power relative to suppliers. The cooperative, sometimes comprised of hundreds of smaller firms, is able to use its combined buying power to bargain with suppliers for better prices and terms. For example, in North America, buyer cooperatives are quite visible in the retail hardware industry as represented by the "Ace", "Hardware Hank", and "True Value" hardware stores. Despite the potentially antagonistic relationship between the firm and its suppliers, suppliers often offer benefits that can improve the firm's competitive position in the industry.

Threat of new entrants

Entrepreneurs represent the threat of a new competitor for existing businesses. It is normally in the interest of existing firms to prevent new competitors from becoming established. Consequently, it is in the best interest of the entrepreneur to learn as much as possible about existing competitive businesses so that the entrepreneur can target their weaknesses. The entrepreneur should also attempt to learn enough about existing businesses so that he/she can anticipate and attempt to minimize the retaliation from existing businesses. Retaliation may take many forms from political actions designed to delay or prevent the new business from opening to deep price cuts intended to force the new business out of the market.

Threat of substitute products

Entrepreneurs often seem unaware of the competitive threat posed by substitute products. One of the reasons entrepreneurs may be unaware of substitute products is that by definition, substitutes come from another industry. Despite all the potential warnings, the retail and recorded music industries were hardly prepared for the consequences when millions of customers switched from CD purchases to downloaded iTunes. Thus, the entrepreneur needs to monitor not only his/her own industry for potential competitors, but also must scan other industries that pose a potential threat.

The intensity of competitive rivalry

The intensity of the rivalry amongst the firms in a given industry will have an effect on the profits of all firms within that industry. Within an industry, when firms are fiercely competitive, the cost of competition will increase because when one firm acts, other firms will feel the need to counteract. Costs for advertising and promotions, profits lost through price reductions, and competitive rivalries occurring over the research and development of new products will erode the profits of competing firms.

The firms within an industry are likely to be plagued by similar problems. One common problem that entrepreneurs prefer to avoid is associated with industries with high fixed costs. High fixed costs are common in manufacturing, communications, and transportation industries. When a product is encumbered by a high fixed cost, the firm will usually make every effort to recover at least a portion of those fixed costs and may resort to offering buyers a range of incentives, from drastic price cuts to rebates, to move the product. These incentives are often met with a swift competitive response on the part of industry competitors. These competitive actions can drive all profits out of the industry.

A problem accompanying, or similar, to high fixed costs can be found in mature industries. When industry growth slows, competition typically heats up. This occurs because the firms within the slow growth industry are competing for the same pool of buyers and often that pool of buyers is in decline. Again, the competitive actions taken by firms to attract this pool of buyers will drive profits out of the industry.

Rivalry also intensifies when consumers see little differentiation between the products offered by firms within an industry. For example, few consumers see the difference between various brands of ketchup and are likely to simply purchase the brand that has the lower price. When consumers see little difference between products within an industry, these products become known as commodities. As expected, rivalry between US ketchup makers Heinz and Hunt's is intense.

High fixed costs, industry maturity, and commodity-like products contribute to a high-level of competition within an industry, but there are often other factors that drive competition. The entrepreneur needs to study and understand the industry and if possible, avoid industries where the level of competition is high as this means the profit potential is low. Still, the entrepreneur may identify an under served niche or a need that the entrepreneur is uniquely qualified to fill, in which case entry into the industry may be profitable for the entrepreneur.

In comparison, firms that are highly differentiated from their rivals often are not engaged in strong competition because these firms know that their product is meeting a need for their consumer base and their customers are going to return to fulfill that need.

Methods of evaluating competitors

Identifying competitors and their relative advantage

An understanding of the industry and the key success factors for the industry allows the entrepreneur to assess the performance of competitive firms. The process starts with the identification of competitors. In many markets competitors will already be known to the entrepreneur. In other markets, the numbers and identities of competitors may be less obvious. Operating under the assumption that the vast majority of businesses need to communicate with the public, the best place to start with competitor identification is with directories and other official and semi-official listings. In many countries, and for most markets, the business telephone directory should be the starting point. City and other directories contain additional information on competitors, including ownership, key employees, and the number of employees. Some products will warrant an Internet search as competition may prove to be regional, national, or even international. After assembling a list of competitors the entrepreneur should develop a method for collecting information on his/her most immediate competitors, i.e. those competitors who will be competing for the same customers. For smaller businesses, simply creating a file folder for each immediate competitor should be sufficient.

The entrepreneur will need to collect more detailed information on his/her most immediate competitors. The entrepreneur should be parsimonious in his/her approach to collecting information and one means of being parsimonious is to focus on information related to the industry's key success factors (KSF). Competitor information may come from a wide range of sources including visits to the competitor's place of operation, word-of-mouth from suppliers and other third parties, competitor's advertisements, newspaper archives, Internet searches, and public records. Since the best indicator of future performance is past performance, the entrepreneur should pay close attention to the longevity and historical performance of competitors.

Having collected information, the entrepreneur is in a position to make comparisons between his/her firm and the firm's immediate competitors. A spreadsheet or table is commonly employed for this assessment. Relevant information beyond key success factors is commonly included in the comparison and may include size measures, reputation, age, largest customers, key suppliers, and almost anything else deemed relevant to the competitive environment.

Competitor Analysis XYZ Industry, 123 Market					
	Entrepreneur's Firm	Competitor A	Competitor B	Competitor C	Competitor D
Key Success factor 1					
Key Success factor 2					

Key Success factor 3					
Key Success factor 4					
Key Success factor 5					
Firm's age					
Manager's reputation					
Market share or ranking					
Other relevant considerations					

The entrepreneur should pay particular attention to the management capabilities of his or her own firm and competing firms. The quality and the style of management will play the major role in establishing the competitive environment. The methods for collecting information on management capability are similar to those used for collecting information on competitors—the firm should rely on word-of-mouth, the Internet (especially management ranking websites, such as www.joost.com), trade publications, civic organization, and industry events. Listening to competing managers will provide an invaluable insight into the industry environment.

Exercise

Use the chart above to complete analysis for the firm and industry of your choice.

Chapter summary

Competitive intelligence is the systematic collection and analysis of publicly available information about an industry and its competitors. Competitive intelligence permits the firm to: (1) understand the industry's structure and its potential impact on the firm's performance, and (2) industry competitors' relative position in the marketplace. The judicious use of competitive intelligence allows the firm to anticipate competitors' actions and act to minimize the impact of those actions. Through the use of competitive intelligence the firm will improve its performance in the marketplace.

References

http://www.census.gov/epcd/www/naics.html

<u>http://www.12manage.com/methods_porter_five_forces.html</u>

Dussauge, Pierre and Bernard Garrette, Will Mitchell (2000). "Learning from competing partners: outcomes and durations of scale and link alliances in Europe, North America and Asia". **Strategic Management Journal**; 21, 2: 99-126.

Davison, Leigh (2001). "Measuring competitive intelligence effectiveness: Insights from the advertising industry". **Competitive Intelligence Review**; Volume 12, Issue 4: 25 – 38.

Dorf, Richard C. and Thomas H. Byers (2008). **Technology Ventures: From Idea to Enterprise**, 2nd edition. New York: McGraw Hill.

Grant, Robert M. (2008). **Contemporary Strategy Analysis**, 6th edition. Malden, MA: Blackwell Publishing.

Johnston, Lisa (2007). "iPod, MP3 Accessories Pile On". **TWICE Magazine**; February 12: 12.

Pinkerton, Richard L. (1994). "Competitive intelligence revisited: A history, and assessment of its use in marketing". **Competitive Intelligence Review**, 5, 4: 23-31.

Young, Greg (1999). "Strategic value analysis for competitive advantage". **Competitive Intelligence Review**, 10, 2: 52-6.

12. Business ethics in a nutshell

Editor: Buie Seawell (Daniels College of Business, University of Denver, USA)

Reviewer: James O'Toole (Daniels College of Business, University of Denver, USA)

Framing the structure and content of business ethics is a presumptuous undertaking, but one I believe to have real merit. The reader might spend a lifetime as student and practitioner in the most exciting field of applied ethics: business ethics.

What is ethics?

Ethics is the branch of philosophy concerned with the meaning of all aspects of human behavior. Theoretical Ethics, sometimes called Normative Ethics, is about discovering and delineating right from wrong; it is the consideration of how we develop the rules and principles (norms) by which to judge and guide meaningful decision-making. Theoretical Ethics is supremely intellectual in character, and, being a branch of philosophy, is also rational in nature. Theoretical Ethics is the rational reflection on what is right, what is wrong, what is just, what is unjust, what is good and what is bad in terms of human behavior.

Business ethics is not chiefly theoretical in character. Though reflective and rational in part, this is only a prelude to the essential task behind business ethics. It is best understood as a branch of ethics called applied ethics: the discipline of applying value to human behavior, relationships and constructs, and the resulting meaning. Business ethics is simply the practice of this discipline within the context of the enterprise of creating wealth (the fundamental role of business).

There are three parts to the discipline of business ethics: personal, professional and corporate. All three are intricately related, and it is helpful to distinguish between them because each rests on slightly different assumptions and requires a slightly different focus in order to be understood. We are looking at business ethics through a trifocal lens: close up and personal, intermediate and professional, and on the grand scale (utilizing both farsighted and peripheral vision) of the corporation.

In spite of some recent bad press, business executives are first and foremost human beings. Like all persons, they seek meaning for their lives through relationships and enterprise, and they want their lives to amount to something. Since ethics is chiefly the discipline of meaning, the business executive, like all other human beings, is engaged in this discipline all the time, whether cognizant of it or not. Therefore, we should begin by looking at how humans have historically approached the process of making meaningful decisions. Here are four ethical approaches that have stood the test of time.

Personal ethics: four ethical approaches

From the earliest moments of recorded human consciousness, the ethical discipline has entailed four fundamental approaches, often called ethical decision-making frameworks: Utilitarian Ethics (outcome based), Deontological Ethics (duty based), Virtue Ethics (virtue based), and Communitarian Ethics (community based). Each has a distinctive point of departure as well as distinctive ways of doing the fundamental ethical task of raising and answering questions of value. It is also important to understand that all four approaches have overlaps as well as common elements, such as:

- **Impartiality**: weighting interests equally

- **Rationality**: backed by reasons a rational person would accept

- **Consistency**: standards applied similarly to similar cases

- **Reversibility**: standards that apply no matter who "makes" the rules

These are in a sense the rules of the ethics game, no matter with which school or approach to ethics one feels most closely to identity.

The Utilitarian approach is perhaps the most familiar and easiest to understand of all approaches to ethics. Whether we think about it or not, most of us are doing utilitarian ethics much of the time, especially those of us in business. The Utilitarian asks a very important question: "How will my actions affect others?" They then attempt to quantify the impact of their actions based on some least common denominator, such as happiness, pleasure, or wealth. Therefore, Utilitarians are also called "consequentialists", because they look to the consequences of their actions to determine whether any particular act is justified.

"The greatest good for the greatest number" is the motto of the Utilitarian approach. Of course, defining "good" has been no easy task because what some people think of as good, others think of as worthless. When a businessperson does a cost benefit analysis, he/she is practicing Utilitarian ethics. In this case, the least common denominator is usually money. Everything from the cost of steel to the worth of a human life must be given a dollar value, and then one just does the math.

The Ford Pinto automobile was a product of just such reasoning. Thirty years ago, executives at the Ford Motor Company reasoned the cost of fixing the gas-tank problem with their Pinto would cost more than the benefit of saving a few human lives. Several tanks did explode, people died, and the company lost lawsuits when judge and juries refused to accept these executives' moral reasoning.

One of the most familiar uses of outcome-based reasoning is in legislative committees in representative democracies. How many constituents will benefit from a tax credit and how many will be diminished is the question before the Revenue Committee at tax rectification time. Representative democracies make most decisions based on the Utilitarian principle of the greatest good for the greatest number. Democratic governments are naturally majoritarian, though in constitutional democracies there are some things that cannot be decided by doing the math (adding up the votes). Some questions should never be voted on. The founders of our nation expressed this fundamental concept with three words: *certain unalienable rights*.

Enter the **Deontological Ethicists**. Immanuel Kant is the quintessential deontological (duty based) ethical theorist. Kant, who lived in eighteenth century Prussia, was one of the most amazing intellects of all time, writing books on astronomy, philosophy, politics and ethics. He once said, "Two things fill the mind with ever new and increasing admiration and awe ... the starry heavens above and the moral law within." For Kant there were some ethical verities as eternal as the stars.

Deontological simply means the study (or science) of duty. Kant did not believe that humans could predict future consequences with any substantial degree of certainty. Ethical theory based on a guess about future consequences appalled him. What he did believe was that if we use our facility of reason, we can determine with certainty our ethical duty. As to whether or not doing our duty would make things better or worse (and for whom), Kant was agnostic.

Duty-based ethics is enormously important for (though consistently ignored by) at least two kinds of folks: politicians and business people. It is also the key to a better understanding of our responsibilities as members of teams. Teams (like work groups or political campaign committees) are narrowly focused on achieving very clearly defined goals: winning the election, successfully introducing a new product, or winning a sailboat race. Sometimes a coach or a boss will say, "Look, just do whatever it takes." Ethically, "whatever it takes", means the ends justify the means. This was Kant's fundamental criticism of the Utilitarians.

For Kant, there were some values (duties) that could never be sacrificed to the greater good. He wrote: "So act as to treat humanity, whether in thy own person or in that of any other, in every case as an end withal, never as a means only." Fellow team members, employees, campaign staffs, customers, partners, etc. are always to some extent means to our various goals (ends), but they are also persons. And persons, Kant believed, cannot be just used, they must also be respected in their own right, whether or not the goal is achieved. He called this absolute *respect for persons* a Categorical Imperative.

In any team situation the goal is critical, but treating team members with respect is imperative. Teams fall apart when a team member feels used or abused (treated as less important than the overall goal itself). Great leaders carry the double burden of achieving a worthwhile end without causing those who sacrifice to achieve the goal being treated as merely expendable means. Persons are never merely a means to an end. They are ends in themselves! We owe that understanding to Immanuel Kant.

It is one thing to understand that there are duties which do not depend on consequences; it is quite another to develop the character to act on those duties. This is where Aristotle (384-322 B.C.) comes in. Aristotle wrote the first systematic treatment of ethics in Western Civilization: *Nicomachean Ethics*.

Today we call his approach to ethics **virtue ethics**. For Aristotle and other Greek thinkers, virtue meant the excellence of a thing. The virtue of a knife is to cut; the virtue of a physician is to heal; the virtue of a lawyer is to seek justice. In this sense, Ethics becomes the discipline of discovering and practicing virtue. Aristotle begins his thinking about ethics by asking, "What do people desire?" He discovers the usual things— wealth, honor, physical and psychological security—but he realizes that these things are not ends in themselves; they are means to ends.

The ultimate end for a person, Aristotle taught, must be an end that is self-sufficient, "that which is always desirable in itself and never for the sake of something else". This end of ends Aristotle designates with the Greek word *eudemonia*, usually translated by the English word happiness. But happiness does not do Aristotle or his ethics justice. Yes, eudemonia means happiness, but really it means so much more. The problem is not with Aristotle's Greek word eudemonia, the problem is in our English word happiness.

Happiness in English comes from the ancient word *hap*, meaning chance, as in happenstance. "Why are you smiling", we ask, "did you win the lottery?" For Aristotle happiness was not something one acquired by chance. Happiness was the grand work of living; the very practice of being all that you can be. Fulfillment and flourishing are far better words to translate the concept contained in the Greek word *eudemonia*. For Aristotle, this state of virtue is achieved not by accident but through intent, reason and practice.

Aristotle thought that one discovers virtue by using the unique gift of human reasoning, that is, through rational contemplation. "The unexamined life is not worth living," said Socrates almost 100 years before Aristotle. Like Aristotle and Aristotle's teacher Plato, Socrates knew that we humans need to engage our brains before we open our mouths or spring into some decisive action. For Aristotle, the focus of that brain work was chiefly about how to balance between the fears and excesses in which the human condition always abounds. Between our fears (deficits) and exuberances (excesses) lies a sweet spot, the *golden mean*, called virtue.

At times of physical peril—say in a big storm on a small sailboat—a crew member may be immobilized by fear and unable to function, thus putting the lives of everyone on the sailboat in danger. Or the opposite could happen. A devil-may-care attitude in the face of real danger can as easily lead to disaster. Courage is the virtue located at the mean between cowardliness and rashness. Yet, identifying such a virtue and making that virtue part of one's character are two quiet different things. Aristotle thus distinguishes between *intellectual virtue* and *practical virtue*. Practical virtues are those developed by practice and are a part of a person's character, while intellectual virtue is simply the identification and understanding of a virtue.

Practice is how one learns to deal with fear; practice is how one learns to tell the truth; practice is how one learns to face both personal and professional conflicts. Practice is the genius of Aristotle's contribution to the development of ethics. He showed that virtues do not become a part of our moral muscle fiber because we believe in them, or advocate them. Instead, virtues become characteristics of our selves by our exercising them. How does one learn to be brave in a storm at sea? "Just do it."

The ultimate goal behind developing characteristics of virtue is eudemonia, a full flourishing of our self, true happiness. Practitioners of the Judaic-Christian tradition tend to think of ethics (or morality) as the business of figuring out how to be good rather than bad. That is not the true end of ethics so far as Aristotle was concerned. The end is a state of fulfillment; the ultimate goal is becoming who you truly are and realizing the potential you were born with—being at your best in every sense.

Just as the virtue of the knife is to cut and the virtue of the boat is to sail, the virtue of the self is to become the best of who it can be. This is happiness (eudemonia). Just as the well-trained athlete seeks to be in the zone (the state of perfect performance achieved by practice), Aristotle wrote about the truly virtuous life and the pursuit of eudemonia. Just as a perfectly trimmed sailboat glides through the water, effortlessly in synch with the waves and the wind, the man or woman in a state of eudemonia has achieved the state of earthly fulfillment.

All three approaches to ethics described above are principally focused on the individual: the singular conscience, rationally reflecting on the meaning of duty or responsibility, and in the case of Virtue ethics, the ethical athlete practicing and inculcating the capacity to achieve the state of eudemonia. **Communitarian Ethics** has quite a different point of departure: the community (or team, or group, or company, or culture) within which the individual engages him/herself is the critical context for ethical decision-making.

The Communitarian asks the important question, "What are the demands (duties) that the community(ies) of which I am a part make on me?" The Scottish ethicists W. D. Ross (himself a student of Aristotle) focused his own ethical reflections on the question of, "Where do ethical duties come from?" His answer was that they come from relationships. We know our duties toward fellow human beings by the nature and quality of our relationships with them. The duties we owe a colleague in the workplace is different from the duties we owe a spouse; those duties are different from the duties we owe our country. The Communitarian asks us to look outward, and to face up to the duties of being social creatures. We define ourselves, and our responsibilities, by the company we keep.

Communitarians are quite critical today of the attitude of so many in our society who, while adamant about their individual rights, are negligent of their social duties. The "me generation" has created a need for a new breed of ethicists who insist that, from family and neighborhood to nation and global ecosystem, the communities in which we live require us to accept substantial responsibilities. Environmentalists, neighborhood activists, feminists, and globalists are some of the groups loosely identified today with the Communitarian Movement.

Amitai Etzioni, in *Spirit of Community: Rights, Responsibilities and the Communitarian Agenda* described the principles of this somewhat disorganized movement. Etizioni's thesis is that we must pay more attention to common duties as opposed to individual rights. Our neighborhoods, he believes, can again be safe from crime without turning our country into a police state. Our families can once again flourish without forcing women to stay home and not enter the workforce. Our schools can provide, "essential moral education" without indoctrinating young people or violating the First Amendment's prohibition of establishing religion.

The key to this social transformation is the communitarian belief in balancing rights and responsibilities: "Strong rights presume strong responsibilities." Etzioni states the Communitarian Agenda:

> *Correcting the current imbalance between rights and responsibilities requires a four-point agenda: a moratorium on the minting of most, if not all, new rights; reestablishing the link between rights and responsibilities; recognizing that some responsibilities do not entail rights; and, most carefully, adjusting some rights to the changed circumstances.*

Here, if nothing else, is a frontal attack on the Libertarian mindset of our age.

Communitarianism is not new, at least if one defines it as an approach to ethics and value referencing significant communities of meaning. Most of the world's great religions are in this sense communitarian. It is from a community of faith that the faithful develops a sense of self and responsibility (or in Confucian thought, the extended family which nurtures this development). Ethics cannot be separated from the ethos of the religious or familial community. The modern communitarian movement may or may not be religiously inclined, yet it is clearly a part of a tradition of ethical approach as old as human association.

In the context of teams, the communitarian approach to ethics has much to commend itself. How much of one's personal agenda is one willing to sacrifice for the overall goal of winning a sailboat race? Under what conditions is one willing to let the values or culture of the team alter one's own ethical inclinations? To what extent do the relationships one has with team members give rise to duties that one is willing to honor? How willing is one to share the credit when the team succeeds? How willing is one to accept blame when the team looses? Under what conditions would one break with the team? If Ross is correct that duties come from relationships, paying attention to such questions about the company we keep may be more than a social obligation; perhaps, our ethical duty.

There are two pervasive ethical approaches not treated here: ethical egoism and The Divine Imperative. Each has a broad and dedicated following and each is deeply problematic to the ethical maturing of any society. Briefly, and with pejorative intent, here is what these extreme, yet interestingly similar approaches assert.

The ethical egoists say that ethics is a matter of doing what feels right to the individual conscience. If one asks, "Why did you do that?" The answer is, "Because I felt like it." The approach is often dressed up with statements about being true to yourself: "let your conscience be your guide", or "do the right thing". But how does one know what is true for the self? How does one develop a conscience? How is one to know that doing what is right (what feels right to you) is the right thing to do?

If nothing else, ethical egoism is a conversation stopper! How does one communicate to colleagues, friends, children or any other human being when the reference point of behavior or ethical judgment is just about how one feels inside? How does a civil society emerge if we civilians cannot deliberate in common, understandable language about our motives, intents, values, or duties? In essence, ethical egoism is the ethics of teenagers rebelling against being answerable to outside authority. To teenagers, to enter the ethical dialogue is to take the radical risk of having one's values and actions challenged. Apparently, there are many of us who are just not grown up enough to risk that! Better to repeat the mantra: "I did what my conscience dictated."

Just as there is no possible meaningful ethical dialogue with the Ethical Egoist, nor is there much hope of creative engagement with Divine Imperialists. For this growing community, ethics is the simple business of doing what God tells one to do. There is therefore no reason or need for discussion. The issue is conversion, not conversation. In a constitutional democracy like ours with a fundamental commitment to "the non-establishment of religion", the Divine Imperialist is stuck with a difficult dilemma: either to make all ethical inquiry "personal" (that is, no social or political value deliberation), or take the ayatollah approach and bring no state into conformity with the revealed will of God. Divine Imperialists do not deliberate. They dictate, simply because there is nothing to deliberate about. God has spoken. It is in the book.

The flaw in the Divine Imperialists' approach is quite clear to everybody but them: If God is good, then He must reveal only good laws and rules. This creates two alternatives. The first is that there is a reference for "good" apart from the Divine itself. The only other, that God is undependable; that God is arbitrary; surely this is unacceptable. God is not only good, but God wills the good. God's will, then, becomes a reality discoverable even apart from belief in a particular represented manifestation of God. Religion, at its best, should understand that faith confers no special status of ethical insight. Believers, agnostics, non-believers can, and do, contribute to the culture's continuing struggle to understand what is good, what is just, what is true. That is why democracies (as opposed to states founded upon some "Divine Right of Kings") survive.

A Postscript on Narrative Ethics. Among the professions, particularly medicine, law and counseling, narrative has become a powerful tool in developing ethical insights and perspective. To tell a story is to invite participation from the hearer, and it is to also a means of communicating the richness and complexity of human dilemmas. Narrative Ethics is simply diagnosis through story. Its benefit over the four traditional ethical approaches is that story invites both ethical engagement and ethical creativity.

In business, as in law, a great deal of teaching is done through the use of cases. This is nothing more or less than using the pedagogy of narrative ethics. The narrative invites the hearer into the complexity of issues involved in personal, professional and organizational dilemmas, and provides a road through the complexity to the simplicity on the other side.

Oliver Wendell Holmes, an American jurist who wrote stunningly comprehensible decisions, even in some of the most complex cases imaginable, has a famous quote: "I would not give a fig for simplicity this side of complexity, but I would give my life for the simplicity that lies on the other side of complexity." It is the role of narrative to lead us through the thickets of overwhelming complexity, to the clarity of enriched simplicity.

Of course, there are some people who congenitally can not stop to ask for directions when lost in life's thickets. For them, storytelling is a waste of time. The male mantra, "just cut to the chase" comes to mind. This may in part explain why women (feminist like Margaret Wheatley, for example) have such a fondness for narrative. At all stages of the ethical decision-making process, narrative is a useful tool of analysis for exposing the facts, conflicts, feelings, and values that are the stuff of the human predicament.

Management: the meta profession

In 1912 Louis D Brandeis addressed the graduating students of Brown University. Tradition dictated that the graduating class was divided between those receiving *learned degrees* in the professions of law, medicine and ministry from those in the *skill based disciplines*, such as business management. The future Supreme Court justice did an interesting thing that graduation day: he turned away from the professional degree candidates toward the business degree candidates, and said:

Each commencement season we are told by the college reports the number of graduates who have selected the professions as their occupations and the number of those who will enter business. The time has come for abandoning such a classification. Business should be, and to some extent already is, one of the professions.

Brandeis minced no words in defining what professionalism was all about. It was:

> *An occupation for which the necessary preliminary training is intellectual in character, involving knowledge and to some extent learning, as distinguished from mere skill; which is pursued largely for others, and not merely for one's own self; and in which the financial return is not the accepted measure of success.*

Spoken to clergy, physicians and lawyers in 1911, these words would have had a familiar—if unheeded—ring. But to businessmen? Brandeis' intuition about the decisive character of business management for human welfare has been borne out across the tortured years of this past century. His argument, however, that business management was essentially professional in character is debated still.

The three characteristics of professionalism cited by Brandeis address detail the nature of the requisite responsibility, and are the crux of why it is still controversial to call business management a profession:

- First. A profession is an occupation for which the necessary preliminary training is intellectual in character, involving knowledge and to some extent learning, as distinguished from mere skill.

- Second. It is an occupation which is pursued largely for others and not merely for one's self.

- Third. It is an occupation in which the amount of financial return is not the accepted measure of success.

Within Brandeis' three paradoxical pronouncements lies the answer to what it means to be a professional in business.

The paradox of skill

All professions require unique skills. While demonstrated proficiency in particular skills is necessary for admission into a profession, skill mastery alone is not sufficient to define the professional. If it were, a surgeon would be simply a plumber employed to mend human pipes and valves; a lawyer simply a carpenter crafting together legal words and phrases into motions, wills or contracts; a teacher simply an actor skilled at presentation or lecturing. While the surgeon must be extraordinarily skilled in the crafts of incision and suturing, while the lawyer must be adept at the craft of legal word-smithing, and the teacher a master of the practical arts of communication, such skills are not the essence of who they are as professionals, nor are they the be and end all of their practices. Understanding this difference is the key to the classic distinction between a trade and a profession.

Both trades and professions require the practice and perfection of significant skills, but a trade is completely defined by its commensurate skill; a profession is not. As Brandeis explains: "A profession is an occupation for which the necessary preliminary training is intellectual in character involving knowledge, and to some extent learning, as distinguished from mere skill." I would add that it is not just in "preliminary training" that intelligence and learning are required, but in all aspects of the practice of the continuing professional life.

In a time when everyone wants to be called professional, a real danger lurks in Brandeis' distinction, an elitism ('mere skill'), a snobbery, a class bias that is inappropriate both to the tradesperson and the professional. Once, the trades were a source of enormous pride and distinction. Through Medieval guilds a revolution in human worth and work was set in motion and the foundations of the industrial and technological revolutions laid. Through the guild structure, the skills of trades were passed from generation to generation, and the pride of association with quality and integrity maintained.

But the professions were something else entirely. Called The Learned Professions as the Middle Ages yielded to the Renaissance, the Priesthood, Law, and Medicine obviously required rigorous training in particular skills, but the application of these particular skills required a dimension of commitment and integrity not necessitated of a trade. The wisdom to counsel human beings in the midst of spiritual, emotional, physical or legal crisis necessarily requires more than technique. It requires a learned and practiced wisdom: an ethic. It is one thing to entrust your bathroom to a plumber, another thing entirely to entrust your life to a heart surgeon. Those willing to assume the unique burdens of the spiritual, physical, and legal care for humans in existential need were designated, or set apart, as learned professionals.

As I write this chapter, I am in the process of recovering from open heart surgery. The experience of putting my life in the hands of a physician is vivid. I am also sitting in my home that is being extensively remodeled. I am fortunate to have a relationship with two excellent persons: Dick, my heart surgeon and Craig, the skilled construction craftsman (carpenter, plumber and electrician) restoring our home. Both are highly skilled and wise men. Dick, however, is integral to the care and counseling that guided me and my family through my decision to "go under the knife". Craig is full of sage wisdom about the public and foreign affairs of our times, but in no sense is my life vulnerable to his lively and wise insights that we share while he restores my kitchen and replaces the bedroom window.

Exactly three weeks ago Dick, sat on the side of my bed in a Denver, Colorado hospital surrounded by twelve members of my family and talked to me about the alternatives for dealing with a most unexpected heart problem. He showed me the very worrisome pictures of several partially blocked arteries, and told me that, in his opinion, I had no choice but to have quadruple bypass surgery. Dick said he would send my file to anyone I wished for a second opinion, but felt I should reach a decision soon. My kids asked all sorts of nervous and caring questions and he responded openly and fully. Never have I been with someone as obviously open and trustworthy at a time when so much was at stake for me.

As I made my decision to move forward with this personal ordeal, I would learn from friends in the community that Dick was one of the most skilled surgeons in the country. That was reassuring. But I already knew he was a professional: a person wise and caring enough for me to trust my life to.

The paradox of the public pledge

A profession is literally so called a profession because the aspirant to the office is orally sworn to specific public commitments—he/she professes publicly legal and ethical obligations unique to the vocation of lawyer, physician, counselor or priest. The public pledge is the portal condition into the unique relationships afforded the vocation. Be clear, it is not primarily a privilege the professional assumes, rather it is fundamentally self-imposed burdens. No one is forced to swear they will put another's interest above their own, yet this is the condition of all professionalism.

There is a tension between a profession's public responsibility and its commitment (also made publicly) to the private, vulnerable client. Brandies includes both in the observation that, "A profession is an occupation which is pursued largely for others and not merely for oneself". The paradox of "the other" is the paradox of the public pledge.

Quite a great deal is made of the special relationship between professionals their parishioners, patients, or clients—the sanctity of the confessional, the doctor patient relationship, or the lawyer client relationship—each special, private and protected both in law and ethics. Thinking of the confessional booth, the examination room, and the lawyer's office the idea of a uniquely protected privacy, of almost a sacred space, emerges. Assuredly the priest, doctor and lawyer are sworn to hold sacred the disclosures within this zone of professionally protected communication. Being a professional means nothing less than willingly and publicly affirming that the client's, patient's or parishioner's interest shall come before one's own interests.

For many professionals the matter stops with the pledge: "I swear the patient's interests comes first, end of discussion." Yet this commitment to the vulnerable client is only half the issue, as the business and professional crises of our times illustrate. Not only is the priest sworn to care for particular souls, he is also sworn to see to the care of "the people of God", the moral welfare of the parish, the salvation of the world. Not only is the doctor sworn to put the interest of the patient above his own, but the health of the patient's family, neighborhood, and the public is also his professional obligation. The lawyer is not simply employed to represent the particular client, but also sworn to be an "officer of the court". While accountants may be employed by Arthur Anderson to do the books for the Enron Corporation, they also are sworn to keep the interests of the public uncompromised (after all, we call the profession Certified *Public* Accountants).

I know of no professional comfortable with the tension inherent in this public pledge. No one likes hard choices; no one likes moral ambiguity; each of us wishes to live in a world where things can be reduced to some least common ethical denominator (for example, a single duty). When teaching business students, the mantra of Milton Friedman is the droning undertone of almost every class discussion: "the business of business is business", the sole responsibility of the business executive is to increase shareholder return.

Yet, the very essence of professional responsibility is to address the difficult and unavoidable ethical tensions between public and private interest—the priest who hears the confession of a disturbed and homicidal parishioner intent on killing yet again; the lawyer who discovers that a client has misrepresented the facts of his case, and is asking for a plea to the court based in lies and distortions; the doctor who is asked to prescribe extraordinarily expensive treatments to a patient too ill, or old to have any reasonable chance of curative benefit; or the engineer who is told that she is bound by a confidentiality agreement, in spite of her certain conviction that a plane, bridge, or space shuttle is likely to fail and potentially cause extensive loss of life. These are not plot summaries for Hollywood; in an infinite variety, they are the stuff of professional life in the complex world of the twenty-first century.

It is by design, and not by accident, that professionals are thrust continually into such Hobson choice predicaments. The professional's public pledge is an acceptance of ethical burdens not incumbent on the rest of society. It is an acknowledgment of the reality of human existence where things do not come out even, where real ethical insight must be exercised and where benign outcomes are far from assured. Someone must live in the land between the rock and the hard place, and those who do so are designated "professional".

I think of professionals as the value bearers for society, those particularly burdened and practiced to address the most difficult and sensitive human ethical dilemmas. I do not mean to imply that a business person, lawyer, doctor, psychiatrist, or teacher is better in some moral sense than anyone else. Instead, that they have agreed to assume a unique ethical burden, to work at the transaction point where issues of significant human value are on the line. The professional is sworn not to desert this post, to be there to counsel, reflect and bear with the human condition in the midst of transition and crisis. This is, to me, the essence of professional practice—the practice of raising the value content of human decisions and choices. That is the professional's sworn burden, it is the very nature of the ethic that defines who the professional is.

All this said, it astounds me that anyone would want the title of professional. But to make sure this point is underlined, let us consider the "Paradox of pay", perhaps the most complexing of all to the business professional.

The paradox of pay

I am watching a sports show on the evening news. A local sportscaster is interviewing a member of the Harlem Globetrotters, who are in town for a game. The interview goes something like this:

Sports Guy: Al, I was surprised you never turned pro.

Al: What do you mean? I am a pro, I get paid pretty good for playing ball.

Sports Guy: Well yeah? But I meant you never tried out for the NBA.

Al: Oh, well I like playing for the Globetrotters better ...

Almost everyone assumes that being professional means getting paid (and paid well) for one's work. There are professionals and there are amateurs, the former get paid, while the amateurs do it for the love of it. Well, no. Originally, the professions were too important to receive wages in the usual sense. Professionals were not paid for their work; instead, professionals received an honorarium, a gratuity from the community intended both to honor and disassociate the vocation from the necessities of the market, to free the vocation for the selfless task of caring for others.

Three days before my heart surgery I happened to watch a Sixty Minutes piece on a cardiology group in California which was prescribing and performing unnecessary bypass surgery in order to increase their practice's revenues. It was chilling. I thought of a case we use in business school about how Sears some years ago pressured employees in their auto servicing division to increase revenues by pushing unneeded air filters, mufflers, and break re-linings, etc. But, heart surgeons re-aligning ethical responsibility due to market dependency? I think the Medieval notion of honoraria for professionals may make a lot of sense in this time of triumphant capitalism. There are some values the market is not designed to dictate.

I love to tease business students about the matter of pay and the power of money. I ask, "Considering the 'oldest profession' what had you rather be known for: doing it for money, or doing it for love?" In the realm of love making, most us prefer to have non market forces determine the dimensions of our intimate lives. Let us hear it for true amateurs!

In a real sense, professionals indeed do it for love. It is difficult to imagine bearing the burden of a physician, lawyer, counselor, or a professor without having a deep and effusive passion for what one does. Professionals cannot leave their work at the office, because what they do is who they are. As I have discovered, teaching is the most rewarding thing I can think of doing. I do not just teach; I am a teacher. I am glad I am paid for my work, but truth be known I would do it for free. I walk away from a class where the students and I have really "lit it up", and I do not even have words to say how good it feels. I can describe historically and intellectually what a professional should be, but even better, I also know what it feels like. No amount of money can compensate for that feeling.

Consider the burdens of true professionalism that skill alone is not sufficient to qualify: one is publicly pledged to work on the unrelenting tension between the welfare of the client and the good of the society; and that is not the criteria by which success will be judged—why would one choose to "turn pro?" I have only one answer: professions are rightly designated as vocations. We become priests, lawyers, physicians, professors because we cannot do anything else; who we are cannot be achieved outside the realm of what we are impelled to do.

Corporate Social Responsibility

The legal and historic roots of the modern corporation reach well back into the eighteenth century, but it was in the Industrial Revolution of the nineteenth century that this truly extraordinary form of human organization came into its own and, the twentieth century, became the dominant economic force on earth. Consider its amazing characteristics concentration of management, accumulation of capital, shielding of ownership from liability, and being granted a legal existence not necessarily bounded by either space or time—both ubiquitous and eternal! As well, however, consider its fearsome prospects vis-à-vis its lack of accountability, its deficit of democratic governance, its often-uncivilized competitive engagement with all other sectors of society, not to mention its transcendence of both national sovereignty and legal jurisdiction. And there you have it. Is the Trans-national Corporation the answer to the fundamental issues of human survival, or the fundamental threat to life itself? In short, will the corporation of the twenty-first century be a corrupt Robin Hood, or a virtuous Sheriff of Nottingham?

Corporations are not natural persons. Corporations are fictitious, corporations are juridical persons created by law. The point is this: the ethical considerations one might use when dealing with a friend, associate, or stranger, are significantly different when the subject is the corporation.

Getting this straight is critically important to an adequate understanding of business ethics. People—their behavior and the products of their work and intellect—are judged ethically and legally based chiefly on their intentions. Ethical analysis of the behavior of natural persons begins with considerations of what a person meant by what he or she did, said, or produced. In contrast, ethical analysis involving the entity we call "the corporation" must forever begin and end in law and public policy. With reference to the political economy that brought forth the beast. The legal entity, known as the corporation, was created to shield investors from liabilities beyond the limit of their investment (a result that neither sole proprietorships nor partnerships could accomplish) with the legislative intent of facilitating the aggregation of private capital. This legal experiment begun 19th century has succeeded spectacularly.

For people to survive, they need physical and emotional nourishment, and familial and social support. Corporations survive solely by their ability to return value to their shareholders. Hence, corporations are consequential critters, Utilitarian to the core. A friend may forget a lunch date and hurt your feelings, but when he says, "I'm really sorry, I can't believe I forgot." You say, "Hey I missed you, but it's OK. Let's try again next week." When a company launches a new product and if the 100 million dollar venture tanks, shareholders do not want to hear about how sorry management is that things did not work out, or that management meant well. It will do the CEO no good to say, "My heart was in the right place."

When we talk about the ethical criteria for judging the behavior of corporations we speak not of intent, but responsibility: quite literally, the capacity to respond. Corporate ethics is the ethics of corporate social responsibility (CSR), not corporate personal responsibility. The responsibility of a corporation is shaped by two realities: the obligations created by society through (1) law and public policy (legal responsibilities), and (2) the obligations created by corporate culture, i.e. stakeholder (customers, employees, neighborhoods, natural environments) obligations. The two overlap and reinforce each other, but their limits lie within the boundaries of a company's tangible capacities.

Corporate ethics is really about gaining understanding of what are called "mixed motives". When natural persons have mixed motives—you give a hundred bucks to the opera because you want your boss, who supports the opera, to think well of you—we somehow know that this is not an unambiguously laudable act. But when a company that makes computers gives 100 laptops to the public school system, and does so with the hope that exposing children to their brand of computers will lead to increased sales—this "doing good to do well" is not only laudable, it is responsible—responsible both to shareholders and the stakeholders.

Corporations as a matter of fact, can only act with "mixed motives". By law, they are created to serve the bottom line of returning wealth to investors. The law says corporations have a fiduciary responsibility (fiduciary = the highest standard of loyalty and trust owed by agents to principles) to their shareholders, who are the legal owners of the corporation. To do good, a corporation must do well. As a business ethicist, I argue the reverse: to do well, a corporation must do good. People have consciences, and some would say souls; corporations have neither. Corporations are creatures of law and public policy, they are cultural creations; as such, they have unique cultures of their own. Corporate ethics is therefore really about the creation of a culture of responsibility within the corporation.

Dr Lynne Payne of Harvard University has made a major contribution to the understanding of CSR and how it is achieved in her distinction between compliance based organizations and integrity based organizations. In reality, CSR is a product of both compliance (legal and regulatory constraints) and integrity (the internal culture and self regulatory environment). This is underscored by new laws such as *Sarbanes-Oxley Act of 2002* and the almost two decade old US Federal Sentencing Guidelines (policy guidelines established in part to determining corporate criminal punishment in US Federal Courts).

Sarbanes Oxley is particularly interesting given Payne's compliance/integrity construct, in that it requires both integrity structures (such as a corporate board of ethics, and internal protections for whistleblowers) and increases fines for violation of anti-trust and other federal statutes regulating inter-state corporate behavior. Thus, corporations are creatures of law and policy and are regulated externally. Corporations have no conscience per se, but like any social system can develop a guiding culture, maintained through education and reinforced by the habits and interactions of the people within the corporation.

In a world of over six billion people, there is little alternative to large and complex organizations designed to feed, house, heal, and help meet basic human needs. The multinational corporation is here to stay; the issues of how these behemoths are guided and controlled is far from settled. How the humans who work and manage these organizations maintain their own integrity within the Utilitarian cultures of the multinational corporation is a chapter of history we are only beginning to write.

The Social Contract between society and the multinational corporation today is being radically renegotiated. The cascading collapses of the Dotcoms, the Enron, Worldcom, and Aldelphia scandals, and now, the meltdown of capital markets across the globe portends a turbulent future indeed for both the corporation and the business professional. Yet, it is in such times that fundamental changes most often emerge. Those who dare to ride these currents of change will emerge in a new order of political economy.

13. Adding products and services

Editors: George M Zinkhan, Anastasia Thyroff, Anja Rempel, and Hongbum Kim (The University of Georgia, USA)

Reviewer: Bettina Cornwell (University of Michigan, USA)

Learning objectives

After reading this chapter, you should:

- understand the strategic importance of adding and deleting products. understand some methods which can be applied to assist in this decision-making process

- understand some different approaches for generating new product ideas

- be familiar with various ways of classifying products and innovations

- be able to discuss innovations related to business models

- know the basic methods for evaluating innovations

- be able to discuss the related topics of failed innovation and product deletion

Introduction

The twenty-first century marketplace is dynamic and fast changing. As a result, organizations are under pressure to evaluate their existing product line and to make continuous decisions about adding new products or deleting existing products. For instance, the graph in Exhibit 45 shows how an organization must establish a series of successful products, if that organization wants to maintain a consistent stream of sales or else grow sales over time. One reason for this pattern is the product life cycle. As shown in the graph, no product lasts forever, and sales levels can fluctuate dramatically over time. The company illustrated in Exhibit 45 has marketed 8 different products over time. In the past, four of these products have been deleted (the products labeled as A, B, C, and F). As a result, the sales level in the most current period depends upon the success of the remaining four products. If the firm has a goal to increase sales in the coming years, then it is imperative for that firm to introduce a new group of successful products.

Organizations invest a lot of money to create new products that perform effectively. Nonetheless, firms often struggle to convince people to incorporate these new products into their routines (Arts 2008). For example, it took 18 years for microwave ovens to gain acceptance in Greece (Tellis, Stremersch, and Yin 2003). The ultimate success of new products depends on consumers accepting them (Arts 2008).

The term "product" refers to both goods and services. A product is anything that can be offered to a market to satisfy a want or need. There are a number of ways to classify products, and those methods are discussed later in the chapter. In this chapter, we discuss the following topics: (a) Where do innovations come from? (b) product categories; (c) Innovation through business models; (d) Evaluating innovations; (e) When innovation fails: deleting products; and (f) chapter summary. In the next two sections, we briefly discuss innovations and their origins.

Sales of individual products and total sales

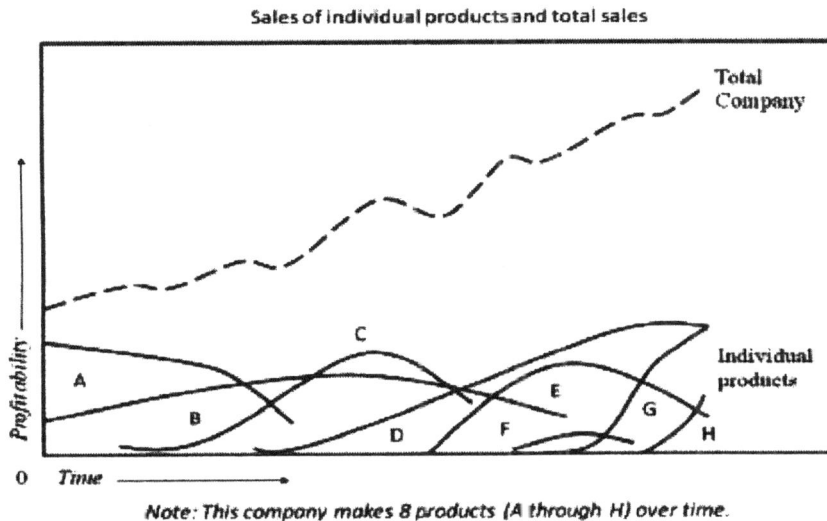

Note: This company makes 8 products (A through H) over time.

Exhibit 45: Sales of individual products and total sales

Where does innovation come from?

We define "innovation" as an idea or product that is new to the sponsoring organization. A "discontinuous innovation" has the potential to alter existing consumption patterns, or else create new ones. For example, portable audio equipment has evolved from the radio, to the cassette tape player, to the compact disk players and to the digital audio player. At the extreme, a discontinuous innovation results in the creation of a new generic category of products, such as the GPS navigation system.

In contrast, "continuous innovations" involve introducing a new entrant into an existing category. Continuous innovations do not challenge established patterns of consumption behavior. A good example of this type of innovation is the smart phone. For this product, consumers already know what a phone is and how to operate it. From this perspective, the operation of a smart phone can be viewed as a combination of the functions associated with a mobile phone and the functions of a personal digital assistant (PDA). In a more recent offering, a smart phone combines the functions of PCs and Macs through applying the software and operating systems of each. As a result, consumers can access their current knowledge about existing products and then easily grasp the "smart phone" concept.

On the one hand, the process of innovation is the life blood of an organization. New product innovations are responsible for employment, economic growth, technological process, and high standards of living (Souder 1987). In a marketing context, innovation is crucial for the development of successful new products (both goods and services). On the other hand, it is a challenge to develop and evaluate these innovations. In brief, where do innovative ideas come from? We describe five sources of innovation: technical breakthroughs, non-technical idea development, ideas that emerge from environments, serendipity, and purposeful development. These various strategies are outlined in Table 10 and described in more detail in the following section.

Technical breakthroughs refer to product innovations that result from technical developments. New brands that have emerged from this process include MP3 players, GPS navigation devices, and cell phones. In the long run, it is consumers who decide how new technologies will be used. For instance, Guglielmo Marconi created the radio-telegraph so that ships could communicate with each other on the high seas in 1894. However, other applications emerged, and everyday uses eventually multiplied. For instance, in 1921, the RadioShack Corporation was formed in Boston to sell equipment to "ham" operators. The company took its name from the small wooden building for radio equipment on ships. As more families adopted radios, it was a real challenge to develop content. Eventually, the advertising business model was created, and the funds that were provided by advertisers were used to sponsor the development of popular content (e.g. music, dramatic shows, variety shows) (Zinkhan 2005).

Non-technical development is another path to product innovation. This approach involves finding a niche in the market without making radical changes to the basic product category (i.e. in terms of the underlying technology). "Build a Bear Workshop" provides a good example of this style of innovation. Unlike other conventional stuffed animal manufacturers, the Build a Bear Workshop allows customers to choose their bear's body, sound, clothing, stuffing, and heart. For example, a customer can choose, a lower-priced paper heart with their wish, or they can invest in a higher-priced electronic heart. After customers make choices, they then observe the production process in the shop. In this way, customers create their own custom-designed toy. This business model does not rely on developing new technology. However, there is a modified production process, as the stuffing and sewing machine are located in the retail store.

Ideas that emerge from environments refer to innovations that result from importing products from other cultures. Good examples of this style of innovation are Wal-mart in China and IKEA in the United States. Traditionally, there were no large-scale retail stores in Asian nations, such as Japan, Korea, China or India. Instead, small retailers or mom-and-pop stores dominated. Large-retail stores are now achieving success in Asian nations, through importing the idea of economies of scale, which, in turn enable one-stop shopping and lower prices. Similarly, IKEA achieved great success in the US and China through importing the idea of a warehouse-type retail setting from Europe. IKEA offers high-quality furniture and home interior products for lower prices. Consumer assembly is often required.

Serendipity plays a role in product innovation. The word serendipity derives from "serendip," which means "Sri Lanka" in Persian. The fairy tale, The Three Princes of Serendip, tells the story of three men who continuously discover something that is completely unrelated to what they originally set out to find. Thus, the term "serendipity" describes a situation where one accidentally discovers something fortunate, while looking for something else entirely. For example, penicillin was discovered quite by accident when Alexander Fleming discovered that a mold contaminating one of his experiments possessed powerful antibacterial properties.

Purposeful development occurs when there is a strong need for certain goods or services. As described by Plato in The Republic: "Necessity is the mother of invention." In other words, this type of innovation occurs when existing product lines cannot satisfy current needs or current demand. As a result, organizations are willing invest considerable funds (e.g. in terms of research and development or marketing research) to create a successful innovation. A good example of purposeful development is the heavy investment that pharmaceutical firms make to discover new prescription drugs. For inspiration, pharmaceutical scientists rely upon current developments in chemistry, physics, plant biology, and folk healing methods. In some instances, this kind of innovation might result from marketing research, where considerable demand is forecast in the marketplace.

Table 10: different sources of innovation

Source of Innovation	Definition	Examples of Innovation
Technical breakthrough	Innovation that results from technical development.	MP3 players; GPS navigation system; Wireless Internet service
Non-technical idea development	Finding niche markets without making radical changes to the basic product category. Does not rely on new technology.	'Build a bear workshop;' Frozen yogurt stores
Idea from outer environment	Importing ideas from other cultures, places, and settings	IKEA in the US; Yoga or Taekwondo in Western nations
Serendipity	Innovation through an accident, when looking for something else	X-rays; Penicillin
Purposeful development	Innovation that derives from heavy investment, once strong demand is recognized	Prescription drugs; Pencils with erasers

It is also possible to create a new business model. Wal-Mart is a good example here, as the retailer applies the philosophy of low prices and cost cutting to every aspect of its operations, including logistics, employee compensation, managerial philosophy, packaging, merchandising, negotiations with suppliers, and so forth. This manner of innovation is discussed in more detail in the section which follows, "Product Categories."

Product categories

There are a number of ways to classify products (see Table 10 and Exhibit 46). For instance, a product can be classified by durability and tangibility. Packaged goods are tangible and are consumed in one or a few uses, such as in the case of beer, soap, or fuel. Durable goods are tangible and survive many uses. Consumer examples include furniture, TVs, computers, clothing and automobiles. According to one convention, a durable good lasts more than one year. Non-durable goods are tangible, but they provide benefits for a short time. Good examples include: gum, shaving cream, gas, batteries, and cosmetics. There are also controlled goods which are often restricted by government action, due to their potential danger or addictive nature. Good examples include: cigarettes, alcohol, tobacco, firearms, and even some over-the-counter drugs.

Business-to-business (B2B) products refer to goods bought by individuals or organizations for further processing or for use in doing business. Examples in B2B include: buildings, flour purchased by a commercial baker, crude oil, steel for automobile manufacture, insurance policies for company buildings, and business consulting services. Business-to-customer (B2C) products refer to goods that individual customers purchase for personal and family use, such as passenger cars, hairdryers, TVs, medical insurance policies, and carpet cleaning services for the home.

Convenience products are products that consumers want to purchase frequently, immediately, and with a minimum of effort. Examples here include: soft drinks, cigarettes, fast foods, newspapers, public transportation and candy bars. Shopping goods are purchased only after consumers make comparisons with competing goods based on such attributes as price, quality, style, or color. Examples in this category include: MP3 players, passenger cars, clothing, furniture, and houses. Specialty products are products with unique characters. Buyers often prize such goods and make a special effort to obtain them. Examples in this group include collectable items, engagement rings, vacation homes, yachts, art works, luxury cars, and special concert tickets.

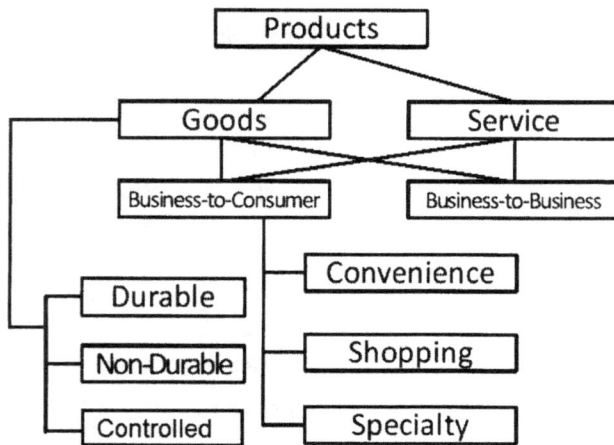

Exhibit 46: Rough Classification of Products

Table 11: Classifying products

Category Name	Definition	Example
Good	A tangible physical entity	Table, electronics, soda, candy bar
Service	An intangible result of the application of human and mechanical efforts to people or objects.	Haircut, dry-cleaning, gardening
Durable	Products that provide benefit for a long time and are not used up when used once.	Automobile, house, machines
Non-durable	Products that provide benefit for a short time.	Milk, laundry detergents, tissue paper
Controlled Goods	Products that need to be regulated due to their potential danger or addictive potential.	Tobacco, alcohol, firearms, pharmaceuticals

Business-to-business	Goods bought by individuals or organizations for further processing or for use in doing business.	plastics for a car manufacturer, insurance plan for plants
Consumer	The goods individual consumers purchase for personal or family use.	Canned soup, medical insurance
Convenience	Products that consumers want to purchase frequently, immediately, and with a minimum of effort.	Chewing gum, beer, cigarettes, fast food
Shopping	Products purchased only after the consumer has made comparisons with competing goods on such bases as price, quality, style, or color.	TV, automobile, house
Specialty	Products with unique characterizations that cause the buyer to prize them and make a special effort to obtain them.	Luxury sports car, jewelry,

Innovation through business models

A good business model is a story that explains how an enterprise is designed to work (Margretta 2002). A business model identifies sources of competitive advantage and describes the firm's pathway to profitability and success. From a marketing perspective, the business model describes customers and what they value. From a managerial perspective, the business model describes how an organization makes profit. See Exhibit 47.

In this section, we review some emerging models in the music industry, in order to illustrate how such models can serve as a source of innovation. That is, a traditional way for organizations to remain profitable is to introduce a series of related goods. As shown earlier in Exhibit 45, the organization introduces eight products (labeled A through H). Over time, the sales for product A begin to decline, so the organization is under considerable pressure to introduce new successful products. If Exhibit 45 represents the cumulative sales for a record label, then product A might be a hip-hop CD, while product B is a CD created by a rock artist. In this section of the chapter, we present an alternative source of innovation—the innovation that results from successfully introducing new business models. All our examples are derived from the music industry, but related industries (e.g. films, books) are undergoing similar transformations and creating similar opportunities for entrepreneurs.

Examples of business models from the music industry

Since the late 1990s, the availability of online music has caused a lot of confusion in the marketplace. Traditional business models are no longer applicable for explaining the current business opportunities. The music industry in the twenty-first century provides a classic illustration of a "disruptive technology", whereby new technologies drive out established technologies and established ways of doing business.

Here, we briefly review eight business models in the music industry. We distinguish among these models via five characteristics: current implementation, feasibility, legality, consumer satisfaction, and record label satisfaction (See Table 3). Note that some of these models are currently implemented, while others are speculative in nature.

Traditional business model

In this business model, the artists create music and try to be signed by a record label. After the artist is signed by a record label, then that organization provides a number of services, including financing music recording and production; organizing concert tours; producing and selling merchandise; marketing the band's creation; promoting the band through exposure on mass media; and more.

Next, the record label delivers the recorded music to manufactures who reproduce and package the music. The supply chain members are in charge of distribution, including an effort to gain cooperation from key retail outlets. Finally, the retailers market and sell the packaged goods to the final consumers (Slater, Smith, Bambauer, Gasser, and Palfrey 2005; see Exhibit 47).

Exhibit 47: Six-step model

Digital music stores

This model suggests that the retailers move online and offer content directly to consumers through websites. This approach is similar to the traditional model, but there is an emphasis on the online delivery of content (Slater et al., 2005). Amazon was one of the first companies to implement this model in the 1990s. Since the debut of this model, two major modifications have been made. First, consumers can now purchase digital downloads of the music, rather than receiving a physical product, such as CDs. This offers an intangible and instantaneous approach to buying music. The second large modification is also related to digital downloading, as users no longer have to buy an entire CD. Many digital music stores offer free sampling of each song which allows customers to preview tracks that they want to purchase. The Apple's iTune store successfully implements this model in the twenty-first century.

Open content

This model is derived from the "Ancillary Products and Services" model that the Berkman center formulated in 2005 (Slater et al. 2005). One main assumption here is that nothing can be done to stop the illegal sharing of music. In order for the model to be successful, the content creator, record companies, and consumers must encourage the use of peer-to-peer networking. Thus, every music download from this business model is free of charge. This model is different in that free file sharing is encouraged. However, there is a concerted effort to find other sources of revenue (Berkman Center 2003). Other sources of income may include touring, selling band paraphernalia, endorsements, and fan clubs. This model is illegal under current laws in the US and many other countries as it violates existing copyrights. Note that, in most contexts, open-content sharing is legal as long the owner signs a contract that allows such distribution.

There are conflicting viewpoints on the open content model. On one extreme, there people like Lars Ulrich, the Drummer for Metallica, who is outraged that this could even be an option. According to Ulrich, "The argument I hear a lot, that music should be free, must then mean the musicians should work for free. Nobody else works for free, why should musicians (Ulrich and McGuinn 2000)?" On the other extreme are people who argue that copyrights are irrational since they deny consumers the right to use creative works and suffocate the creativity of Internet users (Lessig 2004).

At first glance, the open-content model appears to be very radical, as it differs so much from other models. Nonetheless, it has gained considerable attention in the last few years. This approach is very satisfying for customers, but is a major threat for record labels and channel members.

Artist-centered website hub

This business model uses one large website as a database for music. Content creators contact the website directly and set the price of their music. The website sets a minimum downloading fee to cover costs; the fee is set on a monthly basis (or on a per-download basis). Customers access the website and purchase all the music they want, knowing that the artist receives most of the profit.

Some websites are already implementing this model. For instance, CD Baby sells independent music that comes directly from the artist. Since this model cuts out several middlemen, CD Baby claims that artists receive USD 6-12 per album versus the USD 1-2 that artists typically receive through their record labels. There are currently 248,891 artists on CD Baby and over USD 87,052,087 dollars have gone directly to the artist since the company opened for business in 1998 (Hefflinger 2008).

Artist's personal website

Another potential model encourages users to access the artist's personal websites to purchase music. This approach allows the artists to have the most control over their music. The band Radiohead tested this model during the debut of their seventh album "Only in Rainbows." The band alienated themselves from their record label, EMI, and offered the album solely from their website Radiohead.com. Customers who visited the site where allowed to decide what they were willing to pay for the album (Tyangiel 2007).

Although this model is attractive for popular artists, it is potentially troublesome for artists who are not well known. Lesser known artists have great difficulty standing out in a crowded market. This model also eliminates the record label.

Non-traditional "record labels"

Currently, independent record labels are sprouting up in unexpected places. In 2003, the Cracker Barrel Old Country Store created an American Roots record label called CB music, Ltd (Romero 2003). Starbucks, the eternally popular coffee house launched their own record label in March of 2007. Their plan involves signing artists (e.g. Paul McCartney) and selling records through Starbucks stores (http://www.starbucks.com/).

Tax-the-device model

This model follows the open content model, in that music is provided free of charge for music downloads. However, such downloads are tracked, and a sales tax is placed on all devices that are sold to play back downloaded files. The money generated from taxes is then used to pay back artists. Of course, this model is speculative in nature. At present, there is not a reliable method for tracking all downloads. In addition, devices sold outside of the US would be difficult to tax.

Summary of new business models

A major purpose in describing these music business models is to illustrate how innovations do not have to be tied to the success of a new good or service. Rather, an organization can innovate by introducing a new method of doing business, and such innovation has the potential to "turn the world upside down" (a la Google or Facebook).

Table 12: Music Business Models

Model	Currently implemented?	Feasible?	Currently legal or illegal?	Consumer satisfaction	Record label satisfaction
Traditional	No	Not anymore	Legal	No	Yes
Digital music stores	Yes	Yes	Legal	Yes	Yes
Peer-to-peer Stores	Yes	Yes	Legal	Yes	Yes
Open Source	Yes	Yes	Illegal	Yes	No
Artist centered website hub	No	Yes	Legal	Yes	No
Artist's personal website	Yes	Yes	Legal	Yes	No
Non-traditional "record lables"	Yes	Yes	Legal	Yes if used with other models	No to traditional record labels
Tax-the-device	No	Not really	Legal	?	No

Evaluating new products

When an organization adds a new product, there is both potential benefit and risk. As a result, organizations implement formal systems for evaluating new products. In particular, there is a concerted effort to forecast projected sales and thus reduce some of the financial risk. While evaluating new products, there is also the possibility of generating innovative ideas that can later go through the testing process. Idea generation is an essential part of marketing strategy and is critical to the success of a company. When such product ideas move further along in the process, a key step is to create a prototype or working version of the new offering. Again, market testing is crucial at every stage in the development process.

Here, we briefly discuss three main alternatives for evaluating new additions to the product line: laboratory tests, expert evaluations, and customer evaluations (Urban and Hauser 1993). With respect to customer evaluations, we distinguish between central-location tests and home-use tests (Crask, Fox and Stout 1995).

The laboratory tests provide information regarding the performance of new products in extreme settings. For example, a new copy machine can be tested at various work loads, such as numbers of copies and speed per minute to test the relationship between workload and paper jam. A disadvantage for the laboratory test is that it may not fully represent real-life conditions. Consumers are famous for findings new ways to abuse products, and they are not such skillful operators as lab testers.

Expert evaluators can be used at all phases of the new product development process. For instance, experts can be used to estimate whether or not a new product idea will be accepted in the marketplace before a prototype even exists. Experts also play a role later in the process. For instance, a new passenger car can be tested by a car expert, who provides a (published) review that covers topics such as: handling, comfort, ease of use, styling, acceleration, miles per gallon, and so forth. Expert evaluation is relatively low in cost, as just a few experts can provide estimates about the behaviors of many customers. At the same time, the small number of experts on each project may lead to biased forecasts.

In later stages of development, customers can be recruited to evaluate prototypes. There is an attempt to test new products under conditions that are relatively close to actual use. Here, we distinguish between two types of customer evaluations: central-location evaluation and home-use evaluation.

Central-location tests are conducted at designated locations such as shopping malls, sporting events, and college campuses. Participants are recruited by email, telephone, and print ads. Types of central-location tests include:

- Discrimination test: conducted to determine the percentage of customers who can distinguish between product alternatives.

- Paired comparison test: respondents evaluate a pair of options and then state their preference between the options.

- Round robin test: all possible product pairs are evaluated, using a format where consumers compare two products at a time.

- Blind test: a new product is compared to existing products.

Under the home-use test, customers are invited to use a new product as part of their everyday life. The home use test is usually more expensive than the central-location evaluation, but it is more realistic. Popular types of home-use tests include:

- Paired comparison test: participants evaluate two products in normal usage situation and provide evaluations for both products.

- Single-product home-use test (monadic test): participants evaluate one product after using that product for a specified time period.

- Proto-monadic home-use tests: a hybrid design where participants are asked to use a certain product for a specific time period and then evaluate. Next, participants follow a similar procedure for a second test product.

When innovation fails: deleting products

Product failure

In general, a product fails when it does not meet the objectives that were established by the sponsoring organization. Failure rates vary by industry. For instance, failure rates for new packaged goods range from 75 per cent to 90 per cent (catalinamarketing.com). When considering "innovative" new products, Gourville (2005) estimates that approximately half of all such products fail. It often costs more to launch an innovation nationally than to develop the good or service in the first place.

In the following section, we describe Wal-Mart's failure as it tried to enter the German market. Our purpose is to use this one example to illustrate key reasons that new products fail and subsequently must be deleted. See Table 11 for a listing of major reasons that cause products to be deleted. Table 11 includes a description of 13 reasons that products fail. Note that the Wal-Mart experience in Germany provides concrete examples for 10 of these key reasons. In the table, the reasons for product deletion are divided into 5 groups: (a) Market Structure (MS); (b) Business Model (BM); (c) Culture (C); (d) Politics/regulation (P): and (e) Product failure (PF). These same categories are highlighted in the sections which follow.

Case, example of product failure: Wal-Mart in Germany, 1997 to 2006

Wal-Mart is the biggest food retailer in the world and has a presence in several nations. In some nations (e.g. the US, Canada, China), Wal-Mart is a great success. However, Wal-Mart has failed in some countries (e.g. Germany, South Korea). First, we describe Wal-Mart's failure in Europe's largest economy. Second, we use Wal-Mart's experiences in Germany to illustrate some key principles related to product failure and product deletion (see Table 11). Wal-Mart's experiences are also an example of the importance to adapt to culture when starting a business in a new country.

The German grocery industry

There is fierce competition in the German grocery industry, due to the increasing number of discount supermarket chains (KPMG 2006). As a result, there is low profitability in the food retail sector; profit margins range from 0.5 per cent to 1 per cent which is one of the lowest profit margins in Europe (Frankfurter Rundschau 2007). By contrast, profit margins in Great Britain are 5 per cent, in this same sector. In particular, Metro is a tough competitor, and it already applies some of Wal-Mart's successful strategies (e.g. related to economics of scale and low prices). Of course, Wal-Mart is interested in other metrics beyond profit (e.g. shareholder wealth, market share), but, as indicated above, profitability and margins are of key concern to retailers.

Wal-Mart: strategic concept

Wal-Mart is the world's largest retailer with approximately 6,500 stores worldwide (Business 2006). The main feature of Wal-Mart's business model is to cut costs (continuously) and therefore offer lower prices than their competitors. For instance, Wal-Mart has introduced new logistical technologies such as radio-frequency identification (RFID) to optimize its logistic processes. RFID is an automatic identification method, relying on storing and remotely retrieving data using devices called RFID tags or transponders. Wal-Mart tries to minimize labor costs by offering minimal health care plans. Wal-Mart pressures its suppliers to cut costs, on a continuous basis. In brief, Wal-Mart's managers are constantly seeking out ways to cut costs, and some of their successes are passed on to shoppers, in terms of lower prices.

Wal-Mart's entry into the german market

In 1997, Wal-Mart acquired over 21 stores from the supermarket chain "Wertkauf." One year later, Wal-Mart bought an additional 74 stores from the supermarket chain "Interspar". As a result, Wal-Mart became the fourth biggest operator of supermarkets in Germany (Lebensmittelzeitung 2006). The objective was to expand to 500 stores in Germany. However, the number of stores never exceeded the 95 stores that were originally purchased in the first two years. Wal-Mart's position in the marketplace deteriorated over the years. In 2002, Wal-Mart had some financial difficulties due to a low turnover which resulted in the dismissal of some employees. At the end of 2006, Wal-Mart was bought out by "Metro", one of Germany's largest retail groups. Finally, Wal-Mart left the German market with a loss of one billion dollars before tax (Manager-Magazin 2006).

Mis-steps in the german market

In general, there are five key issues related to Wal-Mart's ultimate withdrawal from Germany: (a) market structure; (b) business model (these first two are discussed together here); c) cultural and communication; (d) politics and regulation; and (e) product/service failure. Each of these issues is discussed in turn. Note also that these five issues are highlighted in Table 11.

Market structure and business model

A retailer that wants to follow Wal-Mart's strategy of low prices needs to expand rapidly. In Germany, there not enough appropriate locations to support such expansion (see Table 11). As previously mentioned, Wal-Mart did not build their own stores but took over 21 existing "Wertkauf" supermarkets that had a totally different business model. The stores themselves were very small and had a limited range of goods. A related problem is that these stores were located far apart, which resulted in high logistical costs.

When entering a new market, it is important to anticipate competitors' reactions. In Germany, Wal-Mart's biggest competitor, Metro, wanted to expand their stores; at the same time, Metro wanted to prevent Wal-Mart from executing their expansion plans (Senge 2004). Many times, a product has to be deleted because the competition is too strong.

With the strategy of "Every day low prices," Wal-Mart is very successful in the United States and also in many other countries. In Germany, there is extreme competition in the retail food sector. Therefore, the German customer is quite accustomed to the low prices that are offered by numerous discount supermarket chains. For this reason, Wal-Mart's strategy of offering low prices did not create sufficient competitive advantage (see Table 11).

Culture and communication

When products are introduced, it is important to consider cultural factors. In this case, corporate culture played a key role. Wal-Mart's top executives decided to operate the German locations from their offices in the United Kingdom. Thus, Wal-Mart's "corporate language" was English. However, many of the older Wal-Mart managers in Germany do not speak English. As a result, there were often breakdowns in communication. Some managers of the acquired stores did not stay on after the Wal-Mart acquisition. Key business connections were lost. As a result, several key suppliers (e.g. Adidas, Samsonite, Nike) declined to work as suppliers for Wal-Mart. Wal-Mart did not just lose important suppliers; they also lost an important part of their range of goods (Senge 2004). The situation could have been improved by retaining and communicating effectively with the German managers who had know-how about the local market (see Table 11).

Politics and regulation

The managers of Wal-Mart were not sufficiently familiar with the laws and regulations in Germany, as they violated them several times. One of Wal-Mart's fundamental principles is to stay union free. However, in Germany, unions have a powerful position. Through collective bargaining and related tactics, they can have a strong influence on political decision making. Ver.di is a German union in the service sector. With 2.4 million members, it is one of the largest independent, trade unions in the world (Ver.di 2008).

According to the German Commercial Code, all incorporated companies are obligated to publish a financial statement, including a profit and loss statement. Due to the fact that Wal-Mart refused to publish their financial statements for the years 1999 and 2000, Ver.di sued in a court of law. Wal-Mart was sentenced to pay a fine. The coverage of this law suit in the German press led to a negative public image for Wal-Mart.

After the expansion strategy failed due to the lack of suitable store locations, Wal-Mart began a price war to drive small competitors out of business. The intention was to take over the stores of the insolvent supermarket chains and convert them into Wal-Mart stores. One part of the price war was to introduce a private label called "Smart Brand" and sell most of these products below manufacturing costs. The reaction of many competitors was to decrease their prices, which led to a profit setback for the entire industry. However, the Federal Cartel Office interceded and stopped the price war because there is a law in Germany that enjoins companies from selling goods below manufacturing costs on a continuing basis (Knorr and Arndt 2003).

Product/ service failure

Wal-Mart planned to introduce a sophisticated customer service program which threatened many of its competitors because German discount supermarket chains often do not provide good customer service. Therefore, good customer service, combined with low prices, could have been a new market niche in Germany. One part of Wal-Mart's customer service program was called the "ten foot rule". Every ten feet, a service employee offered some help to the customer (Knorr and Arndt 2003). However, the customer reaction was rather negative, because customers who normally do their grocery shopping in discount supermarket chains are used to self-service. They do not necessarily expect to talk with employees.

13. Adding products and services

Therefore, the "ten foot rule" was perceived as rather annoying and did not result in a reputation for providing good customer service.

Wal-Mart also imported the idea of placing a "greeter" at the entrance to the store. Again, German customers were not used to this custom, and they did not adopt this "service" with any enthusiasm.

Conclusion of Wal-Mart Mini-case

Wal-Mart tried to apply its US success formula in an unmodified manner to the German market. As a result, they didn't have sufficient knowledge about the market structure and key cultural / political issues. In addition, structural factors prevented Wal-Mart from fully implementing its successful business model. Also, there were some instances of product or service failure. The final outcome was that Wal-Mart had to abandon its offerings in Germany

Table 13: Product failure: examples from Wal-mart's investment in Germany

Reasons for Failure	Examples of Wal-Mart in Germany
Insufficient demand (MS / BM)	Wal-Mart's low price strategy didn't create any competitive advantage since many German local retailers were already using that strategy.
Existing competitors are too strong (MS)	Wal-Mart's biggest competitor, Metro, took specific counter-measures to prevent Wal-Mart from executing their expansion plan.
Failure to develop and communicate unique selling propositions (USP) (BM)	The profit margins in the German retail industry were already low before Wal-Mart entered. Wal-Mart was not able to convince German consumers that their prices were really that much lower than the competition.
Unexpected change in the environment— Economic downturn	N/A for Wal-Mart case
Competing new technology successfully introduced	N/A for Wal-Mart case
Change in culture (i.e. change in corporate culture, change in consumer taste or fashion) (C)	Wal-Mart did not adapt well to the German corporate culture.
Changing standard of government regulations (P)	Managers were not familiar with German laws and regulations, so there were violations. In general, Wal-Mart's anti-union policies conflicted with the strong German union. Wal-Mart also tried to sell their products below manufacturing costs, which is illegal in Germany.
The price is too high, so trial is discouraged	N/A for Wal-Mart case
Poor promotion/communication plan (C)	Language barrier between English-speaking managers and older German business people who don't

	speak English.
In retailing, failure to secure attractive sites (MS)	There were not enough appropriate locations for Wal-Mart stores available in Germany.
Product failure (PF)	tores were often located far apart. As a result, logistics costs were high. One of Wal-Mart's main success factors is to minimize costs, but this goal was restricted by high logistical costs.
Poor service quality—during or after sales (PF)	ome of Wal-Mart's methods for providing service were not accepted by German customers. For instance, the customers did not like the concept of the "greeter".
Failure to get corporation from key supply-chain members (BM)	Several key suppliers refused to supply goods, for fear of tarnishing their corporate image.

Notes for Table 4: The reasons for deletion are divided into five categories according to the following legend:

MS: Market structure; BM: Business model; C: Culture and communication; P: Politics and regulation; PF: Product failure

Chapter summary

New products improve people's lives, change markets, and affect theveryday world around us (Arts 2008). From an organizational point of view, successful new products are essential for the survival of a firm. At the same time, an organization must recognize when it is time to withdraw a product from the market. As shown in Figure 1, this withdrawal may take place after some years of success in the marketplace. Alternatively, such product deletion may occur before the product is even launched (see the section on "Evaluating Innovations"). Sometimes, clear and straightforward reasons exist to explain why consumers do not accept a new product. Other times, a clear answer is missing (Arts 2008). In this chapter, we highlight many of the key managerial decisions associated with adding and deleting products. We emphasize the important role of marketing research and market-based insights.

Discussion questions

➢ Discuss various ways to classify innovations and products. Describe how these classification schemes contribute to managerial knowledge and describe how they are related to the process of innovation.

➢ Using information from the Wal-Mart case that is discussed in the chapter, describe some decisions that management handled well.

➢ Suppose that you are in charge of expanding Wal-Mart's operations to France. Describe some actions that you would take to increase the probability of success in that nation.

➢ Your business partner comes to you with a new product idea. Specifically, she has just returned from a trip to the Netherlands. Based on her experiences there, she wants your company to start exporting a specialty beer (Gulpemer) from the Netherlands to the US. Your firm has specific expertise terms of distributing beer in the eastern United States, and you have some interest in your partner's idea. Describe how you would evaluate this idea of adding of Gulpemer to your product line.

➢ A reporter from the New York Times asks you to forecast which method of distributing popular music will be the most popular in the year 2014. Write a press release on this topic. Be certain to provide a justification for your prediction.

➢ Discuss five business models that are popular for distributing popular films. Predict which of these models will be the most successful, five years from now. Provide a convincing justification for your prediction.

➢ Your nephew is a drummer, and he has just formed an alternative rock band. His band is just beginning to achieve some local success in Seattle, Washington. Your nephew views you as a "new product expert", so he asks your advice about how to increase the popularity and profitability of his band's operations. Make five specific recommendations to help your nephew and to justify your reputation as "an expert".

➢ Table 4 provides a description of some reasons that new products fail. Add three more factors to this list.

➢ Discuss some different ways that firms try to develop innovations. For each method that you identify, provide a specific example of a product that was developed following this approach.

➢ Imagine that you want to start your own business. What product would sell? In two paragraphs, describe your business model.

Case: "Apples: Newton and Pippin"

Apple Inc. (formerly Apple Computer Inc.) was founded in 1976 by Steve Jobs, Steve Wozniak, and Ronald Wayne. Steve Jobs is still very active with the company.

Apple has a long history of adding successful new products to its line up. However, in some instances, Apple products have failed in the marketplace, and, subsequently, they were deleted. For instance, both the hand-held Newton and the gaming machine Pippin were dropped from the Apple lineup. See http://www.forbes.com/2008/10/29/apple-product-flops-tech-personal-cx_ag_1030apple.html.

Using this website and others, gather some information about the Newton and the Pippin. Then, using the information from this chapter (e.g. see Table 4), discuss some reasons that Newton and Pippin failed. To what extent did these two products fail for the same reasons? Identify one of Apple's successful products (e.g. the iPhone, the iPod) and describe how the product managers have been able to avoid some of the problems that sank the Newton and the Pippin.

References

Arts, Joep (2008), Essays on New Product Adoption and Diffusion, Amsterdam: the Free University.

Berkman Center (2003). "Copyright and Digital Media in a Post-Napster World," Research Publication No. 2003-05, GartnerG2 and The Berkman Center for Internet and Society at Harvard Law School. http://cyber.law.harvard.edu/publications.

Business (2006): "World's Biggest Retailer Wal-Mart Closes Up Shop in Germany" http://www.dw-world.de/dw/article/0,2144,2112746,00.html

Crask, M., Fox, R. J., and Stout, R. G. (1995). Marketing Research: Principles and Applications. Eaglewood Cliffs, NJ: Prentice Hall.

Frankfurter Rundschau (2007): "Ende einer Expansion" http://www.lexisnexis.de/e-solutions/academic/de/index.html, 08.01.2008.

Gourville, J.T. (2005), "The Curse of Innovation: Why Innovative New Products Fail," MSI Working Paper Series, 5 (4).

Gutowski, George (2006), "Lessons to be Learned from Walmart's Failure in Korea," Seeking Alpha (May 24), article 11141. http://seekingalpha.com/article/11141-lessons-to-be-learned-from-walmart-s-failure-in-korea-wmt

Hefflinger, Mark (2008), "Online India Music Retailer Acquired," Digital Media Wire, August 5.

Knorr, A; Arndt, A. (2003): "Wal-Mart in Deutschland – eine verfehlte Internationalisierungsstrategie," in: Knorr, A. et al. (Hrsg.): Materialien des Wissenschaftsschwerpunktes „Globalisierung der Weltwirtschaft," Band 25, Bremen 2003.

KPMG (2006): "Status quo und Perspektiven im deutschen Lebensmitteleinzelhandel" http://www.kpmg.de/library/pdf/060904_Status_quo_und_Perspektiven_im_deutschen_Lebensmittel einzelhandel_2006_de.pdf, 20.12.2007.

Lebensmittelzeitung (2006): "Wal-Mart in Deutschland – ein Überblick" http://www.lznet.de/links/hotlinks/pages/protected/show53679.html, 20.12.2007.

Lessig, Lawrence (2004), Free Culture: How Big Media Uses Technology and the

Law to Lock Down Culture and Control Creativity. New York: The Penguin Press.

Manager-Magazin (2006): "Metro übernimmt Wal-Mart Deutschland" http://www.managermagazin.de/unternehmen/artikel/0,2828,428960,00.html, 20.12.2007.

Margetta, J. (2002). What Management Is: How it Works and Why It's Everyone's Business. New York: Free Press.

Press@starbucks.com (2007), "Paul McCartney First Artist Signed to New Hear Music Label," Seattle, March 21,

http://www.starbucks.com/aboutus/pressdesc.asp?id=759

Romero, A. (2003), Cracker Barrel Old Country Store Creates New American Roots Record Label. Retrieved October 1, 2008, from World Music Central: http://worldmusiccentral.org/article.php/20031114174754471

Senge, K. (2004): "Der Fall Wal-Mart: Institutionelle Grenzen ökonomischer Globalisierung." http://www.wiso.unidortmund.de/is/dienst/de/textonly/content/V4/V42/pdf/ap-soz04.pdf,21.12.2007

Slater, D., Smith, M., Bambauer, D., Gasser, U., and Palfrey, J. (2005, July 7). Content and Control: Assessing the Impact of Policy Choices on Potential Online Business Models in the Music and Film Industries. Retrieved September 1, 2008, from The Berkman Center for Internet and Society: http://cyber.law.harvard.edu/

Souder, W. E. (1987). Managing new product innovations. Lexington, MA: D.C. Heath and Company.

Tellis, Gerry, Stephan Stremersch, and E. Yin (2003), "The International Takeoff of

New Products: The Role of Economics, Culture, and Country Innovativeness," Marketing Science, 22 (2), 188-208.

Tyrangiel, J. (2007), Radiohead says: Pay what you want. Retrieved August 15, 2008, from Time Entertainment: http://www.time.com/time/arts/article/0,8599,1666973,00.html

Ulrich, L., and McGuinn, R. (2000, July 1). Lars Ulrich, Roger McGuinn Testify Before Senate Judiciary Committee on Downloading Music on the Internet. (D. Kagen, Interviewer) CNN.

Urban, G. L. and Hauser, J. R. (1993). Design and Marketing of New Products (2nd ed.). Eaglewood Cliffs, NJ: Prentice Hall.

Verdi (2008) http://international.verdi.de/ver.di_fremdsprachig/was_ist_ver.di_-_eine_einfuehrung_auf_englisch

Zinkhan, George M. (2005), "Business Models, Advertising, and Emerging Technology," American Academy of Advertising Newsletter, 1 (No. 4), 4-5.Adding products and services

14. International business for the entrepreneur

Authors: Vlad Malamud, Yevgeniy Rotenberg

Editor: Douglas Allen

Reviewers: Dean Murray Young (Thompson Rivers University, Canada) Timothy B Folta (Purdue University)

Contributing authors: Wesley Scott Cables, Ricardo Cubillos, Mike Davis, Vesselin Dotkov, Loiuse Doyle, Barbara Gabhauer, Glenna Gagliardi, Melissa Harrison Hiatt, Katie Holtmeier, Alisa Jeffrey, Alexia Jennings, Tim Pitner, Ashley Randall, Dag Johan Sundby, Nathalie Tryon, Jeffrey Wiant, Sarah Wilson

Introduction

In Mastuj, a remote area in the Chitral district of Pakistan's North West Frontier Province, a young, recently divorced woman with three children feared that she would not be able to make ends meet. Tradition held that women should not work outside the home, further complicating her efforts to generate income.

Nevertheless, in 1998, she applied to the Aga Khan Rural Support Programme (AKRSP) for training in sewing. Soon after her course, she took out an AKRSP loan, which included business training, to buy a sewing machine. She then set up a business stitching and selling ready-made clothes.

As with all AKAM loans, the credit package included two types of micro-insurance: Rs. 100 (USD 1.60) for loan insurance that paid the outstanding balance in case of her death or permanent disability, and another policy that would ensure a Rs. 10,000 benefit for funeral-related costs in case of her accidental death. The micro-insurance shielded the woman's children from debt should she have suffered death or disability.

Exhibit 48: The credit package included two types of micro-insurance that has shielded the woman's children from debt should she have suffered debt and injury.

She has taken several other loans for machinery and material. Each time she has paid back her loan in full and on time. Her monthly income has risen over six-fold from Rs 1000 (USD 16) to Rs. 7000 (USD 120) in four years (2000-2004). She has been able to send her three children to a private school, extend her one room house, and set up a shop near the home. Hygiene and health have improved thanks to better food and the installation of a proper toilet. As of 2004, she had saved over Rs 30,000 (USD 500).

Perhaps most importantly, she has gone beyond subsistence to help those who are less fortunate than herself. She has hired six employees and conducts sewing classes for other women in the community. In 2004, in recognition of her efforts, Ms. Shahira was the recipient of the top prize in the United Nations Global Entrepreneurship Award for Pakistan.

For Ms. Shahira, globalization can play an important role in her business. With the success of her sewing company in her home country, Pakistan, she now has the opportunity to expand into new markets, partner with another company, and continue to grow her company as a whole. Conversely, globalization has negative implications for her company as well that include increased competition, and the risk of cultural issues that would lead to her company not succeeding in a new market. As an up-and-coming entrepreneur, Ms. Shahira must take into consideration all factors of globalization as she continues to operate her business.

For more information about this case, and others like it, visit the Aga Khan Agency for Microfinance website http://www.akdn.org.

Globalization: opportunities and threats to developing country business

To succeed in business today, it is critical to understand the changing global business world and the environment in which a business operates. Not only are entrepreneurs faced with the internal factors affecting their business, they must also understand the external environment in which they operate.

In the United States and Western Europe, globalization has been highly controversial and sparked protests driven by fears of outsourcing jobs, ceding authority to international organizations and declining labor and environmental standards. Views of globalization in lower income countries, however, are more positive. A recent Pew survey found that there was more enthusiasm for foreign trade and investment in less industrialized countries than in industrialized ones. In sub-Saharan Africa, 56% of respondents thought, "growing global trade and business ties are very good for my country (Dollar, 2003)." In developing countries in Asia, 37% had a positive view of globalization, while only 28% of respondents in the United States and Western Europe had such a view (Dollar, 2003). This section discusses the concept of globalization and its positive and negative implications for developing country business.

This chapter will utilize examples of large corporations, as these firms incorporate all necessary aspects required to run a successful business.

What is globalization?

Globalization is difficult to define because it has many dimensions—economic, political, cultural and environmental. The focus here is on the economic dimension of globalization. Economic globalization refers to the "quickly rising share of economic activity in the world [that] seems to be taking place between people in different countries" (World Bank Briefing Paper, 2001). More specifically, economic globalization is the result of the increasing integration of economies around the world, particularly through trade and financial flows and the movement of people and knowledge across international borders (IMF Issue Brief, 2000).

Case: United States Domestic Automaker, Ford

Nowhere are the effects of globalization seen more drastically than in the automobile industry, especially for the United States "Big 3" automakers: General Motors, Chrysler, and Ford.

Ford's history dates back to the Model T created by Henry Ford, with the goal of building a car for every family. Today, Ford is in dire competition with not only their domestic competitors, but also now foreign car manufacturers such as Toyota, Volkswagen and Hyundai.

At the current pace, the automotive market is approaching a 50/50 split between United States and overseas-based control of the US market. As a result, Ford is challenged to constantly reevaluate and revamp its market strategy. This is evident, as Ford decided that it was more cost-effective to buy existing networks than to start from scratch, by bringing Jaguar, Volvo, Mazda, Aston Martin and Land Rover under its control. However, Ford has recently decided to sell its stake in both Jaguar and Land Rover to the Indian automaker, Tata, and may divest other divisions as well.

Today, Ford faces a number of important questions. As the globalization of the auto industry continues, how should Ford market its vehicles? What target markets should Ford appeal to? How can it continue to improve production and quality and adhere to the needs of even more demanding customers? And, how should Ford position itself, as a company, in the face of formidable competition?

While the future of Ford is uncertain, one thing is clear, globalization will continue to affect the way domestic and foreign companies do business.

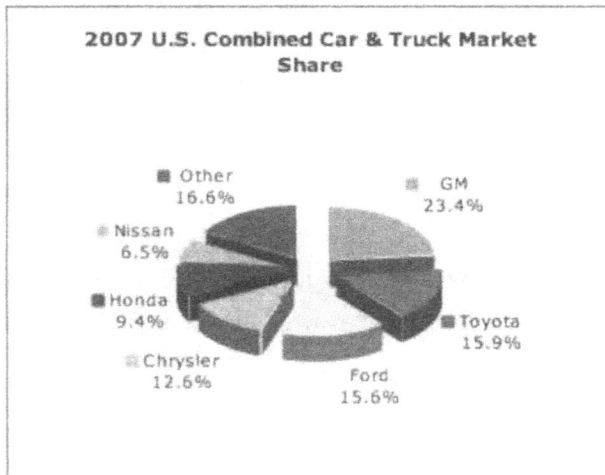

2007 U.S. Combined Car & Truck Market Share

- Other 16.6%
- GM 23.4%
- Nissan 6.5%
- Honda 9.4%
- Chrysler 12.6%
- Ford 15.6%
- Toyota 15.9%

Exhibit 49: Global Market Share, 2007-2008 (Edmunds.com, 2007)As this figure suggests, the "Big Three" must adapt to changes in the market and globalization factors to remain key players in the automotive market. At one point in 2007, for the first time in history, US automaker's share of their home market fell below 50 per cent.

Elements of economic globalization

The growth in cross-border economic activities takes five principal forms: (1) international trade; (2) foreign direct investment; (3) capital market flows; (4) migration (movement of labor); and (5) diffusion of technology (Stiglitz, 2003).

International yrade: An increasing share of spending on goods and services is devoted to imports and an increasing share of what countries produce is sold as exports. Between 1990 and 2001, the percentage of exports and imports in total economic output (GDP) rose from 32.3 per cent to 37.9 per cent in industrialized countries, and from 33.8 per cent to 48.9 per cent in low and middle-income countries (World Briefing Paper, 2001). In the 1980s, about 20 per cent of industrialized countries' exports went to less industrialized countries; today, this share has risen to about 25 per cent, and it appears likely to exceed 33 per cent by 2010 (Qureshi, 1996).

The importance of International trade lies at the root of a country's economy. In the constant changing business market, countries are now more interdependent than ever on their partners for exporting, importing, thereby keeping the home country's economy afloat and healthy. For example, China's economy is heavily dependent on the exportation of goods to the United States, and the United States customer base who will buy these products.

Foreign Direct Investment (FDI): According to the United Nations, FDI is defined as "investment made to acquire lasting interest in enterprises operating outside of the economy of the investor".

Direct investment in constructing production facilities, is distinguished from portfolio investment, which can take the form of short-term capital flows (e.g. loans), or long-term capital flows (e.g. bonds) (Stiglitz, 2003). Since 1980, global flows of foreign direct investment have more than doubled relative to GDP (World Briefing Paper, 2001).

Capital market flows: In many countries, particularly in the developed world, investors have increasingly diversified their portfolios to include foreign financial assets, such as international bonds, stocks or mutual funds, and borrowers have increasingly turned to foreign sources of funds (World Briefing, Paper, 2001). Capital market flows also include remittances from migration, which typically flow from industrialized to less industrialized countries. In essence, the entrepreneur has a number of sources for funding a business.

Migration: Whether it is physicians who emigrate from India and Pakistan to Great Britain or seasonal farm workers emigrating from Mexico to the United States, labor is increasingly mobile. Migration can benefit developing economies when migrants who acquired education and know-how abroad return home to establish new enterprises. However, migration can also hurt the economy through "brain drain", the loss of skilled workers who are essential for economic growth (Stiglitz, 2003).

Diffusion of technology: Innovations in telecommunications, information technology, and computing have lowered communication costs and facilitated the cross-border flow of ideas, including technical knowledge as well as more fundamental concepts such as democracy and free markets (Stiglitz, 2003). The rapid growth and adoption of information technology, however, is not evenly distributed around the world—this gap between the information technology is often referred to as the "digital divide".

As a result, for less industrialized countries this means it is more difficult to advance their businesses without the technical system and knowledge in place such as the Internet, data tracking, and technical resources already existing in many industrialized countries.

Negative effects of globalization for developing country business

Critics of global economic integration warn that (Watkins, 2002, Yusuf, 2001):

- the growth of international trade is exacerbating income inequalities, both between and within industrialized and less industrialized nations

- global commerce is increasingly dominated by transnational corporations which seek to maximize profits without regard for the development needs of individual countries or the local populations

- protectionist policies in industrialized countries prevent many producers in the Third World from accessing export markets;

- the volume and volatility of capital flows increases the risks of banking and currency crises, especially in countries with weak financial institutions

- competition among developing countries to attract foreign investment leads to a "race to the bottom" in which countries dangerously lower environmental standards

- cultural uniqueness is lost in favor of homogenization and a "universal culture" that draws heavily from American culture

Critics of economic integration often point to Latin America as an example where increased openness to international trade had a negative economic effect. Many governments in Latin America (e.g. Peru) liberalized imports far more rapidly than in other regions. In much of Latin America, import liberalization has been credited with increasing the number of people living below the USD \$1 a day poverty line and has perpetuated already existing inequalities (Watkins, 2002).

Positive effects of globalization for developing country business

Conversely, globalization can create new opportunities, new ideas, and open new markets that an entrepreneur may have not had in their home country. As a result, there are a number of positives associated with globalization:

- it creates greater opportunities for firms in less industrialized countries to tap into more and larger markets around the world

- this can lead to more access to capital flows, technology, human capital, cheaper imports and larger export markets

- it allows businesses in less industrialized countries to become part of international production networks and supply chains that are the main conduits of trade

For example, the experience of the East Asian economies demonstrates the positive effect of globalization on economic growth and shows that at least under some circumstances globalization decreases poverty. The spectacular growth in East Asia, which increased GDP per capita by eightfold and raised millions of people out of poverty, was based largely on globalization—export-led growth and closing the technology gap with industrialized countries (Stiglitz, 2003). Generally, economies that globalize have higher growth rates than non-globalizers (Bhagwati and Srinivasan, 2002).

Also, the role of developing country firms in the value chain is becoming increasingly sophisticated as these firms expand beyond manufacturing into services. For example, it is now commonplace for businesses in industrialized countries to outsource functions such as data processing, customer service and reading x-rays to India and other less industrialized countries (Bhagwati et al, 2004). Advanced telecommunications and the Internet are facilitating the transfer of these service jobs from industrialized to less industrialized and making it easier and cheaper for less industrialized country firms to enter global markets. In addition to bringing in capital, outsourcing helps prevent "brain drain" because skilled workers may choose to remain in their home country rather than having to migrate to an industrialized country to find work.

Further, some of the allegations made by critics of globalization are very much in dispute—for example, that globalization necessarily leads to growing income inequality or harm to the environment. While there are some countries in which economic integration has led to increased inequality—China, for instance—there is no worldwide trend (Dollar, 2003). With regard to the environment, international trade and foreign direct investment can provide less industrialized countries with the incentive to adopt, and the access to, new technologies that may be more ecologically sound (World Bank Briefing Paper, 2001). Transnational corporations may also help the environment by exporting higher standards and best practices to less industrialized countries.

C.K. Prahalad and Stuart L. Hart have suggested that the four billion people in the world whose per capita income is less than U.S. $1500 (the people "at the bottom of the pyramid") represent an enormous opportunity for business. Their theory is that the poor in developing countries comprise a vast, untapped market for goods and services, including basic needs as well as more advanced offerings such as financial services, cellular telephones and inexpensive computers.

An example of a successful business that services this market is the Grameen Bank Ltd. in Bangladesh. Founded by Nobel Prize winner Muhammad Yunus, Grameen Bank extends small loans ("micro-credit") to low-income customers. Grameen Bank charges high interest rates of approximately 20% a year, but does not require collateral, which enables even the very poor to obtain credit and gain an opportunity to participate in the formal economy. Grameen Bank's success has stimulated interest in micro-credit around the world.

Although Prahalad and Hart mostly discuss "the bottom of the pyramid" as a potential market for transnational corporations ("TNCs") based in developed countries, this market also offers opportunities to businesses in developing countries. These firms, either alone or in partnership with TNCs, can use their understanding of the needs, and obstacles faced by, the poor to create sustainable enterprises, which will have the added benefit of helping to alleviate poverty.

Exhibit 50: The fortune at the bottom of the pyramid (Prahalad and Stuart)

Globalization and the small business entrepreneur

As the case in the beginning of this chapter demonstrates there are economic, social, and political factors an entrepreneur faces when establishing their business. This chapter will utilize this case, and many others like it, to show how business leaders like Ms. Shahira can incorporate the topics covered in the following pages into their business.

Harnessing technology for global business success

Over the last decade, the Internet has revolutionized the way companies do business. For an entrepreneur, the Internet is a great tool for doing business both internationally and domestically. Information about competitors, market trends, and global industries is also easily accessible and can help determine the path that an organization takes.

Exhibit 51: Technology has become a critical aspect of a company's operating environment.

Types of technology

Internet

The Internet is one of the most cost effective ways to promote products and services around the world. No other advertising medium reaches as many people as the Internet. Using specialized software and other tools, it is now easier than ever to build and run a successful website without a high level of computer skills. Typical information found on a company's website includes a description of the firm, a profile of the management team, products and services offered, and the way customers can contact the company.

Phone, Fax and SMS

Companies in less industrialized countries may not have viable access to the Internet due to a lack of infrastructure. For entrepreneurs facing this issue, phone, fax and SMS text messages are alternative ways in which to do business. Doing business via phone and fax is not difficult. Companies can send marketing materials or receive orders via fax. The use of phone for marketing and sales options is also very useful. Cold calls for marketing are still effective; likewise orders can be made and received over the telephone. Sending and receiving SMS text messages is rapidly becoming a feasible alternative and allows for immediate communication.

Technology for the business entrepreneur

There are multiple ways to implement and leverage technology into a business. If Ms. Shahira chooses to do this, there are inexpensive alternatives with growing benefits for her and her company. By using new techniques to run and establish her business, Ms. Shahira would be able to compete on a greater scale with companies in her industry.

Doing business across cultures

While many similarities exist among businesses, there are dynamics that must be taken into consideration in an increasingly global environment, such as multicultural employees and varying experiences in countries outside that of the business. It is essential to take these differences seriously and not assume that individuals have similar values.

Host country research and cultural implications

Cultural issues can be divided into two categories, explicit and implicit. Explicit culture issues are related to characteristics that one can see or perceive. Implicit culture issues, on the other hand, are related to attitudes and values, symbolized in the figure below.

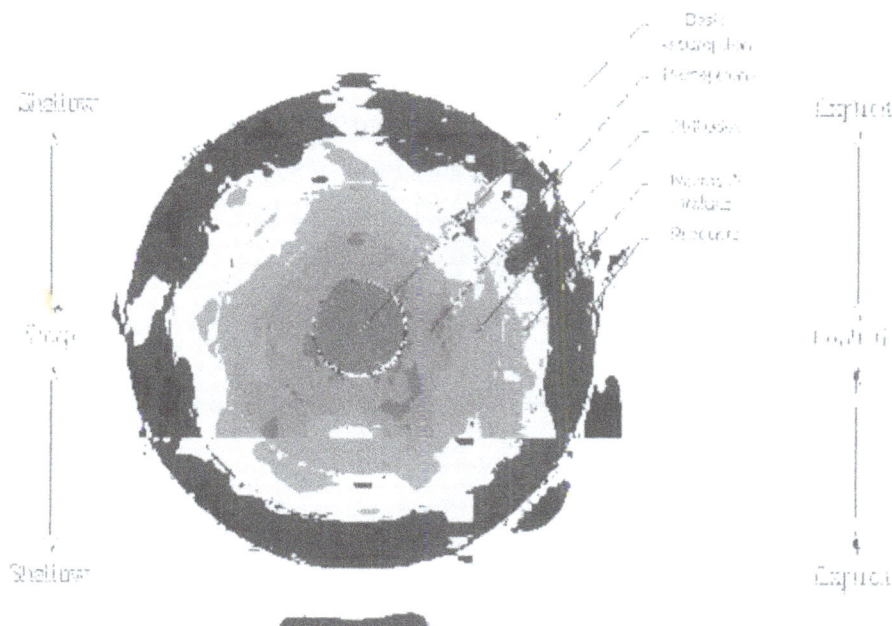

Exhibit 52: The Onion Metaphor of Culture (Ulijn and Fayolle, 2004)

Explicit culture exists on the outer layer and is the observable reality of the language, food, buildings, houses, monuments, agriculture, shrines, markets, fashions and art. These products are visible in people's behaviors, clothes, food, music and theater.

The middle layers include norms, values, and attitudes but are not directly visible. Norms are the mutual sense a group has of what is right and wrong that can develop on a formal level such as written law, or on an informal level such as social control. Values determine good from bad, and are closely related to the ideals shared by a group. A value in one culture may differ vastly from that of another, and therefore these differences must be studied and taken into consideration when doing business across cultures.

Cross-culture training

The creation of a stable and healthy workplace made up of people of varying cultural backgrounds is a matter of increasing importance in the global business environment. Employers must take into consideration the impact cultural diversity can have on both the homogeneity of the workplace and potential legal implications for improper discrimination.

The objective of training programs is to foster the four characteristics of preparedness, sensitivity, patience, and flexibility in managers and other personnel (Czinkota et al, 2005). Methods of training may range from factual preparation involving books and lectures to experiential training involving simulations and field experience. Some topics to be addressed in training might be, but are not limited to:

- comfort levels of trainees' with people of a different background

- impact of trainees' behaviors on others

- understanding stereotypes

- transforming knowledge into empathy

- embracing diversity as a source of strength

- learning a new language

Businesses with diverse cultural backgrounds must maintain an environment suited for every constituent so that the objectives of the business can be efficiently met. Installing cultural diversity training programs can help accomplish this by defining what cultural intelligence is, teaching employees to accept and work effectively with others from different cultural backgrounds, and taking advantage of advice from those who have cross-cultural experience.

Cultural classification

Cultures can either be distinguished according to descriptive characteristics or they can be broken up into value categories, which are essentially dimensions of national culture.

Hofstede's Five dimensions of national culture

Geert Hofstede, a leading expert in cultural values classification, developed a model of five dimensions of natural culture that help to explain basic value differences in culture. The model distinguishes cultures according to the following five different dimensions:

- Power distance

- Individualism/collectivism

- Masculinity/femininity

- Uncertainty avoidance

- Long-term orientation

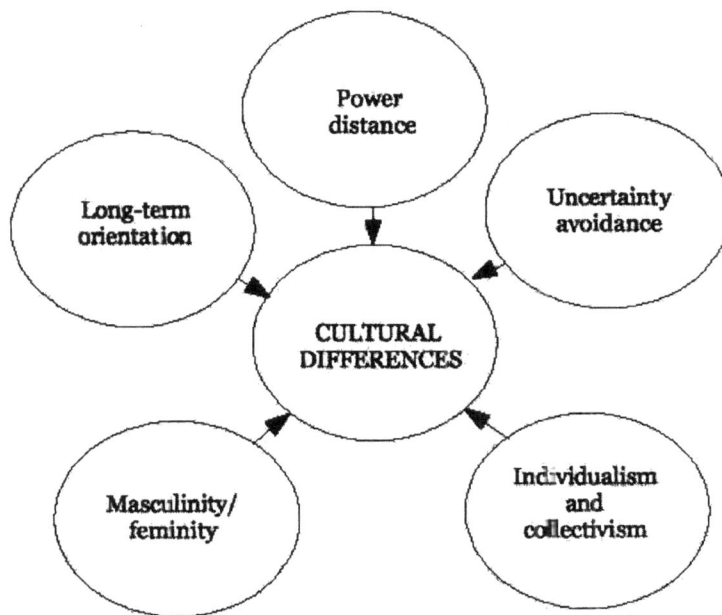

Exhibit 53: Hofstede's five cultural dimensions

Hofstede's 5 Cultural Dimensions

The Power Distance Index (PDI) focuses on the degree of equality, or inequality, between people in the country's society. The Individualism (IDV) focuses on the degree the society reinforces individual or collective, achievement and interpersonal relationships. The Masculinity (MAS) focuses on the degree the society reinforces, or does not reinforce, the traditional masculine work role model of male achievement, control, and power. The Uncertainty Avoidance Index (UAI) focuses on the level of tolerance for uncertainty and ambiguity within the society. These dimensions are measured on a scale from 0 to 100, include 75 countries or regions, and scores are determined by "high" or "low" rankings within each category.

Cultural values determine the way people think and behave. International marketers must understand many subtle differences that may affect the way their marketing is made and perceived in foreign markets. One medium in which many such differences reside is language. Because language is a reflection of culture, some words cannot be cross-culturally translated, which implies that it is often better to have local copywriters write and translate marketing and advertising content to avoid cultural misunderstandings. Because of this phenomenon, global advertising, which is a main component of global marketing, often relies on symbol recognition to convey meaning in their ads, instead of words.

The approach to discussing culture, as it relates to global marketing, in most textbooks is a three-pronged approach. First, the concept of culture is defined, second, the various components of culture are identified, and third, vivid examples of cultural differences are provided. The dire consequences of firms not taking these differences into account are invariably described, as adherence to local culture is considered one of the most important, if not the most important, components of success in international marketing (Hofstede, 1996).

Ethical considerations

Managers of businesses that conduct operations in an increasingly global environment face a dilemma when selecting and applying ethics to decisions in cross-cultural settings. Although ethical values may be similar across cultures in many cases, the application of those values to certain situations may vary. Ethics can be described as the science of human duty. It is upon the ethical standards of a person that judges whether or not an action is right or wrong.

Before a company does business across borders, it must first decide what its motivation is regarding ethical conduct, which will determine what kind of behavior is to be expected from employees.

Political and legal risk in international business

Political and legal risks are two very important aspects of running a business of which an entrepreneur should be aware. Failure to recognize these risks and adjust accordingly could potentially hinder the performance of the overall business.

What is political risk?

Political risk is generally defined as the risk to business interests resulting from political instability or political change. Political risk exists in every country around the globe and varies in magnitude and type from country to country. Political risks may arise from policy changes by governments to change controls imposed on exchange rates and interest rates (Barlett et al, 2004). Moreover, political risk may be caused by actions of legitimate governments such as controls on prices, outputs, activities, and currency and remittance restrictions. Political risk may also result from events outside of government controls such as war, revolution, terrorism, labor strikes, and extortion.

Political risk can adversely affect all aspects of international business from the right to export or import goods to the right to own or operate a business. AON (www.aon.com), for example, categorizes risk based on economic; exchange transfer; strike, riot, or civil commotion; war; terrorism; sovereign non-payment; legal and regulatory; political interference; and supply chain vulnerability.

How to evaluate your level of political risk
Forms of investment and risk

For a firm considering a new foreign market, there are three broad categories of international business: trade, international licensing of technology and intellectual property, and foreign direct investment. A company developing a business plan may have different elements of all three categories depending on the type of product or service.

The choice of entry depends on the firm's experience, the nature of its product or services, capital resources, and the amount of risk it's willing to consider (Schaffer et al, 2005). The risk between these three categories of market entry varies significantly with trade ranked the least risky if the company does not have offices overseas and does not keep inventories there. On the other side of the spectrum is direct foreign investment, which generally brings the greatest economic exposure and thus the greatest risk to the company.

Protection from political risk

Companies can reduce their exposure to political risk by careful planning and monitoring political developments. The company should have a deep understanding of domestic and international affairs for the country they are considering entering. The company should know how politically stable the country is, strength of its institutions, existence of any political or religious conflicts, ethnic composition, and minority rights. The country's standing in the international arena should also be part of the consideration; this includes its relations with neighbors, border disputes, membership in international organizations, and recognition of international law. If the company does not have the resources to conduct such research and analysis, it may find such information at their foreign embassies, international chambers of commerce, political risk consulting firms, insurance companies, and from international businessmen familiar with a particular region. In some countries, the governments will establish agencies to help private businesses grow overseas. Governments may also offer political risk insurance to promote exports or economic development. Private businesses may also purchase political risk insurance from insurance companies specialized in international business. Insurance companies offering political risk insurance will generally provide coverage against inconvertibility, expropriation and political violence, including civil strife (US Small Business Administration). Careful planning and vigilance should be part of any company's preparation for developing an international presence.

Government policy changes and trade relations

A government makes changes in policies that have an impact on international business. Many reasons may cause governments to change their policies toward foreign enterprises. High unemployment, widespread poverty, nationalistic pressure, and political unrest are just a few of the reasons that can lead to changes in policy. Changes in policies can impose more restrictions on foreign companies to operate or limit their access to financing and trade. In some cases, changes in policy may be favorable to foreign businesses as well.

To solve domestic problems, governments often use trade relations. Trade as a political tool may cause an international business to be caught in a trade war or embargo (Schaffer et al, 2005). As a result, international business can experience frequent change in regulations and policies, which can add additional costs of doing business overseas.

China establishes a new employment contract law for 2008 (<u>www.aon.com</u>)

In an effort to promote better employment relationships between employers and employees, and establish stricter guidelines for Employment practices, the Peoples Republic of China (PRC) passed a new employment contract law in June 2007 which became effective on January 1, 2008. This Alert provides highlights of the new law and the effect it will have on employees' rights and their employer's legal liability.

Introduction

On June 29, 2007 at the 28th session of the standing committee of the 10th National People's Congress, a new employment contract law was adopted which took take effect on 1 Jauary 2008. This law requires all employers to enter into contracts with their employees within 30 days of full-time employment and sets out guidelines for their implementation. By incorporating new legal provisions with existing laws from the current PRC labor law, the committee hopes to meet three main objectives: (1) to clarify the employment contract system by clearly identifying both the employer and the employee litigation rights and duties (2) provide protection of an employee's legitimate rights and interests and (3) construct and develop harmonious/stable work relations. All regulations that affect employees such as compensation, work hours, rest, leave, work safety and hygiene, insurance, benefits, employee training, work discipline or work quota management must be approved by the employee representative congress or by all the employees and determined with a trade union (to be established by all employers) or employee representatives. Rules, regulations and decisions having a direct bearing on employees shall be made public or be communicated to the employees by the employer. The labor administration authorities of People's Governments at the county level and above, together with the trade union and enterprise representatives will establish a comprehensive tri-partite mechanism for the coordination of employment relationships. The trade union will also assist employees with employment contracts in accordance with the law.

Increased Legal Liability

Employers

Certain articles in the new law will establish increased legal liability and possible criminal charges for employers whose actions cause an employee to suffer harm, such as:

1. An employer's internal rules or regulations violate the laws.

2. An employment contract is not delivered to an employee or lacks any of the mandatory clauses which the law requires.

3. An employee's resident ID cards, files or contract papers are retained by an employer illegally or the employer collects an unrequired financial guarantee from an employee.

4. An employer uses violence or threats to compel an employee to work, orders them to perform dangerous operations or provides an unsafe or polluted environment resulting in harm.

5. An employer conducts business without the required legal qualifications.

6. An employer terminates a contract in violation of the law.

Employees

Employees that terminate a contract in violation of the Law or breach any confidentiality obligations or competition restrictions stipulated in the contract can be held liable for damages sustained by the other party.

Joint Liability for Employers/Employees and/or Third Parties

1. If an employer hires an employee whose contract with another employer has not yet been terminated or ended, causing the other employer to suffer a loss, it shall be jointly and severally liable with the employee for damages.

2. A staffing firm that violates the law may be subject to fines and have their business license revoked. If the employee(s) they placed suffers harm as a result, both the staffing firm and company that accepted the employee shall be jointly and severally liable for damages.

3. A contractor hiring employees in violation of the law who suffer harm will result in joint liability for the organization that employed such contractor and the contractor.

4. Negligence on the part of a labor administration authority to act in accordance with the law will also result in them bearing liability.

Penalties for an Employer's Non-Compliance

Within the new law there are financial penalties for non-compliance with the terms of employer/employee contract guidelines, which include failure to conclude a written contract within the 30 day period, setting an illegal probationary period, illegally retaining an employee's resident ID card or other papers, etc. An employer that fails to pay an employee his salary, pays below the local minimum wage rate, fails to pay overtime or terminates a contract without paying the employee severance or without cause will also pay varying damages as stipulated in the new law.

Summary

The new employment contract law will enhance employees' rights in striving for better employment terms and working conditions. Therefore, all companies, including foreign companies who have invested in local subsidiary or representative offices in the PRC should re-examine their local and master directors' and officers' liability policies, as well as any employer's liability exposures and relevant local or global policies. Although the level of compliance and the degree to which the new law will be enforced is not yet known, it is important to be fully prepared for a 1 January 2008, not only by reviewing all employment contracts, employee handbooks and internal guidelines, but also by taking stock of any subcontracting agreements or the use of staffing companies and their policies.

Questions

How can the establishment of China's new employment contract benefit other countries that are looking to institute a new law like this one? How would this affect countries trading with China today? How will this new employment contract affect companies doing business in China?

What is legal risk?

Legal risk is the risk arising from failure to comply with statutory or regulatory obligations (http://www.ffiec.gov).

Generally, all laws in the host country will apply to an entrepreneur's local business operations. Examples include filing procedures, employment law, environmental law, tax law, and ownership requirements. The World Bank has a rather extensive country business law library which can be accessed from their website. This can be helpful in the initial phases of considering the legal ramifications of direct investment in a given country.

Many countries limit foreign ownership of assets and legally force foreign companies into a joint venture with a local partner in order to do business there. Poland, for example, limits foreign ownership of farmland and will continue to do so for another decade under agreements with the EU (Dadak, 2004).

It is important to remember that while doing business outside of the home country certain home country laws will still apply. Applicable laws differ from country to country, but one common extension is employment law.

The extent of jurisdiction beyond national boundaries varies widely. In anti-trust for instance, the United States law covers only situations where the violation affects the US, (meaning that it does not matter where the act causing the violation took place), while the EU considers only where the antitrust offense was implemented (Shaffer et al., 2005, pgs 657-664).

In order to minimize exposure to legal risks arising from confusion and excess cost, a company should seek legal advice if possible. In making such arrangements, written contracts should be used. This can minimize confusion in case of litigation.

Political and legal risk for the small business entrepreneur

While Ms. Shahira may be accustomed to a certain set of rules and regulations in her home country of Pakistan, she must anticipate new and other laws when exploring the possibility of expanding internationally. While Ms. Shahira and her small business of running a sewing company faces different political and legal risk than those of a larger company, she is still liable and must understand the laws and regulations that she may face in any country.

Global marketing: assessing potential markets overseas

Case: Toyota has a vehicle for every market

Each market has unique cultural characteristics and contextual circumstances that must be considered. For example, in the United States roads tend to be wide; highways can accommodate a broad array of vehicles with a high number of lanes, and people demand a mix of cars based on their needs. Conversely, in Europe roads tend to be narrow, and the market demands smaller, more fuel-efficient vehicles. Therefore, while a Toyota 4Runner tends to sell extremely well in the United States, it would not be a very popular model in Europe for these very reasons. As a result, Toyota invests billions of dollars every year into market research and market development to make sure they meet the needs and wants of its customers, in each specific country that they sell their vehicles in. This has led to Toyota's success in the US automotive market, as our earlier case suggested. With their #1 selling sedan, Toyota Camry, a wide array of hybrid models, trucks and SUVs to meet the United States constantly-changing expectations, Toyota is, arguably, the strongest player in the automotive industry.

What is global marketing?

One of the inevitable questions that surfaces concerning global marketing is: how does global marketing truly differ from domestic marketing, if at all? There has historically been much discussion over commonalities and differences between global and domestic marketing, but the three most common points of view upon which scholars agree are the following. First, all marketing is about the formulation and implementation of the basic policies known as the 4 P's: Product, Price, Place, and Promotion. Second, international marketing, unlike domestic marketing, is understood to be carried out "across borders". Third, international marketing is not synonymous with international trade (Perry, 1990). Perhaps the best way to distinguish between the two is simply to focus on the textbook definition of international marketing. One comprehensive definition states that, "international marketing means identifying needs and wants of customers in different markets and cultures, providing products, services, technologies, and ideas to give the firm a competitive marketing advantage, communicating information about these products and services and distributing and exchanging them internationally through one or a combination of foreign market entry modes (Bradley, 2005)".

The 4 P'S of the Marketing Mix (NetMBA, 2008)

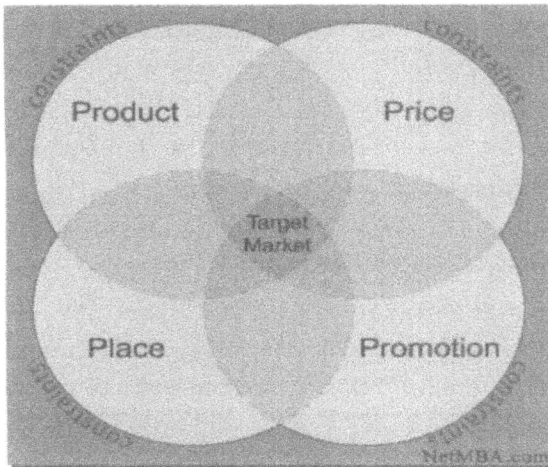

Exhibit 54: he 4 P'S: Product, Price, Place and Promotion are aspects of the marketing mix that are generally controllable

As the following table demonstrates, many decisions affect the marketing mix (NetMBA, 2008):

Table 14: All of these issues must be reconsidered in each market. The marketing mix will appropriately vary as different circumstances dictate.

Product Decisions	Price Decisions
Brand Name	Pricing strategy (price skimming, price penetration, etc.)
Functionality	
Styling	Volume discounting and wholesale pricing
Quality	Seasonal pricing
Safety	Bundling

Packaging Repairs and Support Warranty Accessories and services	Price flexibility Price discrimination
Place Decisions Distribution Channels Market coverage (inclusive, selective, or exclusive distribution) Inventory Management Warehousing Order processing Reverse logistics	Promotions Decisions Push, Pull Strategies Advertising Personal Selling Sales Promotions Public Relations and Publicity

Importance of culture on markets

Because international marketing is closely correlated to the cultures in which a firm wishes to sell its product, culture itself must be analyzed to understand the best way to integrate into both existing and emerging foreign markets. There are five essential areas within which culture must be continually studied in order to achieve success in dealing with culture as it affects international marketing.

These are (Tian, 2008):

- culture impacts on marketing (international versus domestic)
- cross-cultural dimensions of marketing research
- cross-cultural aspects of marketing mix (products, price, promotion, and place)
- cross-cultural marketing education and professional training
- and cross-cultural practice in electronic marketing

Cross-cultural marketing occurs when a consumer's culture differs from that of the marketer's own culture.

Consumer behavior diverges across country lines with increased wealth, globalization, and technology; it does not converge (De Mooij, 2005). This simple fact proves the importance of culture knowledge in cross-cultural marketing endeavors. In fact, the importance of cross-cultural study has inspired a definition separate from that of international marketing. Cross-cultural marketing is defined as the strategic process of marketing among consumers whose culture differs from that of the marketer's own culture at least in one of the fundamental cultural aspects, such as language, religion, social norms and values, education, and the living style (Tian, 2008).

A standardized marketing model utilizes the same functions in all markets. Conversely, a customized marketing strategy adheres to the needs and wants of a particular target market.

Global branding—creation of a marketing strategy

An important decision that international marketers must make is whether to utilize standardized marketing, treating all markets in the same manner, or customized marketing, adhering to local customs and traditions for greater effectiveness. This is an important distinction when analyzing the creation, perception, and trends in global branding. In most countries and cultures, marketers do not compete with individual products, but rather with competing brands markets. Many writers have reasoned that a standardized approach to international markets is the most desirable strategy. The main arguments include that sales will increase when a company can market a consistent product image across different geographical markets, and that cost can be reduced through the formulation and implementation of a single standardized marketing plan. Still others argue that because few markets are comparable across country lines, it is necessary to adapt the marketing mix to ensure that sufficient customization exists to satisfy consumer needs in each market. Additionally, not all companies are able to adopt a standardized strategy as its appropriateness varies from industry to industry. One must remember that even within markets there is great diversity of behavior and taste. In the face of intensely increasing competition and globalization, studies show that people increasingly prefer brands with roots in their national or regional tradition. This would indicate that most firms should lean towards marketing customization in order to satisfy the increasingly nationalistic consumption tendencies of their consumers (Bradley, 2005).

Global marketing and the small business entrepreneur

While marketing the products of the highly successful sewing company that Ms. Shahira has started in Pakistan may not be something that she is looking to do today, it is critical for her, and small businesses like the one she has set up, to understand what it would take to market to a completely different set of clients, in a new country.

Companies like Toyota and Coca-Cola have created a dominant brand across the world with their global branding and positioning strategies, and as a result have sustained tremendous financial benefits from doing so.

Global finance: initial considerations

As the global economy has become more integrated, every company and individual is affected by the developments of the markets and the economies of countries other than their own. Entrepreneurs willing to venture into the global financial marketplace may find lower-cost financing alternatives than are available in their home country. They may also want to obtain financing in the local markets they choose to serve. As a result, with constant economic changes, and fluctuations in the marketplace, along with trade barriers being lowered around the world, the entrepreneurs of tomorrow cannot limit their finance knowledge to just their home country, but can be open to looking at alternative sources to fund their business operations. Entrepreneurs will find that understanding the functioning of the global financial marketplace is a key element of their knowledge and skill base, and a key aspect of furthering their business.

International currency market

Exchange rates

The price of one country's currency in units of another country's currency is known as a foreign currency exchange rate. Exchange rates can be quoted in two ways. One way, known as a direct quote, is to state the number of domestic units of currency per one unit of foreign currency. If an exchange rate is an indirect quote, the exchange rate is stated as the number of foreign units per one unit of domestic currency (Beenhakker, 2001).

For a US company trading US dollars ($) for Swiss Francs (CHF)	
Direct Quote	$0.75/CHF
Indirect Quote	CHF1.25/$

Exhibit 55: Indirect quote example

Foreign exchange market

The foreign exchange (Forex) market is the mechanism, which facilitates the purchase and the sale of foreign currencies. The Forex is a financial market where the participants exchange one monetary unit for another currency. The market operates continuously, 24 hours a day, because a financial center is always open somewhere in the world. The interconnection of the markets makes continuous trading possible (Carrada-Bravo, 2003).

The foreign exchange market is generally divided into five basic currency markets based on pricing procedures ruling the exchange, the time to maturity, the degree of freedom available, the convertibility of currencies, and how the currencies are quoted (Carrada-Bravo, 2003).

In addition, the foreign exchange market is one of the most traded and liquid instruments in the financial world, and serves as a barometer of broader financial market conditions and risk appetite.

Introduction to currency risk

Currency risk is the potential consequence from an adverse movement in foreign exchange rates (Coyle, 2000). Organizations are exposed to currency risk when involved, directly or indirectly, in international trade and finance. Currency risk arises because exchange rates are volatile in the short and the long-term and the future movements of exchange rates cannot be predicted. Companies will as a result suffer losses due to adverse exchange rate movements when exposed to foreign currencies (Coyle, 2000).

Hedging is the term used to describe the actions that reduce or eliminate an exposure to risk (Coyle, 2000). Common ways of hedging currency risk involve:

- transferring the risk to your trading partner by placing the transaction in your domestic currency

- structurally hedging your risk by off setting income against expenditure in the same currency

- purchasing derivatives in the foreign exchange market (Coyle, 2000)

Introduction to derivatives

A financial derivative is a financial instrument where the price is derived from the value of an underlying asset often used to manage risk exposure. There are three classes of derivatives.

Futures: A futures contract is a "commitment to exchange a specified amount of one asset for a specified amount of another asset at a specified time in the future" (Butler, 2003).

Options: An options contract "gives the option holder the right to buy or sell an underlying asset at a specified price and on a specified date" (Butler, 2003).

Swaps: A swap is an "agreement to exchange two liabilities (or assets) and, after a prearranged length of time, to re-exchange the liabilities (or assets)" (Butler, 2003).

Financial derivatives are a very complex system of agreements. It is wise to consult a banking professional for advice on how to implement.

International accounting standards board

The International Accounting Standards Committee (IASC) Foundation, formed in March 2001, is the parent body of the International Accounting Standards Board (IASB). The IASB, formed on April 1, 2001, has assumed accounting standard-setting responsibilities from its predecessor body, the IASC (International Accounting Standard Boards: About Us, n.d.).

The objectives of the IASB are:

- To develop, in the public interest, a single set of high quality, understandable and enforceable global accounting standards

- To help participants in the world's capital markets and other users make economic decisions by having access to high quality, transparent, and comparable information

- To promote the use and vigorous application of those standards

- To bring about convergence of national accounting standards and international accounting standards to high quality solutions (Hussey, 2005).

Exhibit 56: The way the IASB functions
(www.iasb.org)

Even though the IASB standards are not enforced internationally at this time, the standards are quickly being processed. Therefore, a company looking to go international should abide by IASB standards.

Global finance and the small business entrepreneur

With the Aga Khan Rural Support Programme (AKRSP) micro-loan, Ms. Shahira has begun to venture into the global financial marketplace. While the funding from the loan was sufficient for Ms. Shahira's small business at the time, upon expansion, she will require additional sources of capital. Understanding the home country's financial system, and the alternative funding sources available abroad, is a key element of furthering her sewing company.

Organizational structure and human resources management

One of the fundamental challenges facing companies of all sizes is determining how to organize and staff their operations. This task becomes even more complex when a company decides to do business across national borders.

A small business owner may start out as the only employee in his or her company. In this case organization and staffing simply involves the efficient allocation of the owner's time and attention to the various tasks associated with the business. As the company grows, more employees will probably be hired. When this occurs, it is useful to explicitly look at how tasks can be allocated across employees in a systematic way. As the company grows still larger, it is often useful to begin organizing the company into departments.

In many cases, a company's early moves overseas involve reacting to an apparently random or unexpected overseas business opportunity. At first, such business may be conducted anywhere in the organization on an ad hoc basis. As a company extends its operations overseas, it takes on additional complexity as decisions have to be made which address global and local product design, local responsiveness to individual markets, cross-border financing, etc. As the international side of the business grows, many companies conclude that a reorganization of some type can better handle the current international business demands, and better position the company to take full advantage of international opportunities as they arise. In the following section, several common international organization structures are briefly described.

International division

Perhaps the simplest start for many organizations is to adopt what is known as an international division. With the addition of an international division, the domestic organization may remain relatively unchanged while an additional side structure is added. This additional structure (in collaboration with the domestic structure) takes on the responsibility for virtually all international business. This structure assumes that there are skills associated with doing business overseas that will transcend the typical business lines. Market assessments, compliance with export/import regulations, arranging shipping, identification of local representatives, establishment of dedicated sales offices, production facilities, etc. are all examples of tasks often assigned to the international division.

Advantages: The international division is effective in consolidating international activity under one area of responsibility. Such a division develops international expertise that can serve all areas of the organization. This eliminates the need for every part of the organization to master the ins and outs of doing business overseas (this can sometimes be quite complex).

Disadvantages: On the other hand, the existence of an international division encourages the organization to approach their business in an artificially dichotomous manner. Part of the business organization focuses primarily on the home country market, while the international division serves "the rest of the world". In most organizations such a structure lends itself to a continuing preoccupation with the home country market.

As a company becomes more serious about overseas business, it often finds it useful to adopt a more sophisticated global structure. Four examples of such organizations are included below.

Global functional structure

A global functional structure is often adopted by companies with a very limited product scope. A CEO will oversee a number of business functions that have been identified as critical to business operations. Because the product mix is singular or limited, the CEO can coordinate the work of the functions and bring the resources of each to bear on the product line. In this case, the CEO serves as the common denominator between the functions.

Advantages: In many organizations, the primary sources of expertise are functionally based. Therefore, economies of scale can be achieved by grouping these resources by function. In the case of human resources, for instance, a central human resources function can serve as a consultant to all parts of the organization on issues such as pay and performance evaluation. This eliminates the redundancy occurring when multiple parts of the organization attempt to develop such programs on their own. A functional organization also enables the organization to standardize policies, practices and procedures that can be carried out throughout the organization.

Disadvantages: The primary focus on business functional activity, often distracts organizations from specific product requirements, customer needs, and geographic idiosyncrasies. With the top of the organization serving as common denominator and arbiter between the functions, strategies may not reflect realities on the ground as decisions are made without the benefit of close interaction with customers and deep understanding of local circumstances.

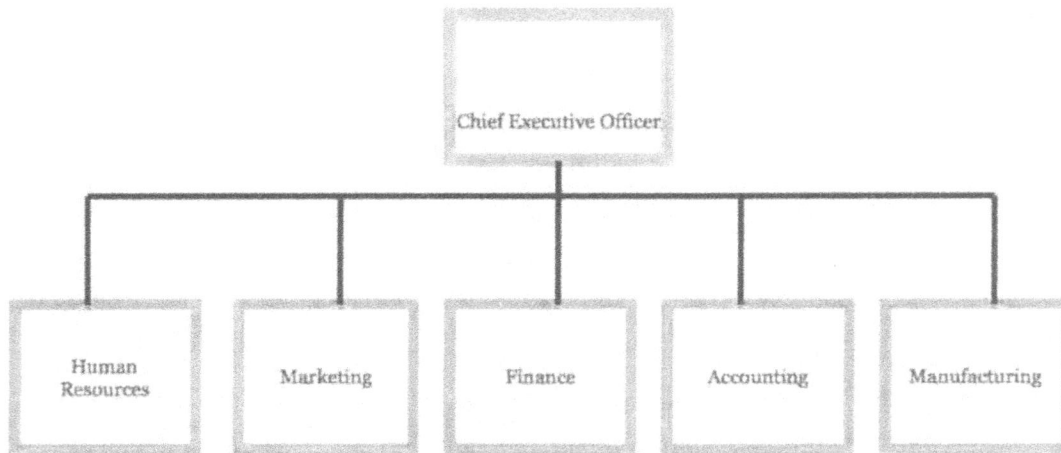

Exhibit 57: A global structure

Product structure

A global product structure is often chosen in companies with an array of diverse product lines. Each product line is assigned to its own organization unit so that decision-making is focused on the product characteristic and the customers who will be targeted. In many cases, the product unit will have its own functional organization—in essence, operating as a stand alone business in the context of the larger organization. In many cases, a product unit will be managed with full profit and loss responsibility.

Advantages: The main advantage of a product structure is that it focuses attention and resources toward a single product and the customers toward which that product is targeted. Decisions are optimized for the success of the product and distractions are minimized.

Disadvantages: Redundancies often exist across product organizations as functional responsibilities are duplicated under each product organization. Economies of scale and scope are more difficult to achieve as this organization structure encourages less cooperation and coordination across the product units.

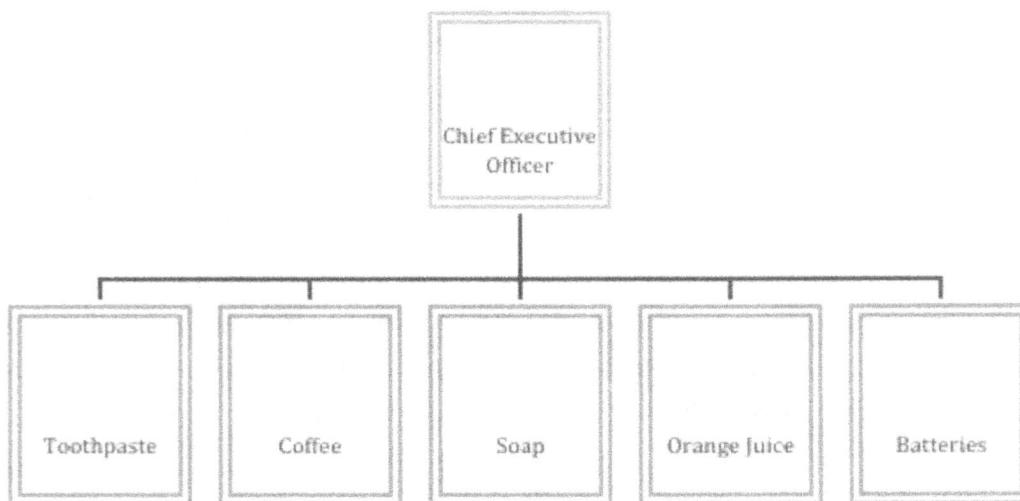

Exhibit 58: A product structure

Area/geographic structure:

An area structure is often chosen by companies who want to emphasize geographically specific strategies and focus decision-making on local needs. Organizations may be divided up into regional and country structures where country managers operate rather autonomous businesses supported by an array of local functions. In this case, the country organization often operates as a fairly self-contained business with substantial local authority as well as profit and loss responsibility.

Advantages: The country organization is capable of sensing and understanding local conditions and is able to formulate strategies which effectively meet the needs of local stakeholders. Policies in areas such as human resource management can be tailored to meet the needs and expectations of local employees, product mix and design can be optimized for local conditions, and the organization can respond more quickly to changing circumstances on the ground.

Disadvantages: The disadvantages of the area structure are similar to those of the product structure. Economies of scale will be harder to achieve as different localities develop and implement very different product strategies on one hand, and invest resources in developing local functional expertise and effort which may well be duplicated unnecessarily across geographic units.

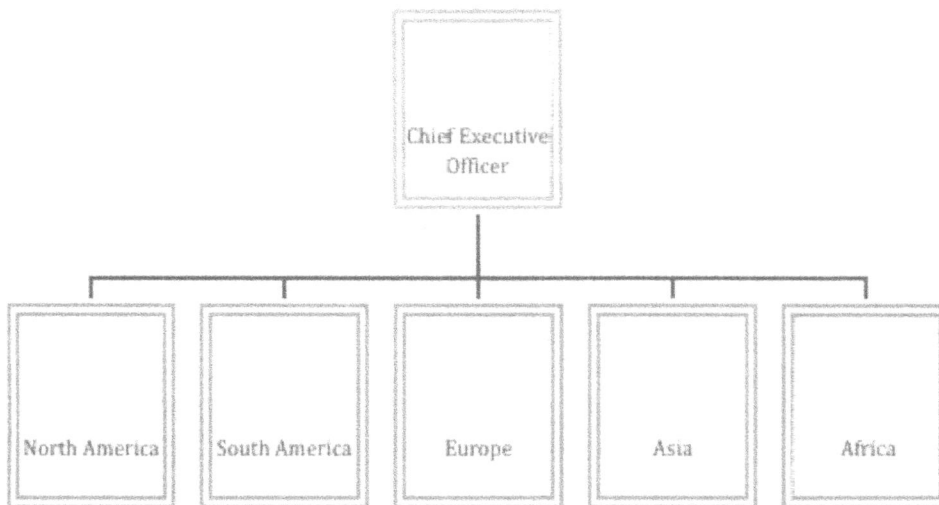

Exhibit 59: Area/geographic structure

Matrix structure:

A matrix structure is often adopted in organizations that would like to optimize decisions across multiple organization dimensions. In other words, they would like to achieve economies of scale where appropriate, but do not want to lose the ability to respond to product/customer and geographic needs more effectively.

A matrix organization simultaneously utilizes two or more dimensions (product, geographic, function, etc.) to organize the company's work. In this case, two or more dimensions may have direct links to the head of the organization (see Exhibit 48) and key individuals throughout the organization may actually report to more than one dimension. As can be seen in Exhibit 48, the orange juice product manager reports to the head of the organization, as does the head of the finance function. In this example, the finance officer in the orange juice product group reports to two individuals: the head of finance and the head of the orange juice group. At the same time, a geographic dimension may require that the function and product heads interact as coequals with any number of country managers or regional heads as well.

Advantages: The matrix allows functional efficiencies to be achieved while also allowing for the management of discrete product lines. Product managers remain focused on specific customer and product issues, yet can tap into the specialized support systems offered by strong functions. Where a geographic dimension is included in the structure, country managers or other local personnel can devote their attention to the development of location specific strategies. Communication and information sharing may be facilitated through the multiple dimensions.

Disadvantages: The matrix is complex and often involves additional coordination costs. Confusion and ambiguity may result from multiple reporting relationships as a single individual may receive conflicting direction from their various supervisors.

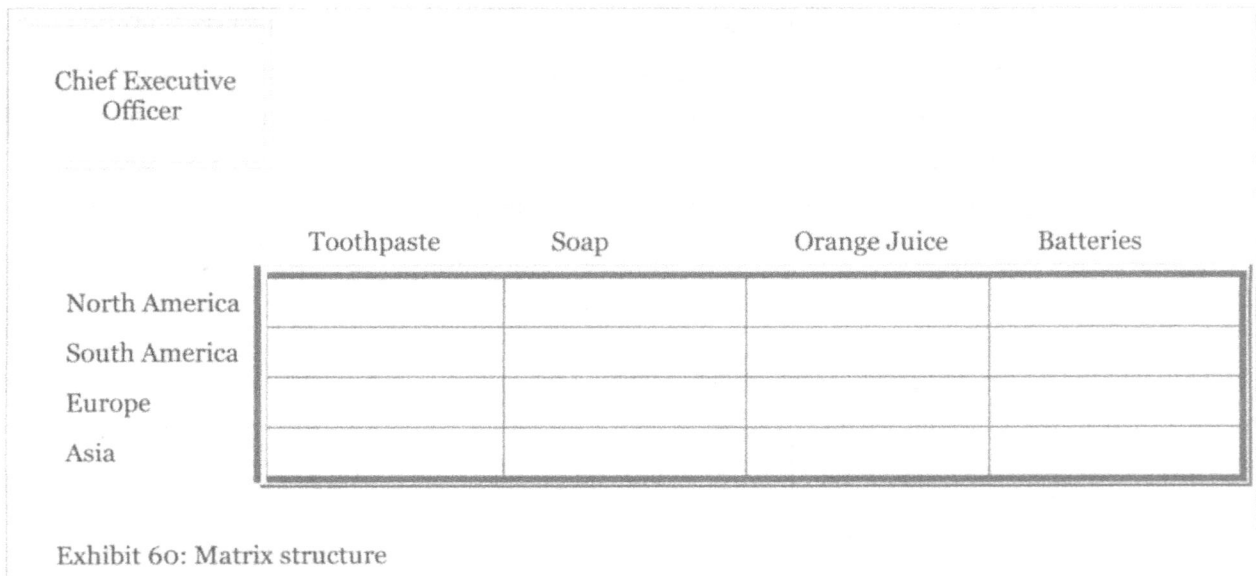

	Toothpaste	Soap	Orange Juice	Batteries
Chief Executive Officer				
North America				
South America				
Europe				
Asia				

Exhibit 60: Matrix structure

Beyond the matrix:

Each of the above organizational choices clearly offers advantages and disadvantages.

While some type of hierarchy exists at the heart of most organization designs, many organizations are finding that the typical pyramid shaped organization no longer meets their needs. They are looking for options that allow greater flexibility and responsiveness. Such organizations may legitimize informal relationships between various organizational parts and levels. They may rely more on teams as coordinating mechanisms and they may actively encourage collaboration and sharing across business units. Successful global organizations in the 21st century will balance hierarchical control (which remains critical in most organizations) on one hand, with less rigidity, more flexibility and emphasis on individual empowerment on the other.

Staffing choices in a globally far-flung company

Staffing choices in a far-flung global company are more complex as well. Issues of cost, cultural savvy, familiarity with local conditions, language skill, family issues, and more must all be considered carefully as staffing decisions are made. In addition to many of the standard human resources challenges that inevitably arise, determining where employees will be sourced from represents one of the most important decisions facing companies as they set up operations abroad. In general, employees may come from any of the following sources: the headquarters (home) country, the host (local) country, or a third country (neither home, nor host). These choices are outlined briefly below.

Ethnocentric staffing involves staffing overseas positions with home country personnel. These "expatriates" are usually assigned to fairly senior or technical positions in the overseas organization. An example of this staffing choice would be when a Japanese company sets up an office in the United States and sends a Japanese executive from their headquarters in Tokyo to staff the new office in Chicago.

Advantages: Home country staff, when sent overseas, are familiar with the home country operations and culture. Because of this, they may be able to better communicate with headquarters, access needed resources, and tap into a home-country network. In addition, the home country may know these people well from past collaboration that can lead to high levels of trust and confidence between the parties. Familiarity with the company often means that these individuals bring special company-specific expertise along with them, as well as technical skills and knowledge related to the company's product offering. They may also bring general technical, or managerial skills that may be in short supply in the host country. Ethnocentric staffing offers the additional benefit of building a global mindset among the home country workforce. Those individuals who are sent overseas as expatriates will often return home with a more globalized perspective.

Disadvantages: Home country employees are expensive. Many companies estimate that sending an expatriate overseas costs about 2-5 times their annual salary. This means that sending an executive and their family overseas can cost hundreds of thousands of dollars or more per year. The home country employee is usually less familiar with the local culture and employment conditions, and the employee and the family may find it hard to adapt to the new local living and working conditions. In fact, according to widely cited research, failure of the spouse and of the family to adapt to local cultural differences are two of the most frequent reasons that an employee assigned to an overseas post will fail to complete their assignment. Ethnocentric staffing practices are also sometimes criticized for preventing talented local employees from filling the positions held by expatriates.

Polycentric staffing involves hiring local personnel to fill needed overseas positions. For example, under this model, a South African company setting up an office in Brazil would hire a Brazilian to fill an open position.

Advantages: A polycentric staffing strategy is much less expensive than the ethnocentric model. Relocation costs are usually much lower and a standard compensation package consistent with the local market is usually sufficient. Local employees are usually more familiar with the local culture and language and may have access to networks and relationships with local stakeholders.

Disadvantages: Talent is often short in host countries. Lack of familiarity with the home country conditions, culture and language may become a barrier to effective communication with the headquarters staff. Lack of familiarity with headquarters operations may make it difficult for the local staff to access needed resources and assistance.

Geocentric staffing involves staffing a location without regard for the employees' place of origin. Companies simply scan their global workforce for the best qualified candidate to fill a position. In this model, a Chinese company might fill a position in their Mexico office with an employee from the United Kingdom.

Advantages: The geocentric model offers the most employment flexibility and choice to the company. The company can search the entire global workforce to find the most qualified candidate for a certain position. Opportunities for cross-cultural development are extended to company employees no matter which country they come from. The additional global interaction taking place can foster teamwork across countries and a better cross-border understanding of company operations. A cadre of globally savvy employees with experience in multiple company locations can be a powerful asset as the company continues to seek additional overseas opportunities.

Disadvantages: Geocentric staffing can be as expensive as ethnocentric staffing practices. Employees and families often have to be relocated across country boundaries and long distances. Geocentrically placed employees may be unfamiliar with local practices.

Regiocentric staffing involves staffing within a global region. In this case, a Korean company might fill a position in Italy with a Spanish employee.

Advantages: Moves are often made over shorter distances as employees are relocated. Cultural and linguistic differences may be less pronounced. Employees gain the benefits of cross-cultural experience as they work outside their home country.

Disadvantages: Costs of relocation often remain fairly high. While cross-cultural perspective is built, a truly global perspective may still be lacking. It is also important to note that cultural and language differences will often be significant factors even within region.

All of the above models have strengths and weaknesses which must be seriously considered. In most companies with multiple employees in overseas locations a mixed strategy will often make the most sense both in terms of efficiency and effectiveness. A few select positions may best be filled with either home country or third country nationals while the vast majority of employment positions are usually filled by local employees. Because cross-cultural difference will be encountered in almost any overseas staffing configuration, significant investment in cross-cultural skills training will be extremely valuable.

Trends and challenges in a global HR environment

HR leaders in the 21st century will be challenged to address a number of issues to ensure availability of skilled staff, regardless of which staffing option the MNC pursues. As the global environment continues to develop, MNCs are challenged to address the shortage in global skills and cross-cultural communication barriers. The successful MNC will be able to adapt to the changing environment by globalizing their HR systems and function, and globalizing the workforce mindset. These efforts must also be aligned with business and organizational objectives and will require HR professionals to adopt a new way of thinking to identify and implement new ways of getting work done.

HR systems in the MNC must be aligned with global business imperatives both in terms of pay and performance systems. As the number of overseas transfers increases, MNCs must look to develop general policies and compensation packages rather than negotiating these on a case-by-case basis in order to obtain efficiency and consistency of process. Systems must also be in place for succession planning on a local level as well as a global level. Currently many MNCs are not operating an effective expatriate pipeline, either not sending the most effective individuals to host countries or failing the repatriate them effectively. The trend towards increasing reliance on integrated systems should contribute to better access across borders and regions to better serve expatriate relocation and business decisions.

Another opportunity for MNCs in regards to creating a global workforce will be to standardize and revisit current expatriate compensation packages to include soft benefits. Until now, individuals have often not been willing to take positions abroad because the incentives are solely financial. Historically, systems have not been in place to repatriate smoothly the individual and family following completion of their overseas assignment. Many employees find themselves out of their home HR system, and therefore are not made aware of possibly enticing job opportunities at home. This can be improved greatly simply by creating alignment and communication between the home and international HR department.

Corporate Social Responsibility and sustainable development in the global environment

The topics surrounding Corporate Social Responsibility (CSR) have become more complex due to the globalization of the economy and the issues that arise from companies competing in international markets. Companies are manufacturing goods, hiring local labor, utilizing raw materials and resources extracted from the environment in international locations.

This heightened awareness of CSR and sustainable development has been endorsed by an increased responsiveness to ethical, social, environmental and other global issues. In recent years, companies have been the center of scandals regarding accounting practices, damages to the environment, inadequate treatment of employees and workers and the effect of its products on the society.

For example, in January 2009, the Chairman of one of India's largest technology companies, Satyam Computer Services Ltd., said he fabricated key financial results, including a fictitious cash balance of more than USD 1 billion (Sheth, 2009). Cases like this, and others such as Enron Corporation and Worldcom in the United States, prompt concerns about corporate governance and accounting standards globally. Further, corporate fraud puts into question one of the fundamental reasons of why shareholders invest in public companies, the need for transparency.

As a result, companies are responding to increased public expectations of responsibility and incorporating the concept of CSR into their operating plans and strategy.

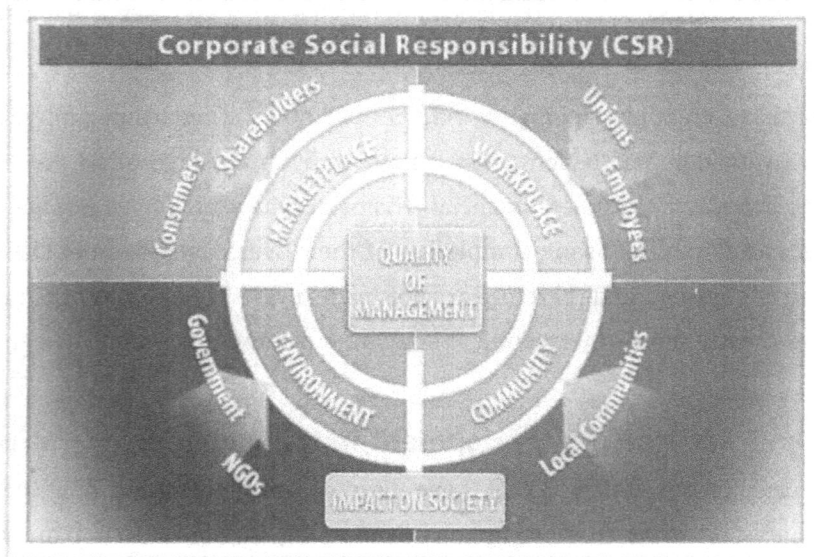

Exhibit 61: Corporate Social Responsibility (CSR) is a concept whereby companies integrate ethical, social, environmental, and other global issues into their business operations and in their interaction with their stakeholders (employees, customers, shareholders, investors, local communities, government), all on a voluntary basis

Source: industryplayer.com

Corporate Social Responsibility and sustainable development defined

Traditionally, CSR has been defined as the corporation's responsibility to comply with the laws and responsibilities to its shareholders. This concept of CSR has evolved to include the organization's responsibility for its impact on different stakeholders such as employees, customers, investors, local communities, and government.

A broader concept is that CSR involves the commitment on the part of the company to adopt behavior that will result in the improvement of the quality of life of its stakeholders while contributing to the economic development of its business. To improve the welfare of its community, the company may take on broad environmental and social endeavors.

The World Business Council for Sustainable Development defines CSR as "the continuing commitment by business to behave ethically and contribute to economic development while improving the quality of life of the workforce and their families as well as of the local community and society at large" (wbcsd.org). This definition outlines the role of enterprises as active partners in the communities in which they operate, rather than the more traditional view of enterprise as a separate, self-regulating, profit-making entity.

CSR Positives and Negatives

Milton Friedman, in his book, *Capitalism and Freedom*, argues that:

"There is one and only one social responsibility of business—to use its resources and engage in activities designed to increase its profits so long as it stays within the rules of the game, which is to say, engages in open and free competition without deception or fraud."

Stockholder wealth maximization commands that corporate management should aggressively seek to maximize stockholder returns by working to increase share prices and to continually grow the dividends paid to shareholders (Czinkota, 2005).

Conversely, according to Professor Archie B. Carroll:

"Corporate social responsibility involves the conduct of a business so that it is economically profitable, law abiding, ethical and socially supportive. To be socially responsible then means that profitability and obedience to the law are foremost conditions when discussing the firm's ethics and the extent to which it supports the society in which it exists with contributions of money, time and talent" (Carroll,1983).

Carroll's CSR model contains four categories of corporate responsibility organized from most to least important. According to Carroll, the "history of business suggests an early emphasis on the economic and then legal aspects and a later concern for the ethical and discretionary aspects" (Carroll, 1979). Economic obligations are, therefore, seen to be moderated by ethical responsibilities or social expectations and norms. Discretionary responsibilities go beyond ethical responsibilities and include philanthropic measures. In 1991, Carroll presented his CSR model as a pyramid, and suggested that although the components are not mutually exclusive, it "helps the manager to see that the different types of obligations are in constant tension with one another" (Carroll, 1979).

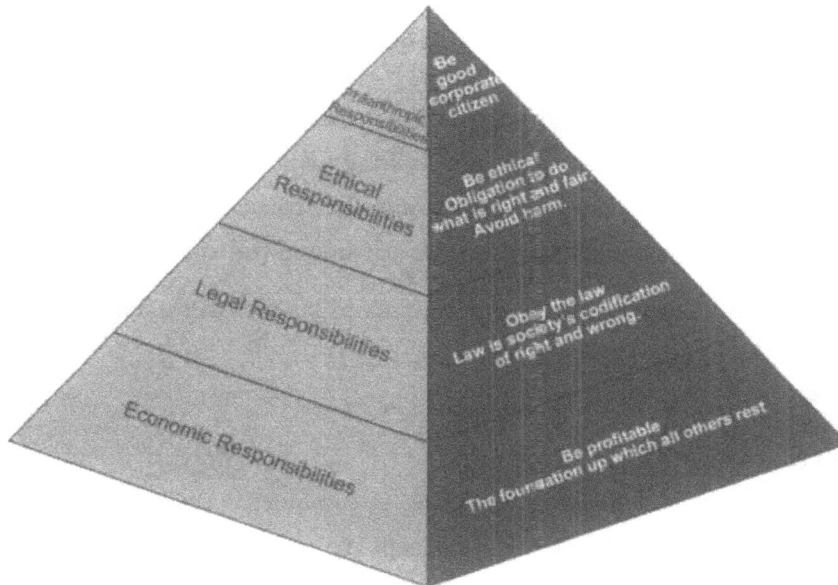

Carroll's CSR Pyramid

Exhibit 62: Carroll's CSR Pyramid: A three-dimensional conceptual model of corporate social performance.

There is no indication that CSR (corporate wealth maximization) and profitability (stockholder wealth maximization) are mutually exclusive (Czinkota, 2005). Corporate wealth maximization suggests that companies consider and balance short-term goals against long-term societal goals of continued employment, community citizenship and public welfare needs (Czinkota, 2005). The successful multinational enterprises of the coming century will be those that find the unique balance between financial objectives and CSR.

CSR and Sustained Development initiatives

There are a number of projects and initiatives that are shaping the goals and principles of corporate social responsibility and sustainable development, such as:

- *OECD (Organization for Economic Cooperation and Development)* is an international organization with 35 industrialized countries as participants, which account for 76 per cent of the world trade. The themes that this organization addresses include environmental, human rights, labor issues, and information disclosure.

- *UN Norms on the Responsibilities of Transnational Corporations and Other Business Enterprises with Regard to Human Rights*. The completion of these norms was possible through discussions with unions, business, and NGOs. The norms include clarification of corporate social responsibilities of companies in countries where they operate, and also refer to human rights in the workplace.

- *ILO (International Labor Organization)* and its *Tripartite Declaration* focuses on the "social aspects of the activities of multinational enterprises, including employment creation in the developing countries" (Governing Body of International Labor Office, 204th session). The principles established by this organization are adopted voluntarily, and thus its reach is limited since non-compliance cannot be sanctioned.

- United Nations' Global Compact was established in 1999 by United Nations' Secretary Kofi Annan as a voluntary international initiative. Participant companies are asked to demonstrate their support to ten different international principles of human and labor rights, anti-corruption and environmental protection, to seek solutions to the challenges of globalization and promote responsible corporate citizenship. The initiative has more than 2,500 business participants from 90 countries around the world.

- *Kyoto Protocol* was agreed on in 1997 to reduce greenhouse gas emissions by 2012. A total of 1968 countries and the EEC have ratified the protocol (envroliteracy.org, 2007).

CSR and corporate strategy

A distinction must be made between charity and CSR. Charity refers to a company's efforts to donate money or resources to an organization or a cause, promoting and allowing employees to volunteer in the community, and the establishment or endorsement of foundations. Conversely, CSR is a concept that involves a company taking into consideration the different stakeholders involved when making a business decision. The Organization for Economic Cooperation and Development identified CSR to be an integral part of a company's value system and strategy (intranet.csreurope.org). For a company to fully integrate CSR, top management must integrate social responsibility into the strategic level of the decision-making process in order to develop a framework for economic decisions made at different levels of the organization's hierarchy.

The problem that a company will encounter if CSR is not integrated into the organization strategy is that management and employees could bypass social responsibility considerations and CSR becomes personal ethics rather than CSR. To adopt a CSR strategy the organization needs to take the following steps:

- Define CSR for their particular business.

- Understand motivations underlying its commitment.

- Establish policies and goals to achieve CSR.

- Establish measures to monitor their accomplishments in CSR (bsr.org).

Case: Built to Last by Jim Collins

How important is Corporate Social Responsibility (CSR) as a core value for the top companies in the world?

In the book *Built to Last*, by Jim Collins the results of a six-year research project into what makes enduring great companies is outlined. Collins listed 18 companies identified as "visionaries" .A visionary company is defined as one that is a leader in its industry, is widely admired by knowledgeable businesspeople, made an imprint on the world, had multiple generations of CEO's, had multiple product/service life cycles, and was founded before 1950. The list of 18 included companies such as Ford, General Electric, Johnson & Johnson, Sony, and Wal-mart.

From 1926 through 1990 these companies outperformed the general stock market by fifteen times.

A key attribute of the findings is that all of these highly profitable companies have sound social values and CSR is an important component of their success. This study shows the relevance of CSR and the importance of strong core values for a successful organization.

Successful Implementation of CSR and Sustainable Development

Tetra Pak Colombia worked with a small recycling company in Colombia to develop a technology they named Ecoplak. The technology utilizes 100 per cent of the residuals of tetra pack carton packages to obtain the material that can be used in the production of roofs and chipboards. With this technology, Tetra Pack has built 24 houses for low-income families to date.

This company did not only take into consideration environmental issues in the recycling of waste from packages; but it also worked with a local recycler to produce this technology. Additionally, this initiative created jobs, developed knowledge in local businesses, and helped families in the community who probably would not have had access to a home. Each house was built using 1 million packages and consisted of 2 bedrooms, 1 bathroom, 1 kitchen, and a living room. The houses were also provided with electricity and water.

Tetra Pak Colombia is currently working with the government to coordinate this effort and is still building houses that are periodically awarded to low income people of the community (tetrapak.com).

CSR, Sustainable Development, and the Future of Businesses

Peter Drucker, in his article, *The New Meaning of Corporate Social Responsibility*, explained that "the proper social responsibility of business is to tame the dragon that is to turn a social problem into economic opportunity and economic benefit, into productive capacity, into human competence, into well-paid jobs, and into wealth" (Berkhout,2007).

As evidenced in the case of Tetra Pack Colombia, a company with CSR and sustainable development aligned into its strategy can be effective in working with its community to solve a social problem. In this case, Tetra Pack Colombia was able to utilize waste that impacted the environment; worked with the government to coordinate efforts to improve the welfare and the quality of life of its community; worked with companies in the community to develop knowledge and new technologies; and create new jobs and alternative, environmentally friendly new sources of material.

According to the World Business Council for Sustainable Development, "By 2050, 85% of the world's population of some nine billion people will be in (less industrialized) countries. If these people are not by then engaged in the marketplace, business cannot prosper and the benefits of a global market will not exist. Clearly it is in our mutual interest to help societies shift to a more sustainable path."

Companies will increasingly be called upon to participate to address challenges of social and environmental roots, both locally and globally. Sustainable development business opportunities exist everywhere and in all forms. Such opportunities include recycling, reducing, and reusing. Improved efficiencies, biotechnology, and miniaturization are other ideas. Innovative leadership in life equality issues is becoming more and more of a trend today. It is no doubt that unique economic and environmental needs exist in industrial and less industrialized countries. CSR opportunities and challenges include promoting good labor practices and diversity, supporting health and education programs in the community. There are few limits in the design and implementation of socially responsible initiatives for a company.

CSR and the small business entrepreneur

For a small business entrepreneur, like Ms. Shahira, her company profits from its relationship with the community. Its stakeholders, which include customers, the local community, and the government, are all critical aspects to the company's growth in the future. As a result, Ms. Shahira must consider social and environmental impacts of her decisions, in addition to the ways that they will make an economic impact to her business.

Chapter summary

This chapter presents the types of global challenges that Ms. Shahira's business could be presented with in the future. As she has done so effectively in her home country, internationally Ms. Shahira has the opportunity to grow her company, and even present her model to other small entrepreneurs to integrate into their businesses. It is important to note however, that the issues discussed only begin to present the common challenges among new entrepreneurs. This is just an introductory start into the journey of extending a small business into new, international markets.

References

"Aga Kahn Agency for Microfinance." 2008, available at http://www.akdn.org/akam_case.asp.

AON Global Risk Alert. "China Establishes a New Employment Contract Law for 2008." AON, 2007, available at www.aon.com/about/publications/global_riskalert/gra_2007-oct-01.jsp

AON Group, Inc. "Political and Economic Risk Map." Aon Global Corporate Marketing and Communications, 2007, available at http://www.aon.com//about/publications/pdf/issues/2007_P&E_Risk_Map.pdf.

"Assessing Globalization." World Bank Briefing Papers, 2001, available at http://www1.worldbank.org/economicpolicy/globalization/issuesbriefs.html.

Bartlett, Christopher A., and Sumantra, Ghoshal, and Birkinshaw, Julian."Transnational Management, Fourth Edition." McGraw Hill: Irwin, 2004.

Beenhakker, Henri. "The Global Economy and International Financing."

Quorum Books, 2001.

Berkhout, Tom. "Corporate Gains." Alternatives Journal, 2005.

Bhagwati, Jagdish, Arvind Panagariya and T.N. Srinivasan. "The Muddles Over Outsourcing." Journal of Economic Perspectives, Fall 2004, 93-114.

Bhagwati, Jagdish and T.N. Srinivasan. "Trade and Poverty in the Poor Countries." American Economic Review Papers & Proceedings, May 2002.

Bradley, Frank. "International Marketing Strategy". Prentice Hall, Toronto, Fifth Edition. 2005.

"Business Social Responsibility." 2007, available at www.bsr.org.

Carrada-Bravo, Francisco. "Managing Global Finance in the Digital Economy."

Praeger Publishers, 2002.

Carroll, Archie. " A Three Dimensional Conceptual Model of Corporate Social Performance." Academy of Management Review, 1979.

Carroll, Archie. "Corporate Social Responsibility: Will Industry Respond to Cut-Backs in Social Program Funding?" Vital Speeches of the Day, 49, 604-608,1983.

Collins, Jim. "Built to Last." HarperBusiness: 1st Edition, October 26, 1994.

"Corporate Social Responsibility." available at www.industryplayer.com.

Coyle, Brian. "Hedging Currency Exposure." Glenlake Publishing, 2000.

Coyle, Brian. "Introduction to Currency Risk." Glenlake Publishing, 2000.

"CSR Europe." 2007, available at www.intranet.csreurope.org.

"CSR: Meeting Changing Expectations." 1999, available at www.wbcsd.org.

Czinkota, Michael and Moffett, Michael and Ronkainen, Ilkka. "International Business." Thomson Southwestern: 7th Edition, 2005, 62.

Czinkota, Michael, and Rivoli, Pietra and Ronkainen, Ilkka. "International Business – 6th Edition." The Dryden Press, 2002.

Dadak, Casimir. "The case for foreign ownership of farmland in Poland." Cato Journal, Vol. 24, No. 3, Fall 2004, available at

http://www.cato.org/pubs/journal/cj24n3/cj24n3-6.pdf

De Mooij, Marieke. "Global Marketing and Advertising. Understanding Cultural Paradoxes". Sage Publication: Second Edition, 2005.

Dollar, David. "The Poor Like Globalization." YaleGlobal, June 23, 2003, available at http://yaleglobal.yale.edu/article.print?id=1934.

Edmunds Auto Observer. "A Historic Year for US Vehicle Sales." 2007, available at http://www.autoobserver.com/2008/01/2007-a-historic-year-for-us-vehicle-sales.html.

"Environmental Literacy Council." 2007, available at www.enviroliteracy.org.

Federal Financial Institutions Examination Council (FFIEC). "Legal Risk." Available at http://www.ffiec.gov/ffiecinfobase/booklets/Retail/retail_03e.html.

Friedman, Milton. "The Social Responsibility of Business is to increase its Profits." New York Times Magazine, 1970.

"Globalization: Threat or Opportunity?" International Monetary Fund Issue Brief, April 12, 2000 (corrected January 2002), available at http://www.imf.org/external/np/exr/ ib/2000/041200.htm.

Hofstede, Geert. "Cultures and Organizations: Software of the Mind: Intercultural Cooperation and Its Importance for Survival." McGraw-Hill, 1996.

Hussey, Roger and Ong, Audra. "International Financial Reporting Standards Desk

Reference." John Wiley & Sons, 2005.

"International Accounting Standards Board: About Us." available at www.iasb.org/About+Us/About+Us.htm.

Kautz, Gerhard. "Take your Business Global. How to Develop International Markets". Entrepreneur Press, 2004.

Lawson, J. "Delivering on Strategy." Spectra-Journal of the MC, June 2006.

NetMBA:Business Knowledge Center. "The Marketing Mix: The 4 P's of Marketing." 2008, available at http://www.netmba.com/marketing/mix.

Perry, Anne C. Article; "International versus Domestic Marketing: Four Conceptual Perspectives." European Journal of Marketing, 1990, 41-54.

Prahalad, C.K. and Stuart L. Hart. "The Fortune at the Bottom of the Pyramid." Strategy + Business, available at http://www.strategy-business.com/press/article/ 11518?pg=all&tid=230.

Qureshi, Zia. "Globalization: New Opportunities, Tough Challenges." Finance & Development, March 1996, 30-33.

Schaffer, Richard, and Earle, Beverley and Agusti, Filiberto. "International Business Law and its Environment: 6th edition." West Legal Studies in Business, Thomson Corp, 2005.

Sheth, Niraj and Range, Jackie and Anand, Geeta. "Corporate Scandal Shakes India." Wall Street Journal, A-1, 2009.

Stiglitz, Joseph E. "Globalization and the Growth in Emerging Markets and the New Economy." Journal of Policy Modeling 25, 2003, 505-524.

Tian, Robert Guang, Ph. D. Article; "Marketing in the 21st Century: Cross-cultural Issues". 2008, available at www.studyoverseas.com/america/usaed/crosscultural.htm.

"Tetra Pak." 2007, available at www.tetrapak.com.

Ulijn, Jan and Fayolle, Allaine. "Toward Cooperation between European Start Ups: The position of the French, Dutch, and German Entrepreneurial and Innovative Engineer." In Terrence Brown & Jan Ulijn (Eds.), Entrepreneurship, Innovation, and Culture, 204-232, 2004. Cheltenham: Edward Edgar.

Watkins, Kevin. "Making Globalization Work for the Poor." Finance & Development, March 2002, available at http://www.imf.org/external/pubs/ft/fandd/2002/03/ watkins.htm.

Wild, Susan Ellis. . "Webster's New World Law Dictionary." Wiley Publishing, 2006.

Yusuf, Shahid. "Globalization and the Challenge for Developing Countries." World Bank Development Research Group, June 2001, available at http://www1.worldbank.org/economicpolicy/globalization/documents/wps2168.pdf.

More references

Butler, Kirt. "Multinational Finance." South-Western College Pub, 2003.

Multinational Finance provides a concise treatment of the investment and financial decisions facing the multinational corporation. The text provides a framework for evaluating the opportunities, costs and risks of multinational operations so readers can see beyond the algebra and terminology to general principles. It is distinguished by its logical organization, superior pedagogy, and clear, non-technical writing style. It includes the traditional international finance topics of foreign exchange, currency and derivatives markets, currency risk (transaction, operating and translation) management, country risk, taxation, capital structure, cost of capital, and international portfolio diversification. It also has unique chapters on multinational treasury management, options on real assets, corporate governance, asset pricing, and international portfolio management.

Moyer, Charles, McGuian, James, and Kretlow, William. "Contemporary Financial

Management." Thomsan Southwestern:10th Edition, 2006.

Focusing on shareholder wealth maximization, international aspects of financial management, ethics, and the impact of the Internet, this introductory textbook covers: determinants of value; capital investment decisions; the cost of capital, capital structure, and dividend policy; and, working capital management and financial forecasting. Topics like lease financing, financing with derivatives, international financial management, and corporate restructuring are also discussed. An enclosed CD provides access to a companion web site. The authors are scholars of management and investment consultants.

World Bank. "Doing Business: Economy Rankings." 2007. Available at http://www.doingbusiness.org/EconomyRankings/

14. International business for the entrepreneur

The Doing Business project provides objective measures of business regulations and their enforcement across 181 economies and selected cities at the subnational and regional level.

15. Growth strategies for start-ups

Translated and reprinted with permission from Dowling/Drumm Gründungsmanagement[31]

Editors: Michael Dowling, Hans Juergen Drumm (University of Regensberg)

Reviewer: Timothy B Folta (Purdue University)

Learning objectives

- define what constitutes a growth firm

- describe the problems of growth and growth strategies

- describe growth mistakes and solutions

Overview

In this chapter we investigate possible strategies for the growth of start-up firms. First, we describe growth as a phenomenon and basic problem for such firms. In particular we analyze the problem from the viewpoint of new start-ups which plan from the outset to grow larger quickly. We then examine different growth strategies which firms can pursue. In the second part of the chapter we present the most well-known mistakes made by start-ups during the growth phase, and suggest ways to correct or—even better—avoid them. To conclude, we provide recommendations for how entrepreneurs can profit best from growth. In this chapter we refer most often to firms with "products" but the strategies and pitfalls reviewed here also apply to service companies.

Definition and models

Definition and statistics

We start by defining what we mean by growth and growth-oriented firms. Criteria such as growth in the number of employees, or sales growth are generally used by researchers. The Kaufmann Center for Entrepreneurial Leadership, a leading institute of entrepreneurial research in the USA, for example, defines high-growth firms as being those with over 30 per cent growth in sales or over 20 per cent growth in the number of employees for each of the three preceding years. Other US researchers (Siegel/MacMillan 1993) define strong growth as over 25 per cent growth per annum over a three-year period.

The number of high-growth firms is no doubt limited. Even in the USA, only 5 per cent of firms each year are estimated to take on extra staff (cf. Sexton/Bowman-Upton 1991, p. 12). However, these fast-growing firms have a disproportionate significance for the increase in the number of jobs. In the USA, for example, it is estimated that only 12-15 per cent of all businesses are responsible for 100 per cent of the employment growth in the US economy

---

31 Translated and reprinted with permission from Dowling/Drumm Gründungsmanagement (Entrepreneurship)
    Springer Verlag, 2003.

(cf. Sexton/Bowman-Upton 1991, p. 10). Research studies in Germany have also shown that businesses with 50 to 250 employees recorded the greatest increase in employment (cf. Kühlhorn/Wissdorf 2001). International comparative data can be found in the Global Entrepreneurship Monitor (GEM). Based on a survey of all start-ups from 1999, the GEM presented the share of high-growth start-ups (see Exhibit 63). (cf. Sternberg 2000).

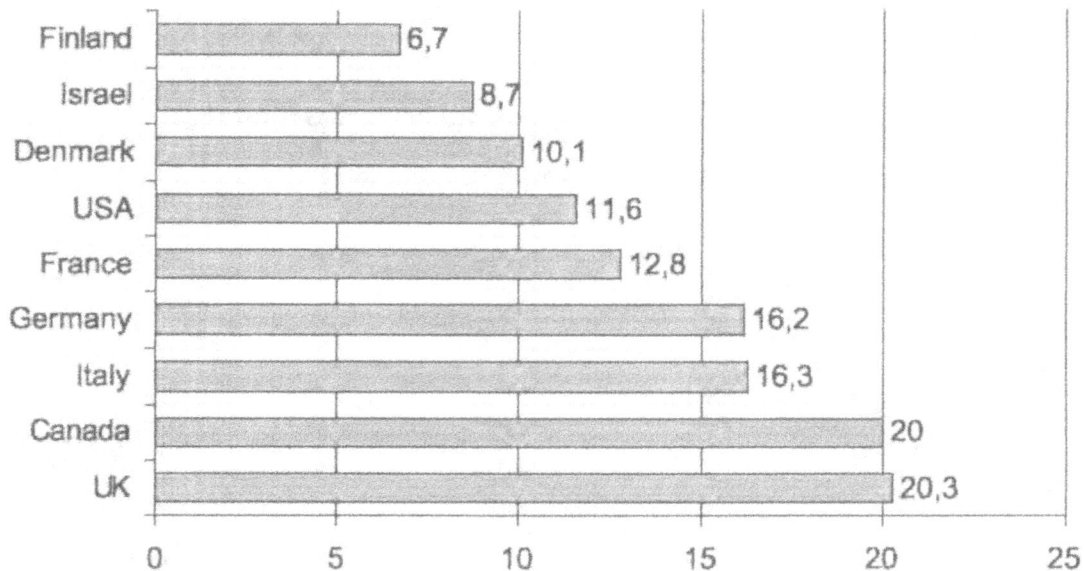

Exhibit 63: Countries in comparison: Share of high-growth start-ups compared to total start-ups. (*Source:* Sternberg 2000)

Growth models

In the field of entrepreneurship research, life cycle models are often used to describe the entrepreneurial process. These models are also used in research into growth problems. Kazanjian and Drazin (1980), for example, developed a four-phase growth model, and identified the typical growth problems of fast-growing firms in each phase.

Phase 1, Concept and development: Focus on the invention and development of a service or product. Main problems:

- developing the idea

- testing a prototype

- finding investment support for the idea

Phase 2, Commercialization: Developing the product for introduction to the market. Main problems:

- setting up the organization and production

- solving technical problems

- market entry

Phase 3, Growth: The fast-growth phase is characterized by its focus on the market.

Main problems:

- Producing larger quantities

- Guaranteeing quality

- Expanding market share

- Personnel problems

Phase 4, Stability: In this phase the focus lies on consolidating the market position with the initial product, and developing further products.

Main problem:

- Simultaneously managing the market entry of new products without losing the competitive advantages of older products.

Although life phase models like these can help the decision-making process in research and practice, they also have their pitfalls. In a review of such models, Sexton and Bowman/Upton (1991) warned that economic phenomena cannot always be compared to biological phenomena (life cycles). Firm growth does not always develop through the phases of such models in a straightforward, linear way, for example. Particularly in fast-growing industries involving technological change, growth is more chaotic than ordered. Moreover, well-known growth models with a bell-shaped, concave, or plateau structure are only useful as ideal reference patterns for actual growth processes.

Building on this criticism, Covin and Slevin (1997) suggest another growth model from the complexity management perspective. This model emphasizes that growth occurs through certain market factors in combination with internal competences and resources. The main problem for entrepreneurs is overcoming the increasing organizational and external complexity. In the following sections of this chapter we will define possible strategies for start-up growth. See Exhibit 64 below.

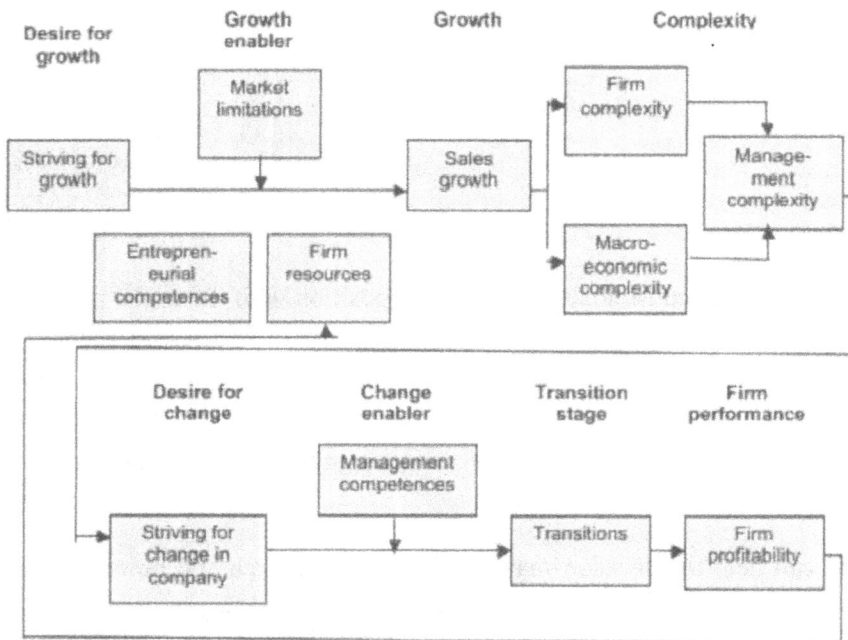

Exhibit 64: The "complexity management" growth model

Industrial change is often triggered by technological changes, for which there are many examples: the substitution of digital technologies in a whole range of analog products, from office equipment to telephones, and the Internet as a communication medium. Technological changes like this enable start-up firms developing new technologies and introducing them to the market to take over the positions of their established competitors.

A second catalyst for industrial transformations is change in consumer behavior. The increasing technological competence of customers, for example, has enabled the growth of direct computer sellers like Dell. Customers are prepared to get information about even high-technology products from the Internet and order them online instead of asking for advice in a shop.

Deregulation or liberalization can also be a reason for industrial transformation and change. In recent years industry deregulation has created opportunities for start-up firms and growth opportunities in general in various industries, such as the air traffic, telecommunications, or financial service sectors.

Changes in technologies, customer preferences, or regulations offer opportunities for transformation and change, but it is up to entrepreneurs to make use of them. At the beginning of a transformation period, firms must experiment with different strategies to tap the growth potential of the industry situation. We have seen many different such experiments with Internet technologies in the last few years. Many of them came to nothing, but several successful business models have survived. We have already given the example of Dell as a successful direct provider of PCs via the Internet. Further examples are US company Auto-By-Tel's sale of cars to traditional car dealers via the Internet, or E-Bay, the Internet auctioneers.

A period of experimentation is followed by a stabilization phase. In the literature, innovation management researchers talk about "dominant designs". A dominant design stabilizes a particular industry structure, and the positions of competitors. There is generally a consolidation phase in the industry, and failed experiments lead to certain firms disappearing from the industry. However, successful business models can mean even faster growth for the survivors, as they can take over shares of the market from other competitors.

Growth through buying out other companies

The entrepreneurship management literature generally refers to internal growth. However, small, fast-growing companies also have the possibility of growing by acquisition. These opportunities have become even more frequent in recent years due to the increasing availability of venture capital, and of capital resources from initial public offerings (IPOs). An acquisition strategy for a fast-growing start-up can bring many advantages. First of all, just like large firms, small firms can try to obtain synergies by means of complementary resources from bought-out firms. Sales growth as a result of buying out firms in the same industry could be rendered more efficient by combined resources and the acquisition of competent employees. An acquisition strategy can also be pursued to enable growth in new geographic markets. Moreover, the opportunity for expansion via acquisition is particularly attractive in other countries, where it can be difficult to establish new businesses.

Such a strategy can also offer the opportunity to go into related diversification, i.e. a start-up firm can acquire other products or services which are related to its original ones. Synergy effects and reduced or shared overheads can also be gained here. Firms can also integrate vertically through acquisition, i.e. by buying out suppliers or customers to process more steps in the value chain in-house. Vertical integration can sometimes bring advantages of cost or differentiation. Cost advantages can arise either through buying or building up cheaper distribution channels (forward integration), or cheap inputs (backward integration). Advantages of differentiation can be obtained by distribution channels or inputs which stand out from those of competitors (cf. Porter 1992).

If the firm to be taken over is already successful, the take-over can provide additional financial resources. A further gain from an acquisition may be additional qualified personnel who might also be able to strengthen the original firm. More customers can be won, or acquired more cheaply than if they have to be found using conventional marketing methods. The acquisition of other firms can also be a chance to gain technological know-how, or even new technologies in the form of patents.

Growth through cooperation

A cooperation strategy strikes a balance between internal growth and growth from the acquisition of other companies. Several studies in the USA have proved that fast-growing start-ups sometimes use cooperation with other small firms, and sometimes with large, established firms.

This cooperation is of various types. Licensing is a typical strategy in the biotech industry, for example. Small biotech start-ups generally do not have the necessary complementary resources (cf. Teece 1986) to carry new drugs through all the test phases and then to market them. Such firms often sell licenses to established pharmaceutical firms (the danger of this strategy will be dealt with "Inadequate or incorrect marketing") Other cooperation strategies, such as Research and Development cooperation, or outsourcing production, are possible. Cooperation strategies are pursued more frequently where there are networks of start-ups (cf. Lechner 2001).

Although new firms can gain the complementary resources they lack through cooperation, they still need basic competences in root technologies and key functions. In a study of high-tech start-ups in the USA, McGee et al. (1995) showed that the start-ups which grew fastest were those which pursued cooperation strategies to build on strengths, and not to compensate for weaknesses.

Stopping growth by selling the firm

An acquisition can be regarded as a growth strategy, but the sale of a company leads to a halt in growth. Such a sale does not necessarily have to be described as a loss, however. On the contrary, a trade sale—when a start-up sells itself to another firm—can be seen as the successful end of the entrepreneurial process. A firm has the possibility of continuing to grow as part of another firm, or the founders can use the sales revenue to pursue other activities. There are many examples of so-called "serial entrepreneurs". These entrepreneurs have founded several new companies, helped them to grow, and then sold them in order to pursue other activities. The best example of this is Jim Clark from Silicon Valley. He is currently working on starting his fourth and fifth companies, both in the Internet field. Prior to this he generated several billion USD for himself and his colleagues with three very successful high-tech start-ups: Silicon Graphics, Netscape, and Healthion. Clark recognized a long time ago that he is best at controlling the growth phase of a start-up, but is too impatient to manage a mature organization professionally. He tries to choose the right time to sell new firms to competitors which are better at dealing with the maturity phase (cf. Chong et al. 2000).

Growth through innovation

Times of technological change are an opportunity for start-ups to grow. New firms that use technological changes to introduce new products or services as market leaders can gain competitive advantages quickly. However, technological innovations like these must be able to be protected, or they will not last. The new firms must also possess or acquire the necessary complementary resources for the products and the marketing of them (cf. Teece 1986).

Certain types of innovation are especially advantageous for start-ups. In his book, *The Innovator's Dilemma*, Christensen (1997) differentiates between "sustaining technologies" and "disruptive technologies". Sustaining technologies improve existing product-market structures and are generally introduced most effectively by established firms. Disruptive technologies, on the other hand, which enable new applications for new customer segments, tend to be developed and marketed by start-ups. Christensen takes the example of the computer hard drive industry to show how start-ups have very often seen successful growth over a twenty-year period as spin-offs of established firms. Similar developments can be seen in other sectors.

In the next part of this chapter, we analyze the most frequent growth mistakes in start-ups.

Growth problems

Management mistakes

Of course, start-ups often make management mistakes in pursuing growth.

A classic first mistake is in the choice of a product or service—and/or even worse, a market—with no potential for growth. The only safeguard against this mistake is to conduct careful market and competitor analysis (See Chapter 13) to estimate the total market potential. This analysis must be complemented by the choice of a strategy for capturing the market with which an assumed market potential can be developed, taking into account the given financial restrictions. A second mistake is the failure to choose one of the aforementioned growth strategies early on. A third mistake is to not recruit competent and professional staff to implement the planned strategies. A fourth mistake is not to align product-market growth strategies with the firm's other strategies, especially finance, HR, and organizational strategies. A fifth mistake is to choose the wrong finance model. Here, an almost classic mistake is for firms to refinance long-term fixed capital with short-term returns, or with short-term revolving loans. A sixth mistake is to force growth. If growth occurs too rapidly, the firm is in danger of losing sight of the risks involved in the individual activities of the value chain, even when this growth can be financed. Here, continuous development is better than erratic growth (cf. Hutzschenreuter 2001), because it enables management to fill the gaps in their knowledge. We will go into several of these management mistakes in more detail in the following.

Incompatibility of growth strategies and organizational structure

The growth of start-ups must be planned, and supported by one or more of the above mentioned strategies. It is a significant growth mistake to do without planning and strategic development. However, even when these mistakes are avoided, and growth strategies exist, managers tend to overlook the fact that there is a connection between the chosen strategy and the particular organizational structure of the start-up. This oversight is a serious impediment to growth.

Firms which are still small and striving to grow should choose team structures, or, if necessary, tight centralization as a structure for their organization so that they can handle knowledge management, and decision coordination and implementation better. The lack of team management and networking in the start-up and consolidation phases hinders growth, as the experience of start-ups from Silicon Valley has shown.

If growth is achieved by increasing sales volume, start-ups can defer the adjustment of the original organizational structure until decision deficits, such as delays in decision-making, begin to surface. In growing companies, maintaining the same team structures and management generally leads to a loss of coordination. It also postpones the creation of a clear corporate structure. If the distribution of responsibility in the start-up is unclear, or if the same team management has been continued despite growth, problems will arise due to a lack of coordination. Therefore, the distribution of competences and responsibility must be achieved, depending on the strategies the start-up pursues. If team structures impede this because they are too slow, they must be replaced by hierarchical structures.

Different strategies may be necessary if the company pursues diversification strategies by expanding into new markets, or bringing out new products by expanding the value chain, or into new networks. However, this requires a good knowledge of the industry or industries in which the start-up wishes to diversify. In this case, a more decentralized organizational structure with different, relatively autonomous departments is advisable. However, department decentralization makes coordination essential. Some of the classic mistakes made by young firms are either to wait too long before decentralizing, decentralizing too soon, and/or failing to coordinate the new departments. Each of these mistakes, or a combination, can have a restricting effect on the growth of a firm, and in the worst case can even increase the risk of a young firm's going bankrupt.

Inadequate or incorrect marketing, cooperation, finance, or HR strategies

Growth is also at risk if start-ups fail to develop strategic planning, marketing, financing, risk management, HR management, organization, or policies for internationalization. Growth mistakes made in regard to marketing, financing, and HR management are particularly serious. Many of the following issues have been introduced in previous chapters.

The first group of flawed growth strategies is marketing strategies. Start-ups are particularly susceptible to concentrating on developing a technical or scientific product further and developing new products, but not paying enough attention to marketing. Marketing plans and their extrapolation are a prerequisite for avoiding growth mistakes. If a firm does not conduct market research, identify customer preferences, generate new customer wishes, or segment or capture the market, it will not grow. Start-ups can only find out whether or not they can achieve or have already achieved a dominant position in the market by conducting systematic market research. If they already have a dominant position, they could try to push competitors out of the market or prevent them from entering it in the first place. Depending on the financial resources available, e.g. after a successful IPO, it could even make sense to buy out competitors and grow in this fashion.

A second group that can hinder growth is cooperation strategies, such as when a start-up becomes overly dependent on a more established company as a senior partner, for example, when a small biotech firm depends on a large pharmaceutical company to market its products. If larger established companies really commit themselves to their junior partners and are successful, then cooperation often ends up with the senior partner taking over the start-up. This only ensures the growth of the senior partner. Transferring licenses to larger firms before a product is fully developed is also dangerous—this is a particular problem for biotech start-ups if the government has not yet approved a new drug. However, what is much more common is opportunistic behavior by the senior partner, where it is paid well by the junior partner for its marketing activities, but then it does not in fact aggressively market the junior partner's products. Such a flawed marketing strategy is also a huge hindrance to growth.

A third group of flawed growth strategies concerns the financing of growth. In the initial phases of the life cycle of start-ups, growth can scarcely be financed out of their profits, nor can it generally be financed alone by the founders' equity. Start-ups in particular are often undercapitalized. The only alternative that remains is seeking outside capital.

To finance growth strategies start-ups sometimes borrow long-term debt which is to be paid back with interest from the revenues from implementing the strategy. Likewise, some start-ups redeem loans and interest payments step-by-step over a long period by taking out revolving, short-term loans. Both financial strategies jeopardize growth considerably, or even hinder it completely if the firm does not generate the planned revenues, or if no new short-term loans are available to pay off part of the long-term loan at the right time. In addition, start-ups with high growth potential in certain industries, can trade partial ownership in their firms for "venture capital".

Start-ups can also make another growth mistake in financing by launching their IPOs on the stock market too soon and simply using this revenue to repay debt or venture capital and replace it with equity from the capital market. What is even more serious after an IPO is when firms make the growth mistake of merely increasing their cash management or randomly buying out other firms, rather than using their IPO funds to finance wise growth strategies.

The fourth group of related business strategies where serious mistakes can be made is Human Resource strategies. In many cases the founders and employees of start-ups are in their thirties, and sometimes only in their twenties, and are frequently highly qualified university or college graduates (cf. Frank/Opitz 2001, p. 454). The homogeneity of the age distribution of managers and employees often leads to start-ups acquiring new personnel from the same age group. However, a homogeneous age distribution may lead to a decline in motivation as employees age at the same time. Start-ups must therefore be particularly careful to achieve a heterogeneous age distribution in their personnel. They must also attempt to acquire older employees with experience in the industry and with management competences from other successful companies. It can be of great value to acquire more senior managers who enjoy the new challenge of working for a start-up before they retire. Lack of loyalty in their personnel should lead start-ups to think about how to retain their particularly talented employees. If start-ups fail to consider these points, obstacles to growth are a matter of course.

Much more important, however, is developing the knowledge and competences of the entire staff depending on the start-up's chosen growth strategy. The knowledge and competences necessary for formulating and implementing the growth strategies must be forecast as part of qualitative Human Resource planning, and then provided by Human Resource development or by acquiring external personnel (cf. Drumm 2000). If this does not happen, start-ups face a growth barrier which is hard to overcome. The failure to implement strategy-oriented HR development and build up and maintain internalized motivation of the employees through attractive work and working conditions is a barrier to growth which is often overlooked.

Inadequate or incorrect internal accounting

All firms, whether young or mature, need cost accounting systems which can report costs and—as far as they are specifically attributable—revenues per cost unit, cost center, and department. It is important that start-ups establish systems for unit cost accounting, cost center accounting, and breakeven analysis (cf. Scherrer 1999) in order to be able to assess economic inefficiencies and sources of loss by means of target/actual comparisons and profit margins. If the competition is fierce, firms should also establish target costing to be able to undermine competitors by adjusting price policy.

Doing without any kind of cost accounting leads not only to the fact that sources of loss remain undiscovered, but also that profit potentials stay hidden as well. Both of these points represent possible growth risks. Start-ups must therefore avoid this risk by establishing cost and profit accounting, and a breakeven analysis as quickly as possible.

Dependence on third parties

Many start-up, survival, and growth strategies lead almost inevitably to the dependence of new firms on third parties. This causes no problem as long as the interests of all people and firms involved are relatively equal and/or compatible. Dependence on third parties functioning as investors, licensors, partners, principal customers in the sales market, or single suppliers does not necessarily lead to growth barriers. However, dependence is a disadvantage if there are diverging interests, or if the partners behave opportunistically. In this case, the growth of the start-up is inhibited and the firm is forced to fight the opportunistic behavior of the partners. For the start-up these defense activities incur transaction costs which arise in the preparation phase of a partnership and in the conclusion of cooperation contracts, and are added to later by transaction costs arising from controlling, and correcting errors.

However, the older the firm becomes, dependence on third parties should be reduced. The dependence on licensors should be compensated for by the firm's own research and development. The dependence on outside investors, on the other hand, is generally unavoidable, but it can be put to positive use by raising risk capital by profit sharing with investors to create homogeneity of interests.

As shown above, dependence on third parties can arise when a firm markets its products. It can, however, also arise in the acquisition of preliminary products, or in financing. It is at its highest in firm networks. Start-ups must therefore ask themselves repeatedly whether these dependencies secure their existence and survival, or whether they are endangering their growth. As long as the firm's survival is secured by suppliers or customers through strategic dependencies, for instance within a network of cooperating firms, the start-up can profit. If such dependencies however, endanger the success and growth of the firm, the start-up must try to extricate itself by building up its own sales or supply channels. Homogeneity of interests must also be taken into account when building an external network in order to minimize transaction costs which stunt growth.

Acculturation problems when buying companies

Growth as a result of acquiring companies in the supply chain, or diversifying into other sectors not only creates the potential for mistakes due to inadequate knowledge of the industry, but by insufficient acculturation of the companies acquired. Every company develops its own culture from the moment it is founded. This is manifested in the founders' value system in regard to their employees, customers, suppliers, sponsors, and other partners. Founders will always try to transfer their value system onto their employees and thus form their behavior completely or at least partly. Company culture is also manifested in desired forms of behavior, rituals, and accepted processes of analyzing and solving processes practiced by the founders which they in turn would like their employees to implement. Communicating these values and forms of behavior is part of the management process.

If other companies are acquired in the course of planned growth processes, the company also takes on their "foreign" firm cultures. The confrontation between two or more incompatible firm cultures makes acculturation essential. The different cultures must be adapted to each other, or the growth of the entire company and its individual departments due to synergy effects is at stake.

There are three different acculturation strategies to choose from. In the case of usurpation, the management from the bought out firm is replaced by the management team of the firm that bought it out. This model is generally expensive, but can be implemented relatively quickly. In the case of adaptation, the buying and bought out firm(s) get to know and understand each other's cultures in order to change and adapt them step by step. This model is much slower than usurpation, but also cheaper. The synthesis model consists of consciously giving up the old firm culture and creating a new one. This model makes sense if the acquisition means that the markets and thus market-oriented strategies change, or the national orientation of the start-up can be expanded to an international one. Doing without acculturation strategies not only stunts growth, but also increases the risk of bankruptcy.

Chapter summary

Company growth must be planned by both old and young firms. It requires the choice of one or more of the above mentioned strategies to promote growth. Product and process innovations, the differentiation of products and markets, the use of market niches, and networking with other companies are important strategies for start-ups. Growth along the supply chain is a special case in vertical networking strategies. Buying out entire companies is also suitable as a growth strategy, but it presupposes the availability of sufficient capital, and the solution of acculturation problems. Growth can be seriously threatened by the management mistakes discussed above, but also promoted by growth strategies that are well implemented.

References, and further literature

Chong, M.L. et al. (2000): The Silicon Valley Edge, Stanford, CA. pp. 120-121.

Covin, J.G. and Slevin, D.P. (1997): High Growth Transitions. Theoretical Perspectives and Suggested Directions. In: Sexton, D.L, and Smilor, R.W., 1997. pp. 99-125.

Christensen, C.M. (1997): The Innovator's Dilemma. Boston.

Drumm, Hans Jürgen (2000): Personalwirtschaft. 4. Aufl. Berlin usw.

Frank, E. and Opitz, C. (2001): Internet-Start-Ups—Ein neuer Wettbewerber unter den „Filteranlagen" für Humankapital. Zeitschrift für Betriebswirtschaft 71. Jg.: 453-469.

Hutzschenreuter, T. (2001): Wachstumsstrategien. Einsatz von Management-kapazitäten zur Wertsteigerung. Wiesbaden.

Kazanjian, R.K. and Drazin, R. (1990): A stage-contingent model of design and growth for technology-based new ventures. Journal of Business Venturing (5): 137-150.

Kühlhorn, G. and Wissdorf, F. (2001): Jobmotor Mittelstand. Impulse März 2001-05-28: 20-27.

Lechner, C. (2000): The Competitiveness of Firm Networks. Frankfurt usw.

McGee, J.E., Dowling, M.J. and Megginson, W.L. (1995): Cooperative strategy and new venture performance. The role of business strategy and management experience. In: Strategic Management Journal 16(7): 565-580.

Porter, M. (1992): Wettbewerbsvorteile. 3. Aufl. Frankfurt/Main.

Porter, M.E. and Rivkin, J.W. (2000): Industry Transformation. Harvard Business School. Publishing N9-701-008, July 10.

Scherrer, G. (1999): Kostenrechnung. 3. Aufl. Stuttgart.

Sexton, D.L. and Bowman-Upton, N.B. (1991): Entrepreneurship: Creativity and Growth. New York.

Sexton, D.L. and Smilor, R.W. (1997): Entrepreneurship 2000. Dover.

Siegel, R., Siegel, E. and MacMillan, I. (1993): Characteristics distinguishing high growth ventures. Journal of Business Venturing 8(2): 169-180.

Sternberg, R. (2000): Entrepreneurship in Deutschland—Das Gründungsgeschehen im internationalen Vergleich: Länderbericht Deutschland zum Global Entrepreneurship Monitor. Berlin.

Teece, D.J. (1986): Profiting from technological innovation: Implications for integration, collaboration, licensing, and public policy. Research Policy 15: 285-305. Elsevier Science Publishers B.V. (North-Holland).

About the chapter author

Professor Michael Dowling is Professor for Innovation and Technology Management at the University of Regensburg. He received his PhD in Business Administration from the University of Texas at Austin in 1988. His research interests include the strategic management of technology, especially in the telecommunications industry, high technology entrepreneurship, and the relationships between technology, public policy and economic development.

About the chapter editor

Professor Hans Jürgen Drumm is a retired Professor of Business Administration with a focus on Human Resource Management and Organization Theory. He received his doctorate at the Free University of Berlin and his Habilitation at the University of the Saarland.